STATE ARCHIVES OF ASSYRIA

VOLUME IX

COURTESY TRUSTEES OF THE BRITISH MUSEUM

FRONTISPIECE. *Seal of the eunuch Tariba-Issar, depicted as a devotee of Aššur and Ištar.*
BM 89164.

STATE ARCHIVES OF ASSYRIA

Published by the Neo-Assyrian Text Corpus Project
of the University of Helsinki
in co-operation with
Deutsche Orient-Gesellschaft

Editor in Chief
Simo Parpola

Managing Editor
Robert M. Whiting

Editorial Committee
Frederick Mario Fales, Simo Parpola, Nicholas Postgate,
Julian Reade, Robert M. Whiting

VOLUME IX

Simo Parpola

ASSYRIAN PROPHECIES

HELSINKI UNIVERSITY PRESS

Publication of this volume was made possible in part by a grant
from the Research Council for the Humanities of
the Academy of Finland

Set in Times
Typography and layout by Teemu Lipasti
The Assyrian Royal Seal emblem drawn by Dominique Collon from original
Seventh Century B.C. impressions (BM 84672 and 84677) in the British Museum
Ventura Publisher format by Robert M. Whiting
Custom fonts designed and developed by Timo Kiippa and Robert M. Whiting
Electronic pasteup by Simo Parpola

Helsinki University Press
Vuorikatu 3 A 2, FIN-00100 Helsinki, Finland
Tel. 358-9-70102363, Tfx. 358-9-70102374

ISBN 951-570-001-9 (Whole Series, Paperback)
ISBN 951-570-002-7 (Whole Series, Hardbound)
ISBN 951-570-166-X (Volume 9, Paperback)
ISBN 951-570-167-8 (Volume 9, Hardbound)

ASSYRIAN PROPHECIES

by

SIMO PARPOLA

Illustrations
edited by
JULIAN READE
and
SIMO PARPOLA

HELSINKI UNIVERSITY PRESS
1997

FOREWORD

The manuscript for this volume was prepared entirely by Simo Parpola. He has also done almost all of the editing and typesetting work on the volume.

The format of this volume differs somewhat from that of other SAA volume in that there is an extensive Introduction to the corpus of texts edited here. Although the size of the corpus is small, the nature and importance of the texts has warranted a much more thorough discussion of their place in Assyrian life than the other corpora that have been edited in this series. For the same reasons, the critical apparatus is also much expanded over that to be found in other volumes of the series, approaching a full commentary.

This is the first volume of the State Archives of Assyria series that has been produced since the Project has become a Centre of Excellence of the University of Helsinki. We thank the University of Helsinki for this honour and for the financial support that comes with it, and we feel that this volume is a particularly appropriate inauguration for this new status.

Helsinki, December 1997 Robert M. Whiting

PREFACE

The text part of this volume (transliterations, translations, critical apparatus, glossary and indices) took its final shape in 1993 and essentially dates from that year, although work on it had of course begun much earlier, already in the late sixties. The introduction and the notes were finished in 1994-97. It may be asked whether the time spent on them justifies the four-year delay in the publication of the edition proper, which was in proofs already at the end of 1993. In my opinion it does. There would certainly have been many quicker and much easier ways to finish the introduction. However, in that case the complex background studies included in it, without which the texts make little sense, would still remain to be written. They are needed to make this important corpus of prophecies fully accessible not just to a limited circle of Assyriologists but to specialists in religious studies as well.

I wish to thank the Trustees of the British Museum for permission to publish the previously unpublished prophecy texts as well as the illustrative material and photographs included in this volume. I am indebted to the whole staff of the Department of Western Asiatic Antiquities, in particular to Drs. C. B. F. Walker and I. L. Finkel for their help with the photographs, and to Dr. Julian Reade for his help with the illustrations. Professor Othmar Keel of the Institut Biblique, Université de Fribourg, and Dr. Annie Caubet of the Département des Antiquités Orientales, Musée du Louvre, kindly granted publication permission for the objects in their custody used as illustrations in the volume. I am also grateful to Professor Rykle Borger (Göttingen) for communicating to me his join to K 1292 immediately after its discovery, and to Professor Herbert Huffmon (Drew University) for discussing the texts with me on many occasions in the eighties. Professors Ithamar Gruenwald (Tel Aviv), Abraham Malamat (Jerusalem) and Moshe Weinfeld (Jerusalem), and Dr. Martti Nissinen (Helsinki) read the final manuscript and provided important comments and additional references. Drs. Steven Cole and Robert Whiting of the SAA Project read the manuscript from the viewpoint of English and helped with the proofs. Ph. lic. Laura Kataja assisted in the typesetting of the text part. I am very grateful to all of them. Last but not least, I wish to record my indebtedness to Professor Karlheinz Deller (Heidelberg), with whom I worked on the corpus in the early seventies. Our planned joint edition never materialized, but I hope he will find the present volume an acceptable substitute.

I dedicate this book to the memory of my grandfather, the Rev. K. E. Salonen, who understood the significance of Assyriology to biblical studies and whose gentle figure I remember fondly, and to the memory of my mother, Taimi Mirjam Parpola (born Salonen), to whom I had originally hoped to present it as a gift. A devout Christian, she was not disturbed by my work on the origins of Christian beliefs but took an active interest in it until her death. I thought of her often in writing this volume.

Helsinki, December 1997 Simo Parpola

CONTENTS

FOREWORD VII

PREFACE IX

INTRODUCTION XIII

The Conceptual and Doctrinal Background XVIII
The Assyrian Concept of God XXI
Ištar: the Holy Spirit XXVI
The Descent of Ištar and the Ascent of the Soul XXXI
The King as God's Son and Chosen One XXXVI
Assyrian Prophecy XLV
Designations of Prophets XLV
Prophecy and the Cult of Ištar XLVII
The Prophets of the Corpus XLVIII
The Prophecy Corpus LIII
Tablet Types LIII
Manuscripts LV
Authorship Indications and Other Scholia to the Oracles LXII
Structural Elements of the Oracles LXIV
Language and Style LXVII
The Historical Contexts and Dates of the Oracles LXVIII
Appendix: Inscriptions of Esarhaddon Pertaining to the Corpus LXXII
On the Present Edition LXXVI
Notes LXXX
Bibliography of Previous Studies CIX
Abbreviations and Symbols CXIII

TRANSLITERATIONS AND TRANSLATIONS

Oracle Collections 1

1. Oracles of Encouragement to Esarhaddon 4
1.1 Issar-la-tašiyaṭ of Arbela 4
1.2 Sinqiša-amur of Arbela 5
1.3 Remutti-Allati of Dara-ahuya 6
1.4 Bayâ of Arbela 6
1.5 Ilussa-amur of the Inner City 7
1.6 Unknown Prophet 7
1.7 Issar-beli-da''ini, Royal Votaress 9
1.8 Ahat-abiša of Arbela 9
1.9 Unknown Prophet 9
1.10 La-dagil-ili of Arbela 10
2. Oracles Concerning Babylon and the Stabilization of the King's Rule 14
2.1 [Nabû]-hussanni of the Inner City 14
2.2 [Bayâ] of Arbela 14
2.3 La-dagil-ili of Arbela 15
2.4 Urkittu-šarrat of Calah 16
2.5 [Sinqiša-amur of Arbela] 17

2.6 Unknown Prophet 18
3. The Covenant of Aššur 22
3.1 Introduction 22
3.2 First Oracle of Salvation 23
3.3 Second Oracle of Salvation 23
3.4 The Meal of Covenant 25
3.5 Word of Ištar of Arbela to Esarhaddon 25
4. Fragment of a Collection of Encouragement Oracles 30

Oracle Reports 31

Reports to Esarhaddon (5-6) 33
5 An Oracle to the Queen Mother 34
6 An Oracle from Tašmetu-ereš of Arbela 35
Reports to Assurbanipal (7-13) 37
7 Prophecies for Crown Prince Assurbanipal 38
8 Words Concerning the Elamites 40
9 Words of Encouragement to Assurbanipal 40
10 Fragment of a Prophecy 42
11 Report on a Vision and an Oracle to Assurbanipal 42

GLOSSARY AND INDICES 45

Logograms and Their Readings 45
Glossary 47
Index of Names 53
Personal Names 53
Place Names 53
God and Temple Names 54
Subject Index 55
Index of Texts 59
By Publication Number 59
By Museum Number 59
List of Joins 59
List of Illustrations 60
Index to the Introduction, Notes and Critical Apparatus 61
Biblical Passages Cited or Discussed 79

COLLATIONS 83

PLATES 85

Shame on the tyrant city [Nineveh], filthy and foul! No warning voice did she heed, she took no rebuke to heart... Her prophets (*nby'yh*) were reckless, no true prophets. Her priests profaned the sanctuary and did violence to the law.

Zephaniah 3:1-4

INTRODUCTION

In 1875 the British Assyriologist George Smith published in copy an unusual cuneiform tablet from Nineveh which he labeled "addresses of encouragement to [the Assyrian king] Esarhaddon" (680-669 BC). Although a tentative English translation of the text (no. 1 in the present edition) was provided by T. G. Pinches already in 1878, it did not attract much attention initially. The first to recognize its significance was Alphonse Delattre, who in an article entitled "The Oracles Given in Favour of Esarhaddon," published in 1888, defined it as "a series of oracles [from] the prophets of Assur [which] recall to mind the images of the Biblical prophets." He regarded it as "one of the most interesting fragments which Assyrian literature presents," adding: "It is astonishing that it should have attracted so little attention up to the present day."

Little did he know that this statement would still be by and large valid more than a hundred years later! True, Delattre's article momentarily generated considerable interest in the oracles. The tablet containing the "addresses" was recopied and retranslated by Pinches in 1891 (this time labeled "The Oracle of Istar of Arbela"), and in the course of the following fifteen years six new tablets of the same kind (nos. 2, 3, 5 and 7-9 in the present edition) were identified in the collections of the British Museum. By 1915, most of the corpus as known today had been made available in English, French and/or German translations and preliminarily analyzed from the religious, historical and literary points of view (see the bibliography on p. CIX).

However, after World War I interest in the oracles abated drastically. For decades, no further additions were made to the corpus, and except for a few retranslations of no. 1 made for anthologies of ANE texts, no new translations, editions or studies of the published texts appeared between 1916 and 1972. As a result, the corpus as a whole slowly sank into oblivion and became virtually inaccessible to non-Assyriologists. By the seventies, the text editions and studies published before WW I had become so hopelessly dated that they could be used only by a handful of specialists in Neo-Assyrian.

Thus, more than a hundred years after its discovery, the Assyrian prophecy corpus still remains virtually unknown to the great majority of biblical scholars and historians of religion — even though it provides a much closer parallel, at least in time, to OT prophecy than the early second-millennium prophetic texts of Mari, now well known to every serious biblical and ANE scholar.

The marginal attention the corpus has received is not only due to the lack of good editions but also to inaccurate and misleading terminology. While the prophecies of the corpus have been traditionally designated as "oracles" — a term accurate in itself but not specific enough to suggest an affinity to OT prophecy — Assyriologists have applied the labels "oracle" and "prophecy" also to texts totally unrelated to inspired prophecy, such as extispicy queries[1] and predictive texts drawing on standard collections of omens.[2] No wonder that biblical scholars, seeing how little such "prophecies" have to do with OT prophecy, have not found the little-known "oracles to Esarhaddon" worth much attention.

In the course of the past fifteen years, the situation has slowly started to change. Thanks to a series of articles in the seventies by Manfred Weippert, Herbert Huffmon and Tomoo Ishida, who for the first time since Delattre approached the texts as prophetic oracles, interest in the corpus has grown and a number of important studies on it have appeared during the eighties and nineties. Studies by Weippert and Maria deJong Ellis have removed the terminological confusion just referred to and firmly established the nature of the texts as prophetic oracles fully comparable to biblical prophecies. The similarities between the Assyrian and biblical prophecy corpora have been systematically charted and discussed by Weippert and Martti Nissinen, and the relevance of the Assyrian prophecies to OT studies in general has been ably demonstrated by Nissinen.

However, the primary significance of the Assyrian prophecy corpus does not lie in the parallel it provides to OT prophecy but in the light it throws on Assyrian religion. It has hitherto been commonly believed that inspired prophecy was basically alien to Mesopotamia,[3] and that Assyrian prophecy in particular, which seems to appear "out of the blue" in the reign of Esarhaddon, was only a marginal and ephemeral phenomenon possibly related to the large-scale deportations from Israel and Phœnicia under Tiglath-Pileser III and Sargon II, and thus a sort of "import from the West."[4] As we shall see, this view is untenable and has to be emphatically rejected. The prophecies have tight links to the cult of Ištar and Assyrian royal ideology, mythology and iconography, and thus represent a genuinely Mesopotamian phenomenon. The scarcity of prophetic oracles from Assyria and Mesopotamia in general is simply due to the basically oral nature of the phenomenon and cannot be used as an argument for its alleged foreign origin.

How then to explain the affinities of the texts with OT prophecy? And what about the occasional passages in them which have parallels in later Jewish mystical tradition (no. 1.6), Hellenistic mystery cults (no. 7 r.8) and Neoplatonic and Christian doctrines (nos. 1.4, 2.5, and 3.4)? Whence did these prophets draw the self-confidence which enabled them to speak not for but *as* gods, or their fanatic emperor-centric zeal? Why did they constantly proclaim the word of Ištar, the goddess of love, and not the word of Aššur, the national god?

My work on these and other questions raised by the corpus has resulted in a interpretative model which adds a new dimension to and sharply deviates from the traditional understanding of Assyrian religion. The main points of this model can be briefly recapitulated as follows:

1. The prophecies have to be studied as integral parts and products of a larger religious structure, the ecstatic cult of Ištar, which in its essence can be defined as an esoteric mystery cult promising its devotees transcendental salvation and eternal life.

2. Like Shakta Tantrism, the ecstatic cult of the Hindu mother goddess, the cult had a sophisticated cosmogony, theosophy, soteriology and theory of the soul, which were hidden from the uninitiated through a veil of symbols, metaphors and riddles and explained only to the initiates, who were bound to secrecy by oath.

3. The cornerstone of the cult's doctrine of salvation was the myth of Ištar's descent to the netherworld, in which the Goddess plays the role of the Neoplatonic Cosmic Soul. The first half of the myth outlines the soul's divine origin and fall, the latter half its way of salvation through repentance, baptism and gradual ascent toward its original perfection.

4. A central component of this doctrine was the concept of the heavenly perfect man sent for the redemption of mankind, materialized in the institution of kingship. In the Descent of Ištar, the king's redemptory role is expressed by the image of the shepherd king, Tammuz, given as Ištar's substitute to the "netherworld," that is, the material world. This image corresponds to the king's role as the earthly representative of God, and finds another expression in the portrayal of the king as the "sun of the people" (radiating heavenly brightness to the darkness of the world) and as an incarnation of the saviour god, Ninurta/Nabû, the vanquisher of sin, darkness and death.

5. The idea of perfection embodied in the king implied total purity from sin, implicit in the soul's divine origin and personified in the figure of the goddess Mullissu, the queen of heaven, the Assyrian equivalent of the Holy Spirit. Doctrinally, the king's perfection was not self-acquired but heaven-sent. Figuratively speaking, he was the son of Mullissu; and like the Byzantine emperor, he ruled through the Holy Spirit's inspiration. The mother-child relationship between the Goddess and the king, expressed through the image of a calf-suckling cow, is a constantly recurrent theme in the prophecies.

6. The king's perfection, *homoousia* with God, made him god in human form and guaranteed his resurrection after bodily death. For the devotees of Ištar, who strove for eternal life emulating the Goddess, he was a Christ-like figure loaded with messianic expectations both as a saviour in this world and in the next.

7. The central symbol of the cult was the cosmic tree connecting heaven and earth, which contained the secret key to the psychic structure of the perfect man and thus to eternal life. Other important symbols were the seven-staged ziggurat; the rainbow; the full, waning and waxing moon; the eight-pointed star; the calf-suckling cow and the child-suckling mother; the horned wild cow; the stag; the lion; the prostitute; the pomegranate; and so on. All these different symbols served to give visual form to basic doctrines of the cult while at the same time hiding them from outsiders, and thus amounted to a secret code, a "language within language" encouraging meditation and dominating the imagery and thinking of the devotees.

8. Beside transcendental meditation, the worship of the Goddess involved extreme asceticism and mortification of flesh, which when combined with weeping and other ecstatic techniques could result in altered states, visions and inspired prophecy.

9. The cult of Ištar, whose roots are in the Sumerian cult of Inanna, has close parallels in the Canaanite cult of Asherah, the Phrygian cult of Cybele and the Egyptian cult of Isis, all of which were likewise prominently ecstatic in character and largely shared the same imagery and symbolism, including the sacred tree. The similarities between Assyrian and biblical prophecy — which cannot be dissociated from its Canaanite context — can thus be explained as due to the conceptual and doctrinal similarities of the underlying religions, without having to resort to the implausible hypothesis of direct loans or influences one way or another.

10. The affinities with later Hellenistic and Greco-Roman religions and philosophies must be explained correspondingly. These systems of thought were not the creations of an "Axial Age intellectual revolution" but directly derived from earlier ANE traditions, as is evident from the overall agreement of their metaphysical propositions and models with those of the Assyrian religion. While each of these religious and philosophical systems must be considered in its own right and against its own prehistory, it is likely that all of them had been significantly influenced by Assyrian imperial doctrines and ideology, which (taken over by the Achaemenid, Seleucid and Roman empires) continued to dominate the eastern Mediterranean world down to the end of classical antiquity.

The conceptual and doctrinal background of the prophecies will be analyzed and discussed in more detail in the first three chapters of this introduction. The aim throughout has been to concentrate on issues essential to the understanding of Assyrian prophecy as a religious phenomenon and to correlate the Assyrian data with related phenomena, especially OT prophecy, Gnosticism and Jewish mysticism. I am fully aware that the issues tackled are extremely complex and would require several volumes, not a brief introduction, to be satisfactorily treated. Nevertheless, I have considered it essentially important not to limit the discussion to the Assyrian evidence alone but to take into consideration also the comparative evidence as fully as possible. The different sets of data are mutually complementary and it is not possible to understand one without the others. The intricate connection between mystery religion, esotericism and emperor cult, crucial to the understanding of ANE prophecy and the origins of ancient philosophy, emerges with full clarity only from the Assyrian evidence. On the other hand, the Assyrian sources, especially their symbolic imagery, cannot be fully understood without the supporting evidence of related traditions.

* *
*

Reconstructing the religious and doctrinal background of the corpus has been a slow and complicated process extending over more than 25 years, and the relevant methodology cannot be adequately discussed here since it would require a monograph of its own. Briefly, the process as a whole can be compared to the piecing together of a giant jigsaw puzzle. The "pieces" of the puzzle were the data found in the corpus, supplemented by those found in other Mesopotamian sources, both written and iconographic, earlier, contemporary and later. The "cover picture" used as an aid in analyzing, interpreting and piecing together these disconnected and fragmentary bits of evidence was the comparative evidence provided by related religious and philosophical systems, some of which survive to the present day through uninterrupted oral and written tradition and can thus be better understood as coherent systems.

Initially, the corpus was analyzed in light of contemporary Assyrian evidence only, in order to establish a reliable point of departure and to identify areas of interpretation requiring further study in light of other kinds of evidence. Next, the texts and the preliminary interpretive model were systematically correlated and compared with OT and Mari prophetic oracles and ANE prophecy in general. This study firmly established not only the independence and antiquity of Assyrian prophecy as a phenomenon, but above all the close ties of ANE prophecy in general to the cult of the "mother goddess" and its esoteric doctrines of salvation. The realization that this cult provides the key to the understanding of Mesopotamian/ANE prophecy as a cross-cultural phenomenon finally necessitated a systematic study of the cult of Ištar in light of the comparative evidence provided by the "mystery cults" of classical antiquity and related religious and philosophical systems (including Gnosticism, Jewish mysticism and Neoplatonism).

I would like to emphasize that while the comparative evidence has certainly played an important role in the reconstruction process and is frequently cited both in the introduction and notes in order to illustrate the nature of Assyrian prophecy as part of a wider cross-cultural phenomenon, it plays only a marginal role in the reconstruction itself, which in its essence is firmly based on Assyrian evidence.

The Conceptual and Doctrinal Background

For all their similarities, Assyrian and biblical prophecies have one conspicuous difference, and it appears to be fundamental. While the biblical prophets proclaim the word of Yahweh, the god of Israel presented as the only true God, the Assyrian prophets do not proclaim the word of their national god, Aššur. In most cases the oracular deity is *Ištar*, the goddess of love, but other deities, both male and female, also appear in this capacity in the texts. Aššur speaks only once in the corpus.

As far as I can see, nobody seems to have ever been bothered by this state of affairs. On the contrary, it seems to have been taken as the most natural thing in the world, a simple reflection of the contrast between the *monotheistic* religion of Israel on the one hand, and the "pagan" *polytheistic* religion of Assyria on the other. From this point of view, the prominence of Ištar and other female deities as oracular gods in Assyria of course constitutes no problem: it simply indicates a close connection of Assyrian prophecy to "fertility" and "vegetation cults," again implying a fundamental contrast to biblical prophecy, which supposedly had a different background.

However, a closer acquaintance with the texts reveals a number of difficulties with this view. Leaving aside the fact that the content of the prophecies has absolutely nothing to do with "fertility" or "vegetation cults," the multiplicity of oracular deities appearing in them is largely illusory. Thus the incipit of no. 2.4, "The word of Ištar of Arbela, the word of the Queen Mullissu" is followed by an oracle in the first person singular; here Mullissu, elsewhere known as the wife of Aššur/Enlil, is clearly only a synonym or another designation of Ištar of Arbela.[5] The same situation recurs in nos. 5, 7 and 9, where the deity, always speaking in the first person singular, is alternatingly identified as Ištar of Arbela or Mullissu, or both. The other two female oracular deities occurring in the texts, Banitu ("Creatrix") and Urkittu ("the Urukite"), are likewise well known from contemporary texts as appellatives of Ištar denoting specific aspects of this universal goddess.[6]

In oracle 1.4, the deity first speaks as Bel, then as Ištar of Arbela, and finally as Nabû, the son of Bel and the keeper of celestial records.[7] It is as if in this short oracle the deity were repeatedly putting on new masks to suit the changing themes of the discourse,[8] and one cannot help being reminded of the Holy Trinity of Christianity, where the Father, the Son, and the Holy Spirit are explained as different hypostases of one indivisible Divine Being.[9] Similar shifts in the identity of the oracular deity are also observable in other oracles of the corpus as well as in other contemporary texts.[10]

FIG. 1. *A triad of gods on the winged disk. See p. XVIII and n. 8ff.*
WA 89502.

Most important, in no. 3, a collection of oracles referred to in the text as "the covenant tablet of Aššur," the identities of Aššur and Ištar blend in an unexpected and absolutely baffling way.

The text consists of five interrelated oracles, all by the same prophet, four of which are identified or identifiable as "words of Ištar of Arbela."[11] The middlemost oracle (3.3), however, deviates from the pattern. It begins with reference to the king's cry for divine help ("Hear me, O Aššur!"), states that the plea was heard, describes the subsequent destruction of the king's enemies through a rain of hail and fire, and ends with a self-identification of the deity: "Let them see (this) and praise me, (knowing) that I am Aššur, lord of the gods."[12]

This oracle, which powerfully recalls Psalm 18, is the only oracle in the whole corpus ascribed to Aššur. In its subscript, it is defined as an oracle of well-being placed before "the Image," doubtless that of Aššur himself, and it is certainly no accident that the reference to the "covenant tablet of Aššur" occurs immediately after it. Note that in Isaiah 45, a similar self-presentation of Yahweh is linked with a similar demonstration of God's power in support of Cyrus, "his anointed," and compare Yahweh's covenant with David (Psalm 89), which in 2 Samuel 7 is conveyed to the king through the prophet Nathan.

Clearly then, oracle 3.3, in accordance with its central position in the text, constituted the essence of the "covenant tablet of Aššur." However, in the very next oracle (3.4), it is not Aššur but Ištar of Arbela who actually concludes the covenant. In a scene reminiscent of the Last Supper, the Goddess invites "the gods, her fathers and brothers" to a covenant meal, in the course of which she addresses them as follows: "You will go to your cities and districts, eat bread and forget this covenant. (But when) you drink from this water, you will remember me and keep this covenant which I have made on behalf of Esarhaddon."

The formulation of the passage makes it clear that Ištar is not acting as a mere mediator here. The covenant in question is between her and the other gods — it is *her* covenant with "the gods, her fathers and brothers." Accordingly, the phrasing of oracle 3.4, considered with 3.3, unquestionably implies that, in a way or another, Aššur and Ištar were considered *identical* by the author of the text.[13] On the other hand, in no. 3.2 and other oracles of the corpus, the Goddess refers to Aššur in the third person and thus evidently as a distinct divine entity. This creates a theological problem that seems serious indeed: How can two gods at the same time appear as identical yet distinct entities in one and the same text?[14]

FIG. 2. *Aššur/Enlil, Ištar/Mullissu and Ninurta/Nabû on Esarhaddon's Senjirli stela (see n. 59).* MESSERSCHMIDT, VS 1 Beiheft Tf. 7 (VA 2708).

The Assyrian Concept of God

The solution to the problem lies in the Assyrian concept of God, which defined Aššur — "the only, universal God"[15] — as "the totality of gods."[16] Aššur himself was beyond human comprehension.[17] Man could know him only through his powers pervading and ruling the universe, which, though emanating from a single source,[18] appeared to man as separate and were accordingly hypostatized as different gods.[19] On the surface, then, Assyrian religion, with its multitude of gods worshiped under different names,[20] appears to us as polytheistic;[21] on a deeper level, however, it was monotheistic,[22] all the diverse deities being conceived of as powers, aspects, qualities, or attributes of Aššur,[23] who is often simply referred to as "(the) God."[24] On the human level, the underlying doctrine of God's "unity in multiplicity" mirrored the structure of the Assyrian empire — a heterogenous multi-national power directed by a superhuman, autocratic king, who was conceived of as the representative of God on earth.[25]

Just as the exercise of the king's rule was effected through a state council presided over by the king personally, so was God's rule over the universe visualized in terms of a divine council presided over by Anu, the first emanation and "mirror image" of Aššur.[26] This council is referred to in oracle 9 and other contemporary texts as "the assembly of all the gods" or "the assembly of the great gods," and it is described as functioning like its human counterpart, with issues raised by individual council members and decisions made after sometimes long debate.[27] The human analogy must not, however, obscure the fact that the image of the council essentially was a metaphor meant to underline the unity of the divine powers and their organic interaction.[28] Aššur himself never appears as a "council member" for the simple reason that the council in fact *was* Aššur — "the totality of gods."[29]

The idea of God as "the sum total of gods" is attested in various parts of the ancient Near East already in the sixth century BC, and later in several Hellenistic and Oriental philosophies and religions (e.g., Platonism, Orphism, Neoplatonism, Hinduism, Tantrism).[30] It certainly also was part and parcel of first-millennium BC Jewish monotheism, as shown by the biblical designation of "God," *elōhîm*, which literally means "gods."[31] What is more, the idea of a divine council is well attested in the Bible and unquestionably formed an essential component of the imagery of Jewish prophets from the earliest times through the end of biblical prophecy.[32] Consider, for example, the following passage, quoting words of the mid-ninth-century prophet Micaiah:[33]

> Now listen to the word of the LORD: I saw the LORD seated on his throne, with all the host of heaven in attendance on his right and on his left.[34] The LORD said, "Who will entice Ahab to attack and fall on Ramoth-gilead?" One said one thing and one said another; then a high spirit came forward and stood before the LORD and said, "I will entice him." "How?" said the LORD. "I will go out," he said, "and be a lying spirit in the mouth of all his prophets." "You shall entice him," said the LORD, "and you shall succeed; go and do it." You see, then, how the LORD has put a lying spirit in the mouth of all these prophets of yours, because he has decreed disaster for you.

FIG. 3. *Israelite sacred tree from Kuntillet 'Ajrud (c. 800-775 BC). See p. XLII and nn. 199-202.* P. BECK, *Tel-Aviv* 9 (1982), fig. 4.

The key elements of this vision — God, seated on his throne, presiding over and conversing with a heavenly council or court — not only recur in most major biblical prophets and Job,[35] but in later Jewish and Christian traditions as well, from post-exilic times down to medieval Kabbalah.[36] Several further elements of biblical celestial imagery (e.g., a furnace or lamp burning at the throne of God, a succession of heavens and heavenly palaces, ladders leading to them, heavenly gates and gatekeepers, and a heavenly city and kingdom)[37] likewise continue as integral elements of later Jewish and Christian traditions,[38] and what is particularly important in this context, they also figure prominently in the Assyrian prophecy corpus and Mesopotamian cosmic geography at large.[39] We shall return below (p. XXVI and n. 136) to other important features in the passage just cited relevant to the understanding of Assyrian prophecy; for the present, it will be enough simply to note that both Judaism and Christianity share many apparently polytheistic concepts and features with Assyrian religion. Interestingly, the relevant imagery is generally not felt to be at variance with the basically monotheistic nature of either religion, while it is commonly taken as diagnostic of the basically polytheistic nature of Assyrian religion.

The various celestial beings or spiritual entities populating the heavens in Christianity and Judaism are explained partly as creations, partly as hypostases of God.[40] In Christian dogma, angels and saints belong to the former category; God the Father, Christ, and the Holy Spirit to the latter. In early Jewish mysticism, by contrast, angels are conceived as *powers of God,* and they are actually invoked as (quasi) independent gods in Jewish magical texts of the early first millennium AD.[41] The fundamental unity of all divine powers is, however, basic to Judaism, and is encoded in its central symbol, the menorah, now well established as derived from the Ancient Near Eastern sacred tree or "Tree of Life."[42] Though the Tree itself is well known from the Bible and has a prehistory reaching long back into pre-exilic times, its precise

FIG. 5. *Anthropomorphic tree from Assur (see n. 47).*
O. KEEL, *The Symbolism of the Biblical World* (Winona Lake 1997), fig. 153 (VA Ass 1358).

FIG. 4. *Assyrian sacred tree, probably from Iran.*
After A. MAHAZARI, *Der Iran und seine Kunstschätze* (Genève 1970), p. 21.

symbolism was long kept secret from the masses and therefore surfaces only in medieval Jewish mysticism, Kabbalah.[43]

The Tree of Life of Kabbalah is a multi-layered symbol in which the metaphysic structure of the universe (macrocosm) and the model of the perfect man (microcosm) converge as the "image" of God. It is composed of ten divine powers called sefirot ("[primordial] numbers," lit., "countings"), defined as aspects or attributes of God and systematically associated with parts of his "body," so as to constitute an anthropomorphic whole.[44] It thus effectively depicts God as the "sum total" of his divine powers, "gods." From the viewpoint of Assyrian prophecy, it is of crucial importance that the tree with its entire associated doctrinal apparatus can be shown to be based on a Mesopotamian model perfected in Assyria in the second millennium BC.[45] That this model could be made an integral part of Jewish religious thought underlines the basic similarity of the Assyrian and biblical concepts of God.[46]

The Assyrian sacred tree (figs. 4-8 and 13f), which occasionally takes an anthropomorphic form, can be analyzed as consisting of the "great gods" of the Assyrian pantheon and taken as a schematic representation of the "divine assembly," with Ištar occupying the "heart" of this divine "body."[47] Like the sefirot, the "great gods" making up the tree were prominently associated with numbers. This fact gives the tree an important mystical dimension, to which we shall return later on (see p. XXXIV).

Equipped with this information, we can now return to the problem of the identity of Aššur and Ištar left pending above. On the surface level, we have

FIG. 6. *Assyrian sacred tree from the palace of Assurnasirpal II, early ninth century BC (cf. fig. 13f).* WA 124580.

a scene in oracle 3.4 in which the prophet, personifying Ištar, administers a ritual meal to gods summoned from various cities and districts of Assyria to participate (along with the respective governors and vassal kings) in a divine covenant in favour of Esarhaddon. On the allegorical level, this corresponds to a meeting of the divine council, convened to terminate a period of divine wrath with Assyria and to initiate a new era under the rule of a saviour king, Esarhaddon. On a deeper, mystical level, the passage describes a process taking place within Aššur himself, with Ištar, the "heart" of his cosmic body, playing a key role in the process.[48] The same pattern of thought is reflected in Tablet XI of the Gilgamesh Epic, which tells that the *heart* of the convened great gods induced them to cause the Flood, and later specifies that it was Ištar who commanded it.[49] Thus, while Ištar in the oracle appears as the *primus motor* of the covenant, it was the council in its entirety, that is, Aššur himself, who concluded it.[50]

It can be argued that a similar mode of thinking is reflected in the Last Supper, and the striking affinities of the latter with oracle 3.4 can be explained accordingly.[51]

In sum, the perspective of oracle 3.4 is that of the divine council in which the prophet participated as a manifestation of Ištar, and this explains its particular formulation. In the preceding oracle (3.3), the situation is different. Here God speaks to man directly through his magnificent deeds. On this level, no metaphors are called for and Aššur is the only God.[52]

All things considered, the conceptual framework of Assyrian prophecy emerges as largely identical with that of ancient Israelite prophecy. Both shared the same basic concept of God as "the sum total of gods" and the same religious concepts and imagery. The worship of a multitude of deities ("the host of heaven") in state religion is well attested for pre-exilic Israel and Judah.[53] No biblical prophet denied the existence of these "hosts of heaven,"[54] though their basic position was that God transcended these powers,[55] which on their own were neither omnipotent nor omniscient, but limited in function.[56] This was also the position of the Assyrian prophets and Mesopotamian religion in general.[57]

Of course, in a religion of this type, the borderline between the surface level (polytheism) and the deeper level (monotheism) is subtle, and the distinction between the two was certainly often lost in practice.[58] Examples are not lacking in Assyrian texts and iconography where Aššur appears as if he were just one god among many — granted, the most exalted one, but still on the same level with other gods.[59] In the prophecies, state cult, and royal inscriptions, however, he is always strictly set apart from his emanations. In accordance with his special status, he is represented as a winged disk hovering over the "Tree of Life."[60] His fundamental unity with his powers is, however, made clear by his seal, where he is said to "hold a cosmic bond binding together the great heavens and the Igigi and Anunnaki gods."[61]

The risk of losing the distinction between God and his powers is likewise inherent in the kabbalistic concept of God, as illustrated by the following passage stressing the importance of the daily recitation of Shema' Israel (Deut. 6:4) for the unification of the divine powers:

> Since you know that the Sefirot are designated as attributes, and they are not [limited] in attribute by their nature, but from our perspective, you ought to unify all of them twice during the day... let him direct [the thought] as if he will cause all of them to enter the [Sefirah of] Keter, from whence they were emanated.[62]

FIG. 7. *Winged disk hovering over the sacred tree in a Neo-Assyrian cylinder seal.* BM 105111.

An early kabbalistic text asserts:

> All the Sefirot will be unified in [Israel's] pure thought and will be linked to each other until they are drawn [up] to the source of the endlessly sublime flame... And this is the secret of the unification [done] by a man in the morning and evening prayer, causing the elevation of all the Sefirot into one bundle and their union.[63]

The bitter attacks of biblical prophets against idolatry and the worship of heavenly bodies and foreign gods[64] have in my opinion to be seen in this light — as attacks against the nation's excessive worship of divine powers at the cost of God himself, which was seen as the root cause of her demise,[65] not as attacks against the contemporary concept of God as such, which did not differ essentially from its Assyrian counterpart.[66]

Ištar: the Holy Spirit

If this is so, why then are the Assyrian oracles called "words of Ištar" and not "words of Aššur," as one would be inclined to expect on the basis of the biblical analogy, "word of YHWH"?

The answer should be evident by now. Ištar, who in the oracles addresses the king as her child, is *Aššur revealed in his* ***mother aspect.*** In speaking through the prophet, she, however, is at the same time also an entity *distinct* from Aššur: a divine power working in man and thus bridging the gulf between man and god. Though distinct from the prophet as well, she unites with him or her, thus making him or her momentarily an agent or limb of God in the sense of p. XXI above and, for a fleeting moment, one with God.[67]

It is important to realize that the Goddess has to be understood concretely in terms of her human manifestation: she is the emotion (*libbu*) moving the prophet, the breath (*šāru*) issuing from his or her "heart," and the voice (*rigmu*) and words (*dibbī*) emerging from his or her mouth. There is a definite correlation between her human manifestation and her place in the divine "body" (the anthropomorphic tree and the divine assembly, see p. XXIIIf above). In both cases she occupies *the heart*, the center of the body universally regarded as the seat of emotions, love and affection, and synonymous with spirit, courage and the essence of anything.[68]

Accordingly, Ištar can be viewed as the "spirit" or "breath" of Aššur (= God) — a concept well-attested in Neo-Assyrian texts.[69] Going a step further, one can say that Ištar of the prophecies is the spirit of God, who, residing in the heart of the prophet, *spirits* him and speaks through his or her lips.[70] In other words, she is the functional equivalent of the biblical Spirit of God (also called the spirit of YHWH, the Holy Spirit, or simply the Spirit), who plays a similar role in biblical and early Christian ecstatic prophecy.[71]

I am well aware that this interpretation, which has not been suggested before, will strike many as bold, ill-considered, and totally out of the question. After all, Ištar is commonly regarded as an aggressive "goddess of war, fecundity, and sexual love"[72] — all notions apparently incompatible with those commonly attached to the Holy Spirit, who especially in Western

FIG. 9. *Ištar with her eight-pointed star behind a eunuch devotee. Neo-Assyrian cylinder seal.*
FRIBOURG 103.

FIG. 8. *Ištar, armed with quivers and swords and holding a bow and arrows, facing a eunuch official (see p. XLVI).*
BM 89769.

Christianity is an elusive, predominantly male entity void of any feminine characteristics.[73] However, a closer look at the facts will soon reveal that the equation rests on good grounds.

It should be noted, first of all, that the male notion of the Spirit in Christianity is a late, secondary development. In the Hebrew Bible, the "Holy Spirit" (*rwḥ qdš*) and its equivalents (*rwḥ ʾlhym, rwḥ yhwh, hrwḥ*) are consistently construed as feminine nouns, which indicates that it was conceived as a feminine entity.[74] In the Nicene Creed (AD 381), the Holy Spirit is defined as the "life-creating power" — i.e., the equivalent of the Mesopotamian "mother goddess" — and the role of the Spirit in the immaculate conception of Jesus Christ, as defined in the Apostles' Creed, corresponds to that of Ištar/Mullissu in the conception of the Assyrian king (see below, p. XL). In the apocryphal Gospel According to the Hebrews (2nd cent.), Jesus calls the Holy Spirit his *mother,*[75] while in the gnostic treatise *On the Origin of the World*, the Spirit is presented as a *virgin* sitting on the left of the throne of Sabaoth, with Jesus Christ enthroned on its right.[76] Correspondingly, in second-century Gnosticism, the later Christian trinity (like the Assyrian trinity in oracle 1.4) appears as a triad made up of the Father, the *Mother*, and the Son.[77]

The gnostic Holy Spirit is a much more complex figure than the faceless and demythologized Spirit of Christianity and shares numerous important features with Ištar/Mullissu. She is the female aspect and "consort" of the Father, the "Mother of the Universe, whom some call Love";[78] she is the first "Thought that dwells in the Light, a Voice, who gradually put forth the All";[79] she is the "androgynous Mother-Father, the Womb that gives shape to the All, the ineffable Word, a hidden Light pouring forth a Living Water, a male Virgin by virtue of a hidden Intellect."[80] She manifests herself in many forms and is, like Ištar, called with many names. She is usually called Sophia, "Wisdom," which corresponds to Ištar's designation as "Daughter of the moon" (see below), but she is also known as the "fallen Sophia" and, like Ištar, referred to as "whore."[81] These characteristics link the gnostic Holy Spirit with the Logos of John 1 and the personified Wisdom of Proverbs 8 on the one hand,[82] and with the ancient Near Eastern "mother goddesses" in general on the other.

The dove, the Christian symbol of the Holy Spirit, was consistently associated with goddesses of love and procreation in the ancient world. In the Greco-Roman world, it was sacred to Venus and Aphrodite;[83] in the apocryphal Acts of Thomas, it is invoked as "the hidden mother."[84] In the Song of Songs, the "dove" refers to the bride,[85] that is, the hidden Wisdom and Beauty of God presented as his consort in Proverbs 8.[86] A talmudic passage compares the Spirit of God hovering over the waters in Gen. 1:2 to a dove hovering over its young ones.[87] In Mesopotamia, the dove's generative potency and incessant groaning and moaning associated it with the mother goddess mourning the fate of her creatures perishing in the deluge.[88] This association is also implicit in Romans 8:26, "The Spirit comes to the aid in our weakness... Through our inarticulate groans the Spirit himself is pleading for us." Incidentally, the Hebrew word for "dove" in the Song of Songs, *yonah*, literally means "the groaning one."[89]

With regard to the traditional notion of Ištar as a "goddess of war and sexual love," it should be noted that while it is technically accurate in a sense, it totally misses the essence of the Goddess. As recently observed by Rivkah Harris, "[Inanna-Ishtar] embodied within herself polarities and contraries, and thereby transcended them... [She] was far more than simply the goddess of fertility, of love and war, and the Venus star."[90] Her complex figure, which combines features of the madonna with those of a whore and a warlord, has been aptly characterized by Harris as a "paradox and a coincidence of opposites." A paradox indeed, for her seemingly contradictory features find a coherent explanation once — and only when — she is recognized as an equivalent of the Holy Spirit and considered in this light from the perspective of later esoteric traditions.

Irrespective of her mythological role, the most common notions attached to Ištar (and other goddesses equated with her) in Mesopotamian texts are purity, chastity, prudence, wisdom and beauty. From the earliest times on, her standing epithets are "pure/holy"[91] and "virgin."[92] She is the "daughter" of Anu (god of heaven), Ea (god of wisdom) and Sin/Moon (god of purity and prudence).[93] She is a veiled bride, "beautiful to a superlative degree."[94] In Assyrian iconography, her most common symbolic representation is the eight-pointed star,[95] and she is often depicted as a female figure surrounded by intense radiance (Fig. 10f).

As recently observed by Irene Winter, "Things that are holy, or ritually pure/clean, are described in terms of light [in Mesopotamian texts and arts], and if the sacred is manifest as luminous, then that which is sacred will shine."[96] Thus the prominence given to the luminosity of the Goddess in visual arts corresponds to the notion of her holiness stressed in contemporary texts. The same is true of the epithet "virgin," which, as is well known, is a universal symbol of purity and chastity. The bearded, androgynous figure of the Goddess in Assyrian texts and iconography has correspondingly nothing to do with virility or martiality but rather symbolizes sublime purity and perfection, as in Gnosticism and Syriac Christianity.[97]

The brilliance and beauty of Ištar corresponds in Jewish mysticism to the brightness and glory of God (*kavod*), revealed to the mystic as a divine light,

FIG. 10. *Ištar, standing on a lion and surrounded by divine radiance (melammu), appearing to the governor Nabû-uṣalla.*
K. WATANABE, *BaM* 23 (1992) 357.

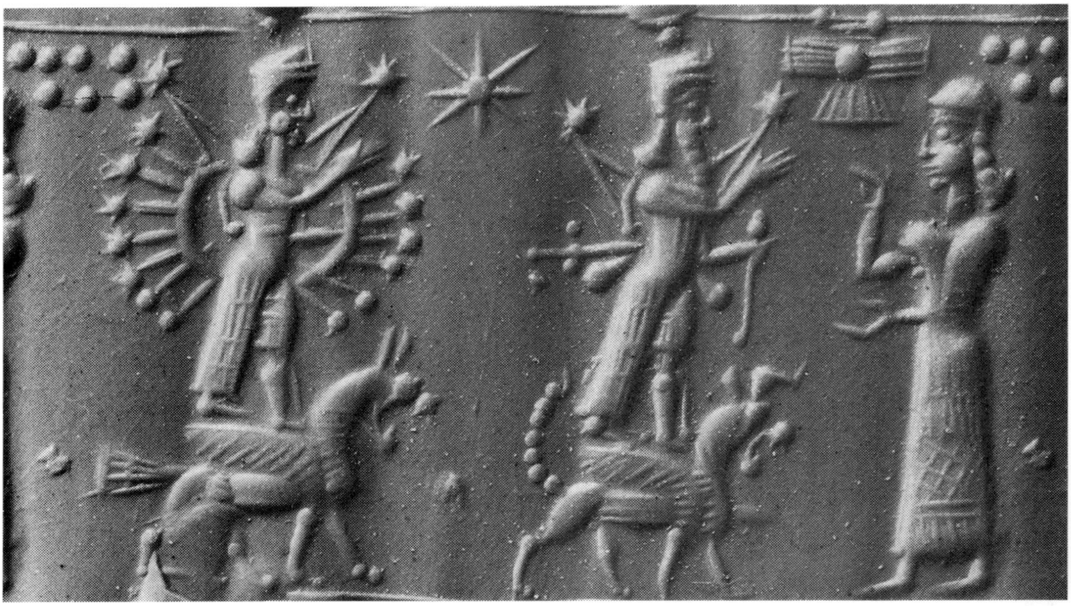

COURTESY MUSÉE DU LOUVRE

FIG. 11a. *Ištar and Aššur-Enlil blessing a eunuch official.*
AO 1510.

b

COURTESY TRUSTEES OF THE BRITISH MUSEUM

c

COURTESY TRUSTEES OF THE BRITISH MUSEUM

d

COURTESY TRUSTEES OF THE BRITISH MUSEUM

e

COURTESY VORDERASIATISCHES MUSEUM, BERLIN

f

COURTESY TRUSTEES OF THE BRITISH MUSEUM

FIG. 11b-f. *Epiphanies of Ištar. b = Neo-Assyrian cylinder seal,* WA 89810. c = *Achaemenid seal from Gorgippa, N shore of the Black Sea,* D. COLLON, *First Impressions, London 1987, no. 432.* d = *Detail of a Neo-Assyrian relief,* WA 124867. e = *Silver medallion from Sam'al, Das Vorderasiatische Museum,* ed. L. Jakob-Rost, Berlin 1987, Abb. 38. f = *Neo-Assyrian cylinder seal,* WA 89632.

often taking the form of a beautiful feminine apparition, *Shekhinah*, "the virgin of light."[98] Unable to approach God directly, the mystic could unite himself with his Shekhinah (lit., "indwelling"), believed to exist also without form, as a voice. Mystical union with God, referred to allegorically as the "bridal chamber," constituted the highest sacrament in Gnosticism (see n. 120 below); as noted above, the same imagery is also found in the Song of Songs, an allegory par excellence for mystical union. The Song of Songs has close parallels in Assyria, with Ištar and other goddesses playing the part of the "bride"; the outspokenly erotic language of these compositions, which served to describe the bliss of the encounter with the godhead, of course has little if anything to do with carnal sexuality.[99] We shall return to the question of sexuality in the cult of Ištar in detail below. Here it may be briefly noted that while sexuality did play a conspicuous part in the cult of the Goddess, it did not, contrary to a widespread modern myth, advocate promiscuity or sexual license, but rather the opposite.[100]

The martial role of the Goddess is a corollory of her role as the divine mother and protector of the king (see p. XXXVI), and has an exact parallel in the role of Yahweh, "the Holy One of Israel," as the warlord of Israel, and of the Madonna, the "Holy Virgin," as the Palladium of Christian armies.[101] The wars she fought were *holy* wars against forces of evil, darkness, and chaos,[102] and they were won not only because the Goddess was on the king's side but because she *spirited* the soldiers of the victorious army, fighting for the just cause.[103]

The role of the Goddess as a prostitute, finally, is explained by the well-known but little understood myth of Ištar's Descent to the Netherworld.[104] This myth contains the key to the religious background of Assyrian prophecy, and must hence be analyzed here in detail.

The Descent of Ištar and the Ascent of the Soul

To understand the *Descent* correctly it is essential to realize that it has nothing to do with "fertility" or "seasonal growth and decay" but, like the gnostic myth of the Fall of Sophia, addresses the question of man's salvation from the bondage of matter. Its protagonist is the "Neoplatonic" Cosmic Soul, personified as the goddess Hekate in the Chaldean Oracles.[105] The first half of the myth presents the soul's heavenly origin and defilement in the "netherworld," i.e. the material world, the latter half outlines her way of salvation.[106] Like Sophia and Hekate Soteira, the goddess of the myth thus is a "two-faced" entity. Descending, she is the holy spirit entering the prison of the body; ascending, she is the penitent soul returning to her celestial home.[107] This double role explains her contradictory figure, which combines the image of the Holy Spirit with that of the prostitute.

The affinity of the gnostic Sophia myth and the Descent of Ištar is borne out by several considerations, most importantly by a Nag Hammadi treatise entitled *The Exegesis on the Soul.*[108] This text has been taken as a rephrasing of the Valentinian myth of Sophia; in actual fact, however, its narrative much more closely follows that of the Descent of Ištar, to the extent that it could be considered a running commentary or a paraphrasis of the latter.[109] In contrast with most gnostic texts, it is written in easily comprehensible, plain language, clearly meant to explain rather than to conceal. It thus offers a most valuable interpretive parallel to the Descent of Ištar, whose heavily metaphorical and allegorical language served just the opposite purpose.[110]

The descent of Ištar is presented in terms of a stripping metaphor. She leaves her home as the queen of heaven, the wise, chaste and pure "daughter of the moon," dressed in her regal attire.[111] At each gate of the netherworld, she has to take off one piece of her clothing, until she in the end arrives in the netherworld completely naked, stripped of all her virtues and powers.[112] Her later ascent is expressed by reversing the metaphor: at each of the seven gates, she gets back a piece of clothing in an order mirroring that of their removal.

In *Exeg. Soul* we read: "As long as the soul was alone with the father, she was virgin and in form androgynous. But when she fell down into a body and came to this life, she fell into the hands of many robbers. Some made use of her [by force], while others did so by seducing her. In short, they defiled her, and she [lost her] virginity. And in her body she prostituted herself."[113] Even though no reference to the removal of garments is actually made in the text, both the context and the use of the word "robbers" imply that the stripping metaphor underlies this passage too.

The same metaphor is also found in Jewish mysticism, where the Torah reveals herself by a process of undressing, while man ascends to higher worlds through a process of dressing.[114] A student of the Torah aspires to become a bridegroom of the Shekhinah, and one who diligently studies the Torah clothes the Shekhinah, for she is naked in her exile in this world. Conversely, every sinner is thought of as one who disrobes the Shekhinah, and in so doing prolongs her exile.[115]

The gates through which Ištar has to pass on her way back from the netherworld correspond in Kabbalah to the gates of the sefirot, through which the soul must pass in order to reach the Divine King.[116] In Gnosticism and in the mysteries of Mithras, they correspond to the seven planetary heavens or spheres.[117] In each case, they are implicitly linked to a clear-cut doctrine of salvation, which we shall now consider.

In *Exeg. Soul*, the way to salvation is opened up by repentance, mourning, prayer, and mercy. Recognizing her miserable condition, the soul begins to call with all her heart upon the name of her father: "Save me, my father, for behold I will render an account for [thee, for I abandoned] my house and fled from my maiden's quarters. Restore me to thyself again." The text adds: "When the father, who is above, sees her in such a state, then he will count her worthy of his mercy upon her."[118]

In the Descent of Ištar, the same idea is expressed through the penitent figure of Papsukkal, who weeps before Ištar's father, and through the creation of the effeminate *assinnu*, who releases Ištar from Ereškigal's thrall. The *assinnu* corresponds to the gnostic "helper" sent by the Father to the suffering soul to comfort it, awaken it, and to provide it with the "food and water of life," the word (*logos*) of salvation (Rudolph *Gnosis*, p. 119ff). The sprinkling of Ištar with the water of life corresponds to the baptism which in *Exeg. Soul* effects the rebirth and cleansing of the soul.[119]

FIG. 12. *Ištar, naked, with her jewelry.*
K. KARVONEN-KANNAS, *The Seleucid and Parthian Terracotta Figurines from Babylon* (Firenze and Helsinki 1995), pl. 5:12 and p. 49a.

In *Exeg. Soul*, the ascent of the soul — the restitution of her original unity with God — is presented in terms of a wedding allegory.[120] The soul is a bride adorning herself for the arrival of the bridegroom, "her man and her brother," to whom she was joined when she was "with the father."[121] The text then explicitly states: "This is the ransom from captivity. This is the upward journey of ascent to heaven. This is the way of ascent to the father ... Then when she will become young again she will ascend, praising the father and her brother, by whom she was rescued."[122]

The ascent of Ištar, too, requires a ransom: Tammuz, her brother and "the husband of her youth," must be given to the netherworld as her substitute.[123] The sacrifice of Tammuz — an etiology for the death of the king as Son of God[124] — constitutes the culmination of the whole myth and must be regarded as a functional equivalent of the redemptory death of Christ.[125] As in Christianity, it paradoxically becomes a promise of eternal life for man. At the end of the myth we are told: "When Tammuz rises, the lapis lazuli pipe and the carnelian ring will rise with him, the male and female mourners will rise with him![126] May the dead rise and smell the incense!"[127]

In sum, it seems certain that the Descent of Ištar contained the basic tenets of an ecstatic mystery cult promising its followers absolution from sins, spiritual rebirth and resurrection from the dead.[128] These rewards were in store for those who were ready to follow the path of the Goddess from prostitution and suffering to the wedding in heaven.[129] In the words of the gnostic document *Thunder*:[130]

I am the first and the last.
I am the honoured and the despised.
I am the prostitute and the holy.
I am the wife and the virgin.
I am the mother and the daughter...
I am the voice whose sound is manifold,

and the *logos* which has many images...
I am shame and boldness...
I am war and peace...
I am the union and the dissolution.
I am what is beneath, and to me will they come up.
I, I am sinless and (yet) the root of sin derives from me...
Give heed then, O listeners—
For many are the sweet forms which exist in numerous
sins and incontinences, and disgraceful passions,
And fleeting pleasures; which people embrace,
Until they become sober and go up to their place of rest.
And they will find me there,
and live, and not die again.[131]

We are poorly informed about the practical details of this cult. As in other ancient mystery cults, those who embarked on it were pledged by oath to lifelong secrecy.[132] The main lines of it can, however, be reconstructed from the available evidence.

The overall goal of the cult was the purification of the soul so that it would regain its original unity with God. This goal was encoded in the Assyrian sacred tree, meditation on which certainly played an important part in the cult. The trunk of the tree, represented as a stylized date palm standing on a rock, symbolized Ištar as the power bridging the gap between heaven (the crown of the tree) and the material world (the base of the tree).[133] The union of the mystic numbers of the crown (1) and of the base (14) equals the mystic number of Ištar (15).[134]

For a spiritually pure person, union with God was believed to be possible not only in death but in life as well.[135] This belief provides the doctrinal basis of Assyrian prophecy: when filled with divine spirit, the prophet not only becomes a seat for the Goddess but actually one with her, and thus can foresee future things.[136]

To achieve the union, one had to emulate the Goddess, particularly her sufferings and agony, which provided the starting point for her salvation.[137]

One way of doing this was self-inflicted bodily pain, whipping oneself to the point of fainting, stinging oneself with pointed spindles, cutting oneself with swords and flint knives, and even turning oneself into a eunuch in a frenzied act of self-mutilation.[138] This ghastly act was widely practiced not only in Mesopotamia but all over the ancient Near East, and illustrates the tremendous power that the cult of Ištar exerted upon its initiates.[139] The purpose of the act — which certainly was the culmination of a long process of spiritual preparation — was to turn the devotee into a living image of Ištar: an androgynous person totally beyond the passions of flesh.[140]

Another important way of emulating the Goddess was incessant weeping, sighing and lamenting.[141] This method was directly prescribed in the Descent of Ištar, and its significance was powerfully augmented by a passage in the Mesopotamian Flood story, where the Goddess bewails the fate of her perishing creations.[142]

Any one of these practices, particularly when continued to the point of exhaustion, is liable to lead to paranormal states and experiences.[143] From the viewpoint of Assyrian prophecy, the prominence of methods involving agitation of the eye (weeping) and the mouth (lamenting) is of particular interest,

FIG. 13. *Assyrian sacred tree with a palmette crown and a mountain base.* WA 89135.

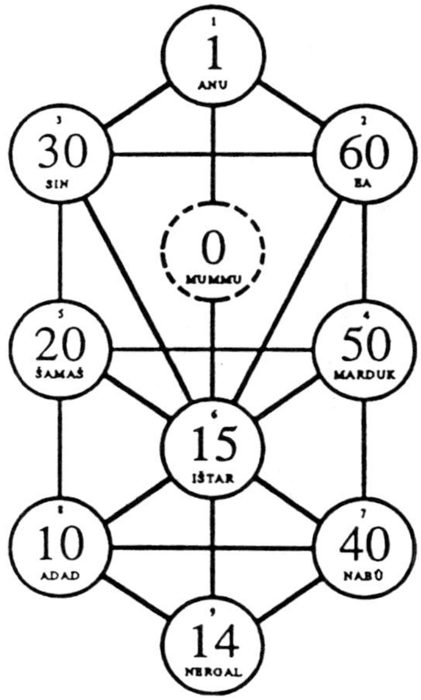

FIG. 14. *The reconstructed numerical structure of the Assyrian sacred tree (cf. n. 48).* PARPOLA, JNES 52 (1993) 183, fig. 9.

for these also play a prominent role in Jewish mysticism and ecstatic Kabbalah.

In his book *Kabbalah: New Perspectives,* Moshe Idel has analyzed in detail the mystical techniques used by kabbalists to induce the mystical union. He reviews several cases of self-induced suffering, weeping, and prayer leading to experiences of the Shekhinah,[144] and then makes an important observation (p. 84f):

> In the cases of Abraham Berukhim, Hayyim Vital, Levi Isaac, and Safrin, weeping preceded the appearance of the Shekhinah... The activation of the eye [here] ends in a visual experience. In the case of Karo and Alkabez, [by contrast], the organ activated was the lips; indeed, [this time] the Shekhinah spoke from the throat of Karo... The correlation between the technique and the nature of the revelation is striking.[145]

The apparition of the Shekhinah as either a vision or a voice, depending on the organ stimulated by the mystic, is indeed striking, and all the more so inasmuch as the same situation is encountered in Assyrian sources, which distinguish between visions and dreams received by seers (*šabrû*) and oracles spoken by prophets (*raggimu*). While male gods, too, could be seen in visions and dreams, only Ištar and other goddesses speak from the mouth of the prophet.

The evidence collected by Idel establishes a similar strong link between prophecy and the Shekhinah. According to R. Moses Azriel ben Eleazar ha-Darshan, "Whoever knows [the divine name] and prays using it, the Shekhinah dwells upon him and he prophesies like the ancient prophets."[146]

An anonymous source quoted by Moses de Cordovero expresses the same in another way:

> Some of the ancients commented that by the combination and permutation of the name ... after a great concentration, the righteous will receive a revelation of an aspect of a *Bat Kol* ... until a great influx will descend upon him, on the condition that whoever deals with this will be a well-prepared vessel to receive the spiritual force.[147]

Commenting on this passage, Idel notes that "in texts written in the ecstatic vein of Kabbalah and Hasidism ... man is regularly viewed as a Temple or a vessel receiving the Shekhinah.[148]

This is no place for a serious discussion of the complex figure of the Shekhinah, but she certainly shares many features with Ištar and gnostic Sophia. Like the latter, she is a "virgin of light,"[149] perceived in visions as a beautiful feminine apparition;[150] she is the supernal holy soul with whom the mystic seeks to unite;[151] she is the presence of God in man;[152] she is the word of God;[153] she is the love of God;[154] and she is also known as the Supernal mother and the Infernal mother,[155] the upper Shekhinah and the lower Shekhinah, paralleling the role of the soul in Ištar's Descent and Sophia's Fall.[156]

In Jewish esotericism, the Shekhinah is closely associated with Malkhut, "kingdom," the receiver and transmitter of the "divine efflux" into the lower worlds.[157] This association corresponds to the special relationship between Ištar and the king in Assyrian religion, which we shall now consider in detail.[158]

The King as God's Son and Chosen One

Throughout the prophecies the king is presented as a semi-divine being, partly man, partly god. On the one hand, he has a human mother who gave birth to him;[159] on the other hand, he is "the son of Mullissu" (the divine queen) and "a creation of Mullissu and the Lady of Arbela."[160] In oracle 2.5, the Goddess declares: "I am your father and mother; I raised you between my wings."[161] The mother-child relationship between the Goddess and the king, implicit in every oracle of the corpus, is elaborated through a set of images and metaphors stressing the king's total dependence on his divine mother and the latter's ardent love for her child or creature. Most commonly, the king is portrayed as a baby suckled, comforted, tended, carried, reared and protected by the Goddess, who now appears as his mother, now as his midwife, wet nurse, or nurse, and tenderly calls him "my calf" or "my king,"[162] while she fiercely attacks his enemies.[163]

Recent studies by Othmar Keel and Martti Nissinen have established that this imagery was by no means limited to the Assyrian prophecy corpus alone but is well attested all over the ancient Near East, including biblical prophecy.[164] In Isaiah 66 and Hosea 11, God's love for Israel is described in terms of a mother-child imagery identical with that of the Assyrian prophecies, and the formulation of Hosea 11:4, "I bent down to feed them [= Israel]," recalls

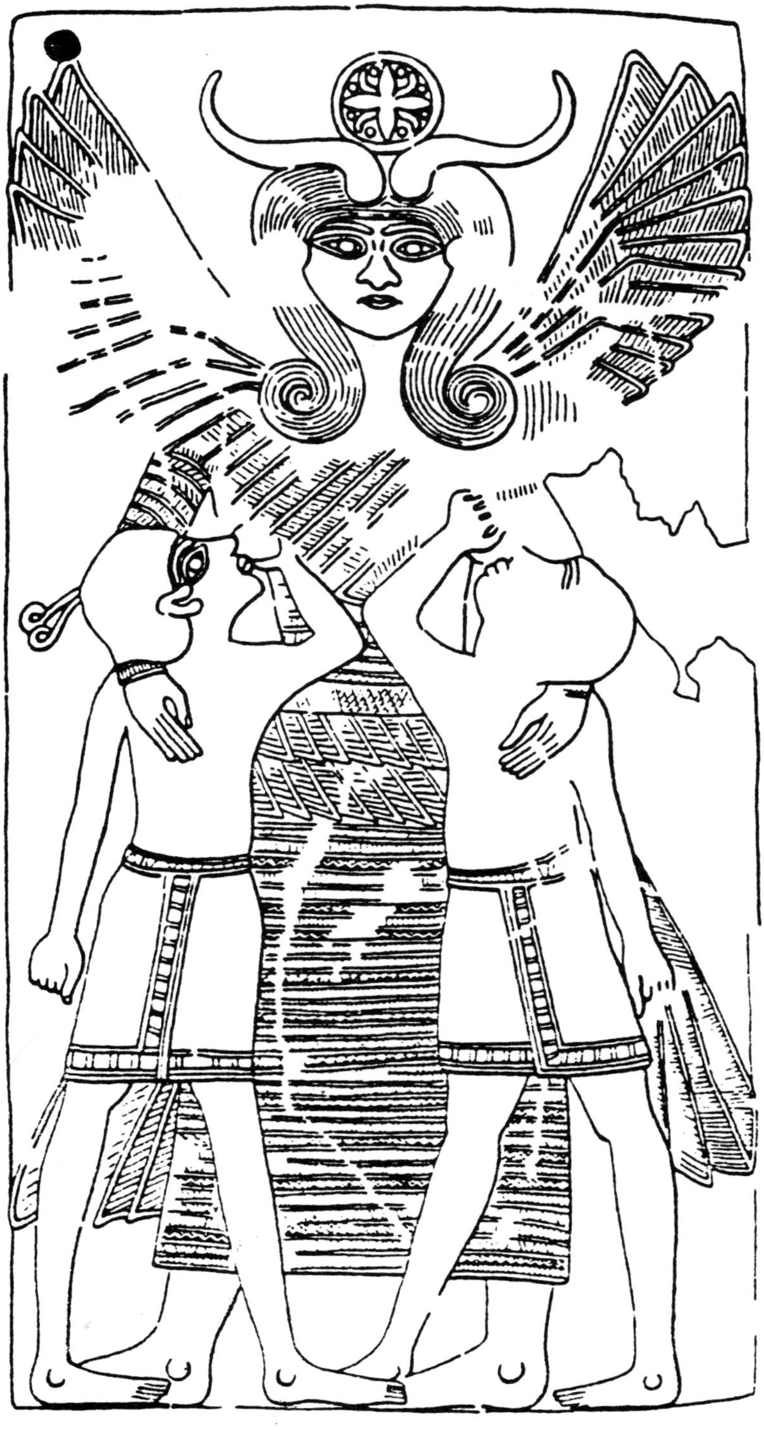

FIG. 15. *Aširtu/Anat nursing the crown prince. Ivory panel from Ugarit, early 13th century BC.*
U. WINTER, *Frau und Göttin* (OBO 53), Abb. 409.

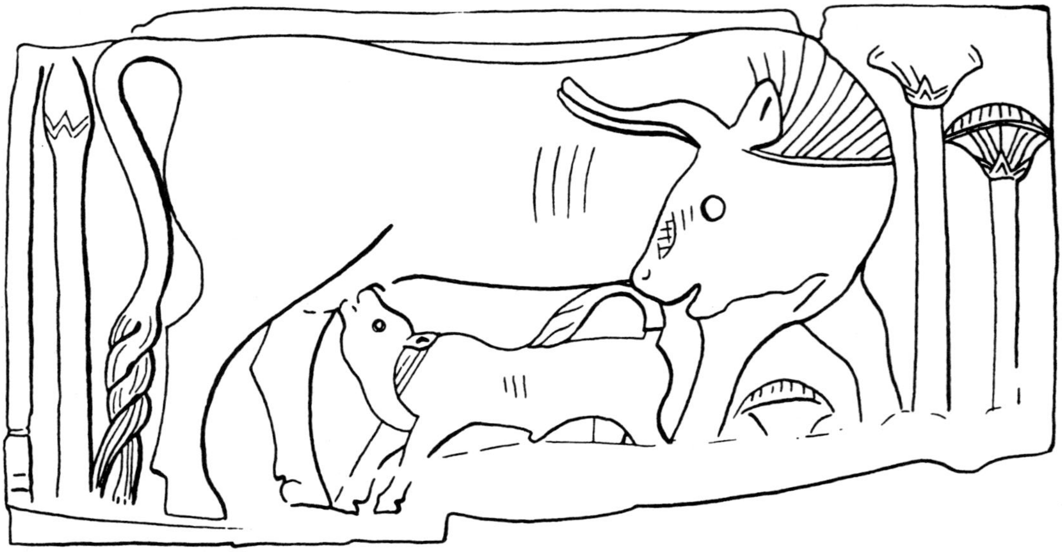

FIG. 16. *Mullissu/Ištar suckling her calf. Neo-Assyrian ivory panel from Nimrud (cf. figs. 19 and 21).*
O. KEEL, *Das Böcklein in der Milch seiner Mutter* (OBO 33), Abb. 118.

the image of a cow bending over its suckling calf, a ubiquitous motif of contemporary visual arts.[165] While in biblical prophecy the role of God's son and chosen one is usually applied to Israel collectively, passages such as 2 Samuel 7 and Psalm 89 leave no doubt that this role was originally reserved for the king alone and ideologically remained the prerogative of the Davidic dynasty for "as long as the heavens endure."[166]

In discussing the meaning of the Assyrian mother-child imagery, Nissinen argues that it was functionally rather than ontologically oriented, and that its primary purpose was to *legitimize* the king's rule.[167] From this point of view, calling the king the son of God would be merely a figure of speech for god-chosen (and thus legitimate) king;[168] and the need to legitimize the

FIG. 17. *Ištar suckling her lamb; notice the cuneiform sign "god" above the ewe. Middle-Assyrian cylinder seal from Assur.*
KEEL, OBO 33, Abb. 87.

kingship of Esarhaddon and Assurbanipal would provide a plausible explanation not only for the existence of the present corpus but for the activity of the prophets in general. In Nissinen's words, "The prophets are always positively disposed towards the king... It was a prophetic *task* [emphasis mine] to convey to the king the divine mother's or midwife's blessing for the legitimation of his kingship."[169]

This interpretation certainly makes good sense, keeping in mind the historical context of the prophecies (see below) and the important role that allegory and metaphor play in Mesopotamian religious language and thought. However, on closer examination it becomes evident that it alone does not provide a sufficient explanation for the existence of the prophecy corpus, nor does it explain Assyrian prophecy as a phenomenon.

First of all, if the prophecies had been delivered and collected simply to back up Esarhaddon's and Assurbanipal's political position, one would expect them to be referred to in royal inscriptions composed at the time when these kings were politically weak. This, however, is not the case. While Esarhaddon does mention that he received encouraging oracles after his victory over his brothers (see p. LXVIII), this statement is found only in inscriptions composed in his eighth regnal year (673), when his power had already long been consolidated. The only reference to prophecies in his early inscriptions is to be found in a context relating to the rebuilding of Babylon (see p. LXIX). And while Assurbanipal takes pains to relate in detail the oracles and visions he received before his war against Teumman, king of Elam (see pp. XLVI and LXX), he does not bother to mention that he had received supporting prophecies as a crown prince or during the Šamaš-šumu-ukin war.[170]

This implies that although both Esarhaddon and Assurbanipal undoubtedly welcomed the support of the prophets,[171] they did not need it to *sanction* their rule. They were no usurpers; on the contrary, they had been promoted to the status of crown prince by divine approval, and their hereditary rights had been fully confirmed by oaths of loyalty imposed on the whole empire.[172] Hence the emphasis of the prophecies on the legitimacy of the king does *not* indicate a need for divine approval but, on the contrary, reflects the exceptional care by which both kings were raised to the status of crown prince.

In the second place, it should be noted that although the doctrine of god-chosen god-raised king certainly was part and parcel of Mesopotamian royal ideology, there is no evidence that it was automatically applied to every Assyrian king (just as not every king of Israel or Judah was automatically hailed as the Messiah).[173] Only relatively few kings refer to themselves as creations of gods, and the inscriptions of Assurbanipal, where this claim is repeatedly made, constitute an exception rather than a rule. Nor is there any evidence that kings who really needed prophetic support actually received it. Excepting Esarhaddon and Assurbanipal, no Assyrian kings mention prophetic oracles in their inscriptions.

Most important, there is every reason to believe that the mother-child imagery of the prophecies was not just metaphorical. We know that Assyrian princes were entrusted as infants to temples of Ištar, almost certainly to be suckled and nursed by hierodules who impersonated the motherly aspects of the Goddess.[174] The ideological background of this practice is provided by the creation myth, *Enūma eliš*, according to which Marduk, the future king of the gods, in his infancy suckled the breasts of goddesses and was tended by a divine nurse.[175] An Assyrian esoteric text related to the cult of Ištar elaborates on the goddesses in question: we learn that Marduk's wet nurse was Ištar of Nineveh, while his dry nurse was Ištar of Arbela.[176] Exactly the same goddesses figure in the prophecies and other contemporary texts as the wet and dry nurses of the king.[177] Moreover, the goddess Mullissu, who in the prophecies appears as the divine mother of both Esarhaddon and Assurbanipal, appears in the same capacity also in contemporary royal inscriptions and hymns.[178] It is thus clear that the distribution of the roles of the goddesses was not fortuitous but had a well-established doctrinal basis shared by contemporary prophecy, mysticism and royal ideology. The application of a celestial pattern of education to royal children, or vice versa, reflects an important dogma already encountered above (p. XXI): the complementarity of the celestial and mundane realms, the latter being conceived of as the mirror image of the former.[179]

Thus when Assurbanipal, in line with oracle 2.5, claims that he "knew no father or mother, and grew up in the lap of [his] goddesses,"[180] and when he calls himself a "product of Emašmaš and Egašankalamma" (the renowned temples of Ištar of Nineveh/Mullissu and Ištar of Arbela),[181] he means what he says. The implication is that he was separated from his physical mother and father in his infancy and brought up in temples of Ištar in Nineveh and Arbela.[182] Nursed by hierodules and educated by initiates in the sacred mysteries he indeed "grew up in the lap of the goddesses" and was "raised between their wings."

By the same token, when the king repeatedly refers to himself as the creation of gods or to Mullissu as "the mother who gave birth to me,"[183] these assertions have to be taken seriously. They imply that he was more than a normal man: a semi-divine being selected and called by gods and miraculously perfected for his office in the womb of his mother[184] — a creature "two-thirds god and one-third man," like the legendary Gilgamesh, the prototype of the perfect king.[185]

Two points in particular are worth close attention in this doctrine, which is attested in Assyrian royal inscriptions since the reign of Tukulti-Ninurta I (1243-1207 BC)[186] and which certainly represented an article of faith comparable to the Christian doctrine of the immaculate conception of Christ.

First, the divine mother of the king, Mullissu, bears the epithet "wild cow" (*rīmtu*) in Assyrian royal inscriptions.[187] This epithet not only connects her with the mother of Gilgamesh, Ninsun the "Wild Cow,"[188] and the calf-licking cow of contemporary visual arts, but also associates her (through the horns of the cow) with the moon, and thus identifies her with the supernal aspect of Ištar, the "Daughter of the moon" or "Ištar of Wisdom,"[189] the equivalent of the Holy Spirit (see pp. XXIX and XXXII above). Created by this goddess, whose very name connoted purity and holiness,[190] the king was a man "conceived of the Holy Spirit"[191]— not just an "adoptive" son of God, but "the offspring of God himself,"[192] the Perfect Man impersonating the Tree of Life and thus fit to rule the world as the "Good Shepherd," God's representative on earth.[193]

Second, whenever the theme of divine creation and choice occurs in Assyrian royal inscriptions, it is always combined with a *historical mission* the king was committed to fulfill.[194] This circumstance gives the choice of a

COURTESY MUSÉE DU LOUVRE

FIG. 18. *Mullissu seated as the Queen of Heaven on her star-lined throne.*
AO 23004.

crown prince a "messianic" dimension also implicit in *Enūma eliš*, where the birth of Marduk in effect signalled the coming of a saviour god, the "avenger of his father."[195] Just as this celestial king-to-be was to vanquish the forces of chaos represented by the raging sea (Tiamat) and to create a new world order, so was the mundane crown prince expected to vanquish whatever forces threatened the empire and to establish a reign of lasting peace and justice. In Mesopotamian mythology, the celestial saviour is consistently identified as Ninurta/Nabû, the heavenly crown prince,[196] who after his victory over the forces of darkness merges with his father and must accordingly be considered as the heavenly paragon of the king in his role as the defender of cosmic order.[197]

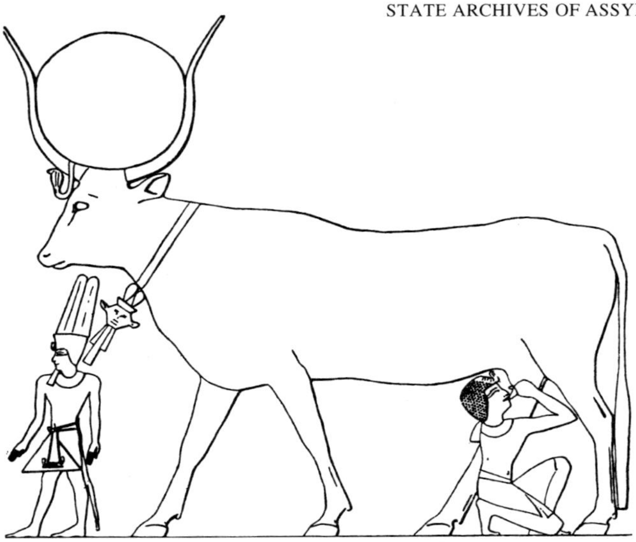

FIG. 19. *Hathor nursing the young pharaoh. 18th dynasty relief from Deir el-Bahri, early 15th century BC.*
KEEL, OBO 33, Abb. 40.

FIG. 20. *Isis as sycamore tree nursing the pharaoh. Wall painting from the tomb of Tuthmosis III, mid-15th century BC.*

Ideologically, then, the god-born god-chosen Assyrian king corresponds to the Egyptian pharaoh (considered the incarnation of Horus) and to the Jewish Messiah. The divine mother of the king, Mullissu, is the perfect equivalent of Egyptian Hathor, defined as the mother and wet nurse of the pharaoh, the wild cow, the queen of heaven, the goddess of love, the mother of gods and the creatrix of all living things, the lady of life, the living soul of the trees, and the ultimate reality.[198] Remarkably enough, the Canaanite equivalent of Mullissu, the goddess Aširtu/Asherah,[199] firmly connected with ecstatic prophecy,[200] is represented as a stylized tree in late second and early first millennium iconography.[201] In 8th-century Israel, Asherah is attested as the consort of Yahweh.[202] Logically, then, she must have functioned as the divine mother of the king in pre-exilic Israel, too, which accords with the mother role of the oracular deity in the Hosea prophecy discussed above (p. XXXVIf).[203]

The king's ideological association with Ninurta/Nabû of course does not imply that every king came to be viewed as, or had to play the role of, a god-chosen "Messiah." On the contrary, the expectations projected upon them as individuals certainly varied greatly depending on the circumstances.

FIG. 21. *The cow-and-calf motif on Pithos A from Kuntillet 'Ajrud.*
KEEL, OBO 33, Abb. 120.

The accession of Esarhaddon was preceded by a period of serious internal crisis for Assyria. The emperor had been murdered by his own sons, the legitimate heir had been driven into exile, and a power struggle in the heart of the land shook the foundations of the whole empire. This state of affairs was interpreted as a manifestation of divine wrath resulting from the upheaval of cosmic harmony.[204] Not only the land of Assyria but the "kingdom of heaven" as well was in a state of war, as the angry gods punished the nation for its wicked deeds.[205]

In this situation the role of Esarhaddon assumed a new, "messianic" significance. There can be little doubt that he had from the beginning been regarded as the legitimate heir by the prophets. In contrast to his brothers, he had been raised by the Goddess; in addition, he had a mother whose name, Naqia/Zakutu ("the pure, innocent one") reminded one of the Holy Goddess herself.[206] In the eyes of the prophets, he was the person chosen to defeat the forces of evil, restore order, and save the country.

A portent received during Esarhaddon's exile, months before the murder of Sennacherib, powerfully added to the nimbus of the prince. This portent not only predicted that the king would be murdered by a son of his but also that the exiled prince would return victorious, ascend the throne, and rebuild "the temples of the great gods."[207] We know that the portent had been communicated to Naqia, and after her pilgrimage to Arbela on behalf of her son (see oracle 1.8) it was doubtless soon propagated all over the empire.[208] With the murder of Sennacherib, the first part of the portent had become a reality; and the swift defeat of the brothers, also preceded by a portent, must have convinced even the last sceptic that Esarhaddon indeed was a tool in the

FIG. 22. *Ninurta/Nabû combatting mythical monsters. Neo-Assyrian cylinder seal with legend reading "Let the one who trusts in you not come to shame, O Nabû!"*
BM 89145.

hand of God — a true incarnation of Ninurta, the "avenger of his father, "shining like sun" after his victory.[209]

Against this background, the oracles to Esarhaddon can be seen as words of divine encouragement and support to a saviour king who had embarked on a historical mission but had not yet completed it, comparable to the messianic oracles delivered to David, Cyrus and Zerubbabel.[210] By defeating the murderers of his father, Esarhaddon had restored the cosmic harmony, but had not yet even gotten started with his grand mission, the restoration of the temples of the great gods, a task that was to occupy him for his entire reign. The message of the prophets was that just as he owed everything to the help of God, he was to proceed fearlessly towards the fulfillment of his mission, knowing that God would be with him in the future too and would not let him come to shame.

We know that Neo-Assyrian prophecy had a long prehistory extending back to the early second millennium BC (see below, p. XLVIII) and that other Assyrian kings also received prophetic encouragement on critical occasions. But just as Esarhaddon's triumphant rise to power against all odds remains without parallel in Assyrian history, the massive prophetic movement in his support is also likely to have been unique. It was the product of a unique historical situation loaded with the expectation of a saviour king, comparable to the one preceding the appearance of Jesus 700 years later.[211]

Assyrian Prophecy

Designations of Prophets

The Neo-Assyrian term for "prophet" was *raggimu* (fem. *raggintu*, "prophetess"), which literally means "shouter/proclaimer."[212] Such a term immediately reminds one of John the Baptist, "the shouting one," and of his 9th-century BC predecessor, Elijah, who epitomize the idealized picture of biblical prophets as ascetics living in the "wilderness." Indeed, there is evidence that asceticism and seclusion from the world played a significant role in the life of Assyrian prophets. In oracle 9 the prophetess presents her concern for the life of the king as the exertions of Gilgamesh; the allusion is to the 9th and 10th tablets of the Gilgamesh Epic, where the hero roams the desert as an ascetic clad in animal skins, again recalling the biblical figures of Elijah and John the Baptist.[213]

The role of the prophets as speakers to the masses is well attested both in the prophecy corpus itself and in contemporary texts. In oracle 2.4 the prophetess declares: "I will speak to the multitudes," and continues: "Listen, sunrise and sunset!," recalling Isaiah 1:2 and other biblical passages. Oracle 3.2 begins, "Listen, Assyrians!," recalling Amos 3 and other biblical oracles addressed to the Israelites collectively. In SAA 10 352 (ABL 437 = LAS 280), a prophetess speaks in "the assembly of the country," while ABL 149 = LAS 317 and CT 53 969 refer to appearances of prophetesses in temples and during religious ceremonies.[214] Oracle 3.5 indicates that the activity of the prophets played a decisive role in winning the population of Assyria over to Esarhaddon's side before his clash with the rebel brothers.[215] The same idea is implicit in lines 108ff of Esarhaddon's succession treaty (SAA 2 no. 6), which show that prophets were considered capable of turning the masses of people against Assurbanipal, Esarhaddon's crown prince designate.[216] Finally, the very fact that prophesying was expressed in Neo-Assyrian through the verb *ragāmu*, "to shout, to proclaim,"[217] implies that prophetic oracles were generally delivered in a loud voice — "shouted" — and hence usually addressed to masses of people rather than to single individuals.

While the deliverers of prophetic oracles are consistently called *raggimu* (*raggintu*) in the prophecy corpus and other Neo-Assyrian texts (letters, treaties, and administrative documents),[218] in Esarhaddon's inscriptions the oracles of Collections 1-3 are referred to as *šipir mahhê*, "messages of ecstatic prophets" (see below, p. LXXIII). The term *mahhû*, "ecstatic prophet,"[219] is well known as a designation of the Mari prophets[220] and also occurs in Ur III, Old Babylonian and Neo-Babylonian texts,[221] as well as in Standard Babylonian literary and lexical texts;[222] it is also attested in Middle Assyrian.[223] By contrast, it is conspicuously absent from purely Neo-Assyrian texts, where it is attested only twice: once in the Succession Treaty of Esarhaddon as a synonym of *raggimu*,[224] and once in a religious commentary, the so-called Marduk Ordeal text.[225] Conversely, the word *raggimu* does not occur outside Neo-Assyrian texts.[226] It is thus clear that *raggimu* was a specifically Neo-Assyrian designation of prophets replacing older *mahhû*, which was retained as a synonym restricted to literary use.[227] Accordingly, the logogram MÍ.GUB.BA, which is given the reading *mahhūtu* in lexical texts,[228] is probably to be read *raggintu* in no. 10, where it seems to refer to the prophetess Dunnaša-amur, the speaker in oracle 9.

Whether the replacement of *mahhû* "ecstatic" by *raggimu* "shouter" reflects a change in the social role of the prophets between the Middle and Neo-Assyrian periods remains unclear.[229] In any case, it is certain that Neo-Assyrian prophecy continued to be ecstatic in character. As already pointed out above (p. XXXIVf), the "possession" of the prophet by the Goddess involved a change in consciousness, purposely triggered by ascetic techniques such as weeping and wailing.[230] In addition to oral prophecy, these techniques also produced visions and dreams. It is certainly no coincidence that *raggimu* "prophet" is equated with *šabrû* "seer, visionary" in a Neo-Assyrian lexical text,[231] and that *mahhû* "ecstatic" is associated with words like "wailer" (*lallaru*), "frenzied" (*zabbu*), "carrier of spindle" (*nāš pilaqqi*), and other ecstatic devotees of Ištar in Babylonian lexical and omen texts.[232] The close connection between visions and prophetic oracles is clearly evidenced by no. 11, which contains an oracular utterance followed by a vision (*diglu*), as well as by several other contemporary texts.[233] At times the borderline between oracular prophecy and visions seems to vanish altogether, as in the following episode in an inscription of Assurbanipal:

> In Ab, the month of the appearance of the Bow star and the festival of the Venerable Lady, the daughter of Enlil, as I was sojourning in her beloved city Arbela to worship her great divinity, they reported me an attack of the Elamites... Because of this insolence ... I turned to Ištar, the Most High; I stood before her, I knelt down under her, and I prayed to her godhead while my tears were flowing: "... He (Teumman) is whetting his weapons in order to invade Assyria. You are the most heroic one of the gods; scatter him like a pack in the thick of the battle and raise a violent, destructive storm against him."
>
> Ištar heard my desperate sighs. She said to me, "Fear not," and encouraged me (with the words): "I feel compassion for the prayer you prayed and [the tears] that filled your eyes."
>
> The very same night as I was praying to her, a seer (*šabrû*) lay down and had a dream. Having awakened, he related to me the nocturnal vision (*tabrīt mūši*) which Ištar had made him see (*ušabrû*):
>
> "The Goddess who dwells in Arbela entered (var. entered me). Quivers hang from her right and left, she held a bow in her hand, and she had drawn a pointed sword to make battle. You stood before her, while she spoke to you like a mother to a child. Ištar, the highest of the gods, called to you and gave you the

following order: 'You plan to make war — I am on my way to where you intend to go.'

You said to her, 'Wherever you go, I will go with you,' but the Lady of Ladies answered you: 'You shall stay here, where your residence is! Eat, drink wine, make merry, and praise my godhead until I go and accomplish that task and make you attain your heart's desire. You shall not make a long face, your feet shall not tremble, and you shall not wipe away sweat in the thick of the battle.'

She sheltered you in her sweet embrace, protecting your entire body. Fire flared up in her face, and she left angrily and impetuously to defeat her enemy, proceeding against Teumman, king of Elam, who had made her very angry."
(Streck Asb pp. 114ff // 190ff // Piepkorn Asb p. 64ff)[234]

In both its imagery and its content the theophany reported here closely resembles the prophetic oracles of the present corpus. However, it differs from them in being a visual and acoustic experience, not direct speech of god, and is accordingly attributed not to a *raggimu* but to a *šabrû*, "seer." The distinction made in the text between *raggimu* and *šabrû* is fundamentally important. While any individual (and especially any devotee of Ištar) could have a vision or a dream and report it,[235] only a few special individuals could qualify as prophets, to speak with the mouth of God. This basic distinction between a "seer" and a "prophet" of course does not preclude the possibility that a prophet could have visions — on the contrary.[236]

Prophecy and the Cult of Ištar

The close connection of Assyrian prophecy to the cult of Ištar has been noted in several earlier studies,[237] and indeed cannot be stressed enough. This close connection is evident not only from the fact that the Assyrian oracles are called words of Ištar/Mullissu; as shown in detail below (p. ILff), the prophets also bear names associated with the Goddess or her cult, and come from three major cult centres of Ištar, viz. Arbela, Calah and Assur (the "Inner City").[238] One of the prophets is a votaress donated to the Goddess by the king.[239] The oracles contain references to the cult of the Goddess or present demands on her behalf.[240] The fact that prophets are closely associated with devotees of Ištar (*assinnu*, *nāš pilaqqi*, etc.) in lexical lists and elsewhere[241] and that they participated in cultic ceremonies[242] strongly suggests that they were permanent members of the temple community. A letter to the king shows that a prophet could be consulted by private individuals during visits to the temple of Ištar in Calah.[243] A Middle Assyrian administrative text from Kar-Tukulti-Ninurta lists prophets and prophetesses as recipients of food rations among other cultic personnel of the Ištar temple of the city.[244]

All this implies that the individuals who became prophets belonged to the community of devotees of Ištar and therefore shared the same religious convictions, doctrines and educational background.[245] Incidental passages in the prophecies show that philosophical and mythological compositions dealing with the ascent and salvation of the soul, such as the myths of Adapa, Atrahasis and Gilgamesh, were well-known to the prophets, to the extent that they affected the imagery and content of the oracles.[246] Other literary allusions in the oracles indicate familiarity with cultic love lyrics and panegyric hymns, royal rituals, and royal penitential psalms and hymns, in other words, texts central to the official cult of Ištar.[247] Most importantly, a number of passages in the oracles have parallels only in esoteric mystical texts relating to the cult of Ištar[248] and Jewish mystical tradition.[249] Such passages imply that the prophets had access to esoteric mystical lore, and the only thinkable context in which such an exposure could have been possible is the cult of Ištar with its secret mysteries and initiation rites.[250]

While all the oracles of the corpus are addressed to or concern the king or his son and display a positive attitude towards the king,[251] it is also certain that other types of prophecies existed. Contemporary letters and other sources reveal that the prophets could also sharply attack the king and his behaviour.[252] Keeping in mind the cultic background of the prophets, it is not unreasonable to suppose that they also propagated the key doctrines of the cult of Ištar, particularly its way of salvation,[253] and consequently also a critique of contemporary morality.[254] While this moral dimension surfaces only occasionally in the extant prophecy corpus,[255] the critical attitude of the prophets towards the "world" cannot be questioned.[256] Such a prophetic activity would help explain the unremitting influx of new devotees to the Goddess. Who else but the prophets would have carried out the "missionary work" generating this influx?[257]

Although no Assyrian prophetic oracles are extant from the time before the 7th century, the existence of prophets and prophetesses (*mahhû* and *mahhūtu*) associated with the cult of Ištar is firmly documented already for the 13th century BC, see p. XLVII above; an oracle of Ištar of Nineveh is actually quoted in the Amarna correspondence (see Tušratta's letter to Amenophis III, EA 23, mid-fourteenth century BC). The Middle Assyrian prophecy, in turn, has a prehistory reaching back, through Mari prophecy, to the early second millennium BC and even beyond. The earliest reference to a prophetic oracle of Ištar seems to occur in an Old Akkadian text dating to reign of Naram-Suen (23rd century BC), see Wilcke, ZA 87 (1997) 16f.

The Prophets of the Corpus

The 28 oracles of the corpus can be assigned, on the basis of the extant authorship indications, to 13 different prophets, four of whom are male and nine female (including two apparently bi- or asexual prophets, see below under Bayâ and Ilussa-amur). The comparatively high number of women is paralleled by the prominence of prophetesses and female ecstatics in Mari and OT prophecy, as well as in Gnosticism and early Christianity.[258] Eight of the prophets come from Arbela, two from Assur, one from Calah, possibly one from Nineveh, and one from a town "in the mountains" (probably near Arbela).

The individual prophets are surveyed below in alphabetic order along with a brief discussion of their names, domiciles and oracles. Outside the corpus, only two more Assyrian prophets (one male and one female) are known by name from contemporary texts.[259] The unnamed prophets and prophetesses (*raggimānu raggimātu*) honoured by the king in ABL 1216 = SAA 10 109:9 almost certainly largely consisted of prophets included in the following list.[260]

1. **Ahāt-abīša** (wr. MÍ.NIN—AD-*šá*), "Sister of her father," a prophetess from Arbela (oracle 1.8). The name, also borne by a daughter of Sargon II (SAA 1 31 r.27, cf. Fuchs Sar. 124:198), can be compared with such NA names as *Rīšat-abīša* "Joy of her father" (ADD 1142:2 and *Hadi-abīša* "Delight of her father" (GPA 248:3), and is unlikely to be an assumed "prophet name" with religious connotations. In a marriage document from Calah (CTN 3 47:4) it is borne by the young girl to be married. The reading of the first element is assured by the NB syllabic spelling MÍ.*a-hat*—AD-*šá* (Tallqvist NBN, p. 3).

Ahat-abiša's short oracle refers to a prayer of Naqia to Ištar on behalf of her exiled son (see p. XLIII above) and closes with words recalling the conclusion of the Lord's Prayer in Matthew 6:13.

2. **Bayâ**, a prophet(ess) from Arbela (oracles 1.4 and [2.2]). The female determinative preceding the name of the prophet in 1.4 is clear on the tablet and is confirmed by MÍ.*ba-ia-a* listed as a "[servant of] Ištar of Huzirina" in STT 406 r. 10. On the other hand, the prophet is clearly defined as a "son" of Arbela (i.e., male) on the tablet, and there is no way of emending the crucial sign DUMU "son" to DUMU.MÍ, "daughter." If oracle 2.2 also originates from Bayâ (see below), the masculine gentilic following the name there would confirm the male sex of the prophet. The female determinative would then imply that the prophet was a "man turned into woman" through an act of self-castration, see above, p. XXXIV. See also below, under Ilussa-amur.

The name of Bayâ is restored in oracle 2.2, but the suggested restoration perfectly fits the extant traces, the available space, and the content of the oracle. Note that 2.2 begins with the same words as 1.4 and shares with it the phrase "the future will be like the past" and the theme of "sixty gods," neither of which occurs in the other oracles of the corpus. Note also that Bayâ is not the only prophet represented by two oracles in the corpus. Collections 1 and 2 also contain two oracles by La-dagil-ili (1.10 and 2.3), and these oracles likewise share common features not occurring in other oracles of the corpus (the beginning words, almost identically worded promises of safety and dynastic succession, and cultic demands). See also below on Sinqiša-amur, the author of oracles 1.2 and 2.5 (and possibly of 9 and 10).

Bayâ's oracles are important for their theological and doctrinal content. The Assyrian concept of God as the "sum total of gods" is clearly articulated in his oracles, which also contain the "Platonic" ship-of-state metaphor and an important Trinitarian allusion (see above p. XVIII). On the exhortation "Do not trust in man; lift your eyes, look to me" (1.4) see below under La-dagil-ili.

3. **Dunnaša-āmur**(wr. MÍ.KALAG-*šá—a-mur*), "I have seen her power(?)," a prophetess from Arbela (nos. 9 and 10). The reading of the logographic element of the name is uncertain (cf. KALAG.GA = *dunnu*, SAA 3 39:34ff), and no syllabic spellings confirming it are available. It is not excluded that one actually has to read Sinqiša-amur ("I have seen her distress"), making this prophet identical with no. 11 below. Note that *sinqu* (= Bab. *sunqu*) in NA meant "hard times, distress" and could hence have been written logo-

graphically with the sign KALAG; cf. MÍ.KALAG.GA = *dannatu* "hard times," and *sunqu* = *dannatu*, LTBA 2 2:340ff.

Reading the name as Sinqiša-amur is supported by the fact that apart from 1.2 (from Sinqiša-amur), no. 9 is the only oracle in the corpus to use the verb *ṭabāhu* "to slaughter" to indicate the annihilation of the king's enemies. On the other hand, Dunnaša-amur would make sense as a "prophet name": the power of the Goddess is stressed several times in NA sources, e.g. oracle 9:3 and ABL 876:9.[261]

In no. 9 the prophetess identifies herself with Gilgamesh roaming the desert in search of eternal life, implying that ascetic denial of the body (lines 12-15) played an important part in her own life, see above, pp. XXXIV and XLV. On this important oracle see further pp. XXI and LXXI, and nn. 18 and 21.

4. **Ilūssa-āmur**, "I have seen her godhead," a prophetess from the Inner City, i.e. Assur (oracle 1.5). The name implies a visionary experience of Ištar and hence probably is a "prophet name." It is otherwise attested only in KAV 121, a small fragment of unknown date from Assur. The rarity of the name makes it likely that this text too refers to the prophetess, and the fact that she appears in the text as a recipient of provisions along with other women suggests that she was permanently attached to a temple (cf. above p. XLVII).

Note that although the name is spelled with the feminine determinative in both 1.5 and KAV 121 (MÍ.DINGIR-*sa—a-mur*), the gentilic adjective in 1.5 is in the masculine gender. See the discussion under Bayâ.

The oracle of Ilussa-amur ends in the words "I am Mu[llissu]," but is otherwise almost completely destroyed.

5. **Issār-bēlī-da''ini**, "Ištar, strengthen my lord!," a prophetess of unknown domicile (probably Arbela) defined as "a votary of the king" (1.7). The name (where "my lord" certainly refers to the donor, in this case the king) may have been given or assumed at the moment of or after the donation. Non-royal votaries to the Goddess apparently did not have comparable names.[262]

Issar-beli-da''ini's fragmentary oracle is addressed to Esarhaddon's mother and is related in content to oracle 1.8, by Ahat-abiša of Arbela, with which it is grouped in Collection 1.

6. **Issār-lā-tašīyaṭ,** "Do not neglect Ištar!," a prophet from Arbela (oracle 1.1). The name is a *hapax legomenon*, but is clearly an equivalent of the contemporary *Lā-teggi-ana-Issār* "Do not neglect Ištar!"[263] If the meaning of the name is to be taken seriously, it suggests that the parents of this prophet had likewise been devotees of Ištar, cf. below under La-dagil-ili.

7. **Lā-dāgil-ili** "One who does not see God," a prophet from Arbela (oracles 1.10, 2.3, [3.1-5]). As already observed by Banks, AJSL 14 (1897/8) 269, "While expecting those who form the mouth-pieces of the gods to bear names implying great piety, we are surprised that Ištar of Arbela spoke through one whose name testifies that he does not trust in God!" Indeed, La-dagil-ili is a surprising name for a prophet. It reminds one of the names given by the prophet Hosea to his children, *Lo-ruhamah* ("Not loved") and *Lo-ammi* ("Not my people"), explained as follows in Hos. 1:

> The LORD ... said [to Hosea], Go, take a wanton for your wife and get children of her wantonness, for like a wanton this land is unfaithful to the LORD... She conceived and bore a daughter, and the LORD said to him, Call her Lo-ruhamah, for I will never again show love to Israel, never again forgive them. After

> weaning Lo-ruhamah, she conceived and bore a son; and the LORD said, Call him Lo-ammi, for you are not my people, and I will not be your God.

Analogously, the name La-dagil-ili would refer to the Assyrian nation or mankind at large who did not seek (or "see") God like the devotees, visionaries and prophets of Ištar.[264] Note the exhortation "do not trust in men, look to me (*dugulanni*)!" in oracle 1.4. A critical attitude to mankind is indeed evident in La-dagil-ili's oracle 2.3: "Mankind is deceitful; I (Ištar) am one who says and does." The name of the prophet could thus be a "prophet name" assumed by La-dagil-ili at some point in his career, or given to him already at birth by prophet parents, as in the Hosea passage just quoted. Cf. the discussion under Issar-la-tašiyaṭ above.[265]

In line with the implications of his name, La-dagil-ili appears to have been a very important prophet, comparable to the great biblical prophets. Like Nathan, he administers the divine covenant with Esarhaddon, and unlike the other prophets of the corpus, he repeatedly demands humility from the king and presents demands on behalf of the cult of Ištar. He has also left more oracles than any other Assyrian prophet. In addition to 1.10 and 2.3, where his name is fully preserved, Collection 3 in its entirety must also be attributed to him.[266]

Like the oracles of Bayâ and Sinqiša-amur, those of La-dagil-ili also contain characteristic elements not found in other oracles of the corpus. Both 1.10 and 2.3 open with the same formula, unique to La-dagil-ili, and the concluding section of 1.10 (also unique to La-dagil-ili) recurs almost verbatim in oracle 2.3, lines 11-14.

8. **Mullissu-kabtat**, "Mullissu is honoured," a prophetess of unknown domicile, possibly Nineveh (oracle 7).

The name of the prophetess as well as the fact that she delivers an oracle of Mullissu suggests that she belonged to the temple of Mullissu in Nineveh, Emašmaš, and thus may have been one of the "goddesses" who nurtured Assurbanipal in his childhood (see above, p. XXXIXf). This would account for the content of her oracle, one of the longest in the corpus, which strikes one as an exceptionately affectionate and tender expression of support for the prince.

9. **Nabû-hussanni**, "Nabû, remember me!," a prophet from Assur (oracle 2.1). Names ending in *hussanni*, "remember me," are rare; besides Nabû, only Aššur is attested as the theophoric element in Neo-Assyrian sources.[267] As restored, the name of the prophet recalls the words of the criminal in Luke 23:42, "Jesus, remember me when you come to your throne (var., come in royal power)." Indeed, its connotation is exactly the same: Nabû is here invoked as the saviour exalted beside his father's throne, to pass judgment on the living and the dead.[268] Restoring the theophoric element as Aššur does not change the basic connotation of the name. It has to be kept in mind that, after all, Nabû was just an aspect of Aššur, see p. XXI and nn. 7ff above.

In his fragmentary oracle, Nabû-hussanni appears to take a position in favour of the restoration of Esaggil.

10. **Rēmutti-Allati**, "Granted by Allatu," a prophetess from a mountain town, Dara-ahuya (oracle 1.3). Allatu was a name of the Mesopotamian netherworld goddess, Ereškigal.[269] Accordingly, the name, which is a hapax legomenon, looks like an assumed "prophet name" referring to its bearer as

a person released from the power of the netherworld, that is, the "world." In her short two-line oracle, the prophetess speaks for the whole community of devotees in Arbela.

11. **Sinqīša-āmur**, "I have seen her distress," a prophetess from Arbela (oracles 1.2 and [2.5]). The name of the prophetess is a hapax legomenon and is clearly an assumed "prophet name"; like the name Ilussa-amur, it refers a visionary revelation of Ištar, specifically as the Creatrix agonizing over the fate of mankind perishing in the deluge.[270] That the suffix *-ša* in the name indeed refers to Ištar is proved by the name *Sinqi/Siniq-Issār* "Distress of Ištar," frequent in contemporary texts.[271] Note that apart from Aššur, Ištar is the only deity combined with the word *sinqu* "distress" in names.[272]

The corpus contains at least two oracles by Sinqiša-amur. The authorship note of the other has been lost, but its attribution to Sinqiša-amur is certain. Both oracles share the same unique address formula and the promise to "bring enemies in neckstocks and vassals with tribute before the king's feet," which does not occur in other oracles of the corpus. In addition, both oracles are largely identical in thematic structure.[273]

The oracles of Sinqiša-amur are important for their doctrinal content: no. 2.5 clearly articulates the concept of the interconnection of the "kingdom of heaven" and the Assyrian empire (see nn. 25 and 204), and the doctrine of Ištar as the power linking the world of gods with the world of men (see nn. 48, 89 and 133). For the possibility that Sinqiša-amur is identical with the author of oracles 9 and 10 see above, under Dunnaša-amur. If so, she would be the only Assyrian prophet known to have remained active for a period of over 31 years.

12. **Tašmētu-ēreš**, "Tašmetu desired," a prophet from Arbela (oracle 6). The name of the prophet is not attested elsewhere and thus may be an assumed "prophet name."[274]

The oracle of Tašmetu-ereš is largely destroyed and contains an intriguing reference to prophetic activity.

13. **Urkittu-šarrat**, "Urkittu is queen," a prophetess from Calah (oracle 2.4). In Sargonid Assyria, Urkittu ("the Urukite [Ištar]") was simply an appellative of Mullissu/Ištar (cf. SAA 3 13:3-22 and r.2f, and 5:8-20), so the name actually extols Mullissu as the supreme goddess, "queen of heaven." Though the name thus suits the prophetess well, it is not necessarily a "prophet name," for names extolling Urkittu were not uncommon in contemporary Assyria.[275]

Note that although the prophetess comes from [the Ištar temple of] Calah, she proclaims the word of "Ištar of Arbela and Queen Mullissu." Her long oracle is political throughout and portrays Ištar as a power directing the course of world history.

The Prophecy Corpus

The Neo-Assyrian prophecy corpus is extant on two kinds of clay tablets, which differ from each other both in size and in shape. Texts 1-4 are relatively large, vertical tablets containing several oracles in two or three columns. Nos. 5-8 are smaller, horizontal in shape and contain only one oracle each (see diagram on p. LIV). By its format, no. 9 belongs with nos. 1-4, although it contains one oracle only; for nos. 10-11 see below, p. LXIf. All the tablets display a fixed length ratio between their horizontal and vertical axes, which remains constant even though the individual tablets vary considerably in size. In the horizontal tablets this ratio is 2:1 (that is, the width of a tablet is twice its height), whereas in the vertical ones it is 1:2 or 2:3, depending on the number of columns into which the tablet was divided.

Tablet Types

Both tablet types are well known from the Ninevite archives. The horizontal format (*u'iltu*) was used for notes, reports, receipts, and memoranda — in short, for information primarily meant for immediate use, not for permanent storage.[276] The vertical, multi-column format (*ṭuppu*) was used for treaties, census lists, balanced accounts and inventories of treasury, as well as for collections of all sorts, including royal decrees and ordinances, recipes, etc. — in short, for documents specifically drawn up for archival storage and reference purposes.[277] The two tablet types rarely overlap in content, but there is evidence that information recorded on horizontal tablets was archivized by copying them onto multi-column tablets, whereafter the originals were routinely destroyed.[278] The archival documents normally have a short heading, short scribal notes interspersed within the text, and a date or colophon at the end. The *u'iltu*s also usually have short notes added to the text, mostly specifying the source of the information.

The tablets of the prophecy corpus share these characteristics. We can thus conclude that nos. 5-8 report freshly received oracles, whereas nos. 1-4 are copies made from reports like nos. 5-8. No. 9 also has to be considered an archival copy because of its vertical format and the formulation of its authorship indication (see below). The careful finish of the tablet, the elaborate wording of the oracle, and the eponym date found at the end likewise clearly distinguish it from the reports. The only respect in which no. 9 formally differs from nos. 1-4 is its single-column format. However, the multi-column format would have been purposeless in a tablet accommodating one oracle

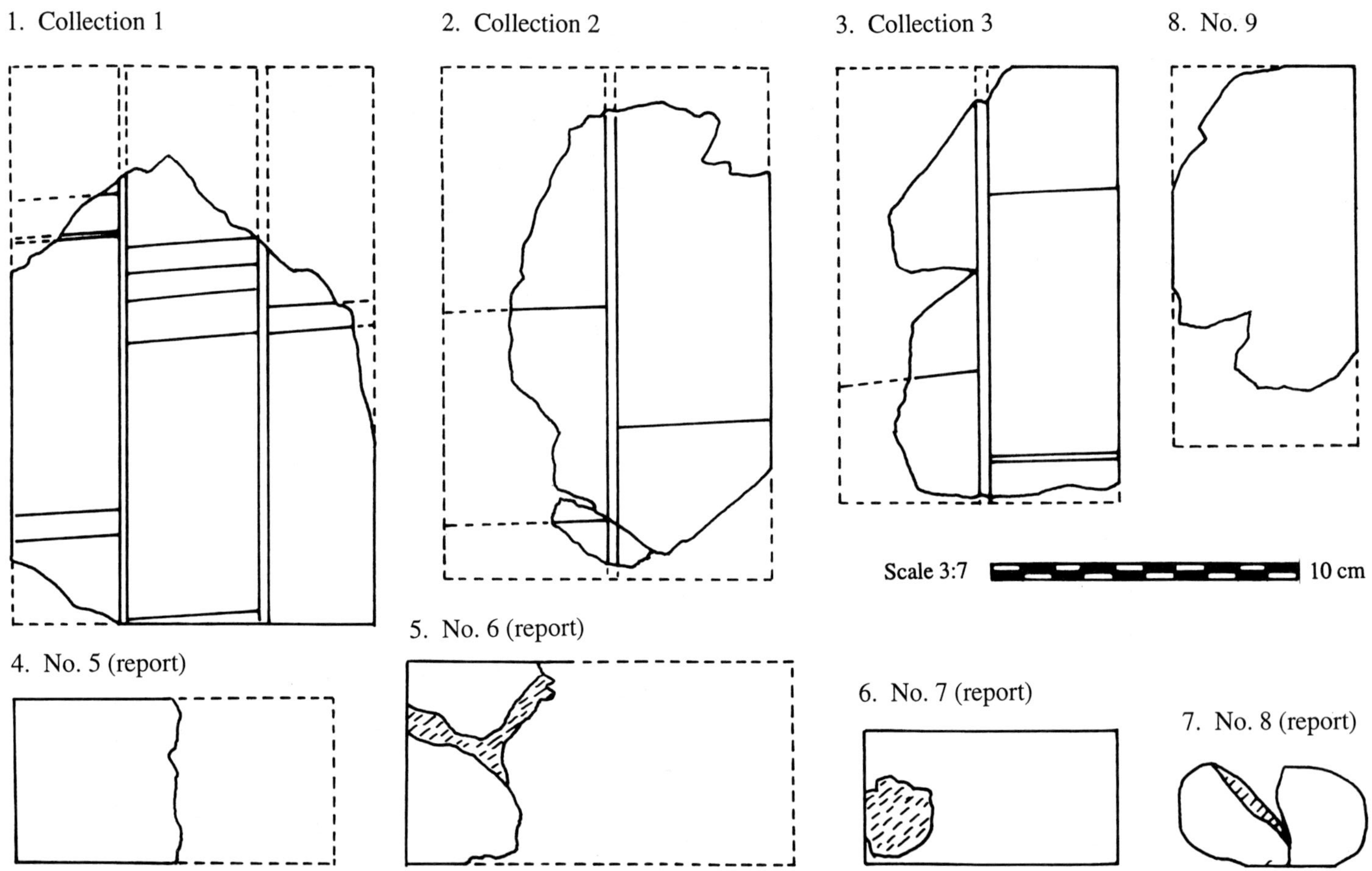

DIAGRAM I. *Outlines of nos. 1-3 and 5-9.*
Note: Broken lines indicate reconstructions, solid lines actual outlines and rulings drawn by scribes.

only. The 1:2 side-length ratio of the tablet is in perfect agreement with the one-column archival standard of Nineveh.

The quotation particle *mā* introducing the oracles in nos. 6-8 and 10-11 confirms that they were not written down by the prophets themselves but by professional scribes.[279] This is also made clear by the colophon of no. 6.

Manuscripts

All the reports certainly originate from different scribes, since the scribal hands are different in all of them. The four oracle collections, however, were all compiled by the same scribe. This can be established with certainty from an analysis of the sign forms and other scribal idiosyncracies occurring in these tablets, as contrasted with the other tablets of the corpus (see Table 1).[280]

Text 1 (Plates I-III)

No. 1 (K 4310) is a three-column tablet measuring 28 mm (maximum thickness) × 118 mm (full width) × 155 mm (extant height). The upper part of the tablet is broken off so the beginnings of all the columns on the obverse and the ends of all the columns on the reverse have been lost. In addition, a small piece has broken away from the lower left corner of the tablet. The columns on the obverse (from left to right) measure 32, 42 and 35 mm in width, those on reverse 33, 42 and 35 mm. The space between columns is 2 and 2.5 mm on the obverse, 2-3 and 2 mm on the reverse.

The portion of even thickness in the middle of the tablet measures 45 mm, the portion of decreasing thickness from there to the bottom of the tablet 65 mm. Assuming an identical curvature for the upper part of the tablet, this implies an original tablet height of 175 mm (= 2 × 65 mm + 45 mm) and a ratio of 2:3 between the horizontal and vertical axis of the tablet, as in nos. 2 and 3.

Vertical script density is 10 signs to 35 mm in cols. I and V, 10 signs to 38 mm in cols. II, III and VI, and 10 signs to 32 mm in col. IV. Allowing for an uninscribed space of 5 mm at the top of the obverse, as on the reverse, the amount of text lost on the obverse can hence be estimated as six lines at the beginning of cols. I and II, and as 14 lines at the beginning of col. III; in addition, another four lines have been lost due to surface damage at the beginning of col. I. Correspondingly, about 14 + 8 + 8 lines have been lost at the ends of cols. IV, V and VI. The lower portion of the last column is uninscribed, but the break at the end may have contained a short colophon and a date (see p. LIII above). The total number of lines lost in the breaks, excluding the colophon, is hence 42. Adding this to the total of extant lines (224), the original line total of the tablet can be established as 266, of which 84.2% are extant. Col. I originally contained 49 lines; col. II and III, 46 lines;

col. IV, 49 lines; col. V, 44 lines; and col. VI, 32 lines of text (+ possibly a colophon and a date).

The individual oracles on the tablet and the authorship indications following them are separated from each other by horizontal rulings. The ruling before oracle 1.1 is a double one, implying that the text before it differed in nature from the rest of the tablet and hence probably did not contain a prophetic oracle. A similar double ruling occurs in no. 3, col. II, where it separates oracle 3.4 from a six-line section of ritual instructions attached to oracle 3.3.

The available data are not sufficient to determine the nature of the introductory passage preceding the double ruling in col. I with any certainty. All that can be said is that it evidently fell into two parts, a ten-line introductory section entirely lost at the beginning of col. I, and a three-line postscript separated from it by a horizontal ruling and closed by the double ruling just discussed. The text remaining from the postscript shows that it cannot have contained an authorship indication, and it is unlikely to have contained ritual instructions. It is possible that the introductory section was preceded by a short 1-2 line heading, see below, p. LXIII with n. 285.

Note that the partially preserved ruling before col. I 1′, which at first glance looks like a double one, almost certainly was a single ruling with an accidentally bifurcated tail. A similar single ruling with a 0.5 mm wide double tail occurs in col. III (between lines 6′ and 7′). In the double rulings preceding oracles 1.1 and 3.4 the space between the rulings is much wider (1.5 mm in the former and 2 mm in the latter).

There are two horizontal impressions of the stylus ten lines apart in the space between cols. VI and V of the reverse, at the beginning of lines v 12 and v 21. The former is accompanied by a superscript winkelhaken ("ten" mark), which may indicate that these impressions were meant to plan the distribution of the text on the tablet. Similar marks are not found elsewhere in corpus.

Apart from the breaks, the tablet is in an excellent state of preservation. The script is clear and for the most part easily legible despite the three-column format, which occasionally caused the scribe problems of space and forced him to exceed the right-hand column margin, especially in col. I (see lines i 6′, 7′, 9′, 10′, 14′, 28′ and 32′, and ii 13′, 20′ and 23′-26′). The handwriting is elegant and experienced, though it betrays traces of haste; erasures and scribal errors occur in i 17′, 20′, 28′, and ii 6′, 8′, 34′ and 39′. It is possible that some of the scribal mistakes derive from textual damage in the originals used. This is suggested by the unusually spelling *na-kar*^{ar}*-ka* "your enemy" in ii 8′, which looks like a misreading for *na-kar-u-ti-ka* "your enemies"; note that *ar* cannot be interpreted as a phonetic complement here, since *kar* was not a polyphonic sign and thus did not need any reading specification. It is interesting that though the scribe evidently has applied his own conventions in the copying process, isolated traces of the orthography and ductus of the originals shine through here and there.[281]

For evidence indicating that the scribe who inscribed the tablet also wrote Collections 2 and 3, see p. LV above with n. 280. On the probable date of the text (late 673), see p. LXIX.

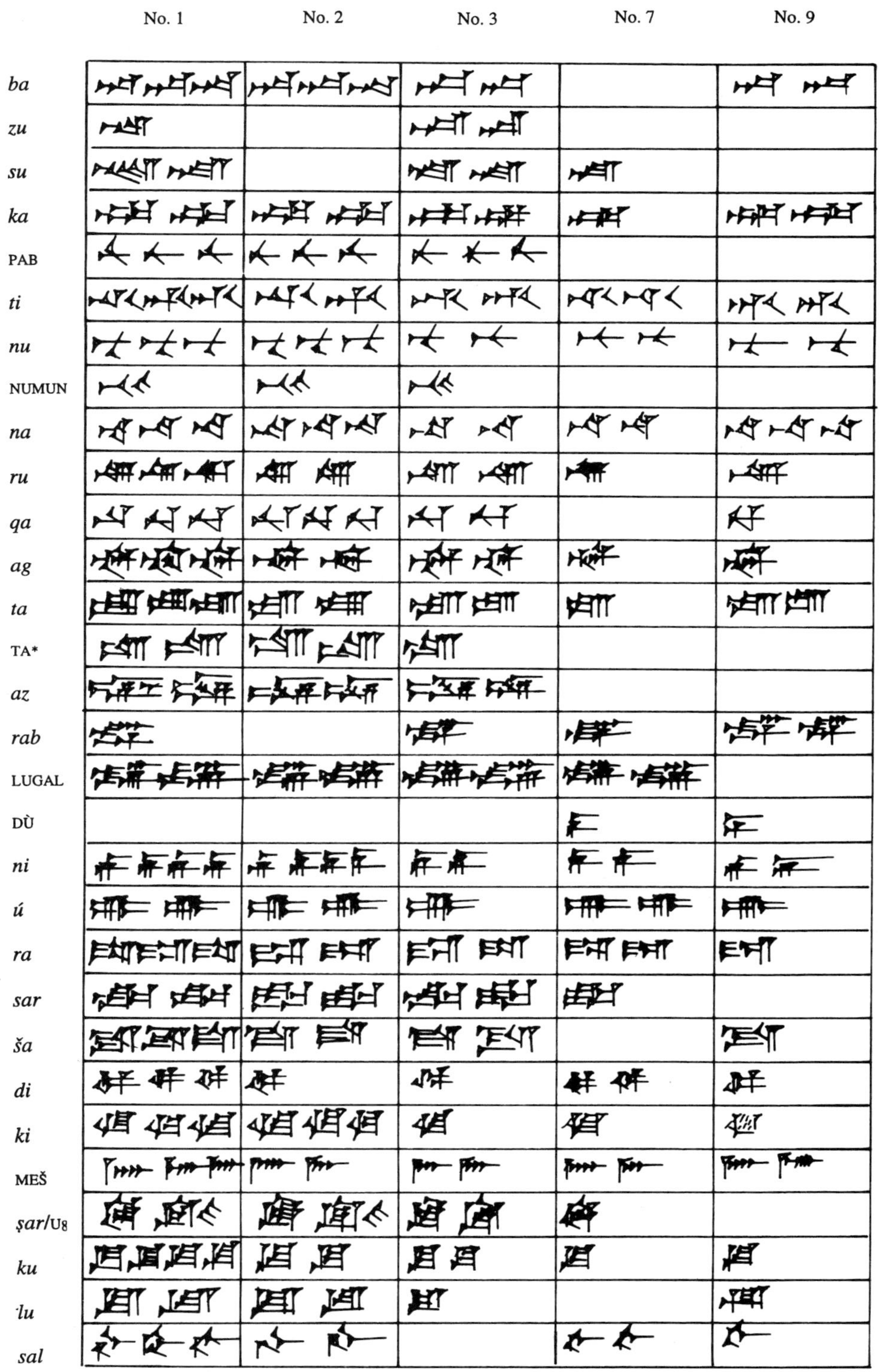

TABLE I. *Sign forms occurring in nos. 1, 2, 3, 7 and 9.*

Text 2 (Plates IV-V)

No. 2 (K 12033 + 82-5-22,527) is a two-column tablet measuring 88 mm × 146 mm. One face of the tablet is flat, the other slightly convex; the flat face is the obverse, as in K 2401 (no. 3). The entire left side of the tablet and the beginnings and ends of all the columns are missing. The right-hand column of the obverse measures 51 mm in width; the original width of the left-hand column can be determined to have been 54 mm on the basis of the restorations in lines 11′-22′, which are certain. As the space between the columns is 3 mm, the original width of the tablet can be reconstructed as 108 mm. On the reverse, the right-hand column (col. III) measures 54 mm, and as the space between the columns here is also 3 mm, the original width of the left-hand column must have been 51 mm.

Assuming that the ratio between the horizontal and vertical axes of the tablet was 2:3, as usual in three-column tablets, the original height of the tablet can be estimated to have been 162 mm.

Vertical script density is 10 signs to 38 mm in cols. I-III (in col. II partly 10 signs to 36 mm) and 10 signs to 40 mm in col. IV. Judging from the curvatures, very little text (about two lines only) has been lost at the bottom of the tablet. The amount of text lost at the top can be estimated as 4 to 6 lines depending on the column. Taking into consideration the lines lost in the breaks, cols. I and II originally contained 45 lines, col. II, 43 lines, and col. IV about 40 lines of text. The original line total of the tablet thus was about 173, of which 145 (= 83.8%) are extant.

As in nos. 1 and 3, the individual oracles are separated from each other by horizontal rulings, but in contradistinction to no. 1, the authorship indications are not correspondingly separated from the oracles. Instead, a blank space is left between the oracle and the authorship indication in 2.1. This space does not occur in other oracles of the tablet.

The scribe is the same as in nos. 1 and 3 (see p. LV). The script is clear but in several places (especially near the breaks) badly damaged and effaced, and therefore at times harder to read than in no. 1. In col. III, recent brushing and scratching has resulted in making the sixth sign in line 8′ illegible beyond remedy. Scribal mistakes occur in lines ii 9′ and 34′, and text is occasionally continued over the column margin as in no. 1, see col. iv 1′, 4′, 13′, 21′ and 27′. On the probable date of the tablet (679 BC) see p. LXIX.

Text 3 (Plates VI-VII)

No. 3 (K 2401) is a two-column tablet measuring 26 mm × 75 mm × 139 mm. As in no. 2, the obverse is flat, the reverse slightly convex. The left side and the lower edge of the tablet are missing; in addition, two small pieces have broken off from the middle of cols. I and III. The right-hand column of the obverse measures 42 mm in width; the space between the columns is 3.5 mm; the original width of the left-hand column can be determined to have been 46 mm on the basis of the restorations in lines 9-13 and 27-34. The original width of the tablet thus was 92 mm. On the reverse, the space between the columns is narrower (2 mm), and the right-hand column a little wider (44 mm) than on the obverse. The left-hand column probably had the same width as that on the obverse (46 mm).

Applied to the reconstructed tablet width (92 mm), the 2:3 axis ratio of two-column tablets yields 138 mm as the original height of the tablet. In actual fact, the tablet measures 139 mm in height, implying that the extant height is very close to the original one. This is confirmed by the curvatures which indicate that very little, possibly only the surface of the edge, is missing at the bottom of the tablet.

Vertical script density is 10 signs to 37 mm in cols. I-III and 10 signs to 35 mm in col. IV. The tablet originally contained a total of 145 lines, of which 139 (= 95.2%) are extant, many of them unfortunately only in part. Each column was originally inscribed with about 37 lines of text (cols. I and III = 37 lines; col. II = 36 lines; col. IV = 35 lines + blank space of two lines).

The individual oracles are separated from each other by horizontal rulings as in nos. 1 and 2; a double ruling separates the first three (coronation) oracles, accompanied by ritual instructions, from the rest of the tablet. In contradistinction to no. 1, but in keeping with no. 2, rulings are not used to separate the ritual instructions from the oracles, and a blank space is inserted before the authorship indication at the end of the tablet. This, as well as the two-column format of no. 2 and 3, indicates that no. 3 is temporally close to no. 2, while no. 1 was written at a different time, as is also implied by the analysis on p. LXVIIIff, which suggests that the tablets date from 680, 679 and 673 respectively.

The scribe is the same as in nos. 1 and 3 (see p. LV). The script is very clear and easily legible throughout.

Text 4 (Plate VIII)

No. 4 (83-1-18,839) is a fragment from the surface of a clay tablet measuring 33 mm (width) by 39 mm (height). The surface of the fragment is entirely flat, which indicates that a multi-column tablet is in question, and the estimated column width (50 mm or slightly less) points to a two-column tablet. Compare the column widths in nos. 2 (51 to 54 mm) and 3 (42 to 46 mm), both two-column tablets, against those in no. 1 (32 to 42 mm), a three-column tablet. The vertical script density is the same as in nos. 2 and 3 (10 signs to 37-38 mm).

The available data are not sufficient to determine the original size of the tablet, but it is likely to have been close to that of no. 2 or 3 and hence probably contained between 170 and 150 lines of text. If the format of the tablet was the same as in nos. 2 and 3, the fragment belongs to the obverse, most probably to the beginning of column II. Since only one line seems to be missing from the beginning, it is unlikely to have contained the very first oracle of the tablet.

The script is clear and easily legible, and the scribal hand agrees with that of nos. 1-3. By its content, the fragment parallels nos. 1-2 and hence a date of composition ca. 680 BC is probable.

Text 5 (Plate VIII)

No. 5 (K 6259) is the left half of a horizontal tablet measuring 25 mm (thickness) × 60 mm (extant width) × 52 mm (full height). The original tablet width can be established as 104 mm on the basis of the 2:1 ratio between the horizontal and vertical axes, which is constant in this type of tablet. Accordingly, more than 40% of text has been lost in each line.

The writing is big; signs measure 5 mm in height on the average, and vertical script density is 10 signs to 60 mm on the obverse and 10 signs to 73 mm on the reverse. Nevertheless, the tablet is in places very difficult to read; many signs, especially on the reverse, are badly obliterated or scratched beyond recognition. The scribal hand does not is not found on other tablets of the corpus.

Text 6 (Plate VIII)

No. 6 (Bu 91-5-9,106 + 109) is a fragment from the left side of a horizontal tablet measuring 26 mm (thickness) × 43 mm (extant width) × 64 mm (height). The original width (twice the height) was 128 mm. Accordingly, more than two thirds of each line has been lost.

The script is clear and easy to read despite occasional surface damage. Vertical script density is 10 signs to 65 mm. The scribal hand is not the same as in no. 5 or other tablets of the corpus.

Text 7 (Plates IX and XIII)

No. 7 (K 883) is an almost complete horizontal tablet measuring 22 mm (thickness) × 82 mm (width) × 41 mm (height). A small chip of 25 mm diameter has broken off the lower left-hand corner of the obverse, and there is minor surface damage in obv. 12 and rev. 1-2 and 11.

Vertical script density is 10 lines to 35 mm. The script is clear and beautiful, and in contrast to nos. 5-6, the text is elegantly distributed over the lines. It is almost certainly an archival copy of a more hastily prepared original, which it seems to have reproduced faithfully, judging from the distinctive features it shares with nos. 5-6 and 8, like the quotation particle *ma-a* (cf. above, p. LV). The scribal hand is not found on the other tablets of the corpus.

Text 8 (Plates X and XIII)

No. 8 (K 1545) is a horizontal tablet pieced together from two fragments; it measures 15 × 62 × 31 mm. A 1-2 cm wide triangular piece is missing from the middle, but otherwise the tablet is complete.

Vertical script density is 10 lines to 40 mm; script is clear and easily legible. Even though the available data are admittedly very limited, it is possible that the tablet was written by Assurbanipal's chief scribe, Ištar-šumu-ereš (cf. the ductus and sign forms, especially those of *iq*, *ša*, *ti*, in LAS 13 and CT 53 84, 177, 594 and 943).

Text 9 (Plates XI-XII)

No. 9 (K 1292 + DT 130) is a vertical single-column tablet measuring 20 mm × 57 mm (full width) × 104 mm (height). The upper left-hand corner and lower part of the tablet are missing. Vertical script density is 10 signs to 35 mm. Assuming that the ratio between the horizontal and vertical axes was 1:2, as is normal in this type of tablet, the original height of the tablet was 114 mm. This means that about 4 lines have been lost at the end of the obverse and a corresponding number of lines at the beginning of the reverse. In addition, the tablet has a coating of very fine clay which has cracked off from the lower left-hand corner of the obverse and from the beginning of the reverse, causing additional loss of text. Altogether, at least 10 lines (= 24%) of the original prophecy have been totally lost.

The tablet is beautifully inscribed and by all criteria represents a library copy rather than a report. The scribal hand closely resembles but is not identical with that of nos. 1-3. The script is very clear and easily legible on the obverse, but badly effaced and at times very hard to read on the reverse.

Text 10 (Plate XIII)

No. 10 (83-1-18,726) is a fragment from the left side of a clay tablet measuring 15 mm (thickness) × 12 mm (width) × 42 mm (height). The curvatures point to a vertical tablet originally measuring ca. 30 × 60 mm. Vertical script density is 10 lines to 41 mm. This implies (including the edges) that the tablet was originally inscribed with about 33 lines of text.

Text 11 (Plate XIII)

No. 11 (K 1974) is fragment of a vertical clay tablet from the upper left part of the reverse measuring 27 mm (width) by 49 mm (height). Curvatures suggest that the original width was ca. 40 mm, and hence the original height ca. 80 mm. Judging from the vertical script density (10 lines to 34 mm), the tablet was probably originally inscribed with about 50 lines of text.

The lines of the tablet are crowded with text, with signs packed tightly against each other, which combined with textual damage makes the reading and interpretation of some lines quite difficult. The scribal hand is not found on other tablets of the corpus.

Authorship Indications and Other Scholia to the Oracles

In addition to oracles proper, all the tablets of the corpus contain other kinds of information as well: brief notes specifying the origin of the oracle and possibly its context and date. The individual tablets exhibit considerable variation in the formulation and placement of such notes, depending on the text type. The reports normally open with a brief note introducing the oracle, while in the collections the notes follow the oracle and are rigorously standardized in formulation. Some of the introductory notes to the reports have close parallels in the biblical corpus.[282]

The Reports

The following introductory notes are attested:

No. 5:1, "The word of Ištar of Arbela [*to the queen mother*]"
No. 6:1, "Ištar of Arbela (has said)"
No. 7:1, "The prophetess Mullissu-kabtat (has said)"
No. 8:1f, "Words concerning [the Elami]tes: [*God*] says as follows"

In addition, no. 6 has a postscript added in smaller script after the oracle: "Tašmetu-ereš, a prophet [...], prophesied (this) in Arbela" (r. 11f). This note has a parallel in collection 3 (iv 31-35) and hence may have been routinely added to many more oracle reports. For the time being it seems, however, that such postscripts were the exception rather than the rule, since two of the reports (nos. 7 and 8) certainly close with the oracle (followed by a horizontal ruling).[283] None of the tablets is dated.

The Collections

Judging from other comparable Ninevite archival texts, it is likely that all the oracle collections opened with a short heading specifying the content of the tablet and ended with a colophon and/or an eponym date.[284] The beginnings of nos. 1-4 are almost completely destroyed, but the breaks offer sufficient room for short (1 to 2 line) headings. The "one-oracle collection" no. 9 begins as follows:

"[*The prote*]*ction* of Mullissu, [...] of the Lady of Arbela."

This could be interpreted as a heading, taking the restored word *kidinnu* as a technical term for "(oracle of) protection," to be compared with the term *šulmu* "(oracle of) well-being" in nos. 3.2 and 3.3 (see p. LXIV below and the commentary on p. 23). However, since the passage is not separated from the rest of the text by a ruling, as is usual in the case of headings,[285] it is more likely to be part of the oracle itself and thus to be interpreted as an address formula in the vocative (see below, p. LXV, and cf. line 22 of the text).

Collections 1 and 2 insert after each individual oracle a stereotypical authorship note which is also found in the "one-oracle collection" no. 9. The note is structurally identical in all three texts ("from/by the mouth of PN + origin") but its exact formulation varies slightly from tablet to tablet. The following variants occur:

1. *ša pi-i* PN DUMU GN "by the mouth of PN, 'son' of GN" (1.1, 1.4, 1.10)
2. *ša pi-i* PNf DUMU.MÍ GN "by the mouth of PNf, 'daughter' of GN" (1.2, 1.8)
3. *ša* KA PNf [DUMU.MÍ] GN "by the mouth of PNf, 'daughter' of GN" (9)
4. *ša pi-i* PNf *ša* GN "by the mouth of PNf of GN" (1.3)
5. *ša pi-i* PNf GN-*a-a* "by the mouth of PNf of GN" (1.5)
6. *ša pi-i* PNf *še-lu-tu* "by the mouth of PNf, votaress" (1.7)
7. TA* *pi-i šá* PN GN-*a-a* "from the mouth of PN of GN" (2.3)
8. TA* *pi-i* PNf GN-*a-a* "from the mouth of PNf of GN" (2.4)
9. [TA* *pi-i*] PN GN-*a-a* "from the mouth of PN of GN" (2.1, 2.2)

Variants 7-9 (especially 7) show that the expression *ša pî* "of/by the mouth" has to be understood literally (cf. above, p. XXVI) and not just as an idiomatic expression for "according to."[286] The fact that the term *raggimu/raggintu* "prophet/prophetess" does not occur in the formula (in contrast to the authorship notes of nos. 3, 6, 7 and 10) indicates that it was superfluous in the context and underlines the basically oral nature of Neo-Assyrian prophecy. Considering that variants 2 and 3 are for all practical purposes identical, it is possible that the scribe of no. 9 was using (the 30-years older) no. 1 as a model when preparing the tablet.

Following the authorship note, no. 9 has an eponym date. If the scribe indeed used no. 1 as a model, it would stand to reason that the latter likewise ended in a date. There is room for 8 lines of text at the end of the tablet, but since the space before the break is uninscribed, it is possible that the uninscribed space extended further down leaving room only for the date in the break.[287] Collection 2, which parallels no. 1 in structure and was written by the same scribe, has a break of about 6 lines at the end of the tablet, which would leave just enough room for the final lines of the last oracle, an authorship note, a ruling, and a date.

Collection 3, which contains several oracles delivered by a single prophet on a very special occasion (see below), does not insert an authorship note after each oracle. Instead, it specifies the author in a postscript resembling that of no. 6:

[La-dagil-i]li, a prophet of [Arbela, prophesied (this) when ......] Ištar [......].

The last two oracles of the tablet (3.4 and 3.5) are separated from the beginning of the text by a double ruling. It could be argued, consequently, that the authorship note pertains only to the last two oracles. However, who would then have delivered the first three? Considering the pains taken elsewhere in the corpus to specify the authors of the oracles, it appears extremely unlikely that the prophet who delivered such important oracles as 3.2 and 3.3 would have been left unnamed. It is therefore perhaps best to accept La-dagil-ili as the author of all the oracles and not to assign undue significance to the double ruling. After all, we do not know what it stood for.

Oracles 3.2 and 3.3 are followed by postscripts defining them as *šulmu*, "(oracles of) well-being," and indicating that copies of them were on display in Ešarra, the temple of Aššur in Assur; the term *šulmu* has to be understood here as referring to the universal harmony restored through Esarhaddon's accession (cf. 3.1 and see above, pp. XXIV and XLIIIf). In addition, the postscript to 3.3 contains ritual instructions showing that the collection, defined as "the covenant tablet of Aššur," was to be read in the presence of the king. Oracle 3.1 seems to describe a procession led by the king to Ešarra; 3.2 addresses a body of Assyrians probably convened in the courtyard of the temple, where a copy of this oracle was placed; and 3.4 refers to a covenant meal administered on the terrace of the temple immediately outside the cella of Aššur. Combining these indications it can be concluded that the oracles were embedded in the coronation ceremonies of Esarhaddon and probably were all publicly delivered by the prophet La-dagil-ili. Considering the date of Esarhaddon's accession (28th Adar, 681, i.e., only a few days before the great New Year's festival of Nisan, where the whole ruling class of Assyria was present), it is possible that the tablet was also read at subsequent New Year's receptions, to impress on the audience the divine support for Esarhaddon's kingship (cf. oracle 3.4 and the biblical passages cited in the commentary to 3 ii 32).

Structural Elements of the Oracles

The oracles consist of a limited inventory of structural and thematic elements (see Chart 1), which could be combined freely. The order of the elements is likewise free, even though certain elements are usually placed at the beginning, others at the end of the oracle. All the elements are optional, though many of them are found in almost all the oracles. Their choice correlates with the contents of the oracles; the "fear not" formula, for example, occurs only in encouragement and support oracles (nos. 1, 2, 4, and 7).

The formulation of the elements can vary considerably, even within oracles by the same prophet. Certain formulations and phrases are attested only in the oracles of certain prophets (see above, pp. IL and LII), while other recur in the oracles of several prophets, note e.g. the "fear not" and praise formulae, and passages such as 1.1:6 = 1.4:34f, and 1.1:15ff = 1.10:7ff. This points to a long prophetic tradition and "professional" education within the context of the Ištar cult.

The following discussion of the elements follows the order of Chart 1.[288] It should be stressed that this order does not fully reflect the reality; although

CHART 1. *Structural and Thematic Elements*

Element	Collection 1										Collection 2						Collect. 3					4	Reports				
	1	2	3	4	5	6	7	8	9	10	1	2	3	4	5	6	1	2	3	4	5		5	6	7	8	9
"word of Ištar"	–	–	–	–		–		–		–		–	–	+	–			–	–	b	b		b		b	–	–
address	b	b	–	+	e	+		+		+	+	+	+	+	b			b	–	+	+	+	+		+	–	b
self-identification	+	+	–	+		b		b		b	+	+	b	–	+	+		–	e	–	+				–	–	–
"fear not" formula	+		–	b		+		+		–	e	b	+	+	+	+	–	–	–	–	–	+			+	–	
past support	+	+	–	+		+		+		+		+			+		–	–	+	–	+				–	–	
present support	e	e	e	–		+	e	e		+		+		+			–	+	–	–	e			+	+	–	+
future support	+	+	–	+		+	+	–		e	+	+	+	+	+	+	–	+	–	–	+	+	+	+	+	–	+
demand for praise	–		–	e				–		+			+			+	–	–	+	–	–		+		–	–	
demand for faith	–		–	+				–		–			+				–	–	–	–	+				–	–	
cultic commands	–		–					–		+	?		+			?	–	–	–	–	+				–	–	
other	–		–					–	–	–							+	+	b	e	+				–	+	

\+ indicates attested element
– " absence of element
? " possible but uncertain element
b " attestation at the beginning of the oracle
e " " at the end " "
lack of +/-/b/e indicates textual damage

some oracles do contain most of elements in the order indicated, the order is quite variable and the full sequence of elements is not actually attested in any of the oracles.

1. The phrase "**word of Ištar**" (*abat Issār*; variant: "word of Queen Mullissu," no. 7:2; cf. also 2.4) occurs in five oracles of the corpus, mostly at the beginning and in combination with an address element,[289] recalling the introductory formula of the royal letters (*abat šarri ana* NN, "the word of the king to NN"). This element corresponds in every respect to the biblical *dbr yhwh*, "the word of YHWH."[290] With one exception (3.5), it is in complementary distribution with the self-identification of the oracular deity.

2. The **addressee** of the oracle is mostly indicated by a name or title in the vocative (e.g., "Esarhaddon!" 1.6), often combined with the "fear not" formula (e.g., "King of Assyria, fear not!" 1.2) or another imperative ("Listen, Assyrians!" 3.2). A dative address ("to NN") occurs in five oracles, usually in combination with the "word of Ištar" formula but once without it ("To the king's mother," 1.8). In three cases the addressee is specified indirectly only ("you," 3.3) or not at all (1.3, and 8). All these forms of address have parallels in biblical prophecies.

3. The "word of Ištar" formula is in most oracles replaced by a **self-identification** of the oracular deity, "I am DN" (*anāku* DN or DN *anāku*), mostly at the very beginning of the oracle (1.6, 1.8, 1.10, 2.3), but also at the end (1.5) and in the middle (1.1, 1.4, 1.6 and often); it may occur repeatedly within a single oracle (1.1, 1.2, 1.4, 1.6, etc.). This element corresponds to the biblical phrase *ʾny yhwh* "I am YHWH," see the discussion above, p. XIX.

4. The exhortation "**fear not!**" (*lā tapallah*) is a ubiquitous element of practically all encouragement oracles, where it is missing only in 1.3 and 1.10. It is often placed at the very beginning the oracle, in combination with the name of the addressee (1.1, 1.2, 1.4, 2.2, 2.5), but it can also occur alone (1.1:24, 2.4:17), at the end (2.1, 2.4, 7) or in the middle of an oracle (1.6, 1.8, 2.5, 4), sometimes several times (2.6, 7). It regularly combines with assurances of divine help, support and protection, and clearly corresponds to biblical *ʾl tyrʾw*, cf. e.g. 2 Chr. 20:15, 'Thus said YHWH: Have no fear, do not be dismayed by the great horde, for the battle is in God's hands."[291]

5. **Past support**. References to divine help and support in the past are found in several oracles. They are regularly paired with promises of future support,[292] and were clearly intended to enhance the credibility of the prophecy, for many of them emphasize that the previous oracles had come true ("What words have I spoken to you that you could not rely upon," 1.1:15ff; "What enemy has attacked you while I remained silent? The future shall be like the past," 1.4:34ff; "Could you not rely on the previous utterance which I spoke to you? Now you can rely on this later one too," 1.10:7-12; "The future shall be like the past; I will go around you and protect you," 2.2:17ff; see also 1.2 ii 2f, 1.8:14-23, 3.3:22-25, 3.5:15-21, and 4:6). For biblical parallels, cf. simply the Isaiah passage cited in the commentary on 1.10:7-12 (p. 10 below).

6. **Present/future support**. The promise of present and future divine support to the king is a theme pervading the entire corpus. Even in 3.3 and 3.4 — the only oracles with no explicit promises for the future — the continuing divine support is implicit in the wording of the text. The individual promises are on the whole very generally formulated (safety, protection, defeat of unspecified enemies, stability of throne); even when names are mentioned (2.4, 3.2, 3.5, 7, 8), one looks in vain for accurate and concrete "predictions." This indicates that the course of history as such was of little or no interest to the prophets. What mattered was whether or not God was with the king; everything else (attainment or loss of power, glory, military victories, etc.) resulted from and depended on this one basic thing. It should be noted that even the references to past events (as in oracles 1.2 and 3.3) are phrased very vaguely throughout.

The predicates of the passages containing promises are regularly in the indicative present.[293] The first person precative forms in 3.3 (lines 17 and 24) and 3.5 (passim) indicate divine will, not promises.

7. **Demand for praise**. Five oracles contain a demand to praise the oracular deity (*na''idanni* "praise me!" 1.4 bis, 1.10 bis, 2.3, 2.6; "let them see and praise me," 3.3; note also "glorify Mullissu!," 5 r.6"). In most cases, this demand accompanies a self-presentation of the deity (1.4, 2.6, 3.3), and is then always combined with a reference to divine support received in the past. In two cases, it is linked with promises of future support (1.4, 2.3).

This thematic element has no direct parallel in biblical prophecy, obviously because only a few of the extant prophecies are addressed to the king. However, several royal psalms praise the greatness of God, and the phrase "Praise YHWH" (*hllw-yh*) occurs frequently in psalms. It may be noted that the hymn of Assurbanipal to Ištar of Arbela and Mullissu (SAA 3 3) could well be a response to a demand for praise presented in an oracle — perhaps no. 9, where this demand is not extant but could well have been included in the portion lost at the bottom of the tablet.

8. **Cultic demands** occur in three oracles of the corpus, all by La-dagil-ili. They include greater veneration of the Goddess (1.10), recognition of the gods of Esaggil (2.3), and provision for the cult of Ištar of Arbela (3.5). It is possible that demands for the restoration of Esaggil were also made in 2.1 and 2.6, but this is uncertain owing to the fragmentary state of these oracles. In any case, cultic demands must have been a fairly regular feature of Neo-Assyrian prophecy, to judge from CT 53 969, a contemporary letter to the king.[294]

Language and Style

Both grammatically and lexically, the language of the oracles is pure Neo-Assyrian, and numerous phonological and morphological details indicate that the prophets spoke it as their mother tongue. The occasional Aramaic loanwords occurring in the oracles (*agappu* 1.1, *hangaru akku* 1.6, *sapāku* 2.1, *ṭullummâ* 2.4, *ṣipputu* 2.5, *izirû* 2.5 and 2.6, *anīna* 3.3, *halputu* 7) are characteristic of Neo-Assyrian in general and cannot be used as evidence for the alleged “Western origin” of the prophecies.[295]

Stylistically, the oracles are half prose, half poetry, characterized by rhythmically structured passages and the use of rich religious imagery, mythological allusions, metaphors and similes.[296] In addition, extensive use is made of “classic” poetic devices such as alliteration, anaphora, antithesis, chiasm, climax, parallelismus membrorum, parataxis and paronomasy.[297] Isolated instances of stylistic *diglossia* are also attested,[298] indicating acquaintance with Babylonian literature. These features, taken together, elevate the diction of the oracles to a surprisingly high stylistic level, keeping in mind that they were written down from oral performance and apparently not subjected to any substantial editing.[299]

It is true that the oracles are on the whole relatively short and that their thematic repertory is somewhat limited and formulaic. However, under no circumstances can they be considered products of untrained ecstatics “prophesying” under the influence of drugs or intoxication. Their literary quality can have been achieved only through conscious striving for literary excellence, and their power of expression reflects the prophets’ spiritual assimilation to the Goddess who spoke through their lips.

The Historical Contexts and Dates of the Oracles

The general date of the corpus is easy to establish: Nos. 1-6 are addressed to Esarhaddon (or his mother, as the mother of the king), nos. 7-11 to Assurbanipal.[300] Determining the exact historical contexts and dates of the individual oracles is more difficult, as only one of the texts (no. 9) bears a date, and the circumstances to which the individual oracles relate are as a rule not specified. Almost all the oracles of collections 1-4, for example, refer to the king's distress and/or battle against his enemies, but such references are in general very elusive. The prophecies concerning Elam, Mannea, Urarṭu and Mugallu of Melid in oracle 2.4 could, in principle, belong to almost any phase of Esarhaddon's twelve-year reign. The promise of victory over [Mel]id and the Cimmerians included in oracle 3.2 is no more specific.

Oracle 1.8, however, offers a concrete, historical fixed point. The first part of it, addressed to the queen mother, contains an unmistakable reference to the time of the murder of Sennacherib (Tebet, 681 BC), when Esarhaddon, the official crown prince, was in exile and his two half-brothers (earlier crown princes) held power in Assyria.[301] The end of the oracle, on the other hand, unequivocally refers to Esarhaddon's triumphal rise to power. It can thus be dated immediately after the end of the civil war, in Adar, 681.

This is a crucially important clue. Clear references to the civil war and the rebel brothers are also found in oracles 3.3 and 3.5. On the other hand, the letters and inscriptions of Esarhaddon inform us that immediately after the war (and possibly already in the course of it, before the decisive battle) the king received encouraging oracles from ecstatic prophets.[302] Since encouragement of the king is indeed the central theme of the oracles included in nos. 1, 2 and 4 (and to some extent no. 3 as well), it seems obvious that they are the oracles referred to in the inscriptions. Considering the scarcity of references to prophecies in Esarhaddon's inscriptions (and Assyrian inscriptions in general), this conclusion can in fact be regarded as virtually certain.

The Dates of the Collections

A careful comparison of the collections with Esarhaddon's inscriptions (see Appendix, p. LXIIff) confirms this hypothesis. It appears that the oracles collected in these tablets were arranged chronologically and, it seems, thematically as well.

Collection 1 begins with an oracle which seems to have been delivered just before the decisive battle fought in 681-XI. The following five oracles

(1.2-1.6) seem to date after the battle but before Esarhaddon's arrival in Nineveh (681-XII-8). Oracle 1.6 refers to an impending crossing of the river (i.e., the Tigris), which represented the last obstacle on the king's journey to the capital; the references to battles yet to be fought indicate that (in contrast to oracle 1.8) the final victory had not yet been achieved. Section 1.9 alludes to the triumphal celebrations arranged after the final victory, and in the last oracle of the collection (1.10) the king already rules in his palace, albeit still in a precarious position.

Collection 2 contains no references to battles, but it is dominated by repeated references to the internal disorder of Assyria (2.1, 2.3-5), the stabilization of Esarhaddon's kingship (2.2, 2.6), the elimination of disloyal subjects and a general feeling of uncertainty prevailing in Assyria (2.4). This fits the political situation of Assyria after Esarhaddon's accession (in the early part of year 680), which is described in Esarhaddon's inscription Assur A composed in early 679.

The central theme of this inscription is the stabilization of the king's rule, the relenting of the gods and the restoration of the cosmic harmony — the very themes which are also central to Collection 2 (especially 2.5). After citing a number of favourable omens, the inscription notes that the king also regularly received oracles from ecstatic prophets "concerning the establishment of the foundation of my sacerdotal throne until far-off days." The oracles are mentioned after a Mars omen that occurred between the 5th and 7th months of the year, but this order does not necessarily have chronological relevance, since the signs received from the gods are grouped in the text in three main categories (portents, oracles, dreams), not in a strict chronological sequence. Most likely the oracles date from the same period as the portents, the first of which (an omen derived from Venus) is datable between the 11th month (Shebat) of 681 and the third month (Sivan) of 680.

At least three oracles of the collection (2.1, 2.3 and 2.5) contain a reference to Babylon and/or its exiled gods and its destroyed temple, Esaggil. The restoration of Babylon and Esaggil was also a central theme of the early inscriptions of Esarhaddon (see Borger Esarh. pp. 12-18, below p. LXXV), and the Jupiter omen cited in support of the project occurred in Sivan, 680.

It seems, accordingly, that Collection 1 contains (in chronological order) oracles relating to the accession of Esarhaddon and dating from the end of year 681, whereas Collection 2 contains oracles from the early part of the next year and relating to the stabilization of Esarhaddon's rule. The existence of two thematic collections of oracles correlating with two separate sets of inscriptions strongly points to a mutual dependency between the two classes of texts; in other words, it seems that the oracle collections were compiled at about the same time as the respective inscriptions. This would date Collection 2 to year 679 (the date of Ass. A) and Collection 1 to late 673 (the date of Nin. A).[303] The temporal difference (six years) between the compilation of the two would explain the slight differences in their formulation, which would be surprising if the texts had been drawn up simultaneously.

The incentive for the compilation of the Nin. A inscriptions, and hence of Collection 1 as well, was certainly Esarhaddon's controversial decision to promote his younger son Assurbanipal as his successor, put into effect in early 672.[304] The detailed account of his own miraculous rise to power served to remind any potential critics of the decision — in the first place, Assurbanipal's elder brother, Šamaš-šumu-ukin, and his supporters — of the fate of those who would try to usurp power against the will of the gods.

Collection 3, which contains the oracles sealing Aššur's covenant with Esarhaddon, is likely to have been recited at the coronation of Esarhaddon and hence is probably the earliest of the three collections, dating from the very last days of 681 or early 680. It is written by the same scribe as nos. 1 and 2 and displays considerable affinity with no. 2 both in its external appearance (tablet format, size, ductus) and orthography.

Collection 4 shares the two-column format and subject matter of nos. 2 and 3 and may thus date from the same time, that is, 680 BC.

The Dates of the Reports

No. 5, addressed to the queen mother, parallels in content 1.8, 1.9, 2.1 and 2.6, and thus is likely to be contemporaneous with the oracles of Collections 1 and 2.

No. 6 opens with a promise to restore order [in Assyria] and hence may be contemporary with the oracles included in Collection 2. Note, however, that the promise "I will restore order" also occurs in no. 11, addressed to Assurbanipal.

No. 7 is addressed to Assurbanipal as crown prince (obv. 3) but before the official promotion ceremony, the girding of the royal diadem (obv. 7), so it must be dated before the prince's introduction to the Palace of Succession, which took place in Iyyar, 672. This agrees with the prophecies of lines 14 and r.5, which date the text between 674 (peace treaty with Elam) and Tammuz/July, 671 (the conquest of Egypt). The Cimmerians (obv. 14) are attested as threat to Assyria's eastern provinces at the time of Assurbanipal's crownprincehood, see LAS II p. 193f; G. B. Lanfranchi, *I Cimmeri* (Padua 1990), pp. 84-108, and A. Ivantchik, *Les Cimmériens au Proche-Orient* (OBO 127, Fribourg 1993), p. 82ff.

Note that the prophecy of line 6 may be echoed in SAA 3 3, Assurbanipal's hymn to Mullissu and Ištar of Arbela, which reads (line 8): "I am Assurbanipal ... whose kingship they made great even in the House of Succession. In their pure mouths is voiced the endurance of my throne."

No. 8 foresees an open military conflict with Elam leading to the complete subjugation of the country, and thus can only date from the reign of Assurbanipal. There are two possibilities: either the war with Teumman in 653 BC, which reduced Elam to a vassal of Assyria (see M. Waters, *A Survey of Neo-Elamite History* [PhD diss., University of Pennsylvania 1997] 84-98), or the aftermath of the Šamaš-šumu-ukin war (647-646 BC), which reduced the country to an Assyrian province (see E. Carter and M. Stolper, *Elam: Surveys of Political History and Archeology* [Berkeley 1984] 51ff). The former alternative is perhaps the likelier one, considering the irate tone of the oracle: note that the war was triggered by an Elamite raid undertaken while Assurbanipal was worshiping Ištar of Arbela — an insult provoking not only the anger of the king but of the Goddess as well (see above, p. XLVI).

No. 9 has an eponym date placing it squarely in the middle of the Šamaš-šumu-ukin rebellion: Nisan 18, eponymy of Bel-šadû'a = April 16, 650 BC.[305] The tone of the prophecy reflects the military situation. Six months before, in Elul II, 651, the Babylonian army had succeeded in capturing Cutha.[306] For the Assyrian king, this was an intolerable setback: a successful rebellion at the heart of the empire represented a serious danger to imperial unity and a direct threat to the emperor himself. Consequently, an Assyrian counteroffensive was launched immediately and Babylon was put under siege on Tammuz 11, 650, less than three months after the date of the text.

The oracle has many affinities with SAA 3 13 (the so-called Dialogue of Assurbanipal with Nabû), and it is likely that both texts emerged from the same historical situation; certainly the same scribe wrote and edited both tablets. SAA 3 13 shows Assurbanipal praying and having a dream in Emašmaš, the temple of Mullissu in Nineveh; the date of no. 9 implies that this took place in the course of or immediately after the New Year's festival of Nisan. The situation in general thus resembles that preceding the war against Teumman, which provoked the oracle and vision cited above, p. XLVI. Note that Mullissu (= Lady of Nineveh) figures as the principal oracular deity in no. 9. It seems very likely that SAA 3 3, Assurbanipal's hymn to Mullissu and Ištar of Arbela, was written in response to no. 9, and it can not be excluded that SAA 3 12, the so-called Righteous Sufferer's Prayer to Nabû, records the prayer that Assurbanipal actually spoke in Emašmaš.

No. 10 cites on its left edge the prophetess who authored no. 9, and may thus date from the same time. Note, however, that Assurbanipal is not mentioned in this fragment; if the name of the prophetess is to be read Sinqiša-amur (see p. ILf), then a date in the reign of Esarhaddon also becomes possible.

No. 11 dates from the reign of Assurbanipal (r. 1), and the promise to "restore order in (all) the lands" may point to the time of the Šamaš-šumu-ukin rebellion (i.e., c. 652-650 BC). However, lines r.4f intriguingly remind one of the theophany reported to Assurbanipal before the war against Teumman (see p. XLVIf). Could this be the original letter reporting it? Note the reference to a (previous) vision in r.6.

Appendix: Inscriptions of Esarhaddon Pertaining to the Corpus

Square brackets enclose explanatory additions to the text (years and months in which the events described took place and →references to the oracles of the corpus).

1. The Civil War of 681 and Esarhaddon's Rise to Power

[Year 683] i 8ff Even though I was younger than my big brothers, at the behest of Aššur, Sin, Šamaš, Bel, Nabû, Nergal, Ištar of Nineveh and Ištar of Arbela, my father duly elevated me among my brothers and declared, "This is my successor." He consulted Šamaš and Adad by extispicy, and they answered him with a firm yes: "He will be your replacement." Respecting their weighty command, he assembled the people of Assyria young and old, my brothers, and the progeny of my dynastic line, and made them swear by the gods of heaven and earth a solemn oath to protect my succession. In a favourable month [Nisan, 683], on an auspicious day, in accordance with their august command, I joyously entered the Palace of Succession [→ 1.2], the awesome place where the fate of kingship resides.

[Year 682] i 23ff Proper guidance was lavished upon my brothers, but they forsook the gods, trusting in their own haughty deeds, and hammered out evil plans. Godlessly they fabricated malicious rumors and untrue slander against me [→ 1.7, 3.3]; spreading unwholesome lies and hostility behind my back, they angered my father's gentle heart with me against the will of the gods [→ 1.8, 3.3], though deep in his heart he felt compassion for me and remained intent on my exercising the kingship.

[Nisan, 681] i 32ff I spoke with my heart and took counsel in my mind, asking myself: "Their deeds are vainglorious and they trust in their own reason; what will they do in their godlessness?" Entreatingly and humbly I beseeched Aššur, king of the gods [3.3], and merciful Marduk, to whom treachery is an abomination, and they accepted my plea. In keeping with the will of the great gods, my lords, they transferred me away from the evil deeds to a secret place and extended their sweet protection over me [→ 1.1, 1.4, 3.3], safeguarding me for the kingship.

[Tebet, 681] i 41ff Afterwards my brothers went crazy (*immahû*) and did everything that is improper before god and man. They planned evil, and godlessly made an armed rebellion in Nineveh, butting each other like young goats in their strife for kingship. Aššur, Sin, Šamaš, Bel, Nabû, Nergal, Ištar of Nineveh and Ištar of Arbela looked with displeasure on the deeds of the usurpers which had been done against the will of the gods and did not stand at their side, but turned their strength into weakness and made them bow to my feet. The people of Assyria, who with water and oil and by the great gods had sworn an oath of allegiance to protect my kingship, did not go to their help [→ 3.5].

[Shebat, 681] [i 53ff] I, Esarhaddon, who cannot be defeated in battle thanks to the support of the great gods, his lords, soon heard of their evil deeds. I cried, "Woe!" [→ 1.1], I rent my princely garment and shrieked a lamentation, I became enraged like a lion, my mind became furious, and I wrenched my wrists to exercise the kingship of my father's house. With raised hands I prayed to Aššur [→ 3.3], Sin, Šamaš, Bel, Nabû, Nergal, Ištar of Nineveh and Ištar of Arbela, and they accepted my prayer, repeatedly sending me, along with their firm 'yes,' this encouraging liver omen: "Go without delay! We will go by your side and slay your enemies!"

[i 63ff] I did no waste a day or two, I did not wait for my troops, I did not look back, I did not review my yoked horses and my fighting equipment, I did not heap up my war provisions, nor did I fear the snow and cold of Shebat and the severity of the winter, but like a flying eagle I spread out my wings to defeat my enemies, and marched labouriously but swiftly towards Nineveh.

[i 70ff] In front of me, in the land of Hanigalbat, the mass of their crack warriors was blocking the advance of my army and brandishing their weapons. Fear of the great gods, my lords, befell them, and when they saw the strength of my onslaught, they went out of their minds (*mahhûtiš*). Ištar, the lady of war and battle, who loves my priesthood, stood by my side, and broke their bows and disrupted their battle array [→ 1.2, 3.3, 3.5]. They said in their ranks, "This is our king!," and by her august command they crossed over to my side, rushing after me and tumbling like lambs to beg for my sovereignty.

[Adar, 681] [i 80ff] The people of Assyria who had sworn loyalty to me by the great gods, came before me and kissed my feet. But those usurpers, instigators of revolt and rebellion — when they heard of the progress of my campaign, they abandoned their supporting troops and fled to an unknown land [→ 3.2].

[i 84ff] I reached the bank of the Tigris and by the command of Sin and Šamaš, the gods of the harbour, made all my troops jump across the broad Tigris as if it were a ditch [→ 1.6]. On the 8th day of the favourable month of Adar, on the *eššēšu* day of Nabû, I joyfully entered my royal city, Nineveh, and smoothly ascended the throne of my father [→ 1.3, 1.7].

[Year 680] [ii 3ff] The south wind, the breeze of Ea, the wind whose blowing is good for exercising the kingship, blew. Good portents appeared in heaven and on earth [→ 3.1]. Messages of ecstatic prophets, the messengers of the gods and the Goddess (*šipir mahhê našparti ilāni u Ištār*), constantly and regularly came in and encouraged me [→ 1.10]. I searched out all the criminals [→ 2.1, 2.3, 2.4] who had induced my brothers to plot evil for taking over the kingship of Assyria, every one of them, imposed a heavy punishment upon them, and destroyed their seed [→ 3.5].

(Borger Esarh. pp. 40-45, Nin. A i 8—ii 11, dated 673-I)

2. *Esarhaddon's First Regnal Year*

[Year 680] i 31ff The twin gods Sin and Šamaš, in order to bestow a righteous and just judgment upon the land and the people, maintained monthly a path of righteousness and justice, appearing regularly on the 1st and 14th days.

i 39ff The brightest of the stars, Venus, appeared in the west in the path of Ea [681-X-29], reached its hypsoma [in Leo] predicting the stabilization of the land and the reconciliation of her gods [680-III-15], and disappeared [680-VII-11]. Mars, who passes the decision for the Westland, shone brightly in the path of Ea [680-V/VII], announcing by his sign his decree concerning the strengthening of the king and his land.

ii 12ff Messages from ecstatic prophets (*mahhû*) concerning the establishment of the foundation of my sacerdotal throne until far-off days were constantly and regularly conveyed to me [→ 1.6, 1.10, 2.1, 2.2, 2.3]. Good omens kept occurring to me in dreams and oracles concerning the establishment of my seat and the extension of my reign. Seeing these signs of good portent, my heart turned confident and my mood became good.

(Borger Esarh. p. 2, Ass. A i 31—ii 26, dated 679-III)

3. *The Gods of Esaggil*

[Year 692] i 18ff Previously, in the reign of an earlier king, evil portents appeared in the land of Sumer and Akkad. Its inhabitants kept answering each other 'yes' for 'no' and spoke lies. They abandoned the rites of their gods and goddesses and embarked on a different course. They laid hand on the property of Esaggil, the (unapproachable) palace of the gods, and traded silver, gold and precious stones for Elamite support.

[Year 689] i 34ff Seeing this, the Enlil of the gods, Marduk, got angry. His mind became furious, and he made an evil plan to disperse the land and its people. His angry heart was bent on levelling the land and destroying its people, and a grievous curse formed in his mouth. Evil portents indicating the *disruption of cosmic harmony* started appearing abundantly in heaven and on earth. The stars in the paths of Enlil, Anu and Ea worsened their positions and repeatedly disclosed abnormal omens. The river of abundance, Arahtu, became a raging current, a fierce surge of water, a violent flood like the Deluge, and swept away the city, its houses and sanctuaries, turning them into ruins. The gods and goddesses who dwelt within it (var. adds: got afraid), abandoned their shrines (var. flew off like birds) and ascended to heaven [→ 2.1, 2.3]. The people who lived there fled elsewhere and took refuge in an unknown land.

[Year 681] ii 2ff Though he had written 70 years [= 1 + 10] as the length of its abandonment, the merciful Marduk quickly relented, reversed the order of the numerical symbols, and ordered its resettlement for the 11th year [= 679]. In order to restore those deeds to their original state, you duly chose me, Esarhaddon, from amongst my older brothers, placed your sweet protection over me, leveled all my enemies like the deluge, killed all my foes, made me attain my desire, and gave me the shepherdship of Assyria to calm the heart of your great godhead and to placate your mind.

[Year 680] ii 24ff At the beginning of my kingship, in my first regnal year, when I magnificently ascended the royal throne, good portents concerning the resettling of the city and the restoration of its sanctuaries occurred to me in heaven and on earth. The angry gods [*relented* and] kept showing me most propitious signs concerning the rebuilding of Babylon and the restoration of Esaggil [→ 2.1, 2.6]. The bright Jupiter, who gives the decision for the land of Akkad, approached in Sivan [680-III] and stood in the place where the sun shines forth. He was bright, his features were red, and his rising was as perfect as the rising of the sun; the angry gods became reconciled [→ 2.4] with the land of Akkad, and there were copious rains and regular floods in the land of Akkad. For the second time, he reached the hypsoma in Pet-Babi and became stable in his seat.

ii 41ff He commanded me to work to complete the cult centres, restore the sanctuaries and set aright the cult of Esaggil. Every month, Sin and Šamaš in their appearances jointly responded with a firm 'yes' regarding the mercy to be shown to the land of Akkad.

(Borger Esarh. pp. 12-18, Bab. A i 10—ii 49, dated 680-II)

On the Present Edition

This volume is essentially a critical edition of the Neo-Assyrian prophecy corpus in the customary SAA style. Because of the exceptional importance of the texts, the introduction and critical apparatus have, however, been considerably expanded over what has been the norm in the previous volumes of the series. It must be stressed that while the introduction deals with questions of fundamental importance to the understanding of ANE prophecy and Assyrian religion, this volume is not a comprehensive study of Assyrian religion, nor is it presented as a "final word" on the matters treated.

Introduction

The introduction deals partly with questions that are concretely related to the prophecy corpus, such as the identity of the prophets, the structure of the texts, or the date and historical context of the individual oracles, and partly with questions relating to the nature of Assyrian prophecy, which are approached holistically in the light of both contemporary Assyrian and diachronic comparative evidence. As noted above (p. XVI), the issues tackled are extremely complex and would actually require several volumes, not a brief introduction, to be properly treated. This made it necessary to refrain from lengthy discussion of specific issues in the introduction itself and to relegate all such discussion to the note apparatus instead.

The introduction and notes thus complement and support each other, and should ideally be read together. The general reader can, however, gladly ignore the notes, even though he will then miss the more detailed and nuanced argumentation and the documentary evidence presented in them. It should be noted that many of the notes contain extensive detailed discussions not only tied to the text but to other notes as well, thus making up a complex network of background information essential to the understanding of the overall discussion. Such interrelated notes are systematically cross-referenced throughout the note apparatus, and both the introduction and the notes are fully indexed.

Texts Included and Excluded

The present volume contains all currently known Neo-Assyrian prophetic oracles included in the extant oracle collections and reports, as detailed above (p. LIIIff). Prophecies quoted in part, paraphrased or referred to in contemporary letters and royal inscriptions have not been included. Such quotations and references are collected and analyzed by Martti Nissinen in a separate study published in the SAAS series as a companion to the present volume.

In addition to texts certainly identifiable as collections or reports, two fragments of uncertain classification (nos. 10 and 11) have also been included for the sake of completeness. No. 10 would by its content qualify for an oracle report but does not have the horizontal format of reports and hence probably is a letter quoting an oracle. No. 11 is almost certainly a letter reporting, besides an oracle, also a vision (*diglu*).

On the other hand, four texts included in an earlier version of this edition (ABL 1249, ABL 1369, CT 53 413 and ABRT I 5f) have been excluded as deemed impertinent for a variety of reasons.

ABL 1249 is a letter from the priest Aššur-hamatia reporting a theophany; although it shares some features with the oracles of the corpus, it cannot be regarded as oral prophecy (see above, pp. XXXV and XLVIf) and accordingly does not belong in the present volume. ABL 1369 is a divine message to the king in the first person singular; although it would qualify as an oracle report due to its horizontal format, it is called a "dispatch" (*šipirtu*) in the text itself and therefore belongs to the category of divine letters edited in SAA 3. CT 53 413 is a fragmentary communication from a votary of Ištar of Arbela to the king; despite its affinities with no. 1.7, it is also explicitly defined as a "dispatch" in the text and accordingly is not a prophetic oracle.

These three texts will be edited along with other letters of Assyrian and Babylonian priests in a forthcoming SAA volume by Steven Cole and Peter Machinist. ABRT I 5f, Assurbanipal's dialogue with Nabû, which shares many features with the oracles of the corpus but cannot be regarded as a specimen of oral prophecy, was edited by Alasdair Livingstone in SAA 3.

The Order of the Texts

The texts are divided by their form and function into two major groups, oracle collections and reports. The collections, most of which predate the reports, are presented first. Within these two major groups, the individual texts are, as far as possible, arranged in chronological sequence. The order of the collections has been determined on the basis of the dates of the individual oracles and the mutual affinities of the texts, ignoring their actual dates of compilation, which cannot be determined with certainty. Thus Collection 1, which is the longest text in the corpus and contains the earliest oracles, is presented first; it is followed by Collection 2, which shares a number of features with it but is shorter and contains later oracles, and this again by Collection 3, which is of a different type and likewise contains oracles later than those in Collection 1. This order probably does not reflect the actual chronological order of the tablets themselves, according to which Collection 3 should have been presented first, followed by Collections 2 and 1 (see p. LXIXf).

Transliterations

The transliterations, addressed to the specialist, render the text of the originals in roman characters according to standard Assyriological conventions and the principles outlined in the Editorial Manual. Every effort has been taken to make them as accurate as possible. All the texts edited have been collated by the editor, most of them several times.

Results of collation are indicated with exclamation marks. Single exclamation marks indicate corrections to published copies, double exclamation marks, scribal errors. Question marks indicate uncertain or questionable readings. Broken portions of the text and all restorations are enclosed within square brackets. Parentheses enclose items omitted by the ancient scribes.

Translations

The translations seek to render the meaning and tenor of the texts as accurately as possible in readable, contemporary English. In the interest of clarity, the line structure of the originals has not been retained in the translation, but the text has been rearranged into logically coherent paragraphs where possible.

Uncertain or conjectural translations are indicated by italics. Interpretative additions to the translation are enclosed within parentheses. All restorations are enclosed within square brackets. Untranslatable passages are represented by dots.

Month names are rendered by their Hebrew equivalents, followed by a Roman numeral (in parentheses) indicating the place of the month within the lunar year. Personal, divine and geographical names are rendered by English or biblical equivalents if a well-established equivalent exists (e.g., Esarhaddon, Nineveh); otherwise, they are given in transcription with length marks deleted. The rendering of professions is a compromise between the use of accurate but impractical Assyrian terms and inaccurate but practical modern or classical equivalents.

Critical Apparatus

The primary purpose of the critical apparatus is to support the readings and translations contained in the edition, and as in the previous volumes, it largely consists of references to collations, scribal mistakes corrected in the transliteration, alternative interpretations of ambiguous passages, and parallels available for restoring broken passages. Conjectural restorations are explained only if their conjectural nature is not apparent from italics in the translation. References to published photographs and copies are given at the beginning of each text, and different interpretations found in earlier editions and translations are commented upon whenever necessary. Collations given in copy at the end of the volume are referred to briefly as "see coll."

In addition, the critical apparatus also contains information more directly relevant to the study and interpretation of the texts, such as discussions of difficult passages, grammatical or lexical problems, or references to discussions in the introduction and notes. Biblical parallels and parallels to individual oracles found in the corpus itself are systematically noted.

Glossary and Indices

The glossary and indices, electronically generated, follow the pattern of the previous volumes. The glossary contains all lexically identifiable words occurring in the texts with the exception of suffixless numbers 1-99. Note that in contrast to the two basic dictionaries, verbal adjectives are for technical reasons listed under the corresponding verbs, with appropriate cross-references.

NOTES

1 See, e.g., W. von Soden, *Herrscher im alten Orient* (Berlin etc. 1954), p. 123 ("Orakelfragen"); M. Weippert, ARINH (1981), p. 99 ("Orakelanfragen"); M. deJong Ellis, JCS 41 (1989) 171 ("oracular queries"); and A. K. Grayson, CAH, 2nd ed., III/2 (1991), p. 129 ("oracle requests"), all referring to the extispicy queries edited in SAA 4. Elsewhere, Grayson uses the term "oracle" to refer the Assyrian prophecy corpus (e.g., BHLT [1975], p. 13f).

2 See E. Weidner, "Babylonische Prophezeiungen," AfO 13 (1939/41) 234-7; A. K. Grayson and W. G. Lambert, "Akkadian Prophecies," JCS 18 (1964) 7-30; W. W. Hallo, "Akkadian Apocalypses," IEJ 16 (1966) 231-42; R. D. Biggs, "More Babylonian 'Prophecies,'" Iraq 29 (1967) 117-32; R. Borger, "Gott Marduk und Gott-König Šulgi als Propheten: Zwei prophetische Texte," BiOr 28 (1971) 3-24; H. Hunger, "Die Tontafeln der XXVII. Kampagne," UVB 26/27 (1972), pp. 82 (W 22307/7 "Prophezeiungen"), 87 and Taf. 25g, and idem, SpTU I (1976) pp. 21-3 and 124; H. Hunger and S. Kaufman, "A New Akkadian Prophecy Text," JAOS 95 (1973) 371-5; A. K. Grayson, *Babylonian Historical Literary Texts* (Toronto 1975), pp. 11-37 ("Akkadian Prophecies"); R. D. Biggs, "The Babylonian Prophecies and the Astrological Traditions of Mesopotamia," JCS 37 (1985) 86-90; idem, "Babylonian Prophecies, Astrology, and a New Source from 'Prophecy Text B,'" Festschrift Reiner (1987), pp. 1-14; see further W. G. Lambert, "History and the Gods: A Review Article," Or. 39 (1970) 170-7, esp. 175ff, and idem, "The Background of Jewish Apocalyptic" (The Ethel M. Wood Lecture ... 22 February 1977, London: The Athlone Press 1978), pp. 1-20. For a detailed exposition of the reasons why the term "prophecy" should not be applied to this type of text see Ellis, JCS 41 (1989) 146ff; cf. also S. Kaufman, "Prediction, Prophecy, and Apocalypse in the Light of New Akkadian Texts," Proceedings of the 6th World Congress of Jewish Studies 1 (Jerusalem 1977), pp. 225f.

3 See, e.g., A. L. Oppenheim, *Ancient Mesopotamia* (Chicago 1964), p. 221: "Ecstasis as a means of communication between god and man did not occupy the important position in Mesopotamia that it did in Syria and Palestine ... The Western concept (Mari—and, of course, the Old Testament) [is] deeply alien to the eastern, Mesopotamian, attitude toward the god-man relationship"; note also A. K. Grayson, BHLT (1975) 14: "Akkadian prophecies are also quite different from biblical prophecy," R. D. Biggs, Iraq 29 (1967) 117: "The [prophetic] practices attested in Mari ... are probably of Western origin and not from Mesopotamia"; and cf. J. Bottéro in J.-P. Vernant et al. (eds.), *Divination et rationalité* (Paris 1974), p. 94f.

4 See H. Tadmor, "The Aramaization of Assyria: Aspects of Western Impact," CRRAI 25 (1982), p. 458, and "Monarchy and the Elite in Assyria and Babylonia: The Question of Royal Accountability," in S. N. Eisenstadt (ed.), *The Origins and Diversity of Axial Age Civilizations* (New York 1986), p. 223f; M. Weippert, "Assyrische Prophetien der Zeit Asarhaddons und Assurbanipals," ARINH (1981), p. 104, and "Die Bildsprache der neuassyrischen Prophetie," OBO 64 (1985), p. 86. A. R. Millard, RHR 202 (1985) 133f, rejects the alleged Western origin of Mari and NA prophecy and regards them as purely Mesopotamian phenomena.

5 Note also the alternation of Ištar and Mullissu in the epistolary formula "may Aššur and Ištar/Mullissu bless the king" (for Aššur + Ištar see ABL 152, 209, 217, 533, 1249, 1415, and CT 53 18 and 500; for Aššur + Mullissu see ABL 87-98, 213, 330, 396-398, 480-483, 547, 562, 577, 1015, 1433 and GPA 240). Cf. also CT 53 235 [Aššur Ištar Bel Nabû] as against ABL 149 = LAS 317 [Aššur Mullissu Nabû Marduk]).

6 See, e.g., the hymn to Nanaya/Ištar published by Reiner, JNES 33 (1974) 224ff, and nn. 10, 130, 183 and 189f below. Both Banitu ("Creatrix") and Urkittu (the "Urukite") are appellatives of Ištar extremely common in Neo-Assyrian personal names but rare in official cultic texts. On Banitu see K. Deller, Assur 3 (1983) 142f; in STT 88 iii 6, she is listed (after Mušabšitu "Creatress") as one of the images of Ištar worshiped in the Aššur temple of Nineveh. For Urkittu cf. Cypris ("the Cyprian"), a frequent appellative of Aphrodite.

7 See in more detail JNES 52 (1993) 204f, AOAT 240 (1995) 398ff, and p. 6, commentary on oracle 1.4. The notion of Nabû as judge over life and death also surfaces in no. 9:20f, to be compared with SAA 3 13:19ff ("Please Nabû, do not abandon me! My life is written before you"). See also below, nn. 41 and 196f on the archangel Michael, the Jewish equivalent of Nabû, and his equation with Christ. References to "the book of life" in the Bible and later Jewish literature are collected in S. Paul, "Heavenly Tablets and the Book of Life," JANES 5 (1973) 345-354. In SAA 3 12 r.9, Nabû is addressed with his name Šiddukišarra (lit., "the accountant of the entire cosmos") in a telling context: "My life is finished; Šiddukišarra, where can I go? I have reached the gate of death; Nabû, why have you forsaken me?"). On this passage see also n. 268 below.

8 In Jewish mysticism, divine names and cognomens are viewed as garments in which God dresses "in accordance with what is appropriate for the moment" (Gikatilla, *Gates of Light*, p. 224; cf. ibid., pp. 170, 177, 209f, 223 and 226, and see nn. 47, 112 and 114 below). It is important to realize that these "names" and "garments" functionally correspond to Assyrian "gods," foreign gods being explicitly defined in this same text as names and garments of YHWH, just as in *Enūma eliš*, Tablets VI and VII, Mesopotamian gods are presented as "names" of Marduk. Cf. the gnostic text Trimorphic Protennoia, where the Logos tells of herself: "I revealed myself in the likeness of their (= the Powers') shape. And I wore everyone's garment and I hid myself within them, and [they] did not know the one who empowers me. For I dwell within all the Sovereignties and Powers and within the Angels ... And none of them knew me, [although] it is I who work in them" (NHC XIII 1, 47, 15ff = Robinson NHL p. 520). Compare the term *prósōpon/persona* (actually, "[actor's] mask") introduced by Hippolytus to refer to the Trinitarian God in his three aspects or manifestations (Kelly *Doctrines*, p. 114f). See also nn. 9, 19, 23, 189, 192 and 248 below.

9 The affinities of oracle 1.4 with the Trinitarian doctrine cannot be brushed off as merely accidental. The final formulation of the latter ("one substance – three persons") has as its point of departure the Neoplatonic hypostases doctrine, which was inspired by the Chaldaean Oracles' triadic view of the universe, particularly their description of the "Father" as a trinity-in-unity (cf. R. T. Wallis, *Neoplatonism* [London 1972], p. 106). A trinitarian concept of God is implicit in the Assyrian doctrine of kingship as a divine institution materialized in the "consubstantial" trinity of the king, the queen, and the crown prince (i.e., father, mother and son), each of the three functioning in different ways as God's representatives upon earth. See nn. 123, 158 and 196f below for the king and the crown prince as images of Enlil/Marduk and Ninurta/Nabû, and n. 159 for the queen as the image of Mullissu/Ištar (the divine mother of the king); see also n. 197 for the consubstantiality of the king and the crown prince, and nn. 25, 179 and 205 for the complementarity of the heavenly and mundane realms. For Mullissu/Ištar as the "Holy Spirit" see pp. XXVIff and XL.

Note that the iconographic representations of Aššur in Assyrian glyptics (the winged disk) occasionally include an anthropomorphic triad of gods: a central figure depicted inside the disk, and two minor accompanying figures riding on its wings, see fig. 1 above and Appendix B in JNES 52 (1993) 201f. The central figure (raising its hand in a gesture of blessing) can be identified as Enlil/Marduk, the figure on the right wing (receiving the blessing) as Ninurta/Nabû, and the figure on the left wing (likewise raising its hand in blessing) as Mullissu/Ištar of Babylon (Zarpanitu), see JNES 52 185 n. 93; for the beard of the female figure, see n. 97 below, and for the scene itself, SAA 3 37 r.24ff. In some representations, the accompanying figures are reduced to mere volutes emerging from the central figure; often a single volute stands for all three figures (see JNES 52 165 n. 25 and App. B). This implies not only that the accompanying figures were conceived as essentially one with the central figure, but that all three together constituted an indivisible, homogenous whole. Hence the configuration Enlil/Marduk–Mullissu/Ištar–Ninurta/Nabû does not just represent a triad of gods but a true "trinity-in-unity" in the Christian and Neoplatonic/Chaldean sense of the concept. Cf. St. John of Damascus, *On the Divine Images* (transl. D. Anderson, Crestwood, NY, 1980), p. 20: "When we speak of the holy and eternal Trinity, we use the images of the sun, light, and burning rays; or a running fountain; ... or a rose tree."

Also note that the Assyrian version of the trinity underlying oracle 1.4 (Father-Mother-Son) is explicitly attested in Gnosticism, e.g. in the treatise Trimorphic Protennoia, where we read: "Now the Voice that originated from my Thought exists as three permanences: the Father, the Mother, the Son" (NHC XIII 1, 37, 20ff = Robinson NHL p. 514); see also The Apocryphon of John, NHC II 1, 9, 10f = Robinson NHL p. 109, and n. 77 below.

10 See notes on oracles 1.6 iii 23-27, 24, iv 14-17; 2.4 iii 16; 3.3 ii 14 and 21; and 9:5. In SAA 3 13, three Ištar figures (Mullissu, Urkittu, Queen of Nineveh) coalesce with Nabû, who in this text (line 15) appears as the progenitor of the king, a role elsewhere ascribed to Ištar. Note the affinities of the passage to the "trinitarian" oracle (1.4) just discussed: "My life is written before you (Nabû), my soul is deposited in the lap of Mullissu." For this passage see also nn. 106 and 268 below.

11 Oracles 3.4-5 are explicitly defined as "words of Ištar of Arbela," the Goddess speaking, as usual, in the first person singular. In the second oracle (3.2), defined as "well-being" in the text, the oracular deity is not identified by name, but the content of the text as well as parallel oracles leave no doubt that Ištar of Arbela is in question (cf. nos. 1.4:30ff and 2.4, and note also 1.9 referring to a "well-being" sent by Ištar to the king). The first oracle (3.1) is very fragmentary but refers to Aššur in the third person and thus parallels no. 3.2.

12 Note, however, that in no. 5:3 the king's cry for help is heard by Ištar, not Aššur, as in the passage Streck Asb p. 78:79ff cited in the note on no. 3 ii 21. Cf. also no. 1 iv 29ff.

13 Note also the interchange of Aššur, Ištar and *ilu* "God" in Assyrian personal names discussed in JNES 52 [1993] 187 n. 187 (see also n. 272 below), and the designation of Ištar of Arbela as *Aššur-Ištar* in the Takultu god-list 3 R 66 r. vii 18 (Frankena Takultu p. 7, cf. discussion ibid. p. 79). The "composite deity" Aššur-Ištar occurs also in line v 24 of the same text between *Aššur-Aššur* "Aššur as Aššur" and *Aššur-Illil* "Aššur as Enlil," on which see n. 59 below.

14 The same problem is of course also inherent in Christianity, whose Trinitarian doctrine has been criticized since antiquity for introducing "a new, more sublime form of polytheism" (Encyclopaedia Britannica, Vol. 16 [1974], p. 282, under "different manifestations of God"). On the history of the Trinitarian doctrine see Kelly *Doctrines*, passim. Note esp. ibid. p. 111ff on God's "immanent plurality" (Hippolytus) and p. 113 on the idea of "distinction" not "division" or "separation" inherent in the concept of the Trinity (Tertullian, quoting "the unity between the root and its shoot, the source and the river, and the sun and its light as illustrations"). See also ibid. p. 265f, and cf. J. Taylor, JSOT 66 (1995) 32 n. 18 on the relationship between Yahweh and "his Asherah" (see n. 199ff below), and G. Scholem, *On the Kabbalah and Its Symbolism* (New York 1969), pp. 105-8, on the relationship between God and "his Shekhinah" (see nn. 98 and 146 below).

15 See the analysis of the name Aššur and its variant spellings in JNES 52 (1993) 205ff.

16 Cf. the name Gabbu-ilani-Aššur "Aššur is the totality of gods" in BaM 24 (1993) 262 no. 18:7 and 18, dated 744/3 BC. See also the discussion in JNES 52 (1993) 187 n. 97 of names like Gabbu-ilani-ereš ("The totality of gods requested") and its abbreviation, Ilani-ereš ("God [lit. "gods"] requested"), alternating with Aššur/Ilu/Ištar-ereš ("Aššur/God/Ištar requested"). As a designation of God, *gabbi ilāni* and its abbreviation *ilāni* "gods" (wr. DINGIR.MEŠ) constitutes a perfect parallel to the biblical *elōhîm* "God" (lit. "gods"), on which see nn. 30f below.

17 E.g., Assurbanipal's hymn to Aššur, SAA 3 1, lines 26-29: "(Even) a god does not comprehend [...] your majesty, O Aššur; the meaning of your [majestic designs] is not understood," and see my discussion in JNES 52 (1993) 185f.

18 See Craig ABRT I 83 // SAA 12 86:7-11, where Aššur is called "creator of himself, father of the gods, who grew up in the Abyss; king of heaven and earth, lord of all the gods, who 'poured out' the supernal and infernal gods and fashioned the vaults of heaven and earth, the maker of all the regions, who lives in the [pur]e starlit heave[ns]"; SAA 3 1:15f, "creator of the creatures of heaven and earth, fashioner of the mountains, [...] creator of the gods, begetter of Ištar"; and Sg 8 314ff, "Aššur, the father of the gods, the lord of all lands, the king over the totality of heaven and earth." Note also En. el. I 14f, where Anšar (= Aššur) is said to have "reflected" Anu as his "heir," and see the discussion in JNES 52 (1993) 191. Cf. also n. 22 below.

19 Note, e.g., the prayer of Tukulti-Ninurta I, KAR 128 (13th century BC), where Šamaš and Adad are respectively invoked as the "radiance" and the "voice" of Aššur. See further n. 23 below.

20 See n. 8 above, and cf. Gikatilla, *Gates of Light*, p. 13f: "There are Names in charge of prayer, mercy and forgiveness, while others are in charge of tears and sadness, injury and tribulations, sustenance and income, or heroism, loving-kindness and grace... When [one] needs to request something from God he should concentrate on the Name designated to handle that question"; cf. also ibid., pp. 166f and 190f.

21 On the problematics of the traditional classification of religions into monotheistic and polytheistic ones see G. Ahn, "'Monotheismus' - 'Polytheismus': Grenzen und Möglichkeiten einer Klassifikation von Gottesvorstellungen," AOAT 232 (1993) 1-24; see also N. Lohfink, "Gott und die Götter im Alten Testament," in K. Rahner et al. (eds.), *Theologische Akademie* 6 (Frankfurt a.M. 1969), pp. 50-71, esp. p. 65. The whole problem disappears as soon as "monotheism" and "polytheism" cease to be viewed as mutually exclusive concepts, in other words, as soon it is realized that God can be at the same time both "one" and "many."

22 Cf. the concept of God of Eastern Christian mysticism, which distinguishes between the "essence of God" and "divine attributes," the latter being regarded as energies that penetrate the universe (see n. 60 below, and cf. nn. 9 and 41). It is good to keep in mind that there is a direct historical link between Christian and Assyrian concepts of God through Neoplatonic philosophy and the Chaldaean Oracles (see nn. 9, 105, 126 and 130ff). Note that Origen's

trinitarian scheme admits the existence of "spiritual beings ... coeternal with the Father [and] in their degree equally entitled to be called gods" (Kelly *Doctrines*, p. 131).

Assyrian "monotheism" was, of course, rooted in earlier Mesopotamian religion, whose concept of God has close parallels in Hinduism and Egyptian religion (see n. 30 below). There is an important difference, however. Whereas in India and Egypt the single transcendent source of the multiplicity of gods could only be defined in negative terms as "non-existence," Assyrian imperial monotheism introduced Aššur as an intermediate entity between non-existence and existence: the infinite metaphysical universe (AN.ŠÁR) engulfing and pervading the physical universe (see JNES 52 [1993] 191). This innovation made Aššur, a "God that created himself," the source of all manifest divine powers (i.e., gods) worshiped in the world, and thus the omnipresent, universal God of the empire (cf. SAA 2 6:393f, "To the future and forever Aššur will be your god, and Assurbanipal ... will be your lord"). Theologically, Aššur corresponds to the *En Sof Or* ("boundless light") of Jewish mysticism, see JNES 52 (1993) 185f and 208, and to the concept of "God beyond the gods" or "greater God" introduced by 20th-century Christian apologists as a reaction to Nietzsche's "death of God."

23 See JNES 52 (1993) 185 nn. 93f for a discussion of the winged disk symbol of Aššur, which unifies several "great gods" (represented symbolically) into a single composite divine being. Note also the text CT 24 50 edited in AOAT 240 (1995) 398ff, which presents 14 "great gods" of the Babylonian pantheon as functions, tools, and qualities of Marduk (the Babylonian national god), as well as KAR 25 ii 3-15, a prayer to Marduk defining various "great gods" as qualities, powers and attributes of Marduk (his "kingship, might, wisdom, victory, strength, counsel, judgment," etc.). The latter text recalls a well-known Talmudic passage (TB *Hagigah* 12a) attributed to the early third-century scholar Rav: "By ten 'words' was the world created: by wisdom, by understanding, by reason, by strength, by rebuke, by might, by righteousness, by judgment, by compassion, and by loving kindness." On this list, which brings to mind the classic kabbalistic decad of divine powers, see JNES 52 (1993) 186 Fig. 10 and 171 n. 49, and nn. 55, 63 and 112 below.

24 See JNES 52 (1993) 185 n. 94 and 187 n. 97, and n. 13 above.

25 This analogy is not accidental, for the empire was conceived of as the counterpart (*tamšīlu*) of the divine world, referred to as the "kingdom of heaven" in oracle 2.5. See nn. 179 and 205 below and my article "The Assyrian Cabinet" (AOAT 240, 1995), passim, and cf. Gikatilla, *Gates of Light*, p. 12: "Our Sages aroused us with the rule: "The Kingdom of earth is the same as the Kingdom of heaven." Note that in the Byzantine empire "imperial ceremonial was the image of the heavenly order" (ODB [1991], p. 1981). Note also Lowell K. Handy, *Among the Host of Heaven* (Winona Lake 1994), who argues that the ANE pantheons functioned as "bureaucracies" and mirrored the social structures of the city states. On the king as God's representative on the earth, see JNES 52 (1993) 167; SAA 10 (1993), p. XVff; and p. XL with n. 193 below.

26 See in detail my article "The Assyrian Cabinet," AOAT 240 (1995) 379-401.

27 Cf. n. 28 and see E. Cassin, "Note sur le *puhrum* des dieux," in A. Finet (ed.), *La voix d'opposition en Mesopotamia* (Bryssels 1975), p. 113; M. deJong Ellis, "Mesopotamian Oracles and Prophetic Texts," JCS 41 (1989) 127-186, esp. p. 139, and A. Malamat, "The Secret Council and Prophetic Involvement in Mari and Israel," in R. Liwak and S. Wagner (eds.), *Prophetie und geschichtliche Wirklichkeit im alten Israel: Festschrift für Siegfried Herrmann zum 65. Geburtstag* (Stuttgart 1991), 231-236, on the divine council in the Old Babylonian prophecies from Eshnunna and Mari; and I. Starr, *The Rituals of the Diviner* (Malibu 1983), pp. 51ff, on the council in OB extispicy texts. The OB Diviners's Prayer (Starr's Text A) portrays the giving of omens as a sitting in judgment of the council of gods; on p. 57f, Starr points out that "there is a marked interplay between celestial and terrestrial judicial roles in ritual of the diviner" (cf. n. 25 above). In the Sumerian Deluge story (Lambert-Millard Atra-hasis p. 142 iv 158), the resolution of the divine council to destroy mankind is referred to as di-til-la, "final sentence," the terminus technicus of Sumerian court decisions.

28 See p. XXV with n. 60ff. R. Gikatilla, in whose *Gates of Light* the divine assembly figures prominently, elaborates on the issue as follows (p. 212f): "One finds that all the Holy Names and their Cognomens ... are intermingled and sustain each other. Irrespective of whether they are from the right or left, each one has the same intention and that is to cleave to the name YHVH... You should not think that the groups to the right and left quarrel with each other, or hate each other, or contradict each other, God forbid. It is only that when you see them disagreeing, they are merely negotiating a judgment to bring the justice of the world's creatures to the light of true justice... All the factions of right and left love each other... All agree on the unification of the Name." Note that the council metaphor was also used in early Christianity to illustrate God's essential unity behind his seeming (trinitarian) plurality: "Tertullian exerted himself to show that the threeness was in no way incompatible with God's essential unity, ... noting that on the analogy of the imperial government one and the same sovereignty could be exercised by coordinated agencies" (Kelly *Doctrines*, p. 113; see also n. 40 below).

29 See AOAT 240 (1995) 385 with n. 17, and Fig. 2 ibid. Note that the Assyrian copies of the Mesopotamian god list An-Anum (Lambert, RlA 3, pp. 275f), which presents the Mesopotamian pantheon as a heavenly royal court, does not include Aššur either but begins with Anu, the "mirror image" of Aššur. Cf. n. 18 above, and see AOAT 240 (1995) 386 and JNES 52 (1993) 179f, 185 and 191.

30 For Iran see S. A. Nigosian, *The Zoroastrian Faith: Tradition and Modern Research* (Montreal: McGill-Queen's University Press 1993), pp. 70-89; for Egypt see J. Baines in B. E. Shafer (ed.), *Religion in Ancient Egypt* (London 1991), p. 188f, and E. Hornung, *Conceptions of God in Ancient Egypt: The One and the Many* (London 1983), and "Die Anfänge von Monotheismus und Trinität in Ägypten," in K. Rahner (ed.), *Der eine Gott und der dreieine Gott* (Munich and Zurich 1983), pp. 48-66; for Ugarit and ANE "Heno/Cosmotheismus" (*hén kaì pân*) see O. Loretz, "Die *Einzigkeit* Jahwes (Dtn 6, 4) im Licht des ugaritischen Baal-Mythos," AOAT 240 (1995) 215-304, esp. 231ff; for classical Greece and Hellenism see O. Kern, *Die Religion der Griechen* II (2nd ed. Berlin 1963), esp. p. 158 with reference to the Orphic logos, "Zeus was the first, Zeus the last... Zeus is the head, Zeus is the middle, everything is Zeus. Zeus is the ground of the earth and the starry heaven," whose antiquity is ascertained by an allusion to it in Plato's *Laws* (785E); cf. R. T. Wallis, *Neoplatonism* (London 1972), p. 104: "Educated pagans were insistent that the supreme deity's glory is best revealed in the multiplicity of subordinate gods he had produced (cf. Enn. II 9.9, 26-42, Porphyry C. Chr. frs. 75-8)." Rudolph *Gnosis*, p. 287, points out that the "monotheistic idea [of God as the summing up of all divinities and divine powers which shape and control the universe] is already found in early Hellenism, as the hymn to Zeus by Cleanthes (about 300 BC) impressively demonstrates." For (Vedic) India, see R. E. Hume, *The Thirteen Principal Upanishads* (2nd ed., London 1931), p. 23ff.

The cuneiform spelling of Iran. *Baga* "God" with the logogram DINGIR.MEŠ "gods" in a LB document from Ecbatana dated 491 BC (mDINGIR.MEŠ–*da-a-ta*, JCS 28 40 no. 28, rendering *Baga-data* "Given by God," see M. Dandamayev, *Iranians in Achaemenid Babylonia* [Costa Mesa 1992], p. 50) implies that Ahura Mazda was understood in the early Achaemenid period as "the sum total of gods," exactly as Aššur centuries earlier (see n. 16 and note Ahura Mazda's takeover of Aššur's winged disk icon in Achaemenid imperial art). The same spelling is also attested for Yahweh in late 5th century cuneiform documents from Nippur (cf. m*ba-na-a*ʾ–DINGIR.MEŠ, BE 9 25:1 and 45:1 [434 BC], corresponding to m*ba-na–ia-a-ma* "Yahweh has created" in CBS 4993+:2 [same person], see R. Zadok, *The Jews in Babylonia* [Haifa 1979], p. 12), establishing a direct link with the equation (Ass.) *ilāni* = (Hebr.) *elōhîm* "God" discussed in the next note.

31 Note that not only is *elōhîm* an exact equivalent of Assyrian (*gabbi*) *ilāni* "(all) gods" as a designation of God (see n. 16), but, like Assyrian *ilāni*, it is also at the same time used in the sense of "(individual) gods, divine agents"; see Enc. Jud. 2 (1972) 956, s.v. angels, with the comment "The Bible does not always distinguish clearly between God and His messenger" (citing as examples Gen. 16:7, 13; 21:17ff; 22:1ff, 11:18; and Ex. 3:2). In the meaning "God," both *elōhîm* and its Assyrian equivalent are construed as singular nouns; the underlying plurality is, however, clearly implied by Gen. 1:26 and 3:22, which in gnostic texts are understood to refer to the divine "rulers" (*archontes*) of the universe, the equivalents of the Assyrian "great gods" (see NHC II 1, 21, 17ff and NHC II 4, 88, 25ff = Robinson NHL pp. 117 and 164f, and cf. n. 44 below). For rabbinical exegesis of Gen. 1:26 and 3:22, see Gen. Rabba VIII 9:11-31. In Ps. 82:1-2, "God takes his stand in the court of heaven to deliver judgment among the gods," and Ps. 95:3, "the LORD is a great God, a great king over all gods" (// Ps. 96:4 and 97:7ff), Yahweh is portrayed as president of the divine council (see just below).

I. Gruenwald (pers. communication) objects to interpreting *elōhîm* as "the sum total of gods," pointing out that "one should distinguish between the many 'names' and 'faces' of God and actual multiplicity. What does it really mean that the OT God had different names? A variety of local traditions, perhaps? Elohim is a plural form, but it indicates as a name the notion of majestatis pluralis." As stated above (n. 21), I do not believe that monotheism and polytheism were mutually exclusive concepts in antiquity, and consequently regard a distinction made between "names and faces of God" and "actual multiplicity" – however relevant from the modern point of view – as artificial and anachronistic when applied to antiquity. As hypostatized divine powers, Assyrian gods (like Jewish angels/gods) could *at the same time* be both "names and faces" and multiple manifestations of God. See further nn. 8, 20 and 28 above, and nn. 33, 41, 47, 55, 58 and 60 below.

32 See H.-J. Fabry, ThWAT V (1986) 775-82, s.v. *sôd* (with detailed bibliography); Enc. Jud. 2 (1972) 957f, sub "Angels as a Group"; H. W. Robinson, "The Council of Yahwe," JTS 45 (1944) 151-7; E. C. Kingsbury, "The Prophets and the Council of Yahwe," JBL 83 (1964) 279-286; J. Gray, *I & II Kings (OTL)*, London 1970, 443ff; E. Mullen, *The Assembly of God* (Chico 1980), p. 205ff; A. Rofé, *The Prophetical Stories* (Jerusalem 1988), pp. 142-52; M. E. Polley, "Hebrew Prophecy Within the Council of Yahwe," in C.D. Evans et al. (eds.), *Scripture in Context* (Pittsburgh 1980), pp. 141-56; A. Malamat, "The Secret Council and Prophetic Involvement in Mari and Israel" (n. 27 above), pp. 231-236; M. Mach, *Entwicklungsstadien des jüdischen Engelglaubens in vorrabbinischer Zeit* (Texte und Studien zum antiken Judentum 34, Tübingen 1992; ref. courtesy I. Gruenwald), and recently H.-D. Neef, *Gottes himmlischer Thonrat: Hintergrund und Bedeutung von* sôd JHWH *im Alten Testament* (Stuttgart 1994; ref. courtesy M. Nissinen).

33 1 Kgs. 22:19-23 = 2 Chron. 18:18-22. For our argument it is immaterial whether the account is historical or "deuteronomistic" fiction. Ahab died in 853 BC according to Reade's calibrated chronology (*Mesopotamian Guidelines for Biblical Chronology*, SMS 4/1 [1981] 8).

34 This verse recalls oracle 1.4 referring to "Sin (Moon), Šamaš (Sun), and sixty great gods" standing with Bel ("Lord") at the birth of Esarhaddon, and oracle 2.2, referring to "sixty gods standing at the [right] and left side" of the oracular deity. Cf. Jer. 8:2 and 2 Kgs. 23:4ff, where "the host of heaven" is similarly associated with Baal, Asherah, the sun and moon, and the planets. On the "host of heaven" see also my remarks in AOAT 240 (1995) 395f and below, nn. 41 and 53.

35 See Isa. 6:1-2; 40:22-26; Jer. 23:18-24; Ezek. 1:22-26; Dan. 7:9ff; Job 1:6-7 and 15:8; note that the council members are here explicitly called "gods" (*bny hʾlhym*). See also Ps. 2:4, 89:5f, 103:19 and 123:1.

36 See Gruenwald *Apocalyptic*, p. 35ff (1 Enoch), 51 (2 Enoch), 56f (Apocalypse of Abraham), 60f (Ascension of Isaiah), 63ff (Revelation of John), 71f (Apocalypse of Paul), 94f (Talmud), 116 (On the Origin of the World), 128ff (Ezekiel the Tragedian), 145 (Hekhalot Zutreti), 153ff (Hekhalot Rabbati), 183 (Maasheh Merkavah), 194 (Sefer Hekhalot), 211f (Masekhet Hekhalot), and 214 (Shiur Qomah); Scholem *Origins* (1987), pp. 145-8; Enc. Jud. 2 (1972) 968ff, sub "Angels in the Talmud and Midrash" ("From the third century, the expression of God's "familia" (*Pamalya*) or the heavenly court of justice is found in the sources. God takes no action without prior consultation with the "familia," ibid. 969); Zohar II 128a and passim; *Gates of Light*, pp. 139, 194 and passim ("the Great Heavenly Court of Seventy-One"). On the latter expression see AOAT 240 (1995) 396ff; note that this court is referred to by Gikatilla (ibid. p. 275) as "the heavenly court known as 'the gods' (*elōhîm*)," and cf. n. 31 above!

37 E.g., Isa. 6:6, Ezek. 10:2, Dan. 7:9 (furnace at the throne of God); Ps. 89:5f, 102:25, 104:2, 148:4 (succession of heavens); Isa. 6:1, Ps. 48:3, 102:19, 104:3 (heavenly palaces); Gen. 28:12 (ladders to heaven); Gen. 28:17, Job 38:10 and 17 (heavenly gates, doors and gatekeepers); Ps. 46, 48, 93:1 and 145:11; 2 Esdras 7:26 (heavenly city and kingdom).

38 See, e.g., the Revelation of John (heavenly Jerusalem), E. Hennecke and W. Schneemelcher, *Neutestamentliche Aprokryphen in deutscher Übersetzung*, Teil II (3rd ed., Tübingen 1964), and Gruenwald *Apocalyptic*, pp. 120f, 142ff, 161f and 209; Gikatilla, *Gates of Light*, pp. 11 and 177.

39 See oracle 1.6 (golden chamber in the midst of the heavens, lamp shining before God), 2.5 (kingdom of heaven), and 3.3 (gate of heaven); see also below, n. 248. For other Mesopotamian texts see Horowitz *Cosmic Geography* (1997), passim; e.g., BWL 136:182f, OECT 6 pl. 12:10, and En. el. V 9 (gates of heaven); SAA 3 39:31f (three heavens, lamp shining before Bel, who sits on a lapis-lazuli dais in a temple in the middle heaven); STT 28 v 13 = AnSt 10 122 v 13, and Starr Barû 30:9 // RA 38 87:11 ([lapis lazuli] ladders to heaven).

40 See n. 9 above and New Catholic Encyclopedia 1 (1967), p. 507 ("Angels are held to spiritual intelligences created by, not emanating from, the divine substance ... A worthy man's spiritualization at the resurrection will make him the angel's equal."). Note that although the Church Fathers decidedly opposed efforts to identify angels with pagan gods, in early Christianity angels were commonly believed to have participated in the creation, to move the stars and to be placed over nations and cities, the four elements, and plants and animals (ibid. p. 511 with refs.).

According to Athenagoras (c. AD 176), "We affirm a crowd of angels and ministers, whom God, the maker and creator of the world, appointed to their several tasks through his Word. He gave them charge over the good order of the universe, over the elements, the heavens, the world, and all it contains" (C. C. Richardson [ed.], *Early Christian Fathers* [New York 1970], p. 309); cf. Enc. Jud. 2 (1972) 963ff and below, n. 41, for similar views in Jewish apocrypha and mysticism. Note also R. J. Hoffmann, *Porphyry's Against the Christians* (Amherst, NY, 1994), p. 84: "You say, 'The immortal angels stand before God, ... and these we speak of as gods because they are near the godhead.' Why do we argue about names? ... Whether one addresses these divine beings as gods or angels matters very little, since their nature remains the same."

41 For angels as powers of God in the Hekhalot texts see J. Dan, *The Revelation of the Secret of the World: The Beginning of Jewish Mysticism in Late Antiquity*, Brown University Program in Judaic Studies, Occasional Papers Number 2 (Providence 1992), p. 17, and idem, *Three Types of ancient Jewish Mysticism* (Cincinnati 1984), p. 17. Note that in J. Montgomery, *Aramaic Incantation Texts from Nippur* (Philadelphia 1913), the Mesopotamian gods Šamaš, Sin, Bel, Nanaya and Nergal are invoked as "holy angels" (*mlʾkʾ*; charm no. 36), while the angel Rahmiel (Ugaritic Rahmaya) is paired with "Dlibat the Passionate," i.e., Mesopotamian Dilibat/Venus (Mandean Libat; charm no. 28), and Metatron, Hadriel, Nuriel, Uriel, Sasgabiel, Hafkiel and Mehafkiel are defined as "the seven angels that go and turn around heaven and earth and stars and zodiac and moon and sea" (ibid. p. 97). In contemporary Greek papyri, Michael, Gabriel, Raphael and other angels are invoked as "gods" (ibid., p. 99). A Hebrew magical-astrological text from Nisibis (M. Gaster, "Wisdom of the Chaldeans," PSBA 22 [1900] 329ff), equates seven angels with the seven classical planets (among others, Michael = Mercury), commenting on Anael = Venus: "This ruler is in the likeness of a woman. He is appointed on all manner of love. On her right arm serves an angel whose name is Arbiel, on the left one called Niniel." Here Anael certainly is the goddess Anat (cf. W. L. Michel, "BTWLH," "virgin" or "Virgin (Anat)" in Job 31:1?," Hebrew Studies 23 [1982] 59-66), while the names Arbiel and Niniel doubtless derive from Ištar of Arbela and Ištar of Nineveh.

The association of angels with planets is not a late phenomenon in Judaism; see above n. 34 on the "hosts of heaven," and note the passage in Ezekiel the Tragedian (2nd cent. BC) discussed by Gruenwald *Apocalyptic* p. 130, where the hosts of heavenly stars fall on their knees before Moses and then march past his throne. In the apocryphal literature angels were not only commonly associated with stars (e.g., 1 En. 18:13ff and 21:33ff; Jub. 19), but there were also angels of the elements, like of the spirit of fire, and of the seasons of the year, of the wind, the clouds, darkness, snow and hail, thunder, and lightning (see Enc. Jud. 2 [1972] 964 for refs.).

In sum, the angels of first millennium AD Judaism in every respect corresponded to Mesopotamian gods. Keeping in mind the Christian definition of angels as creatures of God (n. 40 above), it comes as no surprise that the Church Fathers accused the Jews of "praying not to the God but to angels and practicing magic" (see Gruenwald *Apocalyptic* p. 230 n. 17, discussing the magical treatise Sefer ha-Razim). As pointed out by Gruenwald (ibid.), such practices are, however, not evidence of polytheistic or syncretistic beliefs: they are perfectly in line with biblical and rabbinic monotheism and have to be judged in the light of nn. 8 and 20 above.

It should be noted that the alleged author of Montgomery's charms 8, 9, 17, and 32-33, Joshua ben Perahia (early 1st cent. BC), was an early hero of the Law (cf. Pirke Aboth 1:7) and hence certainly a highly respected member of the rabbinic community. In Sanh. 107b he is associated or confused with Jesus of Nazareth, and not for the assonance of name only: his reputed ascent to heaven reveals him as an emulator of Adam Qadmon, the "perfect man," who as personification of Michael/Metatron was by definition believed to wield extraordinary magic powers (cf. SAA 10 p. XIX and n. 121 below). See further Collins *Scepter and Star*, p. 139.

42 For the derivation of the menorah from the ANE sacred tree see G. Widengren, *The King and the Tree of Life in Ancient Near Eastern Religion* (Uppsala 1951), p. 64ff (with illustration of a menorah-shaped tree in Mesopotamian glyptic); L. Yarden, *The Tree of Light: A Study of the Menorah, the Seven-branched Lampstand* (Ithaca, NY, 1971; rev. ed. Uppsala 1972); C. Meyers, ThWAT IV (1984) 981-7 s.v. *mnwrh*; and recently J. Taylor, "The Asherah, the Menorah and the Sacred Tree," JSOT 66 (1995) 29-54 (ref. courtesy T. Veijola). In Ex. 25:40, the menorah is explicitly associated with "the design (*tbnyt*) which you were shown on the mountain," i.e., the burning bush (Ex. 3: 1f, cf. Deut. 4:15f). According to St. John of Damascus, *On the Divine Images* (transl. D. Anderson, Crestwood, NY, 1980), p. 65, "The burning bush was an image of God's mother (Theotokos)"; cf. nn. 47, 98, 133 and 199ff below.

For the menorah as a distinctive symbol of Judaism in the post-exilic period see Widengren, loc. cit. Note that while in 1 Macc. 1:21 the lampstand occupies a position of central importance among the cult objects carried off from the temple by Antiochus in 169 BC (as 200 years later by Titus), it does not have this status in the lists of booty carried off by Nebuchadnezzar in 587 BC (2 Kgs. 24:13ff and Jer. 52:17ff). This suggests that the menorah was introduced as a religious symbol only in the post-exilic period, in order to distinguish clearly the "deuteronomistic" form of Judaism from its 'idolatrous' predecessor. See p. XXVI with n. 65, and cf. Job 29:2 and Ps. 132:17. See also p. XLII with n. 201f below for the association of the sacred tree with Asherah in pre-exilic Israel, corresponding to its association with Shekhinah and Tiferet in Jewish mysticism (nn. 47 and 133) and with Mullissu and Ištar in Assyria (n. 133), and note that the cherub-flanked tree (n. 98) constituted the principal decorative motif of the temple of Solomon (1 Kgs. 6f, cf. Ezek. 40f) and of the Tabernacle (Ex. 25 and 36).

43 On Kabbalah as a direct continuation of apocalyptic and rabbinic mystical tradition see M. Idel, *Kabbalah: New Perspectives* (New Haven 1988), p. 30ff and I. Gruenwald, "Reflections on the Nature and Origins of Jewish Mysticism," in P. Schaefer et al. (eds.), *Gershom Scholem's Major Trends in Jewish Mysticism 50 Years After* (Tübingen 1993), pp. 25-48. Several central kabbalistic concepts and doctrines are already attested in the Babylonian Talmud (e.g., Maashe Bereshit, Maashe Merkavah, ten divine powers, God's infinite expansion at Creation, the pillars, the story of the Four Sages, Metatron, Sandalphon, the four beasts). The antiquity of the kabbalistic interpretation of the menorah (see n. 44) is confirmed by Philo (Moses 2.102-3), according to whom "the menorah is the symbol of heaven and its lights, of the planets"; cf. Zech. 4:1-14 and Clement of Alexandria, Stromata 5.6.34.9-35.2 ("the lamps symbolize the seven planets and the menorah itself is the sign of Christ"), and see further Morton Smith, *Studies in the Cult of Jahweh* II (Leiden 1996), p. 138. On the relevance of Kabbalah to the study of Assyrian religion see I. Gruenwald, "'How much Qabbalah in Ancient Assyria?' Methodological Reflections on the Study of a Cross-Cultural Phenomenon," in S. Parpola and R. M. Whiting (eds.), *Assyria 1995* (Helsinki 1997), pp. 115-127.

44 See, e.g., Scholem *Origins*, p. 82; Gikatilla, *Gates of Light*, pp. 15, 22, 31f, 221, and passim; Idel *Kabbalah*, p. 113f. On the technical meaning of the term sefirah in the Sefer Yezirah and the writings of Abraham Abulafia ("primordial/ideal number") see Scholem *Origins*, p. 26f, and Idel *Kabbalah*, p. 349 n. 323; according to I. Gruenwald

(pers. communication), the term denotes "notions and entities that have numerical value(s)", as in Pythagoreanism. The sefirotic powers (associated in the *Bahir* with the archangels, see Gottfarstein Bahir, p. 87, and Scholem *Origins*, p. 148) correspond to the gnostic "archons" (the divine powers who rule the physical universe) and to the Assyrian "great gods," both associated with planet(ary sphere)s, see Parpola, AOAT 240 (1995) 390 n. 34 and 397; note that in the gnostic treatise Trimorphic Protennoia, the archons explicitly state they "sprouted from a Tree" (Robinson NHL p. 518 = NHC XIII 1, 44, 20), and that in Lk. 13:18, the "kingdom of God" is compared to a tree. On the association of the sefirot with (planetary) spheres see Scholem, Enc. Jud. 10 (1972) 572f, and nn. 34, 41, 111 and 114-117 below. On the sefirot as an anthropomorphic structure related to the primordial perfect man (Adam Qadmon) see M. Idel, "Un figure d'homme au-dessus des sefirot," Pardes 8 (1988) 129-150. Note also Gikatilla, *Gates of Light*, p. 211: "Through this way one describes the heavenly constellations, the camps and its hosts; some are called by the name 'eye,' some 'ear,' some 'lips,' and some 'mouth,' some are 'hands,' and some 'legs.' And when one refers to them as unity they are called 'Adam.' All these constellations, camps and hosts are interconnected and they receive substance and everflow from each other. All of them receive the illuminating power from Keter."

45 See S. Parpola, "The Assyrian Tree of Life: Tracing the Origins of Jewish Monotheism and Greek Philosophy," JNES 52 (1993) 161-208.

46 In this context also note the prominent role of the pomegranate (the chief symbol of God's "unity in multiplicity," see JNES 52 [1993] 164 n. 21 and above, p. XXI with n. 30) in Jewish mystical thought and religious iconography, e.g. in the ornamental decoration of the robe of the Jewish High Priest, on which see J. Börker-Klähn, RlA 3 620a with reference to Ex. 28:33ff.

47 See in detail JNES 52 (1993) 177ff and AOAT 240 (1995) 385ff; on the anthropomorphic tree from Assur (fig. 5) see JNES 52 (1993) 186 with n.32, and AOAT 240 (1995) 386f. Despite Frayne NABU 1997/23 and Uehlinger NABU 1997/83, following G. Kryszat, AOAT 240 (1995) 201-214, the figure cannot represent a "mountain god," as it lacks the divine crown; its position behind the throne of the highest god in the seal BIF VR 1992.13 (NABU 1997 p. 80) corresponds to that of Enoch/Metatron in Jewish mysticism, see n. 196 below. Cf. also the cylinder seal VA 10537 from Uruk showing the ruler as the "tree of life," with sheep nibbling at the buds of the tree as in the Assur relief (A. Moortgat, *Vorderasiatische Rollsiegel* [Berlin 1940], no. 29).

Note that in Kabbalah, the divine name YHWH, like Ištar (see below, n. 133), is associated with both the trunk of the Tree and its central sefirah (Tiferet, "Beauty"). Cf. Gikatilla, *Gates of Light*, pp. 147, 209 and 223f: "Know and understand that the name YHVH is likened to the trunk of a tree and all the other holy names are like its branches; all are attached to each other from above, below, and all sides... The attribute YHVH stands in the centre line and stands in the middle of all the Names. Thus the name YHVH is the essence of the middle line... This sphere is also called Tiferet... Understand why the letter VAV, which is called the Middle Line and is the Name YHVH, is Tiferet: for it includes all, and it governs all, and it dresses in all the Names in accordance with what is appropriate for the moment" (cf. n. 8 above, and see nn. 112, 114, and 133f below).

The equation of YHVH with Tiferet – on the basis of the position of the names in the Tree – opens an interesting perspective. If YHVH = Tiferet (the essence or "Beauty" of God), then the biblical designation of oracles, "word of YHWH," seemingly so different from the Assyrian one (see above, p. XVIII), turns out to be an exact functional equivalent of the Assyrian "word of Ištar"! Note that in Gikatilla's *Gates of Light*, p. 211, YHVH is not referred to as male but (like Ištar) as *androgynous*, with the remark, "this is the essence of our esoteric beliefs." See p. XXIX with n. 97 and p. XXXVIf on the androgyny of Ištar and the androgynous role of YHWH in biblical prophecy, and see further nn. 98, 133 and 199ff on the association of Ištar, Mullissu, Shekhinah, and Asherah with the sacred tree.

48 Ištar also appears as a convener of the divine council elsewhere in Mesopotamian sources, e.g. in STC 2 pl.78:38 (*Ištar mupahhirat puhri* "convener of the assembly") and, under the name Nisaba, in BBR 89f r. iii 37 (see Lambert-Millard Atra-hasis, p. 154), *mupahhirat ilāni rabûti mupahhirat ilāni daiānī* "convener of the divine judges"; note also Gilg. XI 167 and 205. This role is explained by her nature as the power of love that binds together opposites (cf. below, nn. 90, 130 and 134), and it corresponds to her central position in the tree (above, n. 47) and her representation as an eight-pointed star in Assyrian iconography, the eight points of the star symbolizing the eight other "great gods" of the tree (see JNES 52 [1993] 188 nn. 99 and 101, and fig. 14 above).

49 Gilg. XI 14 and 121f; cf. n. 114 below. Note that the behaviour of Ištar in causing the deluge corresponds to that of Tiamat, who in En. el. I 125f, against her original inclination (cf. I 26-28), is moved to destroy her "noisy offspring." For "noisy" in the meaning "imperfect, sinful," see the note on no. 2 ii 19 below, p. 16, and cf. V. Afanasieva, "Der irdische Lärm des Menschen (nochmals zum Atramhasis-Epos)," ZA 86 (1996) 89-96, esp. 93ff.

50 Cf. the beginning of oracle 3.4 with Lambert-Millard Atra-hasis, p. 121:44ff: "Enlil opened his mouth to speak and addressed the assembly of all the gods: 'Come, all of us, and take an oath to bring a flood.'"

51 Cf. AOAT 240 (1995) 386 with n. 20 on the Pauline doctrine of ecclesia as the corporate body of Christ. Note that the Last Supper, too, sealed a covenant destined to end a period of divine wrath and to initiate a new era in God's relationship with man. The role of Christ in the Last Supper corresponds to that of the Assyrian king, who imposed treaties as the representative of Aššur and sealed them with the God's seal (see SAA 2 p. XXXVI).

52 The choice of the epithet "*lord* of the gods" (rather than the usual "father of the gods") in this oracle was dictated by the political situation (see below, pp. LXIV and LXX), the oracle being certainly addressed as much to the convened vassal rulers and their gods ("let them see and hear") as to the king himself.

53 See G. W. Ahlström, "An Archaeological Picture of Iron Age Religions in Ancient Palestine," StOr 55 (1984) 117-145. For Judah note, e.g., 2 Kgs. 23:4ff (reign of Josiah, c. 637-609 BC); Jer. 2:28 = 11:13, "For you, Judah, have as many gods as you have towns"; ibid. 8:2, "They shall expose them [= the kings of Judah, priests and prophets] to the sun, the moon, and all the host of heaven, whom they loved and served and adored, to whom they resorted and bowed in worship"; Jer. 7:17f, "in the cities of Judah and in the streets of Jerusalem, ... women are kneading dough to make crescent-cakes in honour of the queen of heaven, and drink-offerings are poured out to other gods than me"; cf. Jer. 44:19, "When we burnt sacrifices to the queen of heaven and poured drink-offerings to her, our husbands knew full well that we were making crescent-cakes in the form of her image," and see Weinfeld, UF 4 (1972) 150, n. 137. For Israel note simply Hosea 3:4f, "The Israelites shall live many a long day without king or prince, without sacrifice or sacred pillars, without image or household gods; but after that they will again seek the LORD their God and David their King." On the "hosts of heaven" see also nn. 34f and 41 above.

[54] In addition to the passages referred to in n. 34f, note the prominence of the name "YHWH of Hosts" (*yhwh ṣbʾwt*) in Isaiah, Jeremiah, Nahum, Zephaniah, Haggai, Zecheriah, Malachi, and "God of Hosts" (*ʾlhy ṣbʾwt*) in Hosea and Amos.

[55] Cf., e.g., Isa. 40:26, "Lift up your eyes to the heavens; consider who created it all, led out their host one by one and called them all by their names"; ibid. 45:12, "I alone, I made the earth and created man upon it; I, with my own hands, stretched out the heavens and caused all their host to shine"; ibid. 24:21, "On that day the LORD will punish the host of heaven in heaven"; Jer. 10:12f, "God made the earth by his power (*kḥ*), fixed the world in place by his wisdom (*ḥkmt*), unfurled the skies by his understanding (*tbwnt*)."

The last passage, which refers to powers of God by names that had canonical status in later Jewish mysticism, strongly suggests that the doctrine of divine powers crystallized in the kabbalistic Tree diagram already was part and parcel of Jeremiah's (or his editor's) concept of God. The passage has a close parallel in Prov. 3:19f, implying that this doctrine was by no means confined to the prophet alone: "In wisdom (*hokhmah*) the LORD founded the earth, and by understanding (*tevunah*) he set the heavens in their place; by his knowledge (*daat*) the depths burst forth." What is more, in David's blessing to Solomon (1 Chron. 29:11) we have a sequence of five divine powers that could derive directly from Kabbalah: "Thine, O LORD, is the greatness (*gedullah*), the power (*gevurah*), the beauty (*tiferet*), the victory (*nezah*), and the glory (*hod*)." Not only are the names of the powers identical, but also their order of enumeration is the same as in the later mystical tradition! A similar sequence of divine powers, explicitly associated with the Tree, occurs in Isaiah 11:1-2: "Then a shoot shall grow from the stock of Jesse, and a branch shall spring from his roots. The spirit of the LORD (*rwḥ yhwh*) shall rest upon him, a spirit of wisdom (*hokhmah*) and understanding (*binah*), a spirit of counsel (*atzah*) and power (*gevurah*), a spirit of knowledge (*daat*) and the fear of the LORD" (see Weinfeld, ZAW 88 [1976] 40-42, and for a kabbalistic exegesis of the passage, Gikatilla, *Gates of Light*, p. 330). Note also Jer. 17:7f, "Blessed is the man who trusts in the LORD... He shall be like a tree planted by the waterside" (cf. "Šulgi ... a datepalm planted by the watercourse," Witzel KSt 5 30 ii 1!) and Isa. 61:3, "They shall be called Trees of Righteousness, planted by the LORD for his glory." For a passage in Isaiah (Isa. 30: 30f) linking the sefirah of Hod "glory" with the thunderstorm, see the discussion in JNES 52 (1993) 181.

[56] For the divine powers as God's "hands" (Isa. 45:12) and "agents" see p. XXI above, and my "Assyrian Cabinet," AOAT 240 (1995) 385ff. The imperfect nature of angels and foreign gods and their total dependence upon Yahweh are consistently stressed in later Judaism, from the Apocrypha, Talmud and Midrash through medieval mysticism, see Enc. Jud. 2 (1972) 965 and 969, and note Gikatilla, *Gates of Light*, p. 260f: "You must not believe the vain words of the empty-headed who say there is no power in the gods of other nations and that they are not called elohim. What you must realize is that YHVH ... gave power and dominion to every minister of the nations to judge his people... Know and believe there is no power among the other elohim which are the gods of the nations, except for the power which YHVH gives them to judge and sustain their nation."

[57] See, e.g., Lambert-Millard Atra-hasis, p. 57:198ff: "Nintu opened her mouth and addressed the great gods, 'It is not possible for me to make things, skill lies with Enki.'" Cf. oracle 2.2:24f.

[58] Note the apparent "relapse into polytheism" in a Jewish incantation text of the Talmudic period, discussed by Montgomery, *Aramaic Incantation Texts*, p. 149. For Christianity note simply St. John of Damascus, *On the Divine Images. Three Apologies Against Those Who Attack the Divine Images* (transl. D. Anderson, Crestwood, NY, 1980), pp. 97 and 107: "The unbelievers mock us because we honor the cross, and they infer that because we venerate the holy images, we are idolaters and worshippers of wooden gods... Far be it from us to do this! ... We make golden images of God's angels, principalities and powers, to give glory and honor to Him." Note the very similar distinction made by Porphyry between idolatry and *veneration* of divine images, e.g. "Those who make images as objects of veneration for the gods do not imagine that [God] himself is in the wood or the stone or the bronze used in the making of the image. They do not think for a moment that if a part of the image is cut off the power of God is thereby weakened" R. J. Hoffmann, *Porphyry's Against the Christians* [Amherst, NY, 1994], p. 85).

[59] See, e.g., the anthropomorphic representations of Aššur in Sennacherib's seal of Aššur (SAA 2 p. 28), the Bavian and Maltai reliefs of Sennacherib (SAA 2 Fig. 5 and J. Reade, *Assyrian Sculpture* [London 1983], frontispiece; Thureau-Dangin, RA 21 [1924] 185-197), and the Senjirli stele of Esarhaddon (SAA 2 Fig. 7 = J. Börker-Klähn, *Altorientalische Bildstelen* II [1982], no. 219; Thureau-Dangin, RA 21 196). The identification of the god next to the king as Aššur in all these representations is rendered certain by the inscription on the seal of Aššur (SAA 2 p. XXXVI). It should be noted, however, that anthropomorphic representations of Aššur are rare and virtually limited to the reign of Sennacherib only, who explicitly refers to himself as "maker of the image of Aššur" in his inscriptions (see Tadmor, SAAB 3 [1989] 30). It is hence likely that they have to be considered in the light of this king's efforts to abolish the status of Marduk as a rivalling imperial god by equating him with Aššur, and that Aššur in these representations is portrayed as "Assyrian Enlil" (i.e., the "king of the gods"), a designation making it possible to represent him iconographically in the guise of Enlil/Marduk without compromising his status as a transcendent, universal god. Note that the image of Enlil/Marduk had already long been used in this function in the winged disk icon of Aššur (see above, nn. 9 and 23), and that in the Senjirli stela the pair Aššur/Enlil + Mullissu (topping the stela) makes a triad with Ninurta, who supports the two in a caryatid-like fashion (fig. 2). On Sennacherib's religious reforms see also E. Frahm, AfO Beih. 26 (1997) 282ff with earlier literature.

[60] See JNES 52 (1993) 185. The distinction made between God (the winged disk) and his emanations (the Tree) lives forth in the Eastern branch of Christian mysticism, which distinguishes between the "essence of God" and "divine attributes," regarded as energies that penetrate the universe. Creation is conceived of as a process of emanation, whereby the divine Being is "transported outside of Himself ... to dwell within the heart of all things" (Pseudo-Dionysious the Areopagite, *On the Divine Names*, iv 13).

[61] K 6177 + K 8859 B 8-9, see A. R. George, "Sennacherib and the Tablet of Destinies," Iraq 48 (1986) 133-146, especially p. 142ff.

[62] Idel *Kabbalah*, p. 55.

[63] Ibid., p. 53f; cf. G. Scholem, *On the Kabbalah and its Symbolism* (New York 1969), p. 131. On the unification of the ten sefirot through prayer see also Gikatilla, *Gates of Light*, p. 114. Note that the Alenu le-Shabeah prayer proclaiming the sovereignty and unity of God, now recited at the conclusion of every synagogue service, is taken to be composed by the very same talmudic scholar Rav whose list of ten divine powers was discussed in n. 23 above. On Alenu le-Shabeah and its role in Merkavah mysticism see Gruenwald *Apocalyptic*, p. 182, and Dan, *Three Types of Jewish Mysticism* (1984), p. 13.

64 E.g., Isa. 45:20, 46:6f, 48:5; Jer. 10:3-16, 16:18-21, 18:15, and passim; Ezek. 6:4-8, 8:3-12, 14:3-11, 16:17-22; Hos. 8:5f, 10:5-7, 11:12, 12:10f, 13:2; Amos 5:26; Mic. 1:7, 5:13f (idolatry); Jer. 2:23, 5:19, 7:9, 8:2, 9:14, 11:10-17, 16:11, and passim; Ezek. 8:13-17; Hos. 2:8-17, 7:5, 9:10, 10:5, 12:10f, 13:1; Amos 3:14f, 5:5, 8:14 (heavenly bodies and foreign gods).

65 Similar considerations were behind the Byzantine iconoclasm (eighth to ninth cent. AD), whose organizers maintained that making an image of the sacred reduced it to an apparent, material aspect only, and that "worshipers" of such images violated the cardinal principles of Christianity and committed the mortal sin of idolatry. Note that this effort, and also the iconoclastic crusade of Josiah (2 Kgs. 22f), was organized by the state (the Isauric emperors) with the active support of the clergy, and thus was by no means in conflict with the teachings of the church, but has to be understood in the light of n. 58 above. Cf. also A. A. Bialas, New Catholic Encyclopedia 1 [1967], p. 514 (italics mine): "St. Paul implicitly teaches veneration of angels (1 Cor 11.10; Gal 4.14), but such cult is to be given in a manner that does not derogate from Christ; he shows displeasure at *false or exaggerated* cult to angels. In Ap 22.8-9 St. John is rebuked and corrected for offering *excessive* veneration to an angel but not for venerating him. Fathers of the East and West showed their approval of angelic cult and testified to its early existence. They warned against idolatrous cult of angels (Aristides), condemned latreutic acts of worship toward angels (Origen), defended angelic cult as distinct from adoration reserved to God alone (Eusebius)."

For a contemporary Assyrian text attributing the death of Sargon II to his excessive veneration of the gods of Assyria over those of Babylonia, see H. Tadmor, B. Landsberger and S. Parpola, "The Sin of Sargon and Sennacherib's Last Will," SAAB 3 (1989) 3-51. See also n. 200 below.

66 See pp. XXIf and XXIV with nn. 31ff, 35, 37, and 53ff above; note especially Ezek. 1, whose description of God inevitably recalls Aššur's representation as the "winged disk" (see JNES 52 [1993] 201f and the discussion ibid. pp. 185 and 205). Note also the image of the arrow-shooting YHWH in Zech. 9:14, Ps. 7:12, 18: 14, 64:7, Job 6:4, 16:13, and Deut. 32:42, and compare the arrow-shooting Marduk in SAA 3 37:11-15 and in the winged disk (see JNES 52 [1993] App. B and pp. 165 n. 25, 185 n. 93, and 204; SAA 3 Fig. 2, and often).

67 Cf. A. R. George, RA 85 (1992) 158, who observes, commenting upon the term *ilu sahhiru*, 'prowling god': "Some explanation is needed to suggest how this ecstatic cultic performer comes to be considered a "prowling god"... The idea is that the regular, if temporary, seizure of man by god manifestly demonstrates that individual's divinity. In effect, he personifies a god, and the god is incarnate in him. The divine inspiration of the ecstatic is a notion familiar to ancient Mesopotamia, and may be implicit in the terminology. lú.AN.dib.ba.ra, a term for another kind of ecstatic (Akk. *mahhû*), may be interpreted as "one struck by a passing god." The temporary nature of the frenzy explains the adjective *sahhiru*: the god constantly prowls from place to place like the malignant demons with which this discussion opened, entering now this individual and now that. But unlike those demons he is no foul incubus in search of a victim; instead he seeks a human medium through whose inspiration divine will can be revealed."

68 See, e.g., The Random House College Dictionary (rev. ed. 1975), s.vv. "heart" (4. feeling; love; affection, 5. spirit, courage, or enthusiasm, 6. the innermost or central part of anything, 7. the vital or essential part; core) and "spirit" (1. the incorporeal part of man ... such as the mind or soul, 3. a supernatural, incorporeal thing, as a ghost, 5. an angel or demon, 6. Spirit, the divine influence as an agency working in the heart of man, 7. Spirit, the third person of the Trinity, 8. the soul or heart as the seat of feelings or sympathies, 21. the Spirit, God). For Akkadian *libbu* "heart" as the seat of emotions see CAD s.v., mng. 3c and AOAT 240 (1995) 387.

69 Note the Assyrian personal name *Šār-ilāni-ilā'ī* "The Spirit of God is my god" (APN p. 216), where *šār ilāni* is the perfect equivalent of Hebrew *rūaḥ elōhîm* "Spirit of God"; see n. 31 above for *ilāni* "God", and cf. Akk. *šāru* "wind, breath, flatus" (CAD Š/2 133) with Hebr. rūaḥ "wind, breath, spirit" (HAL p. 1197ff, see also n. 74 below) and Greek *pneuma* "(prophetic) spirit." Note also the names (Ṭab-)šar-Ili/Aššur/Ištar "(Good is) the spirit of God/Aššur/Ištar," Ṭab-šar-Mullissu/Arbail/Sin "Good is the spirit of Mullissu/Arbela/the Moon" (for the latter see n. 174 below), and Ṭab-šar-Nabû "Good is the spirit of Nabû" (APN pp. 216 and 236f; SAAB 5 11:3). Cf. SAA 3 12 r.4f, "O Nabû, where is ... your pleasant breath (*šārka ṭābu*) which wafts and goes over the weak ones (devoted) to you." On the Assyrian term for "soul" (*napšutu*) see nn. 10 and 106.

70 Note KAR 102:15, *ši-kín* KA-*ka be-lum* dIŠ.TAR MUL.MEŠ "your utterance, O Lord, is Ištar of the stars," and see on this text JNES 52 (1993) 240f. Cf. Mt. 10:19, "It is not you who will be speaking; it will be the Spirit of your Father speaking in you." In Rom. 5:5, the Holy Spirit is associated both with God's love and man's heart, as its seat of love ("God's love has flooded our innermost heart through the Holy Spirit he has given us)." Note also Rom. 8:11-17 and Rom. 8:26, "Through our inarticulate groans the Spirit himself is pleading for us."

71 See 2 Chron. 15:1 and 20:14-17; Num. 24:2ff // 15ff; 1 Sam. 19: 20; 1 Cor. 14:1-39; 1 Thess. 5:19-20, etc. Note that the spirit of the LORD (*rwḥ yhwh*) figures in the list of divine powers in Isa. 11:1-2, discussed above, n. 55. See also Isa. 59:21, "My (God's) spirit which rests in you and my words which I have put in your mouth." The Christian (Trinitarian) Holy Spirit has been explicitly equated with the OT prophetic Spirit since the early second century, see Kelly *Doctrines*, pp. 61f, 102f and 257 (citing Athenagoras, Chrysostom, Hippolytus, Justin, Tatian, Theophilus and Athanasius). According to Athenagoras, "the prophets prophes[ied] in a state of ecstacy (*kat' 'ékstasin*), the Spirit breathing through them much as a musician breathes through a pipe," while Chrysostom speaks of St. John and St. Paul as "musical instruments played upon by the Holy Spirit" (ibid., p. 62).

72 See, e.g., G. Leick, *A Dictionary of Ancient Near Eastern Mythology* (London and New York 1991), pp. 96 and 98; M. Gallery Kovacs, *The Epic of Gilgamesh* (Palo Alto 1985), p. 113; S. Dalley, *Myths from Mesopotamia* (Oxford 1989), p. 323; E. Reiner, *Poetry from Babylonia and Assyria* (Michigan 1985), p. 30. All these definitions agree with Ištar's epithets *bēlet qabli u tāhāzi* "Lady of Battle and War" and *bēlet ruāmi/râmi*, "Lady of Love" (Tallqvist Götterepitheta p. 62f).

73 Note the Spirit's appellative "Lord" in the Nicene Creed and the masculine gender of Latin *Spiritus Sanctus* (as against Greek [neuter] *pneûma hágion* and Hebr. [fem.] *rwḥ qdš*), and see Kelly *Doctrines*, p. 94, on the identification of the Spirit with the Son of God; cf. also ibid. pp. 92, 102, 103, 112, 252, 255ff, etc., where the Spirit is consistently referred to as "He." On the masculinization of the Spirit in Western Christianity see A. Baring and J. Cashford, *The Myth of the Goddess: Evolution of an Image* (London 1991), p. 611ff.

74 See, e.g., Isa. 11:1-2, 40:7, Hos. 1:5; Gen. 1:2, Num. 24:2ff, 2 Chron. 15:1, 1 Sam. 19:20; Num. 11:26; the plain *rūaḥ* "spirit" is both feminine and masculine in the Hebrew Bible (see HAL p. 1197b). By contrast, Syriac *rûḥ/rûḥô* "spirit" is usually fem. except when used of the Holy Spirit (*rûḥ qôdešô or rûḥô qadîšô*), see Payne Smith p. 533b.

75 See Warner *Virgin Mary* p. 38, who notes that two prominent Church Fathers, Origen and Jerome, quote this work without criticsm (Origen, *In Jeremiam*, Homily 15:4; Commentary on John 2:12; Jerome, Commentary on Micah 7:16, on Ezekiel 16:13; on Isaiah 11:9). See also below, n. 98.

76 "[Thereafter Sabaoth created] another being, called Jesus Christ, who resembles the savior above in the eighth heaven and who sits at his right upon a revered throne, and at his left, there sits the virgin of the holy spirit, upon a throne and glorifying him" (NHC II 5, 105, 25-31 = Robinson NHL p. 176, see Gruenwald *Apocalyptic*, p. 116). Note also the early second century (AD 116) Book of Elchasai opening with a vision of two enormous angelic beings, male and female, the former one referred to as "Hidden power" (= saviour/Michael), the latter as the "Holy Spirit" (G. P. Luttikhuizen, "The Book of Elchasai: a Jewish Apocalypse," AuOr 5 [1987] 101-6).

77 See n. 9 above and NHC II 1, 2, 14ff (The Apocryphon of John) and XIII 1, 37, 20ff (Trimorphic Protennoia) = Robinson NHL pp. 105ff and 514. Cf. also NHC II 3, 71, 16ff = Robinson NHL p. 152 (The Gospel of Philip, 3rd cent.): "Adam came into being from two *virgins*, from the Spirit and from the virgin earth."

78 NHC III 3 ms. V 9, 5 (Eugnostos, 1st cent. BC) and III 4, 104, 19-20 (Sophia of Jesus Christ, 1st cent. AD) = Robinson NHL p. 231.

79 NHC XIII 1, 35, 1ff (Trimorphic Protennoia, 2nd cent. AD) = Robinson NHL p. 513.

80 NHC XIII 1, 45, 2ff (Robinson NHL p. 519).

81 NHC VII 2, 50, 27f (The Second Treatise of the Great Seth) = Robinson NHL p. 363. See further Rudolph *Gnosis*, p. 81, and R. M. Grant, *Gnosticism and early Christianity* (New York 1966), pp. 50 and 55. For Ištar's epithet *harimtu* ("whore") see Tallqvist Götterepitheta p. 101 and Reiner JNES 33 (1974) 224:ff.

82 See nn. 86 and 192 below.

83 For the dove as Aphrodite's bird, frequently sacrificed to her, see J. R. Pollard, *Birds in Greek Life and Myth* (London 1977), and cf. Flavius Philostratus, *Life of Apollonius* (ed. F.C. Conybeare, Loeb 1912), I 25. On white doves in the cult of the Cypriote Aphrodite (Venus Barbata), see M. Ohnefalsch-Richter, "Der Orient und die frühgriechische Kunst," Orientalisches Archiv 3 (1913) 177, and cf. below, nn. 88 and 97. On white doves in the cult of the Palestinian Aphrodite and on Anat referred to as a dove in Ugaritic texts (// Ps. 68:14f) see M. Weinfeld, "Semiramis: Her Name and her Origin," Festschrift Tadmor (1991), pp. 101ff.

84 M. R. James (ed. and trans.), *The Apocryphal New Testament – Being the Apocryphal Gospels, Acts, Epistles and Apocalypses* (Oxford 1926), p. 388.

85 For verses 1:15 and 4:1 ("How beautiful are you, my dearest, your eyes behind your veil are like doves") see nn. 111 and 117 below; for verses 5:2 and 6:9 ("my dove, my perfect one") see n. 97. For verse 2:14 ("My dove ... let me see your face") cf. the topos of seeing the face of the Shekhinah (God's feminine aspect) in Jewish mystical texts, on which see Idel *Kabbalah*, pp. 80-83 with many examples.

86 See n. 99 below, and cf. nn. 47, 60, 98, 111, 120 and 151. The Hebrew phrase "made me" (*qnny*) in Prov. 8:22 is a pun associating the theme of creation (cf. *qnh šmym wʾrṣ*, Gen. 14:19) with that of acquiring a wife (*qnh ʾšh*, Ruth 4:10) and gaining wisdom (*qnh ḥkmh*) and understanding, cf. Prov. 4:7 "The first thing is to gain wisdom and ... understanding (*qnh bynh*)"; similarly Prov. 16:16 and 17:16. On Wisdom and Understanding as divine powers, see nn. 23 and 55 above; on the association of Wisdom with God's feminine aspect (Shekhinah) in Jewish mysticism see C. Poncé, *Kabbalah* (San Francisco 1973), p. 256f, who points out that "some kabbalists go even as far as to say that when God enters paradise every midnight to converse with the righteous, he also performs a sacred union with his Shekhinah."

87 TB *Hagigah* 15a. Cf. oracle 2.3 in this volume.

88 Note the pun "dove" (tu) = "to give birth" (tu) inherent in the cuneiform sign TU (originally a pictogram of a flying dove) and in the name of the Sumerian mother goddess, Nintu. For cuneiform passages associating doves (TU.MUŠEN) with weeping and moaning (*damāmu*) see, e.g., STT 52:52 (a prayer to Ištar: "he moans like a dove"), Thompson Gilg. pl. 59 K 3200:10 ("the maidens moan like doves") and JNES 33 199:16 ("if the bird (called) 'female mourner' like a dove utters mournful cries"); cf. Gilg. XI 117-125: "Ištar cried out like a woman in labor, the sweet-voiced Belet-ili moaned: '... How could I say evil things in the assembly of the gods, commanding war to destroy my people! It is I who give birth to my people! And (now) they fill the sea like the spawn of fish!' The Anunnaki gods wept with her..." Note that dove bones as well as clay doves, enclosed in offering boxes with pictures of doves, were found in the excavations of the temple of Ninmah (= Belet-ili) in Babylon (see R. Koldewey, *Die Tempel von Babylon und Borsippa*, WVDOG 15 [Berlin 1911], pp. 7 and 19, and E. D. Van Buren, *Clay Figurines of Babylonia and Assyria* [YOR 16, New Haven 1930], nos. 919-20 with literature). For lead figurines representing doves found at the temple of Ištar in Assur see W. Andrae, *Die jüngeren Ischtar-Tempel in Assur* (WVDOG 58, Leipzig 1935), p. 103, Tf. 44 g-k. Several further examples of dove figurines found in Mesopotamian temples of mother goddesses are found in Van Buren, *The Fauna of Ancient Mesopotamia* (AnOr 18, Rome 1939), p. 88f, and K. Karvonen-Kannas, *The Seleucid and Parthian Terracotta Figurines from Babylon* (Monografie di Mesopotamia 4, Firenze 1995), pp. 111 and 199f. Cf. n. 83 above. Note also the white dove hovering over the palm tree in the famous wall painting of the Ištar temple of Mari (Weinfeld, Festschrift Tadmor, p. 101). According to Diodorus, Bibliotheke II 19.2, "the Assyrians worship the dove as a god."

89 HAL p. 402. Cf. Isa. 59:11, "like doves we moan incessantly, waiting for justice, but there is none"; Ezek. 7:16, "like moaning doves"; Nahum 2:8, "their slave girls are carried off, moaning like doves and beating their breasts."

90 R. Harris, "Inanna-Ishtar as Paradox and a Coincidence of Opposites," HR 30 (1991) 261-278, esp. p. 263. Cf. below, n. 130f.

91 E.g., *ellet ištarāti* "the holiest/purest of the goddesses" (Ištar of Nineveh/Mullissu), ABRT I 7:2; *elletu Ištar šaqūtu ilī Igigī* "holy/pure Ištar, the highest of the Igigi gods," Farber Ištar p. 140:31. The epithet *elletu Ištar* "holy/pure Ištar" (Perry Sin pl. 6 K 3447:7, KAR 92 r.9, and passim, see Tallqvist Götterepitheta p. 20) continues Sumerian kù ^{d}innin "holy Inanna" (e.g., BE 31 55:14), attested since the third millennium. See also n. 111 below. Note that the epithet "holy" is attached even to Ereškigal, the sinful aspect of Ištar (nn. 119 and 130), see Inanna's Descent, passim, and cf. Gilg. XII 29 and 48.

92 See Tallqvist Götterepitheta p. 32 and CAD A/2 p. 243 under *ardatu* (e.g., *ardatu Ištar* "virgin Ištar" // ki.sikil ^{d}innin "virgin Inanna," AL^{3}) 134:15f, SBH p. 98 r.17f, TCL 6 51:13). The rendering of *ardatu* as "virgin" is established by its logographic spelling KI.SIKIL, literally, "clean place," and corresponds to Greek *parthenos* "virgin" attested as the epithet of Astarte, Cybele, Rhea, etc., and to the standing epithet of Ugaritic Anat, *btlt* (see Kapelrud *Anat*, p. 29ff, and cf. Hebrew *betūlāh* "virgin," HAL p. 167a). It should be noted that *batultu*, whose basic meaning in Akkadian

simply is "young woman, girl," as shown by its logographic spelling GURUŠ.TUR, is not attested as an epithet of Ištar in Akkadian texts. As noted by Harris, HR 30 (1991) 265, the sexual innocence of Inanna is emphasized by the Goddess herself in Or. 54 (1985) 127, lines 139f: "I (Inanna) am one who knows not that which is womanly – copulating. I am one who knows not that which is womanly – kissing."

93 See n. 111 below.

94 Lambert Love Lyrics, p. 123:20ff.

95 For the eight-pointed star as a symbol of Ištar see U. Seidl, RlA 3 s.v. Göttersymbole, and idem, *Die babylonischen Kudurru-Reliefs: Symbole mesopotamischer Gottheiten* (OBO 87, Freiburg und Göttingen 1989), p. 100f, with previous literature. See also n. 48 above.

96 I. J. Winter, "Radiance as an Aesthetic Value in the Art of Mesopotamia (with some Indian Parallels," B. N. Saraswati et al. (eds.), *Art – The Integral Vision. A Volume of Essay in Felicitation of Kapila Vatsyayan* (New Delhi 1994), p. 123f.

97 On the androgyny of Ištar see B. Groneberg, "Die sumerisch-akkadische Inanna/Ištar: Hermaphroditos?," WO 17 (1986) 25-46 and Harris, HR 30 (1991) 268-70. Note especially the beard of Ištar of Nineveh (Mullissu) and Ištar of Babylon (Zarpanitu) referred to in SAA 3 7:4ff ("O praised Emašmaš, in which dwells Ištar, the queen of Nineveh! Like Aššur, she wears a beard and is clothed with brilliance. The crown on her head gleams like the stars") and in Reiner, JNES 33 (1974) 224ff, strophe I ("In Babylon I am bearded (var. a man), but (still) I am Nanaya"), and cf. the Cypriote Venus Barbata, whose cult involved eunuch priests dressed as women (see n. 139 below). Cf. Rudolph *Gnosis*, p. 80: "For the Gnostics bisexuality is an expression of perfection; it is only the earthly creation which leads to a separation of the original divine unity, which holds for the whole Pleroma." For androgyny as an ideal in early Christianity cf. Mt. 18:1-11 // 19:10-14 // Mk. 10:13-16 // Gal. 3:26-28, and Athenagoras' Plea, ch. 33: "You would, indeed, find many among us, both men and women, who have grown to old age unmarried, [for] to remain virgins and eunuchs brings us closer to God" (C. C. Richardson [ed.], *Early Christian Fathers* [New York 1970], p. 337). See also n. 140 below, and note that many Church Fathers (e.g., Origen) and Byzantine patriarchs were castrates (see n. 139).

98 See p. XXXVI. In biblical and talmudic-midrashic usage, Shekhinah refers to the Divine Presence in the world and in man, which is conditioned by the religious perfection of the people of Israel. In Jewish mysticism, the term has a much more specific meaning: it denotes the maternal or feminine aspect of God hypostatized as a female entity greatly resembling Ištar, especially in her aspect as the queen of heaven, Mullissu (see G. Scholem, *On the Kabbalah and its Symbolism* [New York 1969], pp. 104-8, 114ff and 138-142, and Idel *Kabbalah*, pp. 83ff, 229ff and 315 for many striking examples, e.g. p. 83: "I saw a vision of light, splendor and great brightness, in the image of a young woman adorned with twenty-four ornaments"; for the full context and discussion see ibid., and cf. n. 150 below and JNES 52 (1993) 181 and 198 with nn. 84 and 145). This view of the Shekhinah surfaces only in the Bahir (12th cent.), but passages in earlier mystical literature indicate that its roots are in much earlier times. Note especially 3 Enoch (6th/7th cent.), ch. 5, cited in Gruenwald *Apocalyptic*, p. 50: "From the day when the Holiness expelled the first Adam from the Garden of Eden, Shekhinah was dwelling upon a *Keruv* under the Tree of Life... And the first man (was) sitting outside the gate of the Garden to behold the radiant appearance of the Shekhinah"; another passage cited ibid., p. 186 (Maaseh Merkavah), refers to "gazing at the glory of the Shekhinah."

On the association of the Shekhinah with the tree of life see also below, nn. 133f and 199ff. In Rom. 8:11, the Shekhinah coalesces with the Holy Spirit: "If the Spirit of him who raised Jesus from the dead dwells within you, then the God who raised Jesus from the dead will also give new life to your mortal bodies through his indwelling Spirit." On *kavod* and the related Mesopotamian concept *melammu* see M. Weinfeld, ThWAT IV (1984) 26-39 s.v. *kbwd*.

99 In Jewish mysticism, the Song of Songs is understood as an allegory of the mystical union between God and the soul, its erotic imagery serving to describe the sublime spiritual bliss experienced in this encounter; see Idel *Kabbalah*, p. 227f. Note that the "bride" of the Song of Songs, variously identified with the Torah (= the word of God), the Shekhinah, the Wisdom of God (cf. Prov. 8-9) and the ecclesia of Israel, corresponds in the "Assyrian Song of Songs" (SAA 3 14) to the goddess Tašmetu, the bride of Nabû; this text will be analyzed in detail in M. Nissinen, "Love Lyrics of Nabû and Tašmetu: An Assyrian Song of Songs?" (forthcoming). See further nn. 114 and 120 below.

100 Harris, HR 30 (1991) 273ff, stresses the anomalousness and liminality of the cult of Ištar: "The goddesses's festivals are ... occasions when social rules are in abeyance and deviance from norms is articulated." See also nn. 138ff below. I find it impossible to subscribe to Bottéro's view of Ištar as a goddess of "l'amour libre" (J. Bottéro, *Mésopotamie: L'écriture, la raison et les dieux* [Gallimard 1987], p. 354).

101 For Yahweh see, e.g., Isa. 14:22, 25, 19:2, 43:14; Jer. 25:12, 46:8, 49:35ff, 50:18, 51:44, 51:58; Hos. 8:14, Am. 1:4-8, 2:2f; Ob. 1:8; Mic. 5:10f; Zeph. 1:4, 2:5; Zech. 12:9; and note especially Zech. 9:14, "The LORD shall appear above them, and his arrow shall flash like lightning," to be compared with the winged disk of Aššur shown above Assyrian armies in Assyrian reliefs, with the god Marduk shooting his lightning arrow depicted inside the disk; see the illustration in SAA 3 Fig. 2 and cf. ibid., p. 93:11ff! For the madonna, see Warner *Virgin Mary* p. 304ff with many examples quoted from sixth through seventeenth century sources.

102 See M. Weippert, "'Heiliger Krieg' in Israel und Assyrien," ZAW 84 (1972) 460-493, and B. Oded, *War, Peace and Empire. Justifications for War in Assyrian Royal Inscriptions* (Wiesbaden 1992), pp. 13-18 and passim.

103 Cf., e.g., Streck Asb p. 48 v 95-104, "In the course of my campaign I reached Dur-Undasi, his (Ummanaldasi's) royal city. When the troops saw the river Idide (in its) violent flood, they were scared to cross it. But the Goddess (Ištar) who dwells in Arbela let my troops have a dream in the night and spoke to them as follows: 'I will go before Assurbanipal, the king whom my hands created!' My troops relied upon this dream and crossed safely the river Idide"; SAA 3 3 r.4ff, "Not with my own strength, not with the strength of my bow, but with the power [... and] strength of my goddesses, I (Assurbanipal) made the lands disobedient to me submit to the yoke of Aššur. "

104 For recent translations of the Descent with bibliographies see E. Reiner, *Your Thwarts in Pieces, Your Mooring Rope Cut: Poetry from Babylonia and Assyria* (Michigan 1985), pp. 29-49; Dalley *Myths* (1989), pp. 154-164; Gerfried Müller, TUAT III/4 (1994), pp. 760-766; and B. R. Foster, *Before Muses* (Bethesda 1996), pp. 402-409. The Sumerian version of the myth (W. R. Sladek, *Inanna's Descent to the Netherworld* [PhD diss. Baltimore, University Microfilms 1974]) does not differ from the Akkadian one in its religious content and is taken into consideration in the following whenever it contributes to the understanding of the myth. For attempts to explain the *Descent* in terms of "seasonal growing and decay" see J. G. Frazer, *Adonis, Attis, Osiris* (London 1905); T. Jacobsen, *The Treasures of Darkness*

(New Haven 1976), p. 62; Dalley *Myths* (1989), p. 154; cf. also A. Falkenstein, "Der sumerische und akkadische Mythos von Inannas Gang zur Unterwelt," in E. Graf (ed.), *Festschrift Werner Caskel* (Leiden 1968), pp. 97-110, and A. D. Kilmer, "How was Queen Ereshkigal Tricked? A New Interpretation of the Descent of Ištar," UF 3 (1971) 299-309. According to E. Reiner, "Die akkadische Literatur," in W. Röllig (ed.), *Altorientalische Literaturen* (Wiesbaden 1978), p. 160, "keine Zusammenfassung kann dem Mythos ... gerecht werden, vor allem weil die Interpretation der vollständigeren sumerischen Fassung noch umstritten ist."

105 See Johnston *Hekate* (1990), passim, esp. Chapter IV, pp. 49-70 ("Hekate and the Chaldean Cosmic Soul") and Appendix pp. 152-163 ("Evidence for Hekate's equation with Soul"). Johnston, as a classicist, believes that the figure of Hekate in the Oracles, which substantially differs from the earlier nature of the goddess (ibid. pp. 21-28), is related to the Middle Platonic development of the Platonic theory of the Soul and thus is a creation of Hellenistic (Greco-Roman) philosophy (ibid. pp. 71-75). However, it is abundantly clear from Johnston's analysis that Hekate of the Oracles (an awe-inspiringly beautiful lunar goddess carrying weapons and dressed in armor, a "two-faced" unifier of opposites, center of all powers, mother of the gods, "womb," creatrix, mistress of life, controller of "cosmic sympathy" [= love], Physis, Eris, and an oracular goddess manifesting herself as a light phenomenon and as a voice) directly translates Mesopotamian Ištar.

106 Note SAA 3 13:21, where the soul (ZI.MEŠ, lit. "souls") of Assurbanipal is said to be "entrusted in the lap of Mullissu." In the preceding verse the life of the king is said to be "written before Nabû." The parallelism of the two verses implies that the association of Mullissu with the soul (*napšutu*, the semantic equivalent of Hebr. *nefesh*, see CAD N s.v. *napištu*), was as current at the time as the association of Nabû with judgment over life and death (see nn. 7 and 10 above). The plural "souls" implies the three-graded concept of soul (oversoul, soul, animal soul) of the Chaldean Oracles, Neoplatonism and Jewish mysticism, see n. 133 below. Note that according to Hippolytus, Refutatio V 7.9, "The Assyrians are the first who have held that the soul is divided in three, also one," and cf. Pausanias, *Description of Greece* (ed. W. H. S. Jones, Loeb Classical Library, 1918), Messenia, XXXII 4, "I know that the Chaldaeans and Indian sages were the first to say that the soul of man is immortal, and have been followed by some Greeks, particularly by Plato the son of Ariston."

107 The myth thus works on two levels: 1. the literal level addressed to the broad masses, and 2. the allegorical one addressed to the initiates of the cult of Ištar only. On the surface, the netherworld of the myth is a cosmic locality, the abode of the dead, but on the allegorical level it is the physical world of the humans conceived as a prison or grave of the soul. Note the wings (*kappī*) of the netherworld's inhabitants, corresponding to the wings of the Platonic soul, as well as the dust gathering on the netherworld's "bolted doors" (Descent, line 11), and compare the Sumerian composition "Nungal in the Ekur" (Sjöberg, AfO 24 19ff), where the cosmic mountain (kur) ruled by Enlil is described as "a prison full of weeping, lament and wailing"; cf. further Malul, NABU 1993/100, and Heimpel, NABU 1996/28, and see my remarks on the Etana epic, JNES 52 (1993) 198. Both levels are instrinsically interconnected and equally important to the understanding of the myth.

The two-level oriention of the myth (cosmic soul = human soul) corresponds to that of the tree of life, which simultaneously symbolized both the cosmos and the perfect man; see JNES 52 (1993) 166 and 172f, and AOAT 240 (1995) 384ff. The Tree's association with Ištar (see n. 133 below) leaves no doubt that it played an important role as an object of meditation in her cult, like the "asherah tree" in the Canaanite cult of Asherah, the "yoga tree" in Shakta Tantrism and the "sefirotic tree" in ecstatic Kabbalah (see nn. 133 and 200f below).

108 NHC II 6 = Robinson NHL p. 192ff; the title "Expository Treatise on the Soul" is inserted both at the beginning and the end of the text. The affinities between the Fall of Sophia and the Descent of Ištar have been noted long ago, and several scholars have suggested that the former might be a reflection of the Akkadian myth; see W. Bousset, *Hauptprobleme der Gnosis* (Göttingen 1907), p. 263 n. 3; R. Eisler, *Weltenmantel und Himmelszelt* (München 1910), pp. 102 and 193f; K. Tallqvist, *Madonnas förhistoria* (Helsingfors 1920), p. 59; W. L. Knox, "The Divine Wisdom," JTS 38 (1938) 230-237; T. F. Glasson, "The Descent of Ishtar," Congregational Quarterly 32 (1954) 313-321; R. M. Grant, *Gnosticism and early Christianity* (New York 1966), pp. 84 and 212; J. Doresse, *The Secret Books of the Egyptian Gnostics* (New York/London 1960), p. 218; and especially G. Quispel, "Jewish Gnosis and Mandaean Gnosticism," in J.-E. Ménard (ed.), *Les textes de Nag Hammadi* (Leiden 1975), pp. 89ff. This suggestion is (despite E. Yamauchi, Tyndale Bulletin 29 [1978] 148-150) forcefully supported not only by the structural and functional parallelism of the myths but even more so by the striking affinities between the figures of Sophia and Ištar (see p. XXVIII above, and cf. n. 130f below). Surprisingly, the remarkable affinities between the Descent and Exeg. Soul have, to my knowledge, never been pointed out, let alone discussed before.

109 According to K. Rudolph (*Gnosis*, p. 110), "in its oldest form it (i.e. Exeg. Soul) evidently belongs to a relatively early stage of gnostic literary work" and may have originated in the Samaritan school of Simon Magus (cf. ibid., pp. 255 and 297). The Samaritan background of the text would explain its affinities with the Descent of Ištar, keeping in mind that the city had been part of Syria/Assyria for more than 600 years (between 720 and 104 BC) and that a large part of its population consisted of deportees from Babylonia (see J. D. Purvis, *The Samaritan Pentateuch and the Origin of the Samaritan Sect* [Cambridge, MA, 1968], pp. 89 and 92ff, and note esp. p. 94: "They are said to have become Yahwists while continuing to serve the gods of their homelands..."). See also nn. 125 and 130 below.

110 For ancient myths as "riddles at once unveiling and veiling the ineffable truth" and for an excellent analysis of Hellenistic and early Christian esotericism and the rationale behind it see G. G. Stroumsa, *Hidden Wisdom: Esoteric Traditions and the Roots of Christian Mysticism* (Leiden 1996). While Stroumsa's discussion is limited to classical antiquity, it fully applies to first-millennium Mesopotamia as well, for a concrete example see my article "The Esoteric Meaning of the Name of Gilgamesh" in J. Prosecky (ed.), *Intellectual Life of the Ancient Near East* (CRRAI 43, Prague, forthcoming). The present analysis of the Descent omits, for obvious reasons, the discussion of several "riddles" in the myth not relevant to its overall interpretation. I plan to give a full analysis elsewhere in the near future.

111 The appellative "daughter of Sin (= the moon)" underlines the sublime wisdom and purity of the heavenly Ištar (the Holy Spirit) and provides a concrete link to the gnostic Sophia (= "Wisdom"). For Sin (Moon) as the god of contemplative wisdom, understanding and prudence (corresponding to *Binah* of Jewish mysticism) see the evidence put together and discussed in JNES 52 (1993) 177 n. 70. Note that in Tablet X of the Gilgamesh Epic, which in the structural framework of the epic corresponds to Sin/Binah (see ibid. pp. 193 and 196), Understanding takes the form of a divine barmaid, Siduri, explained as "Ištar of Wisdom" (*Ištār nēmeqi*) in Šurpu II 173. The veiling of Siduri (Gilg. X 4; cf. nn. 85, 110, 117 and 123) emphasizes her chastity; her philosophical discourses with Gilgamesh reflect her

prudence; and the sea by which she lives is the sea of knowledge (Apsû), the abode of Ea (see SAA 10 p. XIX). Cf. Job 38:36, "Who put wisdom in depths of darkness and veiled understanding in secrecy?" The association of the "daughter of the moon" with Wisdom is already attested in the great Inanna hymn of Iddin-Dagan (Römer SKIZ, pp. 128-208 = Jacobsen *Harps* p. 133ff, early 2nd mill.), where the Goddess is not only hailed as the "oldest child of Suen" but also presented as the daughter of Enki, the Sumerian god of wisdom (lines 9 and 23; on this text see also n. 189 below). Note that Ištar appears as the daughter of Ea in the Descent as well (line 28). The notion of chastity implicit in the appellative "daughter of the moon" is underlined by the fact that in several texts (e.g., SAA 3 4 ii 1ff and r. ii 17; Reiner, JNES 33 (1974) 224ff, strophe I; SAA 3 8:20) it is applied to Nanaya/Tašmetu, the bride/spouse of Nabû corresponding to the bride of the Song of Songs (see n. 99 above). Note that in the Song of Songs 6:10, the bride is praised to be "beautiful as the full moon" (*lebanah*), a comparison transferred in medieval church poetry to Virgin Mary, the heavenly bride, "pulchra ut luna."

The concept of purity attached to the moon is illustrated by the inscriptions of Nabunaid, which refer to Sin as "the pure god" ([d]EN.ZU DINGIR *el-lu*, YOS 1 45 ii 34), and by Sin's mystical epithet *ellammê*, "water-pure" (referring to the waters of Apsû conceived as a sea of light), on which see the commentary passages cited in CAD s.v. *ella-mê*. The full moon with its immaculate, shining disk symbolized Ištar, as indicated by her mystic number, 15, coinciding with the full moon day; the darkening of the disk was interpreted in terms of pollution and sin (see Laessøe, *Bît rimki*, p. 95ff, LAS II pp. XXIV, 164f and 176ff, and my remarks in Galter *Astronomie* [1993], p. 54; see also M. Stol in D. J. W. Meijer [ed.], *Natural Phenomena* [Amsterdam 1992] p. 257f on Moon "weeping," full of sorrow, at eclipse, and cf. p. XXXIV and n. 141). Accordingly, the progressive loss of "purity" of the waning moon symbolized the gradual defilement, or "descent," of the Goddess; its total disappearance, total corruption, or spiritual "death"; and the gradual increase of "purity," after the conjunction, ascent and return to the original state of perfection. Cf. the esoteric text I.NAM GIŠ.HUR AN.KI.A (A. Livingstone, *Mystical and Mythological Explanatory Works of Assyrian and Babylonian Scholars* (Oxford 1986), p. 22ff), which, using gematric techniques, associates different lunar phases with different divine powers, and see JNES 52 (1993) 176 n. 66. Cf. Gikatilla's *Gates of Light*, p. 300: "In the language of the Sages this Sphere [Binah] is called Teshuvah ("return, repentance"), the reason being that the souls emanate from this place, for the spirits come from Tiferet [see nn. 47 and 133] and the lower souls from the Sphere Malkhut. They connect with each other until they merit an attachment with the Sphere Binah." On p. 303, ibid., Binah is explained as the Upper Shekhinah (*Shekhinah Aila*), "for she is the essence of our receiving the everflow from the upper world."

The lunar nature of Binah is evident from several passages in *Gates of Light*, e.g., p. 163: "Because this stone is called Binah and dwells above and beyond and yet encircles all the rest [seven spheres], it is called the satellite (SOCHARET)... more clear than pearls and it encircles the seven spheres... it is called the satellite for the rounds it makes." This statement (taking the moon as this highest of the planetary spheres) corresponds to the Mesopotamian order of the seven classical planets, which always began with the moon. Otherwise, too, Gikatilla's exposition of Binah has striking points of contact with Mesopotamian notions of Sin and especially with Tablet X of the Gilgamesh Epic. See, e.g., ibid. p. 164: "The stone called SOCHARET [i.e., Binah] is also known as the higher justice (*zedek elyon*)," and cf. the judicial role of Sin discussed in JNES 52 (1993) 178 n. 70 and AOAT 240 (1995) 391. On p. 334, Binah is called Depth, "meaning the depth of thought" (cf. just above); on p. 216, she is called "waters of death" (*mayim metim*), compare the "waters of death" (*mê mūti*) in Gilg. X 87ff. Note finally p. 305: "The Sphere Binah appeared to enlighten the Sphere Malkhut [Kingdom], purifying it from a number of impurities. This is the essence of the scapegoat that is used on this day (Yom Kippur)," and see n. 124 below.

112 At Gate I, she loses her crown; at Gate II, her earrings; at Gate III, her necklace; at Gate IV, her pectorals (cf. SAA 3 7:8); at Gate V, her girdle; at Gate VI, her bangles; and at Gate VII, her loincloth. Note the progression from top to bottom and the alternation of single and paired pieces of clothing. This agrees with the structure of the Assyrian Tree, the crown corresponding to its palmette crown, the necklace, girdle and loincloth to the three nodes of its trunk, and the earrings, pectorals and bangles to the circles or fruits surrounding the trunk (cf. fig. 12 and JNES 52 [1993] 162ff). Accordingly, the various garments and ornaments can be identified with the divine powers constituting the Tree (see nn. 8, 23 and 44); note that they are explicitly called "powers" (*me*) in the Sumerian version of the myth (lines 14f). The progressive degradation and defilement of Ištar corresponds in Neoplatonic doctrine to the progressive weakening of the Cosmic Soul as it gets more distant from its transcendent origin, the One. On the "gates" of the netherworld see n. 114 below.

113 NHC II 6, 127, 22–128, 1 (Robinson NHL p. 192).

114 Cf. Zohar II 39a, analyzed by Idel, *Kabbalah* p. 227f. In this enigmatic passage the Torah is portrayed as a *rainbow* shrouded in clouds, which removes its outer garments and gives them to Moses, who, dressed in them, is able to ascend the mountain and see the things he saw. The association of the rainbow with the garments removed and with the ascent to the mountain establishes an important link to the Descent of Ištar and Assyrian mysticism in general.

According to Idel, the rainbow, well known from Gen. 9:13 as the bow (*qšt*) of God, is also known in Jewish mysticism as "the bow of Tiferet" and functions there as the symbol of the male sexual member associated with the sefirah of Yesod. This yields the following string of associations: rainbow = bow of God = bow of Tiferet = penis. The same string of associations is attested in Assyrian sources. Bow was a prominent attribute of Ištar, cf. simply the passages cited in CAD s.v. *qaštu* "bow." In *Enūma eliš*, Marduk fashions a bow, designates it as his weapon (IV 35), and defeats Tiamat with it (IV 101); later Anu lifts it up, kisses it, calls it "my daughter," and fixes it as a constellation in the sky (VI 82-92). The constellation in question, "Bow Star" (MUL.BAN), our Canis Maior, rose in Ab (August), a hot month with death and netherworld connotations (see Abusch, JNES 33 [1974] 260f), and its equation with Ištar in her destructive aspect is well attested (e.g., "Ab, the month of the Bow Star, the heroic daughter of Sin," Streck Asb pp. 72 ix 9f and 198 iii 1; "Bow Star = Ištar Elammatu, the daughter of Anu," Mul Apin I ii 7 and KAV 218 B i 17). Consequently, the weapon by which Marduk defeats Tiamat actually is Ištar, and the fact that in the mystical text SAA 3 37:18 Marduk defeats Tiamat with his "penis" (*ušāru*) proves the existence of the bow = penis association in contemporary mysticism. In En. el. IV 49 and 75, Marduk's weapon is called "the deluge," reflecting Ištar's role in bringing about the deluge (see pp. XXIV and LII above). This "deluge bow," which already occurs in the Sumerian myth Angimdimma as Ninurta's weapon (giš.ban a.ma.uru$_5$.mu, "my deluge bow," Angim III 35), is of course nothing but the rainbow. The equation rainbow = Ištar is attested in CT 25 31:8 (see CAD s.v. *manzât*), and both "Bow Star" and "Rainbow Star" are given as names of Venus in LBAT 1564:3 and 1576 ii 7, and equated with Virgo in the Great Star List CT 26 40//, Weidner HBA p. 7, lines 16-18. Broken into its components, the logogram for "rainbow," [d]TIR.AN.NA, signifies "bow of heaven" or "bow of Anu," cf. te-er TIR = *qiš-tum, qa-aš-tum*, A VII/4:83f (MSL 14 467).

The kabbalistic string of associations thus has a perfect parallel in Mesopotamia: rainbow = bow of heaven (Anu) = deluge bow = weapon of Marduk = penis = bow = bow of Ištar = Virgo = Venus = Bow Star = Rainbow Star.

On the other hand, Ištar is addressed as "the ziggurat" (staged temple-tower) in Assurbanipal's hymn to Ištar of Nineveh (Mullissu), SAA 3 7:9. Remains of colouring on the ziggurat of Dur-Šarruken (see V. Place, *Ninive et l'Assyrie* [Paris, 1867-70], II, 79) show that each of its stages was painted in a different colour, the sequence of colours corresponding to the colouring of the seven concentric walls of Ecbatana in Herodotus I 98 (white, black, purple, blue, orange, gold, silver) and probably symbolizing the seven planetary spheres (Venus, Saturn, Mars, Mercury, Jupiter, Sun, and Moon). Through its seven-staged colouring, the ziggurat is associated both with the rainbow and the descent and ascent of Ištar. Its seven colours correspond to the seven garments of the Goddess, so that descent from its silver-coloured top (the Moon! See nn. 111 and 116) would symbolize undressing, while ascending it would symbolize putting on these "coloured garments." Thus the man following in the footsteps of the Goddess would reach the top of the cosmic mountain vested in her "garments," that is, the divine powers (see above, n. 112), just as Moses did in the Zohar passage just quoted. The image of a multicolored seven-staged ziggurat associated with the planetary spheres clearly lies behind the Mithraic ascent of the soul described in Origen's *Contra Celsum* (Meyer *Mysteries*, p. 209): the initiate climbs "a ladder with seven gates," the first (of lead) associated with Saturn, the second (of tin) with Venus, the third (of bronze) with Jupiter, the fourth (of iron) with Mercury, the fifth (of electrum) with Mars, the sixth (of silver) with Moon, and the seventh (of gold) with Sun.

Idel has shown (*Kabbalah*, p. 103ff) that meditation on colours (conceived as "garments" of the sefirot, the divine powers) was widely practiced in Kabbalah, and that visualization of the letters of the Tetragrammaton (symbolizing the sefirot) in colours was a technique for achieving the prophetic state. In pronouncing the daily Shema' Israel prayer (see above, p. XXV), whose objective was the unification of the divine powers, one was supposed to visualize the first Tetragrammaton in colours and circles, "like the colour of the rainbow" (ibid. p. 108). There can be no doubt that the rainbow here symbolized the unification of the divine powers in the sefirah of Keter (the equivalent of Anu, the god of Heaven), cf. *Gates of Light*, p. 227: "Just as Tiferet (Beauty) ascends to the infinite AIN SOF and dresses in the garments of Keter and adorns itself with them, so does Israel, who is attached to Tiferet, ascend with Him." Tiferet is the sefirotic equivalent of Ištar (see n. 47), and the "garments of Keter" correspond to the rainbow, the "bow of Anu." There can be little doubt that the rainbow served as a symbol of the divine unity in Assyrian mysticism, too; note the rainbow arch replacing the palmette crown (the symbol of Anu) in some representations of the Assyrian Tree (e.g., JNES 52 [1993] 200, third row from bottom).

115 See G. Scholem, *On the Kabbalah and its Symbolism* (New York 1969), p. 67. Cf. A. Safran, *Sagesse de la Kabbale. Textes choisis de la littérature mystique juive* (Paris 1987), pp. 38f, 72ff, 76f, 134f and 224, citing Maggid Devarav le-Ya'akov, Nefesh ha-Hayyim, and Likkutey 'Amarim. See also n. 98 above.

116 R. Joseph Gikatilla's guide to meditation on the divine names, *Gates of Light* (13th cent.), presents the sefirot (the divine attributes, "spheres") as a sequence of superimposed gates leading to the Divine light, a sort of celestial ladder; at the same time, they are also presented as limbs, ministers, attributes, and (as in the Descent of Ištar) garments of God, with the explicit caveat that all these images are to be taken allegorically only (pp. 6ff). "A person praying is like someone travelling through perilous terrain; his prayer has to pass among gangs who dwell between heaven and earth and then ascends to the heavens; if he is worthy, the robbers will not harm his prayers" (p. 12). As in the *Descent*, the soul in Gigatilla's scheme originates from and returns to the moon: "If, after she has sinned, she returns and betters her ways, then she ... becomes worthy of ascending to the Sphere Binah (= the moon, see n. 111) which is known as the world to come; thus she returns to the place from which she was lost" (p. 300f).

In earlier Jewish mysticism, the ascending soul was imagined to pass through the gates of seven heavenly palaces guarded by archangels; the God (referred to as the "Divine Glory" or "the King in His Beauty") resided in the topmost heaven corresponding to the sefirah of Binah, which also figures as the location of the Paradise and the seat of Shekhinah and the tree of life; see Gruenwald *Apocalyptic*, pp. 48-62, 152ff and 229f. The 10-11th cent. gaonic sources discussed by Idel *Kabbalah* p. 90f emphasize the psychological nature of the ascent (note especially the responsum of R. Hai Gaon quoted ibid.).

117 See Rudolph *Gnosis* (1987), 171ff. The gnostic imagery closely resembles the Jewish one: the soul passes to the "kingdom of light" through the seven planetary spheres guarded by demonic doorkeepers, whose favour has to be acquired by prayers of entreaty; as in the Descent of Ištar, "the way of ascent is the way of descent" (NHC VII 5, 127, 20 [*The Three Steles of Seth*] = Robinson NHL p. 401, referring to the fall of Sophia). Note that in the gnostic (Naassene) interpretation of the myth of Isis and Osiris, the Goddess, like Ištar, is veiled in "seven robes," which are explained as an allegory for the planetary spheres, the "seven ethereal robes" of nature (Hippolytus, Ref. V 7.23). On the soul's passage through the seven planetary spheres in the mysteries of Mithras, see n. 114 above.

118 NHC II 6, 128, 34–129, 4 (Robinson NHL p. 192f). Cf. Gikatilla, *Gates of Light*, p. 109: "This shrine (i.e., the sefirah of Yesod associated with the material world) ... has a place which is called the Gates of Tears, and God himself opens these gates three times a day. For the penitent, these are the gates where they take consolation and repent their evil deeds. For when the penitent prays, cries and lets tears fall on his prayers, his prayer and his cries enter the Gates of Tears... One should therefore pray with great fervor and weep, if he wants his prayers to be accepted."

119 Note that the main function of the *assinnu* both in the Descent of Ištar and its Sumerian predecessor is to comfort the suffering Ereškigal (the fallen soul), who at this moment is moaning like "a woman about to give birth" (Inanna's Descent, lines 227-33 = 251-7), and compare Exeg. Soul, II 132, 2ff: "Then she will begin to rage at herself like a woman in labor, who writhes and rages in the hour of her delivery." In Inanna's Descent, the *kurgarra* and *galatur* are explicitly said to bring with them "food of life and water of life."

Note also that the word *zikru* used to refer to the *assinnu* in the myth ("Ea, in the wisdom of his heart, created a *zikru*, created the *assinnu*, Aṣušu-namir," lines 92f) explicitly identifies him as a personification of the "Word" (Logos). *Zikru* is a double entendre which can mean both "word" and "man/male," and, by a play with the consonants, also be associated with the word *kezru* "coiffured man" (a devotee of Ištar). The meaning "man" would at the first sight seem to fit the context better (cf., e.g., Dalley's recent [1989] translation of the passage). Upon closer reflection it is excluded, however, because the *assinnu* in fact was not a man but a sexless, probably self-castrated, being (see below, n. 138).

The same double entendre also occurs in the Epic of Gilgamesh ("*zikru* of Anu," Tablet I 83), where it refers to Enkidu as a "helper" sent by the gods for the salvation of Gilgamesh; note Enkidu's epithet *mušēzib ibri* "helper/savior of friend" later in the text. In Gilgamesh's dreams, Enkidu appears as a meteorite (*kiṣru*) falling from heaven, or as an axe (*haṣṣinnu*) loved by Gilgamesh "like a wife," two obvious puns on *kezru* and *assinnu* respectively. The very name Enkidu can be logographically understood as "created by Ea," which makes his origin the same as the *assinnu*'s. Moreover, later in the epic, Enkidu is repeatedly referred to as "the mule," implying that the slaying of the Bull of Heaven culminated in his emasculation (see below, n. 140, and note this passage also involve a pun, *imittu* = "right hand" = "shoulder"). The figure of Enkidu thus coincides with that of the *assinnu* not only functionally but also factually. On his intercourse with the harlot, which parallels the encounter between Ereškigal and the *assinnu* in the Descent of Ištar, see n. 140 below.

It can thus be postulated that the emasculated *assinnus* played an important role in the cult of Ištar as "helpers" of the novices to the cult, heartening them with words of comfort and promise for salvation, and probably also introducing them to the doctrine of the ascent of the soul. In Exeg. Soul, this figure coalesces with that of the bridegroom, "the firstborn of the Father" (see nn. 120 and 123) with whom the reborn soul unites in a "bridal chamber" *before* her final ascent to heaven (see NHC II 6, 132, 7-26; 133, 31-35; 134, 25-27). This suggests that the *assinnus* were responsible for administering the initiands the "sacrament of the bridal chamber," not to be misunderstood as a physical sexual act but as spiritual preparation for the final wedding in heaven (see n. 121).

120 See Rudolph *Gnosis*, p. 245ff, and note especially the Gospel of Philip (Robinson NHL p. 124ff; Meyer *Mysteries*, p. 235ff) where the "bridal chamber" is presented as the highest sacrament, the "Holy of the Holies" (NHC II 3, 69, 24-28), where "one receives the light" (ibid. 86, 4-5; cf. 70, 7-8). The immediate contexts make it quite clear that "the light" here refers to esoteric knowledge relating to the ascent ("he who will receive that light will not be seen, nor can he be detained [sc. during the ascent]," 86, 8-9; cf. ibid. 70, 5ff, "the powers do not see those who are clothed in the perfect light, and consequently are not able to detain them," and see above, n. 116f). It is accordingly probable that "bridal chamber" is a covering term for the whole gnostic initiation, as suggested by W. Eisenberg in Robinson NHL p. 140 (cf. above, n. 119); at the same time, it may also well have functioned as a sacrament for the dying, to prepare them for their final ascent to the Pleroma (see H. G. Gaffron, *Studien zum koptischen Philippusevangelium* [diss. Bonn 1969], p. 185ff).

121 NHC II 6, 132, 8ff. The appellative "first-born" used of the bridegroom identifies him as the gnostic saviour, also called "image of the Father," "son," or "self-originate," and equated with Christ (see Rudolph *Gnosis*, p. 148ff). The role distribution found in the text (bride = soul, bridegroom = saviour/God) corresponds to that in the two wedding-feast parables of Mt. 25:1-13 (the prudent and foolish virgins) and 22:1-14 (the king's feast for his son), and is a commonplace in Jewish mysticism, see Idel *Kabbalah*, p. 209. The apparent "reversal of roles" noted by Idel (the righteous human being playing the part of the bridegroom) is explicable through the *homoousia* of the righteous (= the perfect man) with the saviour (= the king), and hence with God. See nn. 9, 122f, 192 and 196. Note also the passage in Gikatilla's *Gates of Light* quoted above, n. 114, where Tiferet is portrayed as a bride dressing "in the garments of Keter and adorning itself with them" in anticipation of her union with the infinite God.

122 NHC II 6, 134, 13f and 25f.

123 Tammuz was Ištar's "husband" (Desc., line 127; see also Tallqvist Götterepitheta p. 97) but, as the son Ea (ibid. p. 120), also her "brother" (Desc., lines 133ff; on Ištar as the daughter of Ea see n. 111 above). He is thus identical with the saviour figure in Exeg. Soul, who is there called "her (i.e., the soul's) man, who in her brother" (NHC II 6, 132, 8f and 133, 5f). His specification as "husband of her [Ištar's] youth" (*hāmir ṣuhrītiša*, also in Gilg. VI 46) refers to the celestial origin of the fallen Ištar, which is also underlined in Exeg. Soul: "They were originally joined to one another when they were with the father" (133, 4). The patronym "son of Ea," which otherwise exclusively refers to Marduk and Ninurta (see Tallqvist, ibid. 120 s.v. *mār Ea* and 67 s.v. *bukur Nudimmud*), unquestionably identifies Tammuz with the Mesopotamian celestial saviour manifested in the person of the king; see discussion above, pp. XV and XLff.

In accordance with their mythological roles, Ninurta, Marduk and Tammuz represent different aspects of kingship: Ninurta (like Egyptian Horus) is the victorious, triumphant crown prince; Marduk is the ruling king; while Tammuz (like Egyptian Osiris) is the dying/dead king, referred to allegorically as a felled tree (e.g., SAA 3 16 r.19; on the king as the tree of life see n. 193 below), a shepherd killed amid his sheep, a gardener killed in his orchard (ibid. 17f), and similar metaphors. The identities of the god and the king totally merge at the latter's funeral, which culminated in a funeral display (*taklimtu*) identical with that of the god's image during his festival; see LAS 4-6 = SAA 10 9 and 18f, and the commentaries in LAS II p. 7ff; M. Stol, "Greek *deiktérion*: the Lying-in-State of Adonis," in J. H. Kamstra et al. (eds.), *Funerary Symbols and Religion* (Kampen 1988) 127f; J. A. Scurlock, "K 164 (BA 2, p. 635): New Light on the Mourning Rites for Dumuzi?," RA 86 (1992) 53-67.

124 The figure of Tammuz must be understood as an etiology for the death of the king, an explanation of the paradox that the king, the son of God (see p. XXXVIff), had to die. The ascent of Ištar had outlined the way for salvation, but that was not enough. In order to be guided to the right path, the world needed a permanent substitute for the Goddess. This could only be provided through the sacrifice of Tammuz, which is an allegory for the institution of the divine kingship. In materializing the idea of "perfect man" in the human king, God gave mankind an example to follow and a shepherd to guide it to the right path. At the same time, however, he subjected part of his own substance (his own "son") to bodily death.

In this light, it becomes clear that Tammuz had to be sacrificed not for the redemption of the *Goddess* (as a superficial reading of the myth might suggest), but for the redemption of all the fallen souls who would follow her trail. In other words, Tammuz died not for Ištar but for man, and his death can be regarded as a token of God's love for all mankind in the same sense as Christ's redemptory death. Note Aššur's epithet *rā'im tenēšeti* "lover of mankind" in K 1349:10 = Saggs, Iraq 37 (1975) 15, and Ištar's epithet *rā'imat kullat nišē* "lover of all mankind" in PSBA 31 62:4, and cf. 1 John 4:9, "For God is love; and his love was disclosed to us in this, that he sent his only Son into the world to bring us life." It is true that Ištar was "responsible for his (Tammuz's) seizure" (Harris, HR 30 [1991] 265 n. 20), but so is God in Rom. 8:32 ("He did not spare his own Son, but gave him up for us all")!

The doctrinal similarity of the redemptory death of Tammuz to that of Christ emerges with full clarity from the Mesopotamian substitute king ritual, in which the innocent sufferer-king (= the substitute) takes upon himself the sins of the penitent sinner (= the true king) and silently dies for him (see LAS II pp. XXIV and XXX, and my remarks in Galter *Astronomie*, p. 54f). The role of the substitute in this ritual corresponds to that of the "virgin kid" in the medical ritual "Giving a man's substitute to Ereškigal" (see LAS II pp. 127 and 305), which makes the ritual's points of contact with Jesus' trial and suffering ("as a lamb") all the more conspicuous.

125 Apart from the doctrinal similarities between the deaths of Tammuz and Christ, the mythology of Tammuz has striking points of contact with the Passion story, which can hardly be passed over as merely accidental. Just compare the troops of galla demons sent to seize Tammuz (Inanna's Descent, lines 279ff; Dumuzi's Dream, lines 110ff, and the parallels reviewed by Alster, ibid. p. 104ff) with the "great crowd armed with swords and cudgels" sent to arrest Jesus; the betrayal of Tammuz by his friend (Dumuzi's Dream, lines 92-109 and 141-151) with the betrayal of Jesus by Jude; the vain attempts of Utu (the divine judge) to help Tammuz to flee (Inanna's Descent, lines 352-68; Dumuzi's Dream, lines 164-182 and the parallels reviewed by Alster, ibid. p. 114ff) with the attempts of Pilate to let Jesus free; and the weeping of Tammuz's wife, mother and sister (Inanna, Sirtur and Geštinanna) at his death (Jacobsen *Harps*, pp. 57-84) with the role of the three Marys during and after the crucifixion. The cult of Tammuz was widespread in Israel and Judah long after Assyrian times; it was practiced in Jerusalem during the exile (see Ezek. 8:14), and it must have survived until Roman times in Samaria (whose population was half-Babylonian since Assyrian times) and in Galilee, which was annexed to Assyria in 732 BC and reattached to Judea only in 104 BC. According to Jerome (Ep. 58.3), a sacred grove of Tammuz (Adonis) existed in Bethlehem until the reign of Constantine; on the persistence of the cult of Tammuz (Ta'uz) till the 9th century in Harran see T. M. Green, *The City of the Moon God: Religious Traditions of Harran* (Leiden 1992), p. 152. See also S. N. Kramer, *The Sacred Marriage Rite* (Bloomington 1969), p. 133, and n. 126 below.

126 Firmicus Maternus (c. AD 350), De errore profanarum religionum 22.1, describes a mourning scene in a mystery cult, which ends in a similar promise to the devotees: "Be confident, *mystai*, since the god has been saved: you too will be saved from your toils" (see M. J. Vermaseren, *Cybele and Attis: The Myth and the Cult* (London 1977), p. 116; Meyer *Mysteries*, p. 159; Burkert *Mystery Cults*, p. 75). The mourned god, lying on a litter, is not identified in the text, and scholarly opinion as to his identity is divided between Attis and Osiris. Whichever is the case, the affinities between the passage and the concluding words of the Descent of Ištar are certainly not accidental.

Osiris was the Egyptian equivalent of Tammuz (the deceased king), see n. 123 above. Attis was his Phrygian equivalent; as the name of his consort Cybele (= Kubaba of Carchemish, see M. Popko, *Religions of Asia Minor* [Warshaw 1996], pp. 100f, 166f and 181ff) shows, his cult was an import from Syria and had many points in common with that of Tammuz. Like the latter, he was portrayed as a shepherd playing a reed pipe, and in the annual festival commemorating his death, a cut-down pine tree served as his symbolic representation (cf. nn. 123 and 127). His cult was markedly ecstatic and ascetic in character and like that of Tammuz and Ištar, involved self-castration of male devotees (see p. XXXIV with nn. 138ff).

The pine tree representing Attis symbolized immortality, and the castration of his devotees aimed at future bliss. The resurrection of Attis is explicitly confirmed in Firmicus Maternus, De err., 3.1ff). It should be noted that according to Hippolytus (Ref. V 7ff), the gnostic sect of the Naassenes attended the cult of Attis and absorbed its doctrines, whose Mesopotamian origin was commonly known and acknowledged (see especially V 7.6f on the Assyrian/Chaldean origin of the doctrine of the perfect man, 7.9 on that of the three-fold division of the soul, and 7.11f on the higher and lower soul). One wonders whether the apostle Paul, whose home town (Tarsus) must have brought him into contact with the cult of Attis, and whose writings betray clear gnostic influence (see Rudolph *Gnosis*, p. 301ff), originally — before his studies in Jerusalem — belonged to this sect. Cf. above, n. 125.

127 Incense (*qutrinnu*), which ascended to heaven, was an offering expressly destined to celestial gods, as opposed to food and drink offerings presented to their earthly images. Cf. Gilg. XI 160-168, where the gods gather "like flies" to smell the *qutrinnu* of Utnapishtim after the Flood; the offering there marks Utnapishtim's salvation from the Flood and anticipates the eternal life granted to him. The wording of the passage thus implies the resurrection of the deceased devotees of Ištar "together with" Tammuz (that is, at the end of his annual festival, celebrated in the fourth month bearing his name).

Pace Yamauchi, Tyndale Bulletin 29 (1978) 150, Tammuz did not stay permanently in the netherworld. He appears, together with Ningišzida, as the gatekeeper of the highest heaven in the Adapa myth, and an explicit reference to his resurrection is found in a recently published Mari letter (A 1146:42-44, see P. Marello, "Vie nomade," in J.-M. Durand (ed.), *Florilegium marianum*, Mémoires de NABU 1 [1992], p. 119). While the Sumerian myth of Inanna's descent seems to assign to Tammuz a half-year stay in the netherworld (see S. N. Kramer, "Dumuzi's annual resurrection," BASOR 183 [1966] 31, and *The Sacred Marriage Rite* [Bloomington 1969], p. 154ff), the Assyrian evidence suggests that he (like Attis and Adonis) was resurrected soon after his death and burial. See SAA 3 38 r.2ff ([25th day]: "striking"; [26th day]: "wailing"; [28th?]: "Tammuz rises"), and cf. the festival schedules discussed in LAS II p. 9f and Scurlock, RA 86 [1992] 58f (26th day, "wailing"; 27th, "release"; 28th, "Tammuz"), as well as the mourning schedule of Attis: 22nd March, felling of the pine; 24th day, wailing and burial; 25th, resurrection of the buried god.

The commemoration of the resurrection of Tammuz within the Assyrian cultic year does not make him a "periodically rising vegetation god" (cf. n. 104 above). Note that Christ, too, rises from the dead every year within the Christian cultic year, and is not considered a "vegetation god"! The Mesopotamian belief in the resurrection of the king is confirmed by an economic text dated to the 11th month of the last regnal year of Šulgi, which contains the remark "when the divine Šulgi ascended to heaven"; see C. Wilcke, "König Šulgis Himmelfahrt," Münchener Beiträge zur Völkerkunde 1 (1988) 245-55) and by a similar text referring to the resurrection of a later king (Išbi-Erra or Šu-ilišu), see M. Yoshikawa, ASJ 11 (1989) 353 and P. Steinkeller, NABU 1992/4.

128 Note also SAA 3 3:16, "the Lady of Arbela ordered everlasting life for me to live," and OECT 6 p. 72:14, "Mullissu, who gives well-being and life to those who frequent her abode" (prayer of Asb.).

129 Cf. Rom. 8:11-17, "If the Spirit of him who raised Jesus from the dead dwells within you, then the God who raised Christ Jesus from the dead will also give new life to your mortal bodies through his indwelling Spirit... For all who are moved by the Spirit are sons of God... We are God's heirs and Christ's fellow-heirs, if we share his sufferings now in order to share his splendour hereafter."

130 The Thunder (NHC VI 2 = Robinson NHL p. 295ff) has since its discovery been a document "difficult to classify"; however, there is now a growing consensus among scholars that the speaker of this remarkable monologue is "a combination of the higher and lower Sophia." The text's affinities with Isis aretalogies and the self-presentation of Wisdom in Prov. 8 have long been noted, and G. Quispel, in J.-E. Ménard (ed.), *Les textes de Nag Hammadi* (Leiden 1975), p. 105, has adduced a striking parallel from Mandean literature definitely establishing the speaker as the Holy Spirit ("I am death, I am life; I am darkness, I am light; I am error, I am truth; I am destruction, I am consternation; I am the blow, I am the healing," Right Ginza, 207; the speaker is the Mandean "Holy Spirit," Ewat). Quispel dates

the Thunder to the third to first century BC and proposes to identify the speaker as the goddess Anat, the "unorthodox" spouse of Yahweh (ibid., p. 95).

Despite the objections of Yamauchi, Tyndale Bulletin 29 (1978) 148, the analysis of the Descent of Ištar confirms Quispel's suggestions. The speaker of the text is Ištar (or Isis, Anat, etc.) as the coincidence of opposites, the power of love joining the opposites and governing them all. In its first-person monologue format the text parallels the Assyrian prophecies and Chaldean Oracles, and its title recalls the epiphanies of Hekate in the Oracles, preceded by thunder; see Johnston *Hekate*, p. 111ff. See also the important discussion in G. G. Stroumsa, *Hidden Wisdom* (1996), p. 46ff, who interprets "thunder" as an esoteric terminus technicus for "heavenly oral revelation of divine secrets" (p. 51) and draws attention to the designation of two apostles of Jesus as "sons of thunder" in Mk. 3:17. This suggests that the Thunder, like the Exeg. Soul, may have originated in Samaria or in Galilee, which would explain its Mesopotamian affinities (see nn. 108 and 125 above). The text itself has a close parallel in the Sumerian myth of Inanna and Enki (G. Farber-Flügge, Studia Pohl, s.m. 10 [Rome 1973]), which contains a similar long first-person antithetical monologue. Note also the hymn to Inanna edited by Sjöberg, ZA 65 (1976) 161-253, and the Assyrian hymn to Nanaya edited by Reiner, JNES 33 (1974) 224ff, which presents Ištar as a universal goddess worshiped under many names and many (often antithetical) forms.

131 NHC VI 2, 13, 15-20; 14, 12-13 and 29-32; 19, 11-16; 21, 13, and 20-30. Compare the final lines with those of Prov. 8 (lines 32-36): "Now, my sons, listen to me, ... He who finds me, finds life, ... while he who finds me not, hurts himself, and all who hate me are in love with death."

132 Note KAR 139 (Menzel Tempel T1f), r.2ff: "The priest blesses him (the initiate), saying: 'May the heavenly Ištar speak nicely of you [to ...]! As [this] torch is bright, may Ištar decree brightness and prosperity to you. Guard the word and secrets of Ištar! Should you leak out the word of Ištar, you shall not live, and should you not guard her secrets, you shall not prosper. May Ištar guard your mouth and tongue!" Note also the name of the temple of Zarpanitu (Ištar of Babylon) in Assur, É.HAL.AN.KI = *bēt pirišti šamê u erṣeti*, "House of the secrets of heaven and earth," Menzel Tempel T163 line 182.

For passages underlining the secrecy of Hellenistic mystery cults see Apuleius, Metamorphoses XI 21 and 23 (mysteries of Isis); Augustine, City of God, VI 7 (mysteries of Cybele); Diodorus, Bibliotheke, V 48.4 and 49.5 (mysteries of the Kabeiroi and Cybele); C. Kerényi, *Eleusis* (Princeton 1967), p. 47 (mysteries of Demeter); Livy, Hist. XXXIX, 10 and 12f (Bacchic cults); Meyer *Mysteries* p. 50 (mysteries of Demeter). On the secrecy of Chaldean theurgy see Johnston *Hekate*, p. 81, commenting on the oracle fragment 132 ("Keep silent, *myste*"); on Mesopotamian esotericism in general, see my remarks in JNES 52 (1993) 168ff.

133 See Assurbanipal's hymn to Ištar of Nineveh (SAA 3 7), which begins by addressing the Goddess as "date palm, lady (*bēlat*) of Nineveh," and Lambert Love Lyrics, p. 123:18ff, where Ištar of Babylon is addressed as "palm of carnelian." These two passages establish beyond question that Ištar was associated with the palm tree, which in Assyrian iconography constitutes the trunk of the stylized sacred tree (see JNES 52 [1993] 201, App. A, and pp. 173, 187 and 195). Note that the same association is also attested for Canaanite Aširtu/Asherah (see n. 199ff below) and the kabbalistic equivalents of Mullissu/Ištar, Shekhinah (see n. 98) and Tiferet (see n. 47, and note in addition Gikatilla, *Gates of Light*, pp. 304 and 219: "Because it is the source of life, the Sphere Tiferet is called the Tree of Life; meaning that the tree draws life from the highest source. For the Tree of Life was inside the garden – the Middle Line which empties life into the Sphere Yesod. The Sphere that is called Malkhut [Kingdom] receives the everflow of life from the source of life through the Tree of Life ... Through this "Tree," the sphere Binah [see nn. 111 and 116] unites with the sphere Malkhut").

Ištar's association with the Tree is explained by the fact that the three-layered Tree, besides being the image of God and the perfect man (see p. XXIII and n. 193 below), was also an image of the soul. In Kabbalah, its three layers correspond to three grades of the soul: *nefesh*, the animal soul, *ruah*, the moral soul, and *neshamah*, the divine "over-soul" (see Zohar I 205b-206a, and cf. my remarks in JNES 52 [1993] 187 n. 98). The description of Ištar's descent and ascent in terms of the anthropomorphic tree and the seven-staged ziggurat, discussed in nn. 112 and 114, implies that meditation on the tree and its constituents, the divine powers (associated with the different stages of the ascent, see nn. 114 and 116), played an important role in her cult, as later in Kabbalah (see, e.g., A. Kaplan, *Meditation and Kabbalah* [York Beach, 1982], p. 125ff). The same is implied by the two-level (macrocosm/microcosm) orientation of the myth (see n. 107) and by the central role played by meditation on the "yoga tree" and the cosmic mountain in Shakta Tantrism, the ecstatic cult of the Hindu mother goddess, which offers an important living parallel to the cult of Ištar (see in detail T. Goudriaan et al., *Hindu Tantrism* [HdO II/4/2, 1979] 47ff and P. Rawson, *Tantra: The Indian Cult of Ecstacy* [London 1973] p. 25ff.)

134 On the relevant mystic numbers see JNES 52 (1993) 182ff; on the association of the top and base of the Tree with heaven and netherworld and the highest and lowest grades of the soul, see ibid. 187. For Ištar as a power joining the opposites see nn. 48, 89 and 130 above, and cf. Johnston *Hekate*, p. 60: "In Chaldean context, the goddess is given two faces because she is expected to view two specific realms, the Intelligible and Sensible Worlds [i.e., heaven and earth], between which she stands as Cosmic Soul... By facing in both directions and reacting to both the Sensible and Intelligible spheres, Hekate/Soul bridges the gap between them."

This function of Ištar/Hekate corresponds to Augustine's definition of the Holy Spirit as "the mutual love of Father and Son, the consubstantial bond that unites them" (De Trinitate 15, 27); see Kelly *Doctrines*, p. 275, and ibid. p. 276ff on Augustine's use of analogies drawn from the structure of the human soul to explain the Trinity. According to Origen, "The mediator between the only true God, i.e. the ineffable Father, and man is not, in the last analysis, the God-man Jesus Christ, but the Word [i.e., the Holy Spirit] who bridges the gulf between the unoriginate Godhead and creatures" (ibid. p. 157). Note also *Gates of Light*, p. 300 (cited above, n. 111), where Tiferet appears as an intermediary attaching "lower souls" as spirits to their original home, Binah.

135 See nn. 99, 114 and 120, and cf. Johnston *Hekate*, p. 89: "The primary goal of the theurgist was *anagōgē*, the temporary raising of his soul to the "intellectual fire" of the noetic realm while the body was still alive; repeated practice of anagoge purified the soul for its eventual release from Fate when the theurgist's body died." Note also The Gospel of Philip, NHC II 3, 56, 15ff (Robinson NHL p. 144): "Those who say that the lord died first and (then) rose up are in error, for he rose up first and (then) died. If one does not first attain the resurrection he will [[not]] die," and ibid. 73, 1ff (NHL p. 153): "Those who say they will die first and then rise are in error. If they do not first receive the resurrection while they live, when they die they will receive nothing." This corresponds to the situation

in Jewish mysticism, where the ascent of the soul was an established technique for seeking the *unio mystica* in one's lifetime, before absorption into the ocean of divine light after death, see Idel *Kabbalah*, pp. 67-73.

136 Cf. Idel *Kabbalah*, p. 42, citing R. Ezra of Gerona (12th cent.): "The righteous causes his unblemished and pure soul to ascend [until she reaches] the supernal holy soul, [and] she unites with her and knows future things. And this is the manner [in which] the prophet acted, as the evil inclination did not have any dominion over him, to separate him from the supernal soul. Thus, the soul of the prophet is united with the supernal soul in a complete union."

In Jewish mysticism, achieving *unio mystica* after the ascent of the soul is tantamount to being admitted to God's court in the highest heaven; see Gruenwald *Apocalyptic*, passim. Cf. Isaiah 6, where the prophet becomes a participant in the divine council, so that when the Lord (as in Micaiah's vision, above, p. XXI) calls for a volunteer, he actually responds to the call; cf. Jer. 23:18-24 and 2 Cor. 12:1-4. For the same idea in Mesopotamian prophecy, note the Old Babylonian oracle published by M. deJong Ellis, MARI 5 (1987) 235ff, and see n. 27 above.

137 Cf. Burkert *Mystery Cults*, p. 77f: "The worshipers of Isis imitate their goddess, beating their breasts and wailing for Osiris, but bursting into joy when the god has been found again. The castrated *galloi* clearly impersonate Attis... Plutarch says that the suffering of Isis, as enacted in the *teletai*, should be a lesson in piety and consolation."

138 See SAA 3 4 i 2-11; Erra IV 54ff (English transl. in L. Cagni, "The Poem of Erra," SANE 1/3 [Malibu 1977], p. 52); Römer SKIZ, p. 138:53ff (Inanna Hymn of Iddin-Dagan, English transl. in Jacobsen *Harps* [1987], p. 115f), and see the discussion in LAS II (1983) p. 315f. The reference to "fear" in the Erra passage, as well the general context (swords and flint blades) compared with later parallels makes it quite clear that the phrase "turned from men into women" there implies emasculation and not just transvestism (thus CAD s.vv. *assinnu* and *kurgarrû*; Harris, HR 30 [1991] 276f).

Undoubtedly, the *kurgarrû*s and *assinnu*s dressed and behaved like women (see, e.g., UM 29-16-229 ii 4ff = Sjöberg, ZA 65 224, "May she (Inanna) change the right side (male) into the left side (female), dress him/her in the dress of a woman, place the speech of a woman in his/her mouth and give him/her a spindle and a hair clasp"; see also n. 231 below). However, their femininity, like that of the Galli of Cybele and Atargatis, was not transient but permanent, and derived from their emasculation. Note that in OB Lu (below, n. 232), words denoting mutilated persons are associated with ecstatics and frenzied people, implying a correlation between self-mutilation and frenzy, and see n. 220 on emasculated *assinnu*s falling into trance in Mari texts. The androgyny of the *assinnu* is implied by his role in the cult of Ištar, see above, n. 119. The Sumerian equivalent of *assinnu* in the Descent of Inanna, *gala-tur*, means "junior chanter (of lamentations)" and doubtless refers to castrated choirboys; note that Sumerian cultic lamentations, performed by the *gala* chanters, are consistently written in emesal, the Sumerian "women's language" otherwise only used by women and female deities, and cf. I. J. Gelb, StOr 46 (1975) 73.

Several vivid descriptions of acts of self-laceration and emasculation performed by the devotees of the Syrian goddesses Cybele and Atargatis are extant in classical sources, see e.g. Apuleius, Metamorph. VIII 26-28; Catullus, Poem 63; Lucian of Samosata, De dea Syria, 45 and 51; Arnobius of Sicca, Adversus nationes, V 7; Augustine, City of God, II 7 and VII 26. These passages beautifully parallel and complement the cuneiform sources cited above and strikingly illustrate the continuity of the cult of the Mesopotamian mother goddess well into late Antiquity. For a passage indicating that self-laceration (either by sword or whip) was commonly practiced also by biblical prophets see Zech. 13:6, where "scars on chest" are presented as a distinctive feature of a prophet beside "robe of coarse hair." Compare the behaviour of the prophets of Baal and Asherah described in 1 Kgs. 18:26-29 (below, n. 200).

139 Self-castration was an integral part of the cult of Cybele and Attis, which penetrated Rome in 204 BC and thereafter spread to the entire Greco-Roman world (see Meyer *Mysteries*, p. 138f). Though castration of Romans was forbidden by law, in Augustine's times the empire was full of "temples where Galli are mutilated, eunuchs are consecrated, madmen gash themselves ... Effeminates consecrated to the Great Mother [Phœnician Tanit] were to be seen until just the other day in the streets and squares of Carthage with their pomaded hair and powdered faces, gliding along with womanish languor... [the Great Mother] had living men ... gelded by their own hands; [she] introduced eunuchs even in the temples of Rome" (City of God, II 7 and VII 26; see also ibid. VI 7). The fact that the body of resurrected Osiris lacked the male member (Plutarch, De Iside et Osiride, 18 = Meyer *Mysteries*, p. 165) implies that the mysteries of Isis and Osiris also encouraged self-castration. See also L. R. Farnell, *Cults of Greek Statues* II (Oxford 1891-1909), vol. II, pp. 628 und 755, for eunuch priests dressed as women in the Cypriote cult of Venus Barbata (cf. above, n. 97) and A. D. Nock, "Eunuchs in Ancient Religion," Archiv für Religionswissenschaft 23 (1925) 25-33.

The gnostic idealization of androgyny and ascetic denial of the body suggests that self-castration was widespread among the Gnostics; note the urgency of the "struggle against desire" stressed by Isidore, and his positive attitude towards "eunuchs from birth" and "those who have made themselves eunuchs for the sake of the eternal kingdom" (Rudolph *Gnosis*, p. 258; see also ibid. p. 257). These attitudes persisted in the Byzantine empire, where emasculation continued to be practiced until the 11th century despite its prohibition by canon law, "because celibate life was intimately connected with holiness" (J. Herrin, *The Formation of Christendom* [London 1987], pp. 64 and 100). Eunuchs played an important role in the Byzantine church, army, and civil administration, and several patriarchs were castrates. Theophylaktos of Ohrid wrote a defense of the status of eunuchs, demonstrating that "they had always played an important role in the palace and in the church" (ODB 1 [1991], s.v. eunuchs). Cf. the role of the eunuchs in the Assyrian empire, and see my remarks in AOAT 240 (1995) 391 n. 36.

140 See n. 97 above and cf. further Hippolytus, Ref. V 7.14f (Meyer *Mysteries*, p. 149): "For Man, they say, is bisexual. So in accordance with this thought of theirs, the intercourse with woman is in their teaching shown to be most wicked and prohibited. For, he says, Attis was castrated, that is, (cut off) from the earthly parts of the creation (here) below, and has gone over to the eternal substance above where, he says, there is neither female nor male, but a new creature, 'a new man,' who is bisexual." According to Augustine, City of God, VII 26, the castration of the Galli aimed at "a life of blessedness after death." Note that Byzantine "hagiographic texts often represented [angels] as eunuchlike guardians, clad in white, who accompanied the Virgin" (ODB 1 [1991], p. 97 s.v angel). Note also the positive attitude to eunuchs in Isa. 56:3ff: "The eunuchs must not say, 'I am nothing but a barren tree.' For these are the words of the LORD: The eunuchs who keep my sabbaths, who choose to do my will and hold fast to my covenant, shall receive from me something better than sons and daughters ... a name imperishable for all time."

The rationale behind self-castration is illustrated by Mt. 5:29, "If your right hand is your undoing, cut it off and fling it away; it is better for you to lose one part of your body (var., to enter into life maimed, Mt. 18:8) than for the whole of it to go to hell." Compare this with Enkidu's cutting off the "right hand" (*imittu*, a pun on *imittu* "shoulder") of the Bull of Heaven and flinging it at the face of Ištar in Tablet VI of the Gilgamesh Epic, and the myth of Zeus tearing off the testicles of a ram and flinging them into the lap of Deo, as an etiology for the emasculation rites of the cult of Attis (Meyer *Mysteries*, p. 245). In both Mt. 5:29 and Gilg. VI 157, the "right hand" clearly is a metaphor for "penis"; cf. Mt. 19:12 and R. J. Hoffmann, *Porphyry's Against the Christians* (Amherst, NY, 1994), p. 65 n. 45. The ritual "bullfight" (*Taurobolium*), which took place on the "day of blood" on which the Galli castrated themselves (M. J. Vermaseren, *Cybele and Attis: The Myth and the Cult* [New York and London 1977], p. 70ff), almost certainly derived from the Bull episode in Gilgamesh VI. Note that it was carried out above a pit into which the officiant had descended and that it concluded with the offering of the "powers" (= genitals) of the bull to the Goddess, and compare the falling of Enkidu into a pit before the bullfight in Gilgamesh VI. In Tablet X of the epic, Enkidu is several times referred to as "rejected mule" (*kūdanu ṭardu*), implying his emasculation, which could only have occurred in connection with the Bull episode of Tablet VI. For the identification of the Bull with the "id," see JNES 52 [1993] 195 n. 133. See also above, n. 119.

The sexual aspect of Ištar's cult is commonly mistaken for its essence, while it in fact only provided a starting point in the way towards salvation. Doubtless the temples of Ištar provided free sexual services for whover wanted them, in the same fashion as the temples of Aphrodite Pandemos in the Greco-Roman world; however, as a recently discovered text shows (see V. Hurowitz, "An Old Babylonian Bawdy Ballad," in Z. Zevit et al. [eds.], *Solving Riddles and Untying Knots: Biblical, Epigraphic, and Semitic Studies in Honor of Jonas C. Greenfield* [Winona Lake 1995], pp. 543-58), those who took this road would sooner or later discover that fleshly pleasures did not lead to lasting happiness but only to disillusionment, exhaustion, and misery. Their road was viewed as a progressive descent towards hell, from where there was only one escape, that paved by the Goddess herself. Both in the Descent of Ištar and the Epic of Gilgamesh, the decisive turning point is constituted by the encounter with the prostitute and the *assinnu*, which enacted a spiritual rebirth (see n. 119 above). This encounter contained the seeds of a more sublimated conception of love, the true essence of the cult. See G. Held, "Parallels between *The Gilgamesh Epic* and Plato's *Symposium*," JNES 42 (1983) 133-141.

The two aspects of Ištar's cult (physical and spiritual) thus correspond to the two kinds of love distinguished in Plato's Symposium (209E) and associated there respectively with "the Lesser Mysteries" of Persephone and "the greater and more hidden ones" of Heavenly Aphrodite, of which the former were regarded as merely preparatory for the latter (Kerényi, *Eleusis*, p. 45f). Cf. the assessment of the Eleusinian cult in Hippolytus, Ref. VIII 43f (Meyer *Mysteries*, p. 152):

"For the lesser mysteries are those of Persephone here below; and of the mysteries and the road that leads there, which is 'broad and wide' and leads those who are perishing to Persephone, the poet also says: 'But beneath it is an awesome pathway, cavernous and clayey; but this is the best that leads to the pleasant grove of glorious Aphrodite.' This means, he says, the lesser mysteries of birth in the flesh; and when men have been initiated into these they must wait a little before they are initiated into the great, heavenly ones. For those who are allotted these dooms, he says, receive greater destinies. For this, he says, is 'the gate of heaven,' and this is 'the house of God,' where the good God dwells alone, where no unclean person, he says, shall enter, no psychic (unspiritual), no carnal man, but it is reserved for the spiritual alone; and when men come there they must lay down their clothing and all become bridegrooms, being rendered wholly male through the virgin spirit."

[141] For devotees of Ištar sighing and praying within the cult of the Goddess note, e.g., BM 41005 iii 12f (Lambert Love Lyrics p. 105), "The *kurgarrû* kneels down and recites prayers and utter sighs (*inha innah*)," and Farber Ištar p. 64:19, "You have the *assinnu* sit down and utter his sighs" (on behalf of a patient emulating the ascent of the Goddess). Cf. the inscription of Assurbanipal cited above, p. XLVIf, where the king's desperate weeping, sighing and praying lead to epiphanies of the Goddess and promises of divine support, and Erra IV 54ff, where female devotees of Ištar (*kezretu*, *šamhatu* and *harimtu* prostitutes) are referred to as "shouters of lamentations" (*iarurāti*). For further examples see CAD s.v. *nabû* B "to wail, lament" (note that the biblical word for "prophet" may as well derive from this verb rather than from *nabû* A "to call," with which it is traditionally connected; cf. Arab. *naba'a* "to cry, bark," Eg. *nb'* "to rage, to be aroused"; for the association of "ecstatic prophets" with "wailers" see below, n. 232). In Jewish mysticism and in early Christian and Sufi asceticism, weeping functioned as a technique for attaining visions and disclosure of heavenly secrets; see A. Vööbus, *History of Asceticism in the Syrian Orient* II (Louvain 1960), pp. 282ff and 309ff, and Idel *Kabbalah*, p. 75ff and 88 n. 85 with reference to Margaret Smith, *The Way of the Mystics* (New York 1978), pp. 155-157, especially p. 157: "O brethren, will ye not weep in desire for God? Shall he who weeps in longing for his Lord be denied the Vision of Him?"

[142] See nn. 49, 88 and 270.

[143] See, e.g., S. Krippner, "Altered States of Consciousness," in J. White (ed.), *The Highest State of Consciousness* (Garden City, NY, 1972), 1-5, under "States of Rapture" and "Trance States."

[144] Idel *Kabbalah*, p. 80ff. Note especially R. Isaac Yehudah Safrin's report on his vision of the Shekhinah (p. 84), introduced by the following words: "The revelation of the Shekhinah [happens] by means of and following the suffering that one is caused to suffer, by means of which he feels the suffering of the Shekhinah, and the fact that this revelation has a form and an image is on account of his being corporeal." The weeping technique is powerfully expounded by R. Abraham ha-Levi Berukhim, who writes: "When that pious man heard the words of Isaac Luria, he isolated himself for three days and nights in a fast, and [clothed himself] in a sack, and nightly wept. Afterward he went before the Wailing Wall and prayed there and wept a mighty weeping. Suddenly, he raised his eyes and saw on the Wall the image of a woman, from behind, in clothes which it is better not to describe, that we have mercy on the divine glory. When he had seen her, he immediately fell on his face and cried and wept and said: "Zion, Zion, woe to me that I have seen you in such a plight." And he was bitterly complaining and weeping and beating his face and plucking his beard and the hair of his head, until he fainted and lay down and fell asleep on his face. Then he saw in a dream the image of a woman who came and put her hands on his face and wiped the tears of his eyes ... and when Isaac Luria saw him, he said: I see that you have deserved to see the face of the Shekhinah" (ibid. p. 80).

[145] On the ecstatic nature of the eve of *Shavu'ot* when the revelation of Shekhinah was received, see ibid., p. 315 n. 64.

[146] Idel *Kabbalah*, p. 169. Cf. ibid. 39: "According to R. Eleazar, "Whoever cleaves to the divine presence, the divine spirit will surely dwell upon him." This text presupposes the possibility of cleaving to the Shekhinah; from the context, it is not clear whether this entity is identical with God or is to be understood as a manifestation of him [cf. the discussion above, pp. XXff and XXVI!]. Even if the latter alternative is the more congenial interpretation,

assuming a certain independence of the Shekhinah from God, it is nevertheless considered to be a divine entity, cleaving to which was negated in other classical rabbinic texts."

147 Ibid. 169f. Note also the passage in the Collectanaea of Yohanan Alemanno cited ibid., where the influx of the spirit of God is described in terms of a dove: "After ... an inner change and purification from all taint, one becomes as clear and pure as the heavens. Once one has divested oneself of all material thoughts, let him read only the Torah and the divine names written therein... then such a great influx will come to him that he will cause the spirit of God to descend upon him and hover upon him and flutter about him all the day." Cf. oracle no. 2 ii 6 and the discussion above, p. XXVIII! On *bat qol* see D. Sperling, "Akkadian *egirrû* and Hebrew *bt qwl*," JANES 4 (1972) 63-74, A. Malamat, *Mari and the Early Israelite Experience* (Oxford 1989), p. 91, and R. Kesher, *bt qwl* (in Hebrew), Proceedings of the American Academy for Jewish Research 59 (1993) [refs. courtesy A. Malamat]. In Malamat's opinion (letter of August 7, 1997), *bat qōl* ("trace of a voice," usually translated "echo") means "'little' voice (diminutive), i.e. 'lesser' than true prophecy."

148 Ibid. 170.

149 On the "virgin of light" as a denotation for the Shekhinah, see Idel *Kabbalah*, p. 315 n. 58, and idem, "The attitude to Christianity in *Sefer ha-Meshiv*" (in Hebrew), Zion 46 (1981) 89-90. Note that in Jewish mysticism, "Of the ministering angels, those serving God Himself are called youths (*bahurim*), and those serving the Shekhinah are called virgins (*betulot*; J. Israel, *Yalkut Hadash* [1648], nos. 63, 93)" (Enc. Jud. 2, 974).

150 See, e.g., Idel *Kabbalah*, p. 83, citing a vision of R. Isaac Yehudah Yehiel Safrin: "I wept many times before the Lord of the world, out of the depth of the heart, for the suffering of the Shekhinah. And through my suffering and weeping, I fainted and I fell asleep for a while, and I saw a vision of light, splendor and great brightness, in the image of a young woman adorned with twenty-four ornaments... And she said: 'Be strong, my son.'" As noted by Idel (ibid.), this feminine apparition, like Ištar of the Assyrian prophecies (see p. XXXVIff), possesses maternal features – she calls R. Isaac "my son." Cf. n. 152 below and R. Hayyim Vital's "vision of a beautiful woman whom he thought to be his mother" cited below, n. 234.

151 See Scholem, *On the Kabbalah and its Symbolism* (1969), p. 106ff, and Idel *Kabbalah*, p. 43f, quoting R. Menahem Recanati (c. 1300), according to whom the human soul by "cleaving to the supernal soul ... will cleave to the Shekhinah," and cf. n. 136 above (the prophet's soul uniting with "the supernal holy soul"). The term "supernal (holy) soul" (*nefesh elyonah*) corresponds to the Neoplatonic "universal soul" (see ibid., pp. 43 and 290 n. 23) and the Chaldean Soul/Hekate (see n. 134).

152 See above, n. 98.

153 See above, nn. 99 and 114. Note the role of the *neshamah* (the highest grade of the soul often identified with the Shekhinah) as the "speaking spirit" in Zohar III 46b-47a, and cf. Rom. 8:26: "We do not even know how we ought to pray, but through our inarticulate groans the Spirit himself is pleading for us, and God who searches our inmost being knows what the Spirit means, because he pleads for God's people in God's own way." This role of the spirit corresponds to the interceding role of Mullissu and other goddesses in Assyrian texts, e.g., "May Mullissu, the great mother whose utterance carries weight in Ekur, not intercede for him before Enlil at the site of judgment and decision," SAA 2 1 r.5f; "May Mullissu, his (Aššur's) beloved wife ... not intercede for you," SAA 2 6:417f; "(Nikkal) the gracious wild cow (see n. 189 below) ... who intercedes with the luminary of gods, her beloved Sin, who gives good advice and speaks a good word to Šamaš her son, who improves the words of supplication and pleads for the king, who reveres her; the merciful queen, who accepts prayers," ABRT 21:7-10; "May Tašmetu, the spouse of Nabû (see nn. 99 and 111 above), speak unfavourably of him in the presence of her husband Nabû," SAA 11 97:11-r. 1.

154 See Idel *Kabbalah*, p. 57 and 299 n. 151, citing R. David ben Zimra (mid-16th cent.).

155 See, e.g., Zohar I 22a. Note that the Shekhinah is in this context presented as the creatrix of man.

156 See, e.g., Gikatilla, *Gates of Light*, p. 303, where the Upper Shekhinah (*Shekhinah Aila*) is equated with the sefirah of Binah (cf. nn. 111 and 116 above) and the Lower Shekhinah with the sefirah of Malkhut (cf. n. 157). On the identification of the Shekhinah with the soul (*neshamah*) in Jewish mysticism, first attested in the Bahir, see G. Scholem, *On the Kabbalah and Its Symbolism* (New York 1969), p. 106f, and cf. nn. 133 and 153 above.

157 On the interconnection of Malkhut and the Shekhinah see *Gates of Light*, p. 36ff. Note that according to this text, Malkhut/Kingship "is the essence of *ruah ha-qodeš*, the Holy Spirit, from which all the Prophets enter the world of prophecy" (p. 39), as well as the "Tree of Knowledge," which receives the everflow of life from and opens the way to the "Tree of Life," located in the sefirot of Tiferet and/or Binah (ibid., pp. 44 and 219; see nn. 116 and 133 above, and cf. n. 193 below).

158 For the identification of Malkhut/Kingship with Assyrian divine kingship, see JNES 52 (1993) 181. Note further Gikatilla, *Gates of Light*, pp. 15, 31f and 50:

"From YHVH [the emanations] flow through the channel until they reach the name Adonay (= Malkhut) which is where all the strategies of the king are found. For He sustains all through the power of YHVH within him. All governing and ruling are in the hands of Adonay... Know that this attribute, because it [draws] from higher powers, has various qualities: to give life or bring death, to bring up or bring down, to smite or to cure... Since this attribute (Malkhut) is filled with the everflow from those attributes which reside above it, sometimes it is called by the name of one of those attributes from which it is filled at that particular time... At times [Malkhut] is called ELOHIM, for it is filled and draws from the attributes of power and fear, thus bringing judgment into the world... There are times when this attribute draws from the attributes of loving-kindness and mercy."

Compare this with the power of the Assyrian king to "to give life or bring death" (*balluṭu duāku*, e.g., AKA 281:81, ABL 620:4f), and "to bring up or bring down" (*šušqû u šušpulu*, e.g. SAA 10 112 r.29-33) as the image of the Šamaš (the divine judge) and Marduk (the divine king).

159 See oracles 1.4, 1.8, 2.1, etc. Note that the name of the human mother of Esarhaddon, Naqia/Zakutu (lit. "clean, innocent") marks her as the Assyrian equivalent of Mary! See n. 206 below. Note also that in Assyrian imperial art, queens are depicted wearing the mural crown and other attributes (mirror) of Kubaba/Mullissu, obviously in order to portray them as images of the Goddess; this convention was later taken over by the Roman empire, where several empresses but especially Iulia Domna, the Syrian wife of Septimius Severus, are depicted on coins with the mural crown of Cybele. See J. Reade, CRRAI 33 (1987) 139f and fig. 1, for a glazed tile fragment from the temple of Ištar of Nineveh representing a queen with the mural crown, and M. Hörig, *Dea Syria* (AOAT 208, Neukirchen 1979), pp. 129ff and 189ff.

160 See oracles 1.6 iv 6 and 20, 7 r.6, and 9 r.2.

161 Oracle 2.5:26. Cf. Nissinen, AOAT 231 (1991) 289, and n. 97 above.

162 See oracles 1.9:29; 2.6:20; 7:11 ("my/her calf"); 1.3:12; 1.6 iii 13.30; 1.7:9; 1.8:21; 2.4:33; 2.5:22.23.32 ("my king"). See also n. 150 above, on the mother-son relationship between the Shekhinah and the righteous in Kabbalah; in addition to the examples cited there, note also the vision of R. Levi Isaac of Berdichev reported in his *Netiv Mizvotekha*: "And it happened to the holy R. Levi Isaac, that on on the evening of *Shavu'ot* he achieved the vision of the Shekhinah in the image of [a young woman] and she said to him: 'My son, Levi Isaac, be strong, for many troubles will befall you, but be strong, my son, for I shall be with you'" (Idel *Kabbalah*, p. 83f).

163 E.g., oracle 1.1:6-19, 1.2:31f, and often.

164 O. Keel, "Das Böcklein in der Milch seiner Mutter und Verwandtes," OBO 33 (Freiburg/Göttingen 1980); Nissinen, AOAT 231 (1991) 268-98, and 232 (1993) 242-247. The examples cited cover the entire Ancient Near Eastern world from Egypt to Syria, Palestine and Mesopotamia. See also n. 165 below. On Ištar as warlord and mother of the king in Mesopotamian mythology see also Harris, HR 30 (1991) 269f.

165 In Hosea 11, Israel is a boy whom God loves, calls "my son," teaches to walk, takes in his arms, lifts to his cheek like a little child and bends down to feed; in Isa. 66:7-13, Israel is a son of God, who "sucks and is fed from the breasts that give comfort, delighting in her plentiful milk" (cf. SAA 3 13 r.6-8), and is comforted by YHWH "as a mother comforts her son." Note also Isa. 49:15, "Can a woman forget the infant [i.e. Zion] at her breast, or a loving mother the child of her womb?" On the iconographic evidence of the cow-and-calf motif and its variants, ewe-and-lamb and mother-and-child, see Keel, OBO 33 (1980), and note the Ugaritic passage KTU 1.6 = CTA 6 ii 28-30 (Baal and Mot): "As the heart of a cow towards her calf, as the heart of a ewe towards her lamb, so is the heart of Anat towards Baal" (Keel, p. 137), to be compared with the scene of Anat suckling the crown prince on two ivory panels from a royal couch in the palace of Ras Shamra (Gray, Mythology p. 93, both panels flanked by the sacred tree!). See nn. 198ff below. The ewe-and-lamb motif survives in Christianity as the "Lamb of God" of John 1:37, etc.

The importance of the cow-and-calf and mother-and-child motifs to the royal ideology is put beyond doubt by the prominent role they play in the royal ivories of Nimrud and Samaria (see E. Beach, "The Samaria Ivories, Marzeah, and Biblical Text," BiAr 56 [1993] 94-104). Note that the motif of the calf-suckling cow is already attested in Gudea, Cyl. A XIX 24ff: "Like a cow keeping an eye on its calf he frequented the temple in constant worry, like a man feeding his child he did not tire of frequenting it" (áb amar-bi-šè igi-gál-la-gim / é-šè te-te-ma im-ši-du / lú ninda dumu ka-a gub-ba-gim / du-du-e nu-ši-kúš-ù). In Egypt, the calf-suckling cow represents Hathor, the mother of Horus and wet nurse of the pharaoh, the Egyptian equivalent of Assyrian Mullissu (see p. XLII and nn. 187 and 189 below).

166 Note especially 2 Sam. 7:7 ("the judges whom I appointed shepherds of my people Israel"), where the ideological basis of the Israelite monarchy is defined in terms identical with the Mesopotamian royal ideology. See Collins *Scepter and Star*, p. 60ff, and cf., e.g., CH xlii 16, "Let him [the future king] shepherd his people righteously," and see B. Oded, *War, Peace and Empire: Justifications for War in Assyrian Royal Inscriptions* (Wiesbaden 1992), p. 181ff, M.-J. Seux, *Épithètes royales akkadiennes et sumeriennes* (Paris 1967), p. 244ff, and B. Cifola, *Analysis of Variants in the Assyrian Royal Titulary from the Origins to Tiglath-Pileser III* (Naples 1995), p. 189ff; the overwhelmingly spiritual nature of Mesopotamian kingship is underlined by passages such as VAB 4 100 i 9, "(Nebuchadnezzar) who placed fear of the great gods in the mouth of his people." See also n. 124 above. The designation of Jesus as the "Good Shepherd" and as "God's Chosen One, Son of God, and king of Israel" (John 1:34 and 50) unquestionably mark him as a pretender to the Davidic throne. For a suggestion that 2 Sam. 7:12-16 is a "late, tendentious addition" designed to make Nathan's oracle a divine charter for the Israelite monarchy, see Malamat, "A Mari Prophecy and Nathan's Dynastic Oracle," in J. A. Emerton (ed.), *Prophecy: Essays presented to Georg Fohrer on his sixty-fifth birthday* (Berlin and New York 1980), p. 82 n. 82, with reference to an article in Hebrew by I. L. Seeligman, Praqim 2 (1969-74) 302ff.

167 See AOAT 232 (1993) 246, and cf. ibid., p. 234.

168 Nissinen, AOAT 231 (1991) 287f: "Die Rede von dem König als Sohn oder (häufiger) als Pflegekind einer Göttin findet sich in mehreren Sprüchen, und zwar wiederholt in Kontexten, wo ausdrücklich von der Legitimität der Herrschaft des betreffenden Königs die Rede ist... Die Darstellung des Königs als Kind oder Pflegekind einer Gottheit, die ihm eine besondere Liebe erweist, war die beste Garantie für seine Sonderstellung 'vor den grossen Göttern' und vor seinen Rivalen." Note, however, that the king is *not* referred to as the "adoptive child" of the goddess in the prophecies nor in any other Assyrian source; he is always the "son" or "creation" of the god.

169 AOAT 231 (1991) 283; cf. AOAT 232 (1993) 230: "Die beiden Könige haben sozusagen schwarz auf weiß göttliche Garantie für ihr Königtum verlangt, um ihre Machtbefugnis legitimieren zu können. Daraus erklärt sich, daß die Propheten nicht müde werden, ein ums andere Mal zu wiederholen, daß Asarhaddon bzw. Assurbanipal und keiner sonst der von den Göttern erwählte König sei." The issue of legitimation in the Assyrian prophecies is also discussed by Ellis, JCS 41 (1989) 161ff, 173f and 176.

170 An indirect reference to oracle 7 (or 9?) is possibly found in SAA 3 3:1-12: "Exalt and glorify the Lady of Nineveh, magnify and praise the Lady of Arbela! ... I am Assurbanipal, their favourite, ... whose kingship they made great even in the house of succession. In their pure mouths is voiced the endurance of my throne."

171 See, e.g., ABL 1216 = SAA 10 109:7-16, and cf. pp. XLIIIf and LXVIIIff.

172 The brothers of Esarhaddon who usurped the power by assassinating their father did not receive the support of the prophets of Ištar, a circumstance that clearly precipitated their defeat, as noted both in the oracles and Esarhaddon's inscriptions. See p. LXXIII below, and oracles 1.7, 1.8 and 3.5, with relevant commentary.

173 In the Bible, the term explicitly refers to Saul (1 Sam. 12: 3.5, 24:7.11, 26:9.11.16.23; 2 Sam. 1:14.16), David (1 Sam. 16:6; 2 Sam. 19:22, 22:51, 23:1; Ps. 18:51, 89:52, 132:10.17), Solomon (2 Chron. 6:42), Cyrus (Isa. 45:1), and, by implication, to Zerubbabel (Dan. 9:25; for Zerubbabel as the chosen one of God, note Hag. 2:21, "Tell Zerubbabel, governor of Judah, I will shake heaven and earth; I will overthrow the thrones of kings, break the power of heathen realms, overturn chariots and their riders... On that day, says YHWH of Hosts, I will take you, Zerubbabel son of Shealtiel, my servant, and will wear you as a signet-ring; for you it is that I have chosen"). The prophecy in Dan. 9:26 can be taken to refer to the coming of a Messiah in Roman times.

174 See the discussion of the term *piqittu* "charge" in LAS II (1983), p. 109f, and cf. Streck Asb p. 86 x 61, referring to four goddesses (Ištar of Nineveh, the Lady of Kidmuri [= Ištar of Calah], Ištar of Arbela, and the "Lady of Divine Powers") tending the king as a child. According to the Assyrian *Götteraddressbuch* (Menzel Tempel T64), the "Lady of Divine Powers" (*Bēlat/Šarrat parī*) was worshiped in the Bit Eqi temple of Assur, which is connected with the mysteries of Ištar by KAR 139 (above, n. 132).

175 "His father Ea created him, his mother Damkina delivered him; he suckled the breasts of goddesses; a nurse (*tārītu*) guided him, filling him with awesomeness," En. el. I 83-86. Compare this with SAA 3 38:28-31, an esoteric commentary on the infancy of Nabû, the divine crown prince: "The stones which they hide amid the women are the great son of Be[l(!), Nabû], (whom) his father and mother took and hid amid the breasts of the goddesses."

176 SAA 3 39:19-22. The deities are called in the text "Ištar of Durna" and "Ištar of Liburna"; for Durna and Liburna as esoteric names of Nineveh and Arbela see the "Götteraddressbuch" of Assur, lines 189f (Menzel Tempel T165 with discussion). Ištar of Nineveh is attested as Bel's wet nurse also in the Nineveh version of the Marduk Ordeal, SAA 3 35:39: "The milk which they milk before Ištar of Nineveh: because she brought him (Bel) up, he (= Aššur) had mercy on him."

177 See no. 7 r.6 (Ištar of Arbela as king's nurse) and SAA 3 13 r.6-8 (Ištar of Nineveh as king's wet nurse). Note the four teats of Ištar of Nineveh in the latter text and cf. the four eyes and ears of the Goddess in SAA 3 39.

178 See nn. 180, 183 and 186 below.

179 See nn. 25 and 107 above, and cf. p. XLIII with n. 205 below. Note further the Babylonian Diviner's Manual (Oppenheim, JNES 33 [1974] 197-220), lines 39f: "Heaven and earth both produce portents; though appearing separately, they are not separate (because) heaven and earth are interconnected (*ithuzū*)," and cf. Zohar I 156a-b.

180 SAA 3 3:13. Cf. also OECT 6 p. 72:14ff, "O Mullissu, you who give well-being and life to those who seek your abode! I, Assurbanipal, your servant, whom your hands created, whom you, Exalted Lady, raised without father and mother, whom you concealed in your life-giving bosom, protecting my life..."; and ABRT II 21 r.2f, "[I], (Assurbanipal), the representative (of God) beseeching you, whom you, exalted Ištar, created, [whom] you raised in your bosom [like] a real mother, whom you taught to fly [like] a winged [bird]..."

181 SAA 3 3:8.

182 Cf. SAA 3 13 r.6f, "You were a child, Assurbanipal, when I left you with the Lady of Nineveh; you were a baby, Assurbanipal, when you sat in the lap of the Lady of Nineveh."

183 "I, Assurbanipal, ... whom your (Mullissu's) hands created," OECT 6 p. 72:15; "Assurbanipal, ... creation of her (Mullissu's) hands," Streck Asb p. 274; "[I], (Assurbanipal), ... whom you, exalted Ištar, created," ABRT II 21 r.2; "I am Assurbanipal, a creation of Aššur and Mullissu, ... whom Aššur and Sin since times immemorial called by name to kingship and created inside his mother for the shepherdship of Assyria," Streck Asb p. 2 i 1-5; "[Aššur], the father of gods, destined me for kingship inside my mother, [Mul]lissu, the great mother, called me by name to rule the land and the people, [Šer]ua and Belet-ili gave [my stature] lordly features," Streck Asb p. 252ff i 5-7; "The Lady of Nineveh (= Mullissu), the mother who gave birth to me," SAA 3 3 r.14.

184 See the passages quoted in n. 186 and, for Sumerian precedents, J. Klein, "The Birth of a Crownprince: A Neo-Sumerian Literary Topos," CRRAI 33 (1987) 97-106.

185 Gilg. I 42-48.

186 Cf., e.g., RIMA 1 pp. 233, 249 and 254 (Tukulti-Ninurta I: "chosen one of Aššur, whose name Aššur and the great gods duly called" [1], "beloved of the great gods" [8], "beloved of Ištar" [11]); ibid. p. 300 (Aššur-nadin-apli [1206-03 BC]: "king indicated by Anu, desired by Enlil, chosen of Aššur and Šamaš"); ibid. p. 310 (Aššur-reš-iši I [1132-1115]: "desired by the great gods inside his mother and called for guiding Assyria"); RIMA 2 p. 13 (Tiglath-Pileser I [1114-1076]: "beloved prince, your [the great gods'] select one, pious shepherd, whom you chose in your righteous hearts"); ibid., p. 147 (Adad-nerari II [911-891]: "The great gods properly created me, altered my stature to lordly stature, rightly perfected my features and filled my lordly body with wisdom"); ibid. p. 165 (Tukulti-Ninurta II [890-884]: "The great [gods ... looked] kindly [at me] in my mother's womb and changed my stature to lordly stature, ... [perfecting] my features ... [The king whose] honored name Aššur has pronounced eternally [for the control of the four quarters]"); ibid. p. 193ff (Assurnasirpal II [883-859]: "chosen one of Enlil and Ninurta, beloved of Anu and Dagan"); Luckenbill Senn. p. 117 ([705-681]: "Belet-ili, the goddess of creation, looked kindly upon me and created my features in my mother's womb"); Borger Esarh. §§ 27, 82 and 101 ([680-669]: "creation of Aššur and Mullissu, whom the great gods called to kingship to restore [the statues of] the great gods and perfect [their] sanctuaries," "[created in] the womb of my mother who gave birth to me," "Ištar [looked kindly upon me and created my features] in the womb of my mother"); RIMB 2 p. 250 (Šamaš-šumu-ukin [667-648]: "The queen of the gods, Erua, kindly called my name for the priesthood of the people in the womb [lit., 'place of creation'] of the mother who bore me; the great gods looked with pleasure upon me to gather the scattered people of Babylonia and joyfully called me to restore the forgotten cultic practices"); VAB 4 122:23ff (Nebuchadnezzar [605-562]: "After the lordly Erua had created me and Marduk formed my features within my mother, when I had been born and created, I frequented the sanctuaries of God...").

187 dNIN.LÍL *rīmtu Illilītu* "Mullissu cow," Streck Asb p. 78 ix 75; note also *Ištar rīmtu muttakkipat kibrāti* "Ištar, the wild cow who gores the (four) regions," ABRT I 15 i 7 // KAR 57 i 8, and *Ištar rīmtu šaqūtu ša ina mahri illaku* "Ištar, the wild cow who goes in the front," SBH 167:14ff. The visualization of Mullissu/Ištar as a wild cow derives from the unpredictable violence of a wild cow defending her calf (see p. XXXVI), and is to be judged in the light of the discussion above, p. XXXI.

188 MÍ.*rīmat* dNIN.SÚN, Gilg. I 34, and passim. The name Ninsun literally means "Lady Wild Cow."

189 See above, p. XXXII with n. 111. Note that Mullissu shares the epithet *rīmtu* with the moon goddess Nikkal (dNIN.GAL *rīmtu damiqtu ša bunnī namr*[*ūti*] "Nikkal, the gracious wild cow of bright countenance," ABRT II 1:3 = Streck Asb p. 287), and that in Streck Asb p. 1 i 3, Sin (the moon) takes the place of Mullissu as the creator of the king. Also note that in CT 53 17:8 // CT 53 938:8 // ABL 1217:4 and 8, Nikkal alternates with Mullissu as the oracle goddess. Such alternation is clear evidence that the Assyrian gods were not conceived of as separate divine entities but as *names* describing different qualities, aspects and powers of God. See above, pp. XVIII and XXI with nn. 8, 20 and 23.

"Wild cow" as an appellative of the Goddess already occurs in the great hymn of Iddin-Dagan to Inanna (Römer SKIZ p. 137 = Jacobsen *Harps* p. 113f, line 20, cf. line 8, early 2nd mill.) and is there too associated with the moon ("oldest child of the moon," line 9) and wisdom ("her father Enki," line 24). Note that Isis (see nn. 117, 130, 137, 139), who according to Herodotus (Hist. II 41.2) "is a woman with cowhorns," was also prominently associated with the moon: "In the center [of her pitch-black cloak] a mid-month moon breathed forth her floating beams" (Apuleius, Metamorph. XI 4 [transl. J. Lindsay, Bloomington 1962]). Note also the mighty horns and lunar disc of Anat on the Ugarit ivory panels (above, n. 165), and the horns of the prophet of Yahweh in 1 Kgs. 22:10f.

190 The name Mullissu (Mulliltu) probably originally meant "Female Enlil," see S. Parpola, "The Murderer of Sennacherib," CRRAI 26 (1980) 177. However, in Neo-Assyrian times it was almost certainly reinterpreted as "She Who Purifies/Sanctifies" (D-stem fem. participle of *elēlu* "to be pure, holy"), cf. the Neo-Assyrian reinterpretation of Zarpanitu (wife of Marduk) as *Zār-bānītu*, "Creatress of the Seed." The corresponding masculine word (*mullilu*, "purifier") is well known from Assyrian ritual texts, where it denotes the cone-shaped object by which the winged sages purify the sacred tree in royal reliefs, see F. A. M. Wiggermann, *Mesopotamian Protective Spirits* (Groningen 1992), p. 67.

191 Note that in the Byzantine empire, "the emperor, crowned by the Holy Spirit, rules through the Holy Spirit's inspiration" (ODB 1 [1991], p. 1000, s.v. inspiration).

192 John 1:13. Referring to the birth of Christ, the text continues: "So the Word (logos) became flesh," which links up with ibid. 1:1f, "When all things began, the Word already was. The Word dwelt with God, and what God was, the Word was..., and through him all things came to be." This is a reference to the Holy Spirit as the Word of God through which the world was created (ibid. 1:3), and corresponds to the multiple role of Ištar/Mullissu/Hathor/Hekate/Sophia etc. as the divine word, holy spirit, female companion of God, and creatress of the world (see nn. 86, 98, 130 and 165 above). On the affinity of John 1 to the gnostic treatise Trimorphic Protennoia (where the Logos is a feminine entity) see J. D. Turner in Robinson NHL (1990) p. 511ff and K.-W. Tröger (ed.), *Gnosis und Neues Testament* (Berlin 1973), p. 226f. According to Athanasius, "The Son is the selfsame Godhead as the Father, but that Godhead manifested rather than immanent... The Son is the Father's image... Hence anyone who sees Christ sees the Father, 'because of the Son's belonging to the Father's substance and because of His complete likeness to the Father'" (Kelly *Doctrines*, pp. 245 and 247). Cf. n. 158 above and SAA 10 207 = ABL 652 r.12, "The king is the perfect likeness of God."

193 See nn. 166 and 183 above. For the king as the personification of the Tree see JNES 52 (1993) 167f with nn. 32f and AOAT 240 (1995) 384ff and 397 n. 63. See also the Sumerian passages collected and discussed in G. Widengren, *The King and the Tree of Life* (Uppsala 1951), p. 43ff, and my article "The Esoteric Meaning of the Name of Gilgamesh" (CRRAI 43, forthcoming) on Gilgamesh as the perfect king "who equaled the Tree of Balance," and note Erra I 150ff referring to the Cosmic Tree (*mes*) as the "insignia (*simtu*) of kingship." For Ištar/Mullissu as the "trunk" of the Tree see above, nn. 47 and 133f.

As is well known, the "perfect man" of Jewish mysticism, Adam Qadmon, was likewise conceived of as a personification of the Tree of Life. The appellative "Son of Man" by which Jesus refers to himself in the gospels occurs as a designation of Davidic kings in Ps. 80:17 ("Let thy hand rest upon the man at thy right side, the Son of Man [*bn 'dm*] whom thou hast made strong for thy service"); comparison of Mt. 24:64 // Mk. 14:62 // Lk. 22:69 // Dan. 7:13-27 leaves no doubt that this designation referred to the Messiah/King specifically as "the perfect man," and hence as a personification of the Tree. See also Collins *Scepter and Star*, p. 142f, and note Rom. 5:12-14, where Christ is portrayed as the "second Adam," and cf. Mt. 5:48. For Malkhut/Kingship as the Tree of Knowledge and the gateway to the Tree of Life in Kabbalah see nn. 116 and 133 above. In Sabbatian Messianism, "the soul of the King Messiah cleaves to the tree of life" (Idel *Kabbalah*, p. 57).

On the Byzantine emperor as "God's representative on earth" (a status actively fostered by the church) see ODB 1 (1991), p. 989. See also my remarks in AOAT 240 (1995) 397 on Umayyad and Abbasid caliphs as "shepherds of God" and "perfect men," perpetuating earlier Byzantine and Sassanid traditions.

194 See Cifola, *Royal Titulary* (above, n. 166), p. 162ff.

195 See En. el. I 79-104, II [94f, 123f], III 58f, 116f, 138, IV 13, and cf. above, n. 175.

196 See JNES 52 (1993) 204f. Ninurta/Nabû corresponds to the archangel Michael, who in early Christianity (Hermas) was equated with the Son of God, and in Jewish apocalyptic and mystical tradition is known as "the great prince" (*Sar ha-Gadol*) and coalesces with the heavenly scribe, Enoch-Metatron, the "perfect man" (Adam Qadmon); see Kelly *Doctrines*, p. 94f, Gruenwald *Apocalyptic*, pp. 140f and 166 n. 60, and M. Idel, "Enoch is Metatron," Immanuel 24/25 (1990) 220-40, esp. p. 224 n. 15. In Jewish magical texts, Michael, like Ninurta/Nabû, figures as "the healer" and is associated with the planet Mercury. I shall deal with the matter in more detail in an article under preparation. On Marduk = Enlil, Nabû = Ninurta see JNES 52 178f nn. 74 and 76. While the names Ninurta and Nabû were largely interchangeable in the Sargonid period, Ninurta primarily connoted the saviour engaged in the battle against sin and death, whereas Nabû ("the brilliant one") primarily connoted the transformed victor judging men on the day of "accounting."

197 Ninurta/Nabû's triumphal return to his father formed an important element of state religion and was re-enacted on several cultic occasions, in particular the New Year's festival celebrated in Nisan; the triumphal processions in victory celebrations (see p. 10 below, note on oracle 1.9 v 27f, and E. Weissert, "Royal Hunt and Royal Triumph in a Prism Fragment of Ashurbanipal," in S. Parpola and R. M. Whiting [eds.], *Assyria 1995* [Helsinki 1997], p. 339ff) and the ceremonial entry of the crown prince into the Succession Palace (see LAS II pp. 116 and 119f) were also variants of the same mythological pattern. In the latter case, the "return to the Father" symbolized the perfection of the crown prince's education and his transition to full royal status; from now on, he was the "perfect man," consubstantial, and thus "one" with his father (see JNES 52 [1993] 205 and AOAT 240 [1995] 398). In Assyrian mysticism, the same mythological pattern was applied to the purified soul's triumph in heaven, union with God. Note that in Assyrian iconography, the mythical sages purifying the king are furnished with wings and other attributes of divinity, and are occasionally entirely identical with Ninurta in appearance, except for the buckets of holy water and purifier cones that they carry; see the discussion in SAA 10 p. XIXff, and cf. Fig. 4 ibid. with SAA 3, Fig. 29.

198 See F. Daumas, "Hathor," in W. Helck et al. (eds.), Lexikon der Ägyptologie II (Wiesbaden 1977), 1024-33. See also nn. 165, 187 and 189 above.

199 See N. Wyatt, "The Stela of the Seated God from Ugarit," UF 15 (1983) 271-7; note the sacred tree flanking the panels. On the identification of the seated goddess on the ivory pyxis lid from Minet el Beida as Asherah see I. Cornelius, "Anat and Qudshu as the Mistress of Animals," SEL 10 (1993) 33. See also J. Gray, *Near Eastern Mythology* (New York 1985), p. 73 for the representation of Asherah as sacred tree (flanked by caprids) on an unguent box from Ras Shamra.

200 See 1 Kgs. 18:19ff, referring to "400 prophets of the goddess Asherah," and note R. Isaac of Acre's comment on this passage in his *'Ozar Hayyim*, quoted in Idel, *Studies in Ecstatic Kabbalah* (Albany 1988), p. 153 n. 67: "And the matter of 'and they prophesied,' was that they did like those who practice *hitbodedut* [concentration], to negate their physical senses and to remove from the thoughts of their soul all objects of sensation... And the prophets of Baal and those who served the Asherah certainly communed in their thoughts with the queen of heaven, ... for the crown

[i.e., *Shekhinah*] is the queen of heaven, upon whom is placed the rulership of this lower world. But the thought of Elijah's pure soul communed with YaH the Lord God of Israel alone." Thus "making do with concentration on the 'intelligibles' or the Shekhinah would seem to have been thought improper by R. Isaac, who saw it a religious obligation to transfer contemplation and communion to God alone" (Idel, ibid.; cf. pp. XXVI and XXXIV above).

201 See O. Keel and C. Uehlinger, *Göttinnen, Götter und Gottessymbole* (Freiburg im Breisgau 1992), pp. 255-282, and J. Taylor, "The Asherah, the Menorah and the Sacred Tree," JSOT 66 (1995) 29-54. Note that the temple of Solomon, as well as the restored temple of Ezekiel 40f, was "inside and out, from the ground up to the top," decorated with carvings of "cherubim and palm-trees, a palm between every pair of cherubim" (Ezek. 41:17-20; cf. 1 Kgs. 6:29-35 and Gen. 3:24). Note also that the two bronze pillars of the temple, Jachin and Boaz, whose pomegranate-studded ornamentation (1 Kgs. 7:17-22, Jer. 52:17-23) corresponds to the pomegranate-fringed surrounding network the Assyrian sacred tree (see JNES 52 [1993] 163f), in Jewish mystical tradition represent the left and right sides of the sefirotic tree: "The columns ... are [the sefirot of] Netzah and Hod and the two capitals on top of the columns are Gedulah and Gevurah; the two pieces of network to cover the two globes are Hokhmah and Binah" (Gikatilla, *Gates of Light*, p. 144). On the association of the Shekhinah with cherubs and the Tree of Life see n. 98 above.

202 See M. Dietrich and O. Loretz, *"Jahwe und seine Aschera:" Anthropomorphes Kultbild in Mesopotamien, Ugarit und Israel — Das Biblische Bilderverbot* (UBL 9, Münster 1992); J. Hadley, "Yahweh and 'His Asherah': Archaeological and Textual Evidence for the Cult of the Goddess," in W. Dietrich and A. Klopfenstein (eds.), *Ein Gott allein? JHWH-Verehrung und biblischer Monotheismus im Kontext der israelitischen und altorientalischen Religionsgeschichte* (OBO 139, Freiburg [Schweiz] 1994), pp. 235-268; P. Merlo, "L'Asherah di Yhwh a Kuntillet Ajrud," SEL 11 (1994) 21-54; M. Weinfeld, "Feminine Features in the Imagery of God in Israel: The Sacred Marriage and the Sacred Tree," VT 46 (1996) 515-529, esp. 526f.

203 Note that in Zohar I 102a-b, Abraham is presented as the personification of the tree of life.

204 See p. LXIX and the note on oracle 2.3 ii 27 (p. 16). Cf. Borger Esarh., Bab. A-G i 34ff, translated above, p. LXXIV.

205 See oracles 2.5 ("I will put Assyria in order, I will put the kingdom of heaven in order") and 2.4 iii 19f ("I will put Assyria in order and reconcile the angry gods with Assyria"), and Borger Esarh., Bab. A ii 24ff (above, p. LXXV). Cf. R. Yehudah ben Yaʾakov Hunain (late 16th cent, cited in Idel *Kabbalah*, p. 178): "As the war was below, so it was above, because of the sin of Israel; for just as the righteous add force and power in the higher assembly, when they act in the opposite [way], it is as if they weaken the supernal force ... for the lower [entities] are like the root and modus of the supernal [entities]." Note also Gikatilla's *Gates of Light*, p. 121 and 122: "This verse implies that the war was above and below and the war was strong in the heavens ... "He [= Yahweh] waged war with the celestial Egypt and defeated them."

206 Note oracles 1.4 ("When you were small, I took you to me") and 2.5 ("I raised you between my wings"), and see above, p. XXXIX. Unlike his elder brothers, who were apparently born before Sargon had usurped power (see SAA 6 p. XXXIIff) and thus *could not* be entrusted to the care of the Goddess as royal babies, Esarhaddon was born when his father was already crown prince (see Streck Asb p. 5 i 27, and LAS II, p. 231 n. 390) and thus qualified for royal education from the very beginning. The Aramaic or Hebrew name of Esarhaddon's mother, Naqia, means "clean, pure, innocent" (cf. Aram. *naqyā* "rein, klar, hell," *nqy* "reinigen," Dalman Aram. Wb. p. 277; Hebr. *nāqî* "blameless, innocent", *nqh* "to be without blame," HAL p. 720).

207 See S. Parpola, "The Murderer of Sennacherib," CRRAI 26 (1980) 171-82, esp. 179f.

208 See SAA 10 109 = ABL 1216:7-16 and note on oracle 3.5 iii 20.

209 See oracle 3.2 ii 7 and p. XLI with nn. 196ff, above; cf. Mt. 13:43, "Then the righteous will shine as brightly as the sun in the kingdom of their Father. " For Esarhaddon as the "avenger of his father" see Borger Esarh. p. 40:53ff, above, p. LXXIII.

210 For comparable encouragement oracles in the biblical corpus see e.g. Zech. 8:6-13, pertaining to the building of the second Temple, especially verses 9 and 13: "Take courage from the prophets who were present when the foundations were laid for the house of the LORD of Hosts, their promise that the temple is to be rebuilt... Courage! Do not be afraid!"

211 The numerous points which the descriptions of Jesus' career in the gospels have in common with Assyrian royal ideology are too obvious and consistent to be dismissed as accidental. See n. 166 above, and note, e.g., Jesus' royal lineage (cf. n. 193), purity of mother (nn. 159 and 206), immaculate conception (n. 186), omen of kingship (n. 207), birth in the manger (nn. 165 and 187ff), prophetic acknowledgment (n. 172), call for the salvation of Israel (n. 194), and his roles as the good shepherd (nn. 166 and 193), the "perfect man" (nn. 121, 193 and 196) and the Lamb of God (n. 165), his appellative "Lord" (see below), miraculous powers to cure (nn. 41 and 196), subjugation of the stormy sea (cf. oracle 2.2), face shining like sun (n. 209), triumphal entry into Jerusalem (n. 197), innocent suffering (nn. 123ff), wailing by the three Marys (n. 125), resurrection (n. 127), victory over sin and death (n. 196), and eventual exaltation and ascension to the right side of the Father (n. 197) to judge the living and the dead (n. 7). See also n. 9 above, on the doctrine of Trinity. These doctrines and tenets were transmitted to Roman Palestine through various mystery cults (see nn. 109, 125f, 165, etc.), whose doctrine of salvation essentially hinged on the concept of the "perfect man," materialized in the person of the king.

For scriptural evidence suggesting that Jesus himself understood the figure of the Messiah in terms of Mesopotamian royal ideology and his own mission in terms of Michael/Ninurta's fight against sin (nn. 41 and 196), see the well-known and heavily debated passage Mt. 22:41-46 // Mk. 12:35-37 // Lk. 20:41-44 // Ps. 110:1 (see Collins *Scepter and Star*, p. 142), where the appellative "Lord" by which the Messiah is referred to is the standard appellative of the Mesopotamian saviour (see JNES 52 [1993] 205 and AOAT 240 [1995] 398).

212 The nominal pattern *parris* is a variant of the G-stem participle *pāris* (GAG § 55m) with a frequentative nuance approximating that of the pattern *parrās*, used for forming words of profession (GAG § 55o); cf. CAD and AHw. s.vv. *akkilu* "glutton," *šattû* "drunkard," *parriṣu* "criminal" ('one who transgresses habitually'), *giṣṣiṣu* "foe" ('one who gnashes his teeth habitually'), *pallišu* "borer," and *šaṭṭiru* "scribe"; note also *ṣarritu* "(habitual) farter" (SAA 3 29 r.4 and 30:2). For *ragāmu* "to shout, proclaim" see below, n. 217.

213 The description of John the Baptist in the gospels ("coat of camel's hair, with a leather belt round his waist") marks him as an emulator of Elijah (see 2 Kgs. 1:8), and hence as the eschatological prophet (*nabīʾ*) expected by the Qumran community before the coming of the "anointed ones of Aaron and Israel" (*mšyhy ʾhrwn wyšr'l*), i.e. of a priestly and royal Messiah (1 QS 9,11; see H.-P. Müller, ThWAT V [1986], p. 163, s.v. *nbyʾ*). Elijah's "robe of coarse

hair" also occurs as a distinctive feature of prophets in Zech. 13:4. On the "posture of Elijah" (1 Kgs. 18:42) as a technique for achieving visions in later Jewish mysticism see Idel *Kabbalah*, pp. 78ff and 91, and note the occurrence of this posture in the Epic of Gilgamesh (Tablet IV 86; see JNES 52 [1993] 192 n. 120).

214 ABL 149 = LAS 317:7-r.8: "The prophetess Mullissu-abu-uṣri who took the king's clothes to Akkad, has prophesied [in the te]mple: "[The] throne from the te[mp]le [... (Break) ... "Le]t the throne go, I shall catch my king's enemies with it." CT 53 969 reads (obv. 10ff): "The king's sacrifices have been performed... [NN?], the woman [... who] ... during the sacrif[ices], has prophesied (*tarrugum*): 'Why has the orchard and grove of ... been given to the Egyptians? Speak in the king's presence; let them give it back to me, and I will *gi*[*ve*] total abundance [to] his [...].' Cf. Amos prophesying in the temple of Bethel (Amos 7:10ff), Jeremiah in the temple of Jerusalem (Jer. 7:2). See also n. 220 on *assinnus* falling into trance and prophesying in the temple of the goddess Anunitum in Mari.

215 See notes on oracle 3.5 iii 20f and iv 13ff.

216 "If you hear any evil, improper, ugly word which is not seemly or good to Assurbanipal, the great crown prince designate ... from the mouth of a prophet (*raggimu*), an ecstatic (*mahhû*), an inquirer of oracles (*šā'ilu amat ili*), or from the mouth of any human being at all, you shall not conceal it but report it to Assurbanipal..." (lines 108-122).

217 The meanings of *ragāmu* attested in Neo-Assyrian include: 1. "to cry out, shout, shriek" (ZA 45 42:40); 2. "to cry out, shout, raise a cry" (KAV 197:58, ABL 1372:24); 3. "to call, shout to" (AfO 17 287:105); and 4. (in the ventive) "to call up (for questioning)" (ABL 1073:14, KAV 115:23).

218 See oracles 3 iv 31, 6 r.11 and 7:1; SAA 10 352 = ABL 437, LAS 317 = ABL 149, SAA 10 109 = ABL 1216, SAA 10 294 = ABL 1285, SAA 2 6 ⌜185⌝ 10, and SAA 7 9; cf. Nissinen, *AOAT* 232 (1993) 227 and idem, "References to Prophetic Activity in Neo-Assyrian Sources" (forthcoming).

219 The word *mahhû* (Ass., Mari; Bab. *muhhû*) is the D-stem verbal adjective of *mahû* "to become frenzied, to go into a trance" (CAD M/1 115f); hence, literally, "one brought into a trance." Note the Sumerian lexical equivalents of *mahû*, è "to go out (of one's mind)" and e_{11} "to ascend/descend" (cf. nn. 114, 116f and 133 above) in Diri I 158 and 208, as well as the commentary item [È : *šegû* :] È : *mahû* "'to ascend/descend' (= è) means 'to rage, to be frenzied'" in CT 41 28 r.6 (Alu comm.).

220 LÚ.*mu-uh-hu-um ša* ᵈ[*d*]*a-gan*, ARM 3 40 = ARM 26 221:9 and ARM 2 90 = ARM 26 220:16; also ARM 3 78 = ARM 26 221bis:12 (PN LÚ.*mu-uh-hu-ú-um*), ARM 6 45 = ARM 26 201:9 (MÍ.*mu-uh-hu-tim*), and 10 50:22 (MÍ.*mu-uh-hu-tum*); *šumma ina rēš war*[*hi*]*m mu-uh-hu-um ištaqa*[*l*] *a*[*n*]*a ma-he-e-e*[*m*] *ul i*[*reddu*], RA 35 2 ii 22f (Ištar ritual, see ARM 26 p. 386). Note also ARM 10 7 = ARM 26 213, where an *assinnu* named Šelebum (cf. ARM 10 80 = ARM 26 197 and the end of the letter) falls into trance (*im-ma-hu*) in the temple of Anunitum and delivers an oracle of the goddess (in the 1st person) to the king (addressed by name and in the 2nd person, as in the present corpus). For another oracle to the king by an *assinnu* of Anunitum (Ili-haznaya) see ARM 10 6 = ARM 26 212; see also ARM 26 200, where an ecstatic prophetess (*mu-uh-hu-tum*) prophesies in the temple of Anunitum, and ARM 10 8 = ARM 26 214, where a woman falls into trance in the temple of Anunitum and delivers an oracle.

221 E.g., *ana* LÚ.*mah-im ša* DN "to the prophet of DN," TCS 1 369:5 (Ur III); MÍ.LÚ.GUB.BA *ša* DN "prophetess of DN," TCL 10 39:11; PN *mu-hu-um* "prophet," MDP 18 171:14; LÚ.GUB.BA DINGIR.RA "prophet of the god," MDP 10 no. 7:6.9 (all OB); LÚ.GUB.BA, OECT 1 pl.21:38; PN A ᵐLÚ.GUB.BA, YOS 6 18:1.7.8.10, YOS 7 135:6 (all NB).

222 E.g., "If there appear many ecstatic prophets/prophetesses (LÚ.GUB.BA.MEŠ/MÍ.GUB.BA.MEŠ) in a city," CT 38 4 81f, followed (in similar context) by "many cripples" (*akû*), "frenzied people" (*zabbu*), and "male and female seers" (*šabrû* and *šabrātum*); also "If a man (while walking in the street) sees an ecstatic" (NÍ.ZU.UB, followed by LÚ.GUB.BA IGI "sees an ecstatic prophet"), Sm 332 r.5 (both Alu); "If he sees a prophet (*ma-ah-ha-a*)," TDP 4:30 (Sagig); LÚ.GUB.BA ŠUB-*ut* "a prophet will fall down," Boissier DA 211 r.12. For the lexical texts, see below, n. 232.

223 See VS 19 1 i 37f (below, n. 244).

224 See n. 216 above.

225 "The ecstatic (*mahhû*) who goes before the Lady of Babylon is a bringer of news (*mupassiru*); he goes toward her, weeping: 'They are taking him to the river ordeal.' She sends him away, saying: 'My brother, my brother!,'" SAA 3 34:28 // 35:31.

226 Except in an Assyrian lexical text (n. 231) and in the Neo-Babylonian letter SAA 10 109 = ABL 1216, written in Nineveh by an Assyrianized court scholar. The alleged attestation of the word in a MA tablet from Tell Rimah (Saggs, Iraq 30 [1968] 162f on TR 2031:6, cf. H. Huffmon, "The Origins of Prophecy," in F. M. Cross et al. (eds.), *Magnalia Dei, Essays on the Bible and Archaeology in Memory of G. Ernest Wright* [Garden City, NY, 1976], p. 175) must be deleted, since instead of *ra-kin-tu* "oracle priestess" the text actually reads *ra-qi i+na*!.

227 Cf. the use of the word *rakkābu* "express messenger" for normal *kallāp šipirte* in Neo-Assyrian royal inscriptions, etc. Note the occurrence of *mahhû* and *mahhūtu* among the cult personnel of the Ištar temple in the Tammuz ritual Farber Ištar p. 140:31.

228 lú.gub.ba = *mu-uh-hu-um*, mí.lú.gub.ba = *mu*(-*uh*)-*hu-tum*, MSL 12 158:23 (OB Lu); lú.gub.ba = *mah-hu-ú* "ecstatic," ibid. 101f:213 (Lu I); lú.ní.su.ub = *mah-hu-u*, lú.gub.ba = MIN, ibid. 132:117f (Lu IV).

229 In NA royal inscriptions, the verb *mahû* "to be(come) ecstatic" occurs in the pejorative meaning "to be(come) crazy," see Borger Esarh. p. 42 i 41: "my brothers became crazy (*im-ma-hu-ma*)," and ibid. 44 i 73: "seeing my onslaught, they became crazy" (*ēmû mahhûtiš*)"; similarly Streck Asb p. 8 i 84 and 158:19. However, these passages are obvious literary allusions to En. el. IV 8, "Tiamat went crazy/out of her mind" (*mahhūtiš īteme*), and can hardly be taken to indicate that the word *mahhû* itself had acquired a pejorative connotation which would have led to its replacement by *raggimu* in NA times. Cf. the "crazy" behaviour of Israelite prophetes: Isaiah goes about naked and barefoot for three years "as a sign and warning" (Isa. 20:2f); Jeremiah wears cords and bars of a yoke on his neck (Jer. 27:2); Saul lies naked all day in prophetic rapture (1 Sam. 19:20-24); Zedekiah makes himself horns of iron (1 Kgs. 22:10f). Note also Jer. 29:26f: "It is your duty, as officer in charge of the LORD's house, to put every madman who sets up as a prophet into the stocks and the pillory. Why, then, have you not reprimanded Jeremiah of Anathoth, who poses as a prophet before you?"

The respected position of prophets in Neo-Assyrian times is made clear by SAA 3 3:6-12: "A word from their lips is blazing fire! Their utterances are valid for ever! ... In their pure mouths is voiced the endurance of my throne."

230 See LAS II p. 58f and cf. n. 141 above. On fasting as a method for obtaining visions see in Jewish mysticism see Idel *Kabbalah*, p. 80ff and Gruenwald *Apocalyptic*, p. 99f (with reference to Dan. 10, etc.).

231 lú.šabra (PA.AL) = ŠU-*u* (= *šabrû*) = *rag-gi-*[*mu*], MSL 12 226 (Hg B to Hh XV; 4 mss., all from Nineveh). The preceding entries include [lú].zilulu (PA.GIŠGAL) = *sah-*[*hi-ru*] "prowling" (line 132; see n. 67 above) and [lú].UR.SAL

= [*a*]*s-sin-nu* = *sin-niš-a-*[*nu*] "womanish, effeminate" (line 133; see n. 138 above). Cf. also the omens referred to in n. 222, where prophets are associated with "frenzied people" (*zabbu*) and "male and female seers" (*šabrû* and *šabrātum*).

232 See MSL 12 102 (LÚ = *amēlu*, Tablet I), where the entry lú.gub.ba = *mah-hu-ú* "ecstatic prophet" (line 213) occurs between *kalû* "lamentation singer," *munambû* "lamentor," *lallaru* "wailer" (lines 209-212) and *zabbu* "frenzied," *kurgarrû* "self-castrate," *assinnu* "man-woman" and *nāš pilaqqi* "spindle carrier" (see n. 138 above). In Tablet IV of the same series, *mahhû* "ecstatic" and *zabbu* "frenzied" constitute a single semantic section (MSL 12 132:116-23) separated by rulings from other sections; both words are given the same Sumerian equivalents (lú.ní.su.ub, lú.gub.ba, lú.al.è.dè) and grouped together with the word lú.zag.gír.lá denoting a devotee of Ištar equipped with a sword and participating in self-castration scenes. In the OB version of the same series (MSL 12 158:23ff), both words are in addition associated with the word *naqmu/naqimtu* describing a bodily defect. Note also the Ištar ritual referring to the distribution of loaves to a "frenzied man" and "frenzied (woman" (*zabbu zabbatu*) beside a "prophet and prophetess" (*mahhû u mahhūtu*), Farber *Ištar*, p. 140:31. For the omen texts, see above, n. 222. See also A. Malamat, *Mari and the Early Israelite Experience* (1989), p. 85 n. 58.

233 See CT 53 17 (+) 107:8-10 // CT 53 938:8-10; SAA 10 294 = ABL 1285:31-33; Borger Esarh. p. 2:12ff and p. 45 ii 6f; Thompson Esarh. pl. 14 ii 9ff; Streck Asb p. 120 v 93ff.

234 For a previous analysis of this passage see Oppenheim Dreams p. 200f. Compare the following autobiographical confession of R. Hayyim Vital cited in Idel *Kabbalah*, p. 81:

"In 1566, on the Sabbath eve, on the 8th of Tevet, I said Kiddush and sat down to eat; and my eyes were shedding tears, and I was sighing and grieving ... and I likewise wept for [my] neglect of the study of Torah... and because of my worry I did not eat at all, and I lay on my bed on my face, weeping, and I fell asleep out of much weeping, and I dreamt a wondrous dream."

Vital then had a highly elaborate revelation reported as a vision rather than as a dream. He saw a beautiful woman whom he thought to be his mother, and who asked him: "'Why are you weeping, Hayyim, my son? I have heard your tears and I have come to help you.' ... and I called to the woman: 'Mother, Mother, help me, so that I may see the Lord sitting upon a throne, the Ancient of Days, his beard white as snow, infinitely splendid.'" See also nn. 150 and 162 above.

235 Note especially the letter ABL 1249, where a priest of Ištar of Arbela (Aššur-hamatua) conveys to the king a message from Bel. As in the Assurbanipal passage just quoted, this message was not delivered orally but received in a dream or vision, and is hence (despite its affinities with oral prophecies) not included in the present corpus. Cf. Jer. 23:25ff: "I [YHWH] have heard what the prophets say, the prophets who speak lies in my name and cry, 'I have had a dream, a dream!' How long will it be till they change their tune, these prophets who prophesy lies and give voice to their own inventions? By these dreams which they tell one another these men think they will make my people forget my name, as their fathers forgot my name for the name/by their worship of Baal. If a prophet has a dream, let him tell his dream; if he has my word, let him speak my word in truth."

236 See e.g. n. 243 below. For biblical prophecy see just above and cf. e.g. the vision of Ezekiel by the river Kebar (Ezek. 1). The distinction between "prophets" and "seers" (*ḥōzē*) also applies to ancient Israel, see Am. 7:10-17 and Weippert, AOAT 220 (1988) 309.

237 See Weippert, ARINH (1981), p. 74f, OBO 64 (1985), p. 55, AOAT 220 (1988) 303, and most recently and most explicitly Nissinen, AOAT 232 (1991) 228.

238 The extant authorship notes show that the majority of the oracles are by prophets of Ištar of Arbela; oracles 1.5 and 2.1 were delivered by prophets from Assur, and 2.4 is by a prophet from Calah. Though none of the extant oracles can be attributed to a prophet from Nineveh, the importance of the cult of Ištar of Nineveh (Mullissu) implies that this is purely coincidental. Cf. n. 174 above, and the note on oracle 3.5 iii 20, below, p. 26.

239 See oracle 1.7 and the discussion below, p. L.

240 See oracles 1.8, 1.9, 1.10, 2.3, 3.5 and 5, and note also CT 53 969 (above, n. 214) and Thompson Esarh. pl. 14 ii 9-16 (Asb): "The Lady of Kidmuri, who in her anger had abandonded her cella and taken up residence in a place unworthy of her, became relented during my good reign which Aššur had presented and, through dreams and prophetic oracles (*ina* MÁŠ.MI *šipir mahhê*), constantly sent me (orders) to provide for her august godhead and glorify her precious rites."

241 See nn. 222f, 232 and 244.

242 See SAA 3 34:28 // 35:31 (n. 225 above), referring to the New Year's ritual of Babylon. Note also the role played by male and female prophets (*mahhû* and *mahhūtu*) in the Tammuz ritual Farber Ištar p. 140:31.

243 SAA 10 294 = ABL 1285:31f, "[I turned to] a prophet (*raggimu*) but did not find [any hop]e, he was adverse and did not see much (*diglu untaṭṭi*, lit. 'lacked/reduced vision')"; see my article "The Forlorn Scholar" in Festschrift Reiner (1987), pp. 257-78. This passage shows that Assyrian prophecy was not limited to royal prophecy only but that prophets could also be consulted, both on matters of state and on private matters, to prognosticate the future, as in ancient Greece and Israel. The same is implied by lexical passages such as MSL 12 238 (Kuyunjik Professions List), where the word *mahhû* "ecstatic prophet" (LÚ.GUB.BA, Col. ii 7) is associated with *bārû* "diviner/haruspex," *āšipu* "exorcist," and *šāʾilu* "dream interpreter" (ibid. ii 8-12). The reference to a prophet (*raggimu*) lodging with military personnel in SAA 7 9 = ADD 860 r. i 23 further suggests that prophets, like haruspices (see SAA 4 p. XXXf), may have accompanied the army on military campaigns, to predict the outcome of impending battles. Note the passage Streck Asb p. 48 v 95-104: "When the troops saw the river Idide in its violent flood, they were scared to cross it. But the Goddess who dwells in Arbela let my troops have a dream in the night and spoke to them as follows: 'I will go before Assurbanipal, the king whom my hands created!' My troops relied upon this dream and crossed safely the river Idide."

Cf. H.H. Rowley, *Prophecy and Religion in Ancient China and Israel* (1956), p. 9: "There is ... a good deal of evidence that Old Testament prophets were consulted, both on matters of state and on private matters, in the effort to discover the future, or to give wise guidance for the present. Saul went to Ramah to consult Samuel about his father's lost asses [1 Sam. 9:6] ... Hezekiah sent for Isaiah in a time of crisis to know what he should do [2 Kgs. 19:2]." Note further 1 Kgs. 22:6 (Ahab sends for a host of prophets to forecast the issue of the projected war with Damascus); 1 Kgs. 14:1ff (Jeroboam sends his wife to the prophet Ahijah, "the man who said I was to be king over this people," to find out what will happen to his son Abijah who had fallen ill); 2 Kgs. 22:12ff (Hilkiah etc. sent to Huldah the prophetess to consult her on the book of law, "to seek guidance of the LORD"); and Jer. 21:1ff (Zedekiah sends Passhur etc. to Jeremiah with this request: "Nebuchadnezzar ... is making war on us; inquire of the LORD on our behalf. Perhaps the LORD will perform a miracle as he has done in the past times, so that Nebuchadnezzar will raise the siege").

244 "10 homers 4 seahs 5 litres (of barley received by) Aššur-aha-iddina on the 2nd day for the food rations of the prophets, prophetesses and *assinnus* of the Ištar temple" (*a-na* ŠUG-*at mah-hu-e mah-hu-a-te ù* LÚ.SAL.MEŠ *ša* É dU.DAR), VS 19 1 i 37f, see H. Freydank, "Zwei Verpflegungstexte aus Kar-Tukulti-Ninurta," AoF 1 (1974) 55-89. See also p. L on Ilussa-amur (the deliverer of oracle 1.5) as recipient of food rations from a temple in Assur.

245 Cf. n. 220 above.

246 See notes on oracles 1.1:6f, 2.3 ii 19, and 9:8-15. For no. 1.1:6f cf. S. A. Picchioni, *Il poemetto di Adapa* (Assyriologia 6, Budapest 1981), p. 118:43, *Adapa ša šūti kappaša išbir* "Adapa broke the wing of the south wind" (also ibid. 60 and r.5, 7 and 11); W. G. Lambert, "Inscribed Pazuzu heads from Babylon," FUB 12 (1970) 47:2f, IM.ME *lemnu ša* ZI-*šú nanduru* "the evil wind, whose attack is fearsome..." and ibid. 42:4 // STT 149 r.6f, *ēdiššīja a-ra-a-šu-nu/i-zi-ri-šú-nu ušabbir* "By myself I have broken their (the evil winds') wings." Note that a similar allusion to the Adapa myth is also found in Mari prophecy, see ARM 26 no. 200:7ff, and cf. Durand, ibid. p. 406. For "south wind" as a metonym for the cosmic witch (i.e., the powers of darkness in general) see T. Abusch, "Ascent to the Stars in a Mesopotamian Ritual," in J. J. Collins and M. Fishbane (eds.), *Death, Ecstasy, and Other Worldly Journeys* (SUNY 1995), p. 36 n. 10.

247 See notes on oracles 1.10:5, 2.2 i 16f, 2.3 ii 17f, 3.1 i 4ff, 18, 23, 28, iii 2f, and 9:3, 5.

248 See nn. 132 and 175f above. Oracle 1.6 iii 23-27 has a close parallel in the esoteric commentary SAA 3 39:31f: "The middle heaven of *saggilmut* stone is of the Igigi gods. Bel sits there in a high temple on a dais of lapis lazuli and has made a lamp of amber shine there" (*ina parakki uqnî ūšib* GIŠ.*bu-ṣi-(in)* NA_4.*elmeši ina libbi unammir*). Note that while the deity enthroned in the middle heaven is here identified as Bel, in the oracle it is Ištar of Arbela, see nn. 8, 10 and 47 above. The three-layered scheme of heavens and the location of the throne of god (Ištar/Bel) in the middle heaven corresponds to the three-layered structure of the Assyrian tree of life and the position of Ištar in its centre (see fig. 14), as well as to the three-graded structure of the soul (n. 133 above); it is also attested in early Jewish mysticism, see Gruenwald *Apocalyptic*, pp. 34f, 43f, 48 and 91 n. 54 (1 Enoch xiv and lxxi; 2 Cor. 12:2; Testament of Levi iii). The seven-layered scheme of heavens, which is predominant in later Jewish mysticism (cf. Gruenwald, ibid. p. 48), does not represent a later development but is an alternative scheme already attested in second- and first-millennium BC Mesopotamian texts; see Chap. IX in Horowitz *Cosmic Geography*, and nn. 116f above.

249 See just above on oracle 1.6:23ff, and note that the material of the middle heaven (blue *saggilmut* stone) corresponds to that of the firmament underneath God's throne ("sapphire") in Ex. 24:10 and Ezek. 1:26 and 10:1; see Horowitz *Cosmic Geography*, Chap. I, and Gruenwald *Apocalyptic*, p. 35 n. 21.

"The lamp of *elmešu*" of oracle 1.6:23 corresponds to the "lamp of God" of Job 29:2, to the "likeness of *ḥašmal*" of Ezek. 1:4 and 27, and to the fire burning before God in Jewish apocalyptic visions (cf. Gruenwald *Apocalyptic*, pp. 31ff). Note the prominent association of *ḥašmal* with lightning striking from heaven in the Babylonian Talmud (*Hagigah* 13a), to be compared with cuneiform passages such as TCL 15 24 vi 8, "I (Enlil) flash over the country like *elmešu*." The enigmatic *elmešu/ḥašmal* (Septuagint: *elektron*) has now been established as a loanword from Baltic **helmes* "amber," see M. Heltzer, "On the Origin of the Near Eastern Archaeological Amber (Akkadian *elmešu*; Hebrew *ḥašmal*)," Michmanim 11 (Haifa 1997) 29-38.

The notion of God watching (*harādu*) the king from heaven in oracles 1.4 and 1.6 can be compared with the vision of "a Watcher, a Holy One coming down from heaven" to fell the cosmic tree symbolizing the haughty king in Dan. 4:13 and 23 (cf. 4:17). Note that the Aram. verb *'wr* "to wake, watch" (Payne Smith, p. 407), from which the word "Watcher" (*'yr*) of Dan. 4 is derived, is an exact semantic equivalent of NA *harādu* "to wake, watch," and that in kabbalistic tradition, the sefirah of Tiferet (= Ištar, see nn. 47, 114, 121 and 134 above) is called "the Watcher" and associated with the Watchman of Dan. 4 (see Z. Halevi, *The Way of Kabbalah* [Bath 1991], p. 53, and idem, *The Tree of Life* [2nd ed., Bath 1991], p. 40; cf. Idel *Kabbalah*, p. 177, citing R. Meir ibn Gabbay: "When the supernal luminary watches men and sees their good and proper deeds, [then] in accordance with what they stir below, they stir above"). For Ištar as the "Holy One" see above, n. 91, and cf. n. 69.

250 See above, nn. 110, 119, 132, 140 and 244, and note the esoteric dimension of OT prophecy discussed above, n. 55f.

251 See SAA 10 284 = ABL 58 r.1-9; LAS 317 = ABL 149; SAA 10 352 = ABL 437:23-r.3; SAA 10 109 = ABL 1216:9; ABL 1217 r.2-5; ABL 1249; CT 53 969 r.4-17 (n. 214 above); Streck Asb p. 24 iii 4-10 (below, n. 259), 48 v 95-104 and 120 v 93-96 (n. 243); Thompson Esarh. pl. 14 ii 9-16 (n. 240). On the central role of the king in pre-exilic Israelite prophecy see Weippert, ARINH (1981), p. 104ff and Nissinen, AOAT 232 (1993) 230ff. Note also 2 Sam. 24:11ff, "Meanwhile the command of the LORD had come to the prophet Gad, David's seer, to go and speak to David: 'This is the word of the LORD: I have three things in store for you; choose one and I will bring it upon you.' So Gad came to David and repeated this to him."

252 See Nissinen, "Falsche Prophetie in neuassyrischer und deuteronomistischer Darstellung," T. Veijola (ed.), *Das Deuteronomium und seine Querbeziehungen* (Schriften der Finnischen Exegetischen Gesellschaft 62, Helsinki/Göttingen 1996), 172-195, esp. 178ff.

253 Cf. oracles 1.4:38 and 9:8-25, and see nn. 7, 10, 119, 140 and 257.

254 Note that the Mari oracles "are often critical of the king for failing in his duties to various gods and temples. Once the king is even reminded of his duties to promote justice" (H. Huffmon, "The Origins of Prophecy" [n. 226 above], p. 173f, with reference to A. 1121 + A. 2731 [now B. Lafont, "Le roi de Mari et les prophètes du dieu Adad," RA 78 (1984) 7-18] r.49ff: "Am I not Adad, the lord of Aleppo, who raised you in my armpit and returned you to the throne of your father's house? I have never asked you for anything. When a woman or a man who has suffered injustice appeals to you, answer their plea and do them justice"). Note also ARMT 13 113 (enemy invasion seen in a vision attributed to religious indifference of Kibri-Dagan, governor of Terqa), and cf. A. Malamat, "Prophetic Revelations in New Documents from Mari and the Bible," SVT 15 (1966) 207-227.

255 See oracle 1.4:27f.

256 See oracle 2.3:17-19 and the discussion of the prophet name La-dagil-ili, p. Lf. Cf. Isa. 8:5ff: "Once again the LORD said to me: Because this nation has rejected the waters of Shiloah, (...) therefore the Lord will bring up against it the king of Assyria; ... and he warned me not to follow the ways of this people." Cf. also Jer. 5:21 "Listen, you foolish and senseless people, who have eyes and see nothing, ears and hear nothing," and see above, nn. 49, 107, 135 and 139.

257 Compare the missionary activity and outspokenly "prophetic" appearance (long hair, shabby clothes, etc.) of the gnostic "itinerant apostles" (Rudolph *Gnosis*, p. 217), and see n. 213 above. Note in addition the Chaldean Oracles (nn. 130 and 134f above) and the gnostic document Thunder (above, p. XXXIIIf with n. 130), both of which proclaim, in the voice of the Goddess, salvation from the bonds of the material world.

258 See Durand, ARM 26 (1988) 386 and 396; Rudolph *Gnosis*, p. 212ff; Ex. 15:20f, 2 Kgs. 22:14, Neh. 6:14, Isa. 8:3, etc.

259 See ABL 149 = LAS 317:7ff, a letter to Esarhaddon reporting on a prophetess (*ra-gi-in-tu*) named Mullissu-abi-uṣri ("Mullissu, protect my father!"; see n. 214 above), and SAA 7 9 = ADD 860 r. i 23, an administrative text listing a prophet (LÚ.*rag-gi-mu*) named Quqî in military company (cf. n. 243 above).

260 See p. On this letter and its dating see Parpola, LAS II p. 50 and CRRAI 26 (1980) 179.

261 Note also *dunnaša lulli/luštašni* "let me extol her (Ištar's) power," VS 10 214 i 4 and 8 (see B. Groneberg, RA 75 [1981] 107-134).

262 See Iraq 15 56 ND 2316:1-6 and Iraq 16 pl.7 ND 2309:3-9 for two votaresses of Mullissu, acquired and dedicated to the Goddess by officials of the royal harem, and IM 76882 = TIM 11 14:25 for a married and divorced votaress of Ištar of Arbela; see also LAS 158 = SAA 10 194 r.8ff and the discussion in LAS II p. 138.

263 ADD 63 r.10, 105 r.2, 111 r.5 and CTN 3 9:2; note also the name *Lā-teggi-ana-Nanāya*, "Do not neglect Nanaya!," ADD 173:2.

264 Note that the prophet/diviner Bileam is referred to in the Deir Alla inscription as "man who sees the gods" (*ʾš ḥ[z]h ʾlhn*) and see above on the interrelationship of prophecy and visionary experiences (*diglu*).

265 The name La-dagil-ili was also borne by individuals who were not prophets: an oil-presser with this name is known from ADD 775:5, and one La-dagil-ili with no indication of profession occurs as a witness in several legal documents from Calah spanning the period 666-662 BC (see ND 2334:9, ND 3420 r.5, ND 3422 r.22, ND 3423 r. 24, ND 3430 r.14, ND 3435 r.18, ND 3444 r.12, ND 3449 r.14, ND 3451 r.9, ND 3461 r.10, ND 3462 r.10, ND 3463 r.31, and ND 3464 r.18). Since both of these individuals appear to have lived a generation after the prophet, it is not excluded that they were named after him.

266 See p. LXIIIf and the commentary p. 27; note further the cultic demands in 3.5 (otherwise paralleled only by 1.10 and 2.3), the phrase *atta ana aiāši* in 3 iii 25 (which recurs only in 2.3:21), and the rhetorical question in 3 iii 20-24, which has a close (albeit differently phrased) parallel in 1.10:3-9.

267 For other attestations of the Nabû-hussanni, see ADD 238 r.5, 239:17, ADD 491 r.9 (all texts from Nineveh). The name Aššur-hussanni is attested only in texts from Assur.

268 See p. XVIII with nn. 7 and 196f and the commentary on 1.4 below, p. 6). Incidentally, not only the words of the criminal but the last words of Christ as well have striking parallels in Assyrian sources, again in contexts involving Nabû, the equivalent of the archangel Michael. For Mt. 27:46 and Mk. 15:34, "My God, why hast thou forsaken me?" cf. SAA 3 12 r.10f, "I have reached the gate of death; Nabû, why have you forsaken me? Do not abandon me, my lord"; for Lk. 23:46, "Father, into thy hands I commit my spirit" cf. SAA 3 13:20f, "Please, Nabû, do not abandon me; my life is written before you, my soul is deposited in the lap of Mullissu." Regarding the latter passage see also nn. 10 and 106 above.

269 Cf. dEREŠ.KI.GAL = d*al-la-tum*, CT 25 4:24 and 8:8; d*al-la-tum* dU.GUR / PAB *ina* É d*al-la-tum* Menzel Tempel 2 T 149:49f).

270 See p. XXIV and nn. 49, 88 and 114 above; note also Lambert-Millard Atra-hasis, pp. 94 iii 32ff ("the Goddess saw it as she wept..."), 96 iv 4ff ("Nintu was wailing [*unabba*]"), and 100 vi 2-4 ("Let [these] flies be the lapis around my neck / that I may remember it [every] day [and for ever]"), and see A. Draffkorn Kilmer, "The Symbolism of Flies in the Mesopotamian Flood Myth and Some Further Implications," Festschrift Reiner (1987), pp. 175-180. The agony of the Goddess (because of the fate of her sinful creatures) is to be compared with the suffering of the Shekhinah for the sins of mankind in Kabbalah, cf. n. 144 above. For the lapis lazuli flies as a means of self-laceration and mortification (in sympathy for the Goddess), see my remarks in LAS II (1983) p. 315f.

271 E.g., ADD 76:4; 110:3, r.2, 4; 742:6 and 18; 743 r.5; AO 2221:5, 9, 13; PSBA 30 111:14, 112:13.

272 The only exception is the name Sinqi-Aššur (AO 2221 r.14) where Aššur replaces Ištar. See above, pp. XX and XXVI, on the *homoousia* of Aššur and Ištar, and n. 13 on the interchange of Aššur, Ištar and Ilu "God" in personal names.

273 Cf. oracle 1.2:31f (slaughtering the king's enemies) with 2.5:21f; 1.2:35 (rearing the king) with 2.5:27; and 1.2:6f (defeating the king's enemies) with 2.5:32.

274 In SAA 3 14, Tašmetu, the bride of Nabû, plays a role similar to that of the bride (= God in His beauty) of the Song of Songs. Her yearning for Nabû (= the mystic struggling to conquer sin) reminds one of the Jewish parable of the daughter of the King (= God), who, locked high up in the palace, gazes out of a window, yearning to unite with her lover (= the mystic) down on the street. That this parable was current already in Assyrian times is suggested by the "Lady in the Window" motif of the Ancient Near Eastern art (for illustration see, e.g., SAA 3 fig. 11), whose distribution was identical with that of the "calf-suckling cow" (see p. XXXVIII above).

275 E.g., "Urkittu is my god," ADD 232:7; "Urkittu is my wall," ADD 779:2; "Urkittu is able," ADD 619:9; "My heart is with Urkittu," ND 5550:5.

276 See LAS II (1983) p. 65 no. 60:7; L. Kataja, SAAB 1 (1987) 65; and K. Radner, "The Relation Between Format and Content of Neo-Assyrian Texts," in R. Mattila (ed.), *Nineveh 612 BC. The Glory and Fall of the Assyrian Empire* (Helsinki 1995), pp. 70 and 72ff.

277 For treaties, census lists, balanced accounts, and inventories of treasury see the diagrams in SAA 2, p. XLIVf, ZA 64 (1975) 102f, SAAB 6 (1990) 19ff, JNES 42 (1983) 3 (books), as well as the photographs in SAA 7, pls. IIIf. For collections of royal decrees and ordinances, see SAA 12 77 and PKTA 39-40; for collections of recipes, see Oppenheim Glass p. 23 and figs. 1-10, etc.

278 Cf. Veenhof, CRRAI 30 (1986) 7, and Van De Mieroop, ibid. p. 94.

279 Cf. Jer. 36:2ff: "In the fourth year of Jehoiakim ... this word came to Jeremiah from the LORD: 'Take a scroll and write on it every word that I have spoken to you about Jerusalem and Judah and on the nations, from the day that I first spoke to you in the reign of Josiah down to the present day. Perhaps the house of Judah will be warned of the calamity that I am planning to bring to them...' So Jeremiah called Baruch son of Neriah, and he wrote on the scroll at Jeremiah's dictation all the words which the LORD had spoken to him. He gave Baruch this instruction: 'I am prevented from going to the LORD's house. You must go there in my place on a fast-day and read the words of the

LORD in the hearing of the people from the scroll you have written at my dictation.'" On this passage and a similar one from Mari see A. Malamat, "New Light from Mari (ARM XXVI) on Biblical Prophecy III: A Prophet's Need of a Scribe," in D. Garrone and F. Israel (eds.), *Storia e tradizioni di Israele: scritti in onore di J. Alberto Soggin* (Brescia 1991), pp. 185-8.

280 In no. 1, the determinative pronoun is written 29 times with the sign *ša*, 7 times with the sign *šá*. In nos. 2 and 3, *ša* is used 9 times each vs. 5 times each for *šá*; no data are available from no. 4. In sum, the scribe used both signs for writing the pronoun but preferred the sign *ša*, which appears in all authorship notes of these tablets except 2.3. No. 9 likewise uses *ša* in the authorship note and both *ša* and *šá* in the oracle itself. By contrast, the scribes of tablets 5, 6 and 8 used *ša* only for writing the pronoun, those of nos. 7 and 11 *šá* only. In no. 10, both *ša* and *šá* are used, but the latter is more frequent (2 attestations against one of *ša*).

In nos. 1-4, the sign *te* occurs 17 times in final position (including forms with pronominal and enclitic suffixes like *am-ma-te-ia*), vs. 40 spellings with *-ti*. Note that virtually all the spellings with *-te* occur on the obverse of no. 1 (= oracles 1.1-6:14 examples), which indicates that the scribe initially followed the orthography of the reports he was copying but later lapsed to his own conventions (i.e., the almost exclusive use of the sign *ti* in final position; cf. n. 281). In no. 7, there are 3 cases of final *-te* vs. 8 cases of *-ti*; in no. 8, one example of *-te* and *-ti* each; and in no. 9, 3 spellings with *-te* with no examples of *-ti*.

281 Note, e.g., the syllabic spelling *ra-bi-tu* in oracle 1.6 as against GAL-*tu/tú* in 1.1 and 1.3. The sign forms in nos. 1-4 are on the whole uniform, indicating a single scribal hand. However, oracle 1.6 surprisingly contains some sign variants deviating from the norm (see Table 1, p. LVII). This seems to indicate that the scribe, arriving at the middle of the tablet, had for a moment slipped to mechanically reproducing the sign forms of the original. See also n. 280 above.

282 Cf. no. 5:1 with Mal. 1:1 and no. 8:1f with Ob. 1:1.

283 The last line of no. 5 is unclear, but it is unlikely to be a scribal addition.

284 Cf., e.g., CA pl. 3:1-4, "[The n]ew [rites] which [Ass]urbanipal, king of Assyria, [*perfor*]*m*ed from the 16th [of Shebat] through the 10th of Adar, eponymy of Bel-Harran-šadûʾa"; SAA 7 48 = ADD 1075:1-2, "Silver [...] of the queen [mother ...]"; SAA 7 57 = ADD 928:1, "[...] of silver"; SAA 7 60 = ADD 930:1-4, "[These are] the objects [of the god]s of Akkad, [which we]nt [to] Elam"; SAA 7 71 = ADD 687:1, "Silver, collection"; SAA 7 167 = ADD 968:1, "Consignment of [...]"; SAA 11 36 = ADD 1036:1, "[Distribution of t]ribute"; SAA 11 90 = ADD 754:1-2, "Distribution of levy of oxen and sheep."

285 All the headings listed in n. 284 except SAA 11 90 = ADD 754 are followed by rulings. The introductory lines of the reports (nos. 5-8, see just above) are not followed by rulings and thus should not be understood as headings.

286 Thus W. G. Lambert, AfO 17 (1954-56) 320:8 and JCS 16 (1962) 72ff. Note that the authorship indication *ša pî* in the "Catalogue of Texts and Authors" (JCS 16 59-77) basically refers to divinely inspired compositions received in visionary experiences, see SAA 10 p. XVIIf with nn. 18f and 34. For *ša pî* as a term for (authoritative) oral lore see Y. Elman, JANES 7 (1975) 21ff. The proper expression for "according to" was *ana pî* or *kī(ma) pî*, see Hunger Kolophone p. 6, though it should be noted that *ana pî* also had the literal meaning "according to dictation" (Elman, loc. cit., p. 22).

287 Cf., e.g., the last column of 82-5-22,533 = SAA 7 51 (photograph JNES 42 [1983] 20), which contains only a two-line date in the middle of the column; similarly SAA 7, nos. 1, 3 and 5 (note also nos. 159-161, photographs ibid. pl. IX).

288 See also the analysis and discussion in Weippert, "Assyrische Prophetien," ARINH (1981), p. 76ff and tables 3-4.

289 An exception is oracle 2.4, where the phrase follows an introductory rhetorical question and occurs in the middle of the prophecy as well.

290 Jer. 1:2.4.11, 2:1, Hos. 1:1, Joel 1:1, Jon. 1:1, 3:1, Mic. 1:1, Zeph. 1:1, Zech. 1:1.7, 4:6, 6:9, 7:1.8, 8:1, 9:1, 12:1, Mal. 1:1; cf. Isa. 2:1 (*dbr* alone). Note that *dbr yhwh* likewise mostly introduces the oracle and is combined with an address e.g. in Zech. 4:6, "This is the word of the LORD concerning Zerubbabel" (*zh dbr-yhwh ʻl-zrbbl*), and Mal. 1:1, "An oracle. The word of the LORD to Israel through Malachi" (*mśʾ / dbr-yhwh ʻl yšrʾl byd* PN).

291 For further examples see Nissinen, AOAT 232 (1993) 247f.

292 Such a reference is missing only in oracle 3.2, addressed to the Assyrians collectively, which instead begins with a reference to the victories of the king.

293 The only possible exception is *lurr*[*ik*] "I will length[en ...]" in no. 10 r.7 (context fragmentary).

294 See n. 214 above.

295 See W. von Soden, "Aramäische Wörter in neuassyrischen und neu- und spätbabylonischen Texten. Ein Vorbericht. I-III," Or. 35 (1966) 1-20; 37 (1968) 261-71; 46 (1968) 183-197, and note that Aramaic loanwords constitute an integral part of standard Neo-Assyrian vocabulary and are evenly distributed in all types of Neo-Assyrian texts, from treaties to literary and ritual texts.

296 See M. Weippert, "Die Bildsprache der neuassyrischen Prophetie," in H. Weippert et al., *Beiträge zur prophetischen Bildsprache in Israel und Assyrien* (OBO 64, Göttingen 1985), pp. 55-91. Note, however, that contra Weippert (p. 87), the figurative language of the prophecies does not derive from "privatem Lebensbereich zu Hause" or from "Alltag von Menschen, denen ihr gesellschaftlicher Status die Musse zu kontemplativer Naturbetrachtung lässt" but from the traditional imagery of Mesopotamian (and ancient Near Eastern) religion and royal ideology. See pp. XXII, XLVIIf and n. 165 above, and notes on oracles 1.1 i 6.7.9.25ff, 2.2 i 16f, 2.3 ii 6f.9, etc. For the Ship of State metaphor of 2.2 i 16f see also JNES 33 (1974) 278:91 ("like a ship I do not know at which quay I put in"); Cicero, In Pisonem, 9:20 (*navem gubernare et salvam in portu collicare*); Horace, Odes 1.14; and Plato's Republic, where the Ship of State is a leading metaphor (the philosophers being the "true pilots" who lead the ship of state). Note the resurfacing of the metaphor in eighth-century Syria, now applied to the church: "I see the Church which God founded ... tossed on an angry Sea, beaten by rushing waves" (St. John of Damascus, *On the Divine Images* [transl. D. Anderson, Crestwood, NY, 1980], p. 13).

297 For examples see no. 1.6 iv 22-25, 1.7:8f, 2.3:12, 3.5 iii 28f (alliteration); 1.3:11f, 1.4:22/25, 1.6:15f, 1.7:8f, 1.8:22f, 1.10:22-26, 2.4:30, 2.5:33f, 3.1:9-12, 3.2:28-30 and 31-33, 5 3rf, 6:2f, 7:3-6 and r.9f (anaphora); 1.1:22f, 25f and 27, 1.2:3-5, 1.4:24, 27ff and 37, 1.6 iii 31f, iv 1-2 and 29-32, 2.2:17f and 21, 2.3:12 and 17f, 2.4:35f, 2.5:26, 3.2:31f, 7:4f and r.5 (antithesis); 1.1:11f, 1.6 iv 22-25, 3.2:31ff, 3.5:27 (chiasm); 1.4:24-26, 1.6 iv 29-35, 2.2:18-20, 3.2 ii 1-3, 3.3:20ff (climax); 1.4:28f, 1.6 iii 15-18 and iv 29-33, 2.2:18f, 2.4:30, 2.5:21f, 3.2:28-30, 3.3:22f, 3.5 iii

28f and 30f, 7 r.6 (parallelismus membrorum); 1.6 iii 9-11 and 19-22, iv 15f, 1.7:3f, 1.8:22f, 1.10:27, 2.3:4, 2.4:31f, 2.5:33f (parataxis); 1.6 iv 22f and 30, 2.2:19, 5:2, 7 r.1 (paronomasy).

298 E.g. *šarratu Mullissu* 2.4, *kippat erbetti* 3.2, *ṣēru rapādu* 1.8. See also no. 9 (passim).

299 See p. LV.

300 Oracle 3.2 is addressed to Assyrians collectively without mentioning the king by name. However, this oracle unquestionably belongs together with the other oracles of the collection, and the king is certainly identifiable as Esarhaddon from the contents of the oracle.

301 On Sennacherib's murder and the date of Esarhaddon's exile see S. Parpola, "The Murderer of Sennacherib," CRRAI 26 (1980) 171-82, and SAA 6 (1991), p. XXXIV.

302 See SAA 10 109 = ABL 1216:9 and Appendix, p. LXXIIIf.

303 Cf. already M. Jastrow, *Die Religion Babyloniens und Assyriens* II (Giessen 1912), p. 158: "Die Orakel [stammen] zwar aus den ersten Jahren der Asarhaddonischen Regierung, aber die Sammlung [wurde] wohl erst gegen Schluss seiner Herrschaft oder gar nach seinem Tode veranstaltet."

304 See H. Tadmor, "Autobiographical Apology in the Royal Assyrian Literature," in H. Tadmor and M. Weinfeld (eds.), *History, Historiography and Interpretation* (Jerusalem 1984), pp. 36-57, esp. p. 45.

305 For the Julian date see LAS II, Appendix A.

306 See J. A. Brinkman, *Prelude to Empire: Babylonian Society and Politics, 747-626 B.C.* (Philadelphia 1984), p. 96f, and G. Frame, *Babylonia 689-627 B.C. A Political History* (Leiden 1992), p. 146.

Bibliography of Previous Studies

Pre-WW I period (1875-1916)

1875 G. Smith, "Addresses of Encouragement to Esarhaddon," in H. C. Rawlinson (ed.), *The Cuneiform Inscriptions of Western Asia* IV (London), no. 68 [copy of no. 1; see ibid. p. 4].

1878 T. G. Pinches in A. H. Sayce (ed.), *Records of the Past* XI (London), 59 [translat. of no. 1].

1882 J. Halévy, *Documents réligieux de l'Assyrie et de la Babylonie* I (Paris), pp. 197-200 [translit. of no. 1 into Hebrew characters].

1888 A. Delattre, "The Oracles Given in Favour of Esarhaddon," *The Babylonian and Oriental Record* III (London), 25ff [edition of no. 1; uses the word "prophet"].

1891 T. G. Pinches, "The Oracle of Istar of Arbela, addressed to Esarhaddon," in H. C. Rawlinson (ed.), *The Cuneiform Inscriptions of Western Asia* IV (2nd ed., London), no. 61 [revised copy of no. 1; see ibid. p. x].

1891 T. G. Pinches in A.H. Sayce (ed.), *Records of the Past, New Series* V (London), pp. 129-40 [edition of no. 1].

1893 S. A. Strong, "On Some Oracles to Esarhaddon and Ashurbanipal," BA 2, pp. 627-45 [copy and edition of no. 3, cols. ii and iii, and no. 7].

1895 J. A. Craig, *Assyrian and Babylonian Religious Texts*, Vol. I (Leipzig), pp. 22-7, with corrections in Vol. II, pp. ix-x [copy of nos. 3 and 7].

1897 V. Scheil, "Choix de textes réligieux assyriens," RHR 36 206f [translat. of nos. 3 and 7].

1898 E. J. Banks, "Eight Oracular Responses to Esarhaddon," AJSL 14 267-77 [translit., translat., and commentary of no. 1].

1902 F. Martin, *Textes réligieux assyriens et babyloniens* (BÉHÉ 130, Paris), pp. 88-97 and 100-5 [edition of nos. 3 and 7].

1904 C. D. Gray in R. F. Harper (ed.), *Assyrian and Babylonian Literature* (New York), pp. 414-9 [translat. of no. 1].

1907 O. Weber, *Die Literatur der Babylonier und Assyrer* (Leipzig), p. 181ff ["Orakel an Assarhaddon und Assurbanipal"].

1910 H. Zimmern, "Gilgameš-Omina und Gilgameš-Orakel," ZA 24 166-71 [translit., translat. and study of no. 9].

1912 M. Jastrow jr., *Die Religion Babyloniens und Assyriens* II (Giessen), pp. 158-74 ["Das Orakelwesen"; translat. of nos. 1, 3 and 7 with bibliography and commentary].

1912 L. Waterman, "Some Kouyunjik Letters and Related Texts," AJSL 29 12 [copy, translit. and translat. of no. 8].
1913 R. F. Harper, *Assyrian and Babylonian Letters* XII (Chicago and London), no. 1280 [copy of no. 8].
1914 E. Klauber, AJSL 30 253 [translit. and English translat. of no. 8].
1914 S. Langdon, *Tammuz and Ishtar* (Oxford), pls. 2-4 [copy of nos. 2 and 5] and pp. 128-45 [translation of nos. 1-3, 5 and 7].
1915 M. Streck, *Assurbanipal* I (Leipzig), pp. CLXX-CLXXV [paraphrase and discussion of nos. 7 and 9].
1916 F. Schmidtke, *Asarhaddons Statthalterschaft in Babylonien und seine Thronbesteigung in Assyrien 681 v.Chr.* (AOTU 1/2, Leiden), p. 115ff [translit., translat. and discussion of no. 1, "Die an Asarhaddon anlässlich der Thronstreitigkeiten erlangenen Orakel"].

The Years 1917-1968

1926 E. Ebeling in H. Gressmann (ed.), *Altorientalische Texte zum Alten Testament* (2nd ed., Berlin and Leipzig), pp. 281-3 [translat. of no. 1].
1927 D. D. Luckenbill, *Ancient Records of Assyria and Babylonia* II (Chicago), pp. 238-41 (§§ 617-38) [translat. of no. 1].
1930 L. Waterman, *Royal Correspondence of the Assyrian Empire* II-III (Ann Arbor), no. 1280 [translit., translat. and commentary of no. 8].
1955 R. H. Pfeiffer, "Oracles Concerning Esarhaddon," in J. B. Pritchard (ed.), *Ancient Near Eastern Texts Relating to the Old Testament* (2nd edition, Princeton), pp. 449-51 [translat. of nos. 1 and 7].
1956 J. Nougayrol, "Asarhaddon et Naqi'a sur un bronze du Louvre," Syria 33 158f [translation and discussion of no. 2 i 1-14, ii 24-8, iii 1-12].
1968 J. Nougayrol in A. Caquot and M. Leibovici (eds.), *La divination* I (Paris), pp. 67-9 [translat. and discussion of no. 1 ii 16-39].

Years 1969-present

1969 R. D. Biggs, "Akkadian Oracles and Prophecies," in J. B. Pritchard (ed.), *Ancient Near Eastern Texts Relating to the Old Testament* (3rd edition, Princeton), p. 605 [translat. of no. 1].
1970 F. Ellermeier, *Sibyllen, Musikanten, Haremsfrauen* (Herzberg), p. 8f.
1970 R. Labat in R. Labat, A. Caquot, M. Sznyzer and M. Vieyra (eds.), *Les religions du Proche-Orient asiatique: Textes babyloniens, ougaritiques, hittites* (Paris), p. 257f [translation of no. 1 i 4-29, iii 7-iv 6].
1972 K. Deller and S. Parpola, "Neuassyrische Prophetensprüche" (Heidelberg, private circulation) [translit., translat. and commentary of nos. 1-3].
1972 M. Weippert, "'Heiliger Krieg' in Israel und Assyrien," ZAW 84 473f and 481f [translit., translat. and discussion of nos. 1 i 5-25 and 3 ii 10-25].
1973 M. Dietrich, "Prophetie in den Keilschrifttexten," JARG 1 15-44.

1974 H. B. Huffmon, "Prophetic Oracles in the Ancient Near East: Reflections on their Use in Form-Critical Study of the Hebrew Bible" (SBL paper, private circulation) [translat. of nos. 1, 2, 3, 5 and 7].

1976 H. B. Huffmon, "Prophecy in the Ancient Near East," *The Interpreter's Dictionary of the Bible, Supplementary Volume* (Nashville) [nos. 2 ii 29-33 and 3 ii 10—iii 15].

1977 T. Ishida, *The Royal Dynasties in Ancient Israel: A Study on the Formation and Development of Royal-Dynastic Ideology* (Berlin and New York), pp. 90-2 and 114-6 [discussion and translat. of selected passages from nos. 1, 2 and 3].

1977 G. R. Castellino, "Testi sumerici i accadici," in O. Botta (ed.), *Collana "Classici delle religioni," 1: Le religioni orientali* (Torino), pp. 449-54 and 458f [translat. of nos. 1, 3 and 7].

1980 R. R. Wilson, *Prophecy and Society in Ancient Israel* (Philadelphia), pp. 111-9.

1980 M. Dijkstra, *Gods voorstelling: Predikatieve expressie van zelfopenbaring in oudoosterse teksten en Deutero-Jesaja* (Dissertationes Neerlandicae, Series Teologica 2, Kampen), pp. 147-70.

1981 D. J. McCarthy, *Treaty and Covenant: A Study in Form in the Ancient Oriental Documents and in the Old Testament* (Analecta Biblica 21A, Rome), p. 419f [no. 3].

1981 M. Weippert, "Assyrische Prophetien der Zeit Asarhaddons und Assurbanipals," in F. M. Fales (ed.), *Assyrian Royal Inscriptions: New Horizons* (Rome), pp. 75-115 [no. 1 i 5-30, iii 7-iv 35, v 21-3, no. 3 ii 10-32, iii 15-36].

1982 H. Tadmor, "The Aramaization of Assyria: Aspects of Western Impact," in H. Nissen and J. Renger (eds.), *Mesopotamien und seine Nachbarn* (CRRAI 25, Berlin), p. 458 [no. 1.4].

1982 H. Spieckermann, *Juda unter Assur in der Sargonidenzeit* (Forschungen zur Religion und Literatur des Alten und Neuen Testaments 129, Göttingen), pp. 295-303.

1983 M. Weippert in K. R. Veenhof (ed.), *Schrijvend Verleden. Documenten uit het oude Nabije Oosten vertaald en toegelicht* (Leiden), pp. 285f [translat. of nos. 1-3, 5 and 7].

1985 H. B. Huffmon, "Prophetic Treaty/Covenant Mediation in Assyria and Israel" (AOS paper, private circulation) [no. 3 ii 10—iii 33].

1985 M. Weippert, "Die Bildsprache der neuassyrischen Prophetie," in H. and M. Weippert (eds.), *Beiträge zur prophetischen Bildsprache in Israel und Assyrien* (OBO 64, Göttingen), pp. 55-91 [no. 1 iii 7—iv 35, etc.].

1985 A. Millard, "La prophétie et l'écriture: Israël, Aram, Assyrie," RHR 202 125-44.

1986 K. Hecker, "Assyrische Propheten," in O. Kaiser (ed.), *Texte aus der Umwelt des Alten Testaments* II/1, pp. 55-63 [translat. of nos. 1, 3 and 7].

1987 K. van der Toorn, "L'oracle de victoire comme expression prophétique au Proche-Orient ancien," RB 94 63-97.

1988 M. Weippert, "Aspekte israelitischer Prophetie im Lichte verwandter Erscheinungen des Alten Orients," AOAT 220, Neukirchen), pp. 287-319.

1989 M. deJong Ellis, "Observations on Mesopotamian Oracles and Prophetic Texts: Literary and Historiographic Considerations," JCS 41 127-86.

1989 A. Malamat, *Mari and the Early Israelite Experience* (The Schweich Lectures 1984, Oxford, repr. 1992), pp. 70-121: "Prophets, Ancestors and Kings" [see p. 79ff, nn. 43 and 47].

1991 M. Nissinen, *Prophetie, Redaktion und Fortschreibung im Hoseabuch* (AOAT 231, Neukirchen), pp. 77-88, 120 [no. 1 i 6f], 136f [nos. 2.4 and 3.2-5], 146f [no. 3.3], 181f [no. 3.4], 280-304 [nos. 1.4, 1.6, 1.8-10, 2.5, 7, 9].

1992 H. B. Huffmon, "Prophecy: Ancient Near Eastern Prophecy," *Anchor Bible Dictionary* 5, pp. 477-82.

1993 M. Nissinen, "Die Relevanz der neuassyrischen Prophetie für das Studium des Alten Testaments," AOAT 232 (Neukirchen), pp. 217-58.

1993 M.-C. Perroudon, "An Angry Goddess," SAAB 6 41-4 [no. 3 iii 31-34].

1993 A. Ivantchik, "Corrigenda aux textes akkadiens mentionnant les Cimmériens. 2. Oracle de la déesse Mullissu à Assourbanipal," N.A.B.U. 1993/2 40f [translit. and translat. of no. 7].

1996 M. Nissinen, "Falsche Prophetie in neuassyrischer und deuteronomistischer Darstellung," in T. Veijola (ed.), *Das Deuteronomium und seine Querbeziehungen* (Schriften der Finnischen Exegetischen Gesellschaft 62, Helsinki/Göttingen), 172-95.

1996 A. Laato, *History and Ideology in the Old Testament Prophetic Literature* (Coniectanea Biblica, Old Testament Series 41, Stockholm), pp. 173-88 and 271-9.

1997 F. M. Fales and G. B. Lanfranchi, "The Impact of Oracular Material on the Political Utterances and Political Action of the Sargonid Dynasty," in J.-G. Heintz (ed.), *Oracles et propheties dans l'antiquité* (Travaux du Centre de Recherche sur le Proche-Orient et la Grece Antiques 15, Paris), pp. 99-114.

Abbreviations and Symbols

Bibliographical Abbreviations

A	tablets in the collections of Istanbul Arkeoloji Müzereli
ABL	R. F. Harper, *Assyrian and Babylonian Letters* (London and Chicago 1892-1914)
ABRT	J. A. Craig, *Assyrian and Babylonian Religious Texts* (Leipzig 1895)
Ab. Zar.	Abodah Zarah
ADD	C. H. W. Johns, *Assyrian Deeds and Documents* (Cambridge 1898-1923)
AfO	Archiv für Orientforschung
AHw.	W. von Soden, *Akkadisches Handwörterbuch*
AJSL	American Journal of Semitic Languages and Literatures
AKA	L. W. King, *The Annals of the Kings of Assyria* I (London 1902)
AL	F. Delitzsch, *Assyrische Lesestücke* (3rd ed. Leipzig 1885)
Alu	omen series *Šumma ālu*
Am.	Amos
Angim	J. S. Cooper, *The Return of Ninurta to Nippur* (AnOr 52, Rome 1978)
ANET	J. B. Pritchard (ed.), *Ancient Near Eastern Texts Relating to the Old Testament* (3rd edition, Princeton 1969)
AnOr	Analecta Orientalia
AnSt	Anatolian Studies
AO	tablets in the collections of the Musée du Louvre
AOAT	Alter Orient und Altes Testament
AoF	Altorientalische Forschungen
Ap	Apocalypse of John
APN	K. Tallqvist, *Assyrian Personal Names* (Helsinki 1914)
ARI	A. K. Grayson, *Assyrian Royal Inscriptions* (Wiesbaden 1972-76)
ARINH	F. M. Fales (ed.), *Assyrian Royal Inscriptions: New Horizons in Literary, Ideological and Historical Analysis* (Orientis Antiqui Collectio XVIII, Rome 1981)
ARM	Archives royales de Mari
ARMT	Archives royales de Mari (transliterations and translations)
ASJ	Acta Sumerologica (Japan, Hiroshima)
AuOr	Aula Orientalis
BA	Beiträge zur Assyriologie
BaM	Baghdader Mitteilungen

BBR	H. Zimmern, *Beiträge zur Kenntnis der babylonischen Religion* I, II (Assyriologische Bibliothek 12, Leipzig 1896, 1901)
BBSt.	L. W. King, *Babylonian Boundary Stones* (London 1912)
BE	Babylonian Expedition of the University of Pennsylvania, Series A: Cuneiform Texts
BHLT	A. K. Grayson, *Babylonian Historical-Literary Texts* (Toronto 1975)
BiAr	Biblical Archaeologist
BiOr	Bibliotheca Orientalis
BM	tablets in the collections of the British Museum
Borger Esarh.	R. Borger, *Die Inschriften Asarhaddons, Königs von Assyrien* (AfO Beiheft 9, Graz 1956)
Brockelmann Lex. Syr.	C. Brockelmann, *Lexicon Syriacum* (Göttingen 1928; reprint Olms 1995)
BT	field numbers of tablets excavated at Balawat
Burkert *Mystery Cults*	W. Burkert, *Ancient Mystery Cults* (Harvard 1987)
BWL	W. G. Lambert, *Babylonian Wisdom Literature* (Oxford 1960)
CA	G. van Driel, *The Cult of Aššur* (Assen 1969)
CAD	The Assyrian Dictionary of the Oriental Institute of the University of Chicago
CAH	The Cambridge Ancient History
CBS	tablets in the collections of the University Museum of the University of Pennsylvania
Chron.	Chronicles
Col.	Colossians
Collins *Scepter and Star*	J. J. Collins, *The Scepter and the Star. The Messiahs of the Dead Sea Scrolls and Other Ancient Literature* (New York 1995)
Cor.	Corinthians
CRRAI	Rencontre assyriologique internationale, comptes rendus
CT	Cuneiform Texts from Babylonian Tablets in the British Museum
CTA	A. Herdner, *Corpus des tablettes en cunéiformes alphabétiques découvertes à Ras Shamra-Ugarit de 1929 à 1939* (Paris 1963)
CTN	Cuneiform Texts from Nimrud
DA	C. Boissier, *Documents assyriens relatifs aux présages* (Paris 1894-99)
Dalley *Myths*	S. Dalley, *Myths from Mesopotamia* (Oxford 1989)
Dalman Aram. Wb.	G. H. Dalman, *Aramäisch-neuhebräisches Handwörterbuch zu Targum, Talmud und Midrasch* (Göttingen 1938)
Dan.	Daniel
Desc.	Descent of Ištar (CT 15 45ff)
Deut.	Deuteronomy
Diri	lexical series diri DIR *siāku* = (*w*)*atru*
DT	tablets in the collections of the British Museum
Dumuzi's Dream	B. Alster, *Dumuzi's Dream* (Mesopotamia 1, Copenhagen 1972)
EA	J. A. Knudtzon, *Die El-Amarna-Tafeln* (VAB 2, Leipzig 1915)
En.	Enoch
En. el.	*Enūma eliš*
Enc. Jud.	Encyclopaedia Judaica (Jerusalem)

Erra	L. Cagni, *L'epopea di Erra* (Studi Semitici 34, Rome 1969)
Ex.	Exodus
Exeg. Soul	The Exegesis on the Soul (NHC II 127, 18ff)
Ezek.	Ezekiel
Farber Ištar	W. Farber, *Beschwörungsrituale an Ištar und Dumuzi* (Wiesbaden 1977)
Frankena Takultu	R. Frankena, *Tākultu. De sacrale maaltijd in het assyrische ritueel* (Leiden 1956)
Festschrift Reiner	F. Rochberg-Halton (ed.), *Language, Literature, and History: Philological and Historical Studies Presented to Erica Reiner* (American Oriental Series 67, New Haven 1987)
Festschrift Tadmor	M. Cogan and I. Eph'al, *Ah, Assyria... Studies in Assyrian History and Ancient Near Eastern Historiography Presented to Hayim Tadmor* (Jerusalem)
FUB	Forschungen und Berichte
Fuchs Sar.	A. Fuchs, *Die Inscriften Sargons II. aus Khorsabad* (Göttingen 1994)
Gal.	Galatians
Galter *Astronomie*	H. Galter (ed.), *Die Rolle der Astronomie in den Kulturen Mesopotamiens* (Graz 1993)
Gates of Light	A. Weinstein (trans.), Rabbi Joseph Gikatilla, *Gates of Light* (*Sha'are orah*) (San Francisco 1994)
Gen.	Genesis
Gilg.	S. Parpola, *The Standard Babylonian Epic of Gilgamesh* (SAACT 1, Helsinki 1997)
Gottfarstein Bahir	J. Gottfarstein (transl.), *Le Bahir* (Verdier: Lagrasse 1983)
GPA	J. N. Postgate, *The Governor's Palace Archive* (CTN 2, London 1973)
Gray *Mythology*	J. Gray, *Near Eastern Mythology* (New York 1988)
Gruenwald *Apocalyptic*	I. Gruenwald, *Apocalyptic and Merkavah Mysticism* (Leiden 1980)
Hab.	Habakkuk
Hag.	Haggai
HAL	L. Koehler and W. Baumgartner, *The Hebrew and Aramaic Lexicon of the Old Testament* (rev. ed., Leiden and New York 1994-96)
HBA	E. Weidner, *Handbuch der babylonischen Astronomie* I (Assyriologische Bibliothek 23, Leipzig 1914)
HdO	Handbuch der Orientalistik
Hg	lexical series HAR.gud = *imrû* = *ballu* (MSL 5-11)
Hh	lexical series *HAR*.ra = *hubullu* (MSL 5-11)
Horowitz *Cosmic Geography*	W. Horowitz, *Mesopotamian Cosmic Geography* (Mesopotamian Civilizations 8, Winona Lake 1997)
Hos.	Hosea
HR	History of Religions
Hruška Anzu	B. Hruška, *Der Mythenadler Anzu in Literatur und Vorstellung des alten Mesopotamien* (Assyriologia 2, Budapest 1975)
Hunger Kolophone	H. Hunger, *Babylonische und assyrische Kolophone* (AOAT 2, Neukirchen-Vluyn 1968)

Idel *Kabbalah*	M. Idel, *Kabbalah: New Perspectives* (New Haven and London 1988)
IEJ	Israel Exploration Journal
IM	tablets in the collection of the Iraq Museum
Inanna's Descent	W. R. Sladek, *Inanna's Descent to the Netherworld* (PhD diss. Baltimore, University Microfilms 1974)
Isa.	Isaiah
Jacobsen *Harps*	T. Jacobsen, *The Harps that once... Sumerian Poetry in Translation* (New Haven and London 1987)
JANES	Journal of the Ancient Near Eastern Society of Columbia University
JAOS	Journal of the American Oriental Society
JARG	Jahrbuch für Anthropologie und Religionsgeschichte
Jastrow Dict.	M. Jastrow, *A Dictionary of the Targumim, the Talmud, the Talmud Babli and Yerushalmi, and the Midrashic Literature* (New York 1943)
JBL	Journal of Biblical Literature
JCS	Journal of Cuneiform Studies
Jer.	Jeremiah
JNES	Journal of Near Eastern Studies
Johnston *Hekate*	Sarah I. Johnston, *Hekate Soteira. A Study of Hekate's Roles in the Chaldean Oracles and Related Literature* (American Classical Studies 21, Atlanta 1990)
Jon.	Jonah
Josh.	Joshua
JSOT	Journal for the Study of the Old Testament
JTS	Journal of Theological Studies
Jub.	Jubilees
K	tablets in the collections of the British Museum
KAJ	E. Ebeling, *Keilschrifttexte aus Assur juridischen Inhalts* (Leipzig 1927)
Kapelrud *Anat*	A. S. Kapelrud, *The Violent Goddess: Anat in the Ras Shamra Texts* (Oslo 1969)
KAR	E. Ebeling, *Keilschrifttexte aus Assur religiösen Inhalts* (Leipzig 1919)
KAV	O. Schroeder, *Keilschrifttexte aus Assur verschiedenen Inhalts* (Leipzig 1920)
KB	Keilinschriftliche Bibliothek
Kelly *Doctrines*	J. N. D. Kelly, *Early Christian Doctrines* (5th ed., London 1977)
Kgs.	Kings
KSt 5	M. Witzel, *Perlen sumerischer Poesie in Transcription und Uebersetzung* (Keilinschriftliche Studien 5, Fulda 1925)
KTU	M. Dietrich, O. Loretz and J. Sanmartín, *Die keilalphabetischen Texte aus Ugarit, Teil 1: Transkription* (AOAT 24, Neukirchen-Vluyn 1976)
Lambert Love Lyrics	W. G. Lambert, "The Problem of the Love Lyrics," H. Goedicke and J. Roberts (eds.), *Unity and Diversity* (Baltimore 1975) 98-135
Lambert-Millard Atra-hasis	W. G. Lambert and A.R. Millard, *Atra-hasis, the Babylonian Story of the Flood* (Oxford 1969)

LAS	S. Parpola, *Letters from Assyrian Scholars to the Kings Esarhaddon and Assurbanipal* I, II (AOAT 5/1-2, Neukirchen-Vluyn 1970, 1983)
LBAT	T. G. Pinches, A. J. Sachs and J. N. Strassmeier, *Late Babylonian Astronomical Texts* (Providence 1955)
Lk.	Luke
LSS	Leipziger Semitische Studien
LTBA	L. Matouš and W. von Soden, *Die lexikalischen Tafelserien der Babylonier und Assyrer in den Berliner Museen* I-II (Berlin 1933)
Lu	lexical series lú = *ša* (MSL 12)
Luckenbill Senn.	D. D. Luckenbill, *The Annals of Sennacherib* (Oriental Institute Publications 2, Chicago 1924)
Macc.	Maccabees
Mal.	Malachi
MDP	Mémoires de la Délégation en Perse
Menzel Tempel	B. Menzel, *Assyrische Tempel* (Studia Pohl, Series Maior 10, Rome 1981)
Meyer *Mysteries*	M. W. Meyer (ed.), *The Ancient Mysteries. Sacred Texts of the Mystery Religions of the Ancient Mediterranean World* (San Francisco 1987)
Mic.	Micah
Mk.	Mark
MSL	Materialien zum sumerischen Lexikon / Materials for the Sumerian Lexicon
Mt.	Matthew
Mul Apin	H. Hunger and D. Pingree, *MUL.APIN. An Astronomical Compendium in Cuneiform* (AfO Beiheift 24, Horn 1989)
MVAG	Mitteilungen der Vorderasiatisch-Ägyptischen Gesellschaft
NABU	Nouvelles Assyriologiques Brèves et Utilitaires
NBN	K. Tallqvist, *Neubabylonisches Namenbuch* (Helsinki 1905)
ND	field numbers of tablets excavated at Nimrud
Neh.	Nehemiah
NHC	Nag Hammadi Codex or Codices
NL	H. W. F. Saggs, "The Nimrud Letters," Iraq 17 (1955) 21ff., etc.
Num.	Numeri
Ob.	Obadiah
OBO	Orbis Biblicus et Orientalis
ODB	The Oxford Dictionary of Byzantium
OECT	Oxford Editions of Cuneiform Texts
OLZ	Orientalistische Literaturzeitung
Oppenheim Dreams	A. L. Oppenheim, *The Interpretation of Dreams in the Ancient Near East* (Transactions of the American Philosophical Society 46/3, Philadelphia 1956)
Oppenheim Glass	A. L. Oppenheim, *Glass and Glassmaking in Ancient Mesopotamia* (Corning, New York 1970)
Or.	Orientalia (Nova Series)
OTL	Old Testament Library
Payne Smith	J. Payne Smith, *A Compendious Syriac Dictionary* (Oxford 1903)
Perry Sin	G. Perry, *Hymnen und Gebete an Sin* (LSS 2/4, Leipzig 1907)

PKTA	E. Ebeling, *Parfümrezepte und kultische Texte aus Assur* (Rome 1952)
Prov.	Proverbs
Ps.	Psalms
PSBA	Proceedings of the Society of Biblical Archaeology
R	H. C. Rawlinson (ed.), *The Cuneiform Inscriptions of Western Asia* (London 1861-84)
RA	Revue d'assyriologie
RB	Revue biblique
Rev.	Revelation of John
RHR	Revue de l'histoire des religions
RIMA	Royal Inscriptions of Mesopotamia, Assyrian Periods
RIMB	Royal Inscriptions of Mesopotamia, Babylonian Periods
RlA	Reallexikon der Assyriologie
RMA	R. C. Thompson, *The Reports of the Magicians and Astrologers of Nineveh and Babylon* (London 1900)
Robinson NHL	J. M. Robinson (ed.), *The Nag Hammadi Library in English* (rev. ed., Leiden 1988)
Rom.	Romans
Rudolph *Gnosis*	K. Rudolph, *Gnosis. The Nature and History of Gnosticism* (San Francisco 1987)
SAA	State Archives of Assyria
SAAB	State Archives of Assyria Bulletin
SAACT	State Archives of Assyria Cuneiform Texts
Sam.	Samuel
SANE	Sources from the Ancient Near East
Sanh.	Sanhedrin
SBH	G. A. Reisner, *Sumerisch-babylonische Hymnen nach Thontafeln griechischer Zeit* (Berlin 1896)
Scholem *Origins*	G. Scholem, *Origins of the Kabbalah* (Princeton 1987)
SEL	Studi epigrafici e linguistici
SKIZ	W. H. Ph. Römer, *Sumerische 'Königshymnen' der Isin-Zeit* (Leiden 1965)
Sg 8	F. Thureau-Dangin, *Une relation de la huitième campagne de Sargon* (TCL 3, Paris 1912)
Sm	tablets in the collections of the British Museum
SMS	Syro-Mesopotamian Studies
S. of S.	Song of Songs
SpTU	Spätbabylonische Texte aus Uruk
STC	L. W. King, *The Seven Tablets of Creation* (London 1902)
StOr	Studia Orientalia
Streck Asb	M. Streck, *Assurbanipal* I-III (VAB 7, Leipzig 1916)
STT	The Sultantepe Tablets
SVT	Supplements to Vetus Testamentum
Tallqvist Götterepitheta	K. Tallqvist, *Akkadische Götterepitheta* (StOr 7, Helsinki 1938)
TB	Talmud Bavli

TCAE	J. N. Postgate, *Taxation and Conscription in the Assyrian Empire* (Studia Pohl, Series Maior 3, Rome 1974)
TCL	Textes cunéiformes du Louvre
TCS	Texts from Cuneiform Sources
TDP	R. Labat, *Traité akkadien de diagnostics et pronostics médicaux* (Leiden 1951)
TH	J. Fiedrich et al., *Die Inschriften von Tell Halaf* (AfO Beiheft 6, Berlin 1940)
Thompson Esarh.	R. C. Thompson, *The Prisms of Esarhaddon and Ashurbanipal found at Nineveh, 1927-8* (London 1931)
ThWAT	Theologisches Wörterbuch zum Alten Testament
TI	S. Langdon, *Tammuz and Ishtar* (Oxford 1914)
TIM	Texts in the Iraq Museum
TR	field numbers of tablets excavated at Tell Rimah
TUAT	Texte aus der Umwelt des Alten Testaments
UBL	Ugaritisch-Biblische Literatur
UF	Ugarit-Forschungen
UM	tablets in the collections of the University Museum of the University of Pennsylvania
UVB	Vorläufiger Bericht über die ... Ausgrabungen in Uruk-Warka
VAB	Vorderasiatische Bibliothek
VS	Vorderasiatische Schriftdenkmäler der Königlichen Museen zu Berlin
VT	Vetus Testamentum
W	field numbers of tablets excavated at Warka
WA	Western Asiatic Antiquities, British Museum, London
Warner *Virgin Mary*	M. Warner, *Alone of All Her Sex. The Myth and the Cult of the Virgin Mary* (London 1976, 1990)
Weidner Tn.	E. Weidner, *Die Inschriften Tukulti-Ninurtas I. und seiner Nachfolger* (AfO Beiheft 12, Graz 1959)
Weinfeld *Deuteronomy*	M. Weinfeld, *Deuteronomy and the Deuteronomic School* (Oxford 1972)
WO	Die Welt des Orients
WVDOG	Wissenschaftliche Veröffentlichungen der Deutschen Orient-Gesellschaft
YOR	Yale Oriental Series, Researches
YOS	Yale Oriental Series, Babylonian Texts
ZA	Zeitschrift für Assyriologie
ZAW	Zeitschrift für die alttestamentliche Wissenschaft
Zech.	Zechariah
Zeph.	Zephaniah
Zohar	R. Margalioth (ed.), *Zohar* (Jerusalem 1978)

Other Abbreviations and Symbols

ANE	Ancient Near East
Arab.	Arabic
Aram.	Aramaic, Aramean
Asb.	Assurbanipal
Asn.	Assurnasirpal
Ass.	Assyrian, Assur
Bab.	Babylonian, Babylon
Bibl.	biblical
coll.	collated, collation
DN	divine name
e.	edge
Eg.	Egyptian
Esarh.	Esarhaddon
f.	female, feminine
GN(N)	geographical name(s)
Hebr.	Hebrew
imp.	imperative
Iran.	Iranian
LB	Late Babylonian
lw.	loanword
m.	masculine
MA	Middle Assyrian
mng.	meaning
NA	Neo-Assyrian
NB	Neo-Babylonian
Nin.	Nineveh
obv.	obverse
OB	Old Babylonian
OT	Old Testament
PN(N)	personal name(s)
PNf	female personal name
pres.	present
pret.	preterit
pf.	perfect
pl.	plural
r., rev.	reverse
rabb.	rabbinical Hebrew or Aramaic
RN	royal name
rs.	right side
s.	(left) side
Sar.	Sargon
SB	Standard Babylonian
Senn.	Sennacherib
sg.	singular
stat.	stative
subj.	subjunctive

Sum.	Sumerian
Syr.	Syrian, Syriac
unpub.	unpublished
var.	variant
WSem.	West Semitic
!	collation
!!	emendation
?	uncertain reading
∶ ∴ ∷	cuneiform division marks
*	graphic variants (see LAS I p. XX)
0	uninscribed space or nonexistent sign
x	broken or undeciphered sign
( )	supplied word or sign
(( ))	sign erroneously added by scribe
[[ ]]	erasure
[...]	minor break (one or two missing words)
[......]	major break
...	untranslatable word
......	untranslatable passage
→	see also
+	joined to
//	paralleled by or including parallels

TRANSLITERATIONS AND TRANSLATIONS

Oracle Collections

Collection One

FIG. 23. *Walls of Arbela and façade of the temple of Ištar, Egašankalamma (see p. XL).*
AO 19914.

1. Oracles of Encouragement to Esarhaddon

K 4310

I beginning (about 10 lines) destroyed

1′ [*x x x x x x*] *dan-ni-te*
2′ [*x x x x* (*x*)] *rap-šat*!
3′ [*x x x x*] ⌜KI⌝! *dan ni*

4′ [ᵐ*aš-šur*—PAB]—AŠ LUGAL KUR.KUR
5′ [*la t*]*a-pa-làh*
6′ [*a*]*i*!-ʾ*u šá-a-ru ša i-di-ba-ka-a-ni*
7′ *a-qa-pu-šú la ak-su-pu-u-ni*
8′ *na-ka-ru-te-ka*
9′ *ki-i šá-ah-šu-ri ša* ITI.SIG$_4$
10′ *ina* IGI GÌR.2.MEŠ-*ka i-tan-ga-ra-ru*
11′ ᵈGAŠAN GAL-*tú a-na-ku*
12′ *a-na-ku* ᵈ15 *ša* URU.*arba-ìl*
13′ *ša na-ka-ru-te-ka*
14′ *ina* IGI GÌR.2.MEŠ-*ka ak-kar-ru-u-ni*
15′ *ai-ú-te di-ib-bi-ia*
16′ *ša aq-qa-ba-kan-ni*
17′ *ina* UGU-*hi la ta-zi*!!-*zu-u-ni*
18′ *a-na-ku* ᵈ15 *ša* URU.*arba-ìl*
19′ *na-ka-ru-te-ka ú-ka-a-ṣa*!

4 R^2 61

(Beginning destroyed)

i 1 [......] *strong* (f.)
2 [......] *is* wide (f.)
3 [......] ...

1.1 ISSAR-LA-TAŠIYAṬ

4 [Esarh]addon, king of the lands, fear [not]!

6 What wind has risen against you, whose wing I have not broken? Your enemies will roll before your feet like ripe apples.

11 I am the Great Lady; I am Ištar of Arbela, who cast your enemies before your feet. What words have I spoken to you that you could not rely upon?

18 I am Ištar of Arbela. I will flay your enemies and give them to you.

1 Photo pls. I-III. Copy G. Smith, 4 R 68 (1875); Pinches, 4 R^2 61 (1891). Collated by the editor in November, 1966, and in July, 1992. i 1-3 On this passage and the lost introductory lines see Introduction, p. LVI. i 2 The last sign, misread by Pinches, is correctly given as *šat* in Smith's copy. i 3 See coll. The damaged first sign agrees in shape with KI but not with ŠU in line i 9, and thus cannot to be read *šu*, as copied by Smith and Pinches. A faint trace of the initial winkelhaken of KI is visible at the break. i 6 "Wind" is a metonym for "enemy," cf. line 8 and ii 34f. *i-di-ba-ka-a-ni* is here taken as pret. of *tabû* "to rise, attack"; cf. AfO 17 p. 358:14 and FUB 18 p. 47:2f, "the evil/fierce wind whose attack (*te-bu-šú*) is fearsome," and Jer. 51:1, "I will raise a destroying wind against Babylon." Other similar forms of *tabû* are *ú-šá-da-ba*, SAA 5 58:9; *ú-sa-da-bi-šu*, KAV 115 r.7; *nu-sa-da-bi-*[*šú-nu*], CT 53 901:2; note also [*l*]*i-di-bu-*⌜*ku*⌝, NL 93 r.2; *ni-di-bu-ku-ni*, ABL 605 r.3; and *ni-id-di-bu-ú-ku*, BM 132980:17, from *tabāku* "to pour". The verb *edēpu* "to blow, inflate," with which the form has been hitherto connected, is not attested in NA.
The first sign in the line is not [*š*]*u*, as copied by Pinches, nor [*i*]*a* (thus coll. W.G. Lambert *apud* Weippert, ARINH [1981], p. 81), nor [*m*]*a* (coll. Hecker, TUAT II/1 [1986] 56), but ⌜*a*⌝-*a* with an extra horizontal wedge between the two *a*'s in the lower register; see coll. This exceptional form of *a-a*, also found in i 15, ii 2 and 34 (collated), was used in this text for writing the diphthong */ai/*. i 7 An allusion to the "breaking of the wing" (*kappa šebēru*) of the evil winds in the Adapa and Pazuzu myths, see Introduction, p. XLVIIf and n. 246. *a-qa-pu* is hence certainly an alloform of *agappu* "wing," even though no other explicit spellings of the word with *q* are attested. i 9 Lit., "apples of the month Sivan"; cf. SAA 3 14 r.6, where the ankle bones of Tašmetu are likened to "an apple of Sivan" (GIŠ.HAŠHUR ITI.SI[G$_4$]), and Luckenbill Senn. 46 vi 12, "I cut off their hands like the *fruits* of ripe cucumbers," lit. "cucumbers of Sivan" (*qiššê si-ma-ni*). Sivan accordingly was the month in which apples and cucumbers normally ripened in Assyria. Landsberger's suggestion (JNES 8 [1949] 257) that ITI.SIG$_4$ here is a rebus for "proper time" (*simānu*) is unlikely, however, since "proper time" (*simunu*) was in NA phonemically differentiated from the month name Sivan (*Simānu/Simannu*). i 14 *ak-kar-ru-u-ni* is an alloform of *akrurūni* (pret. of *krr*) to be compared, e.g., with *a-da-bu-u-ni* (pret. of *dbb*) in ABL 211 r.10; contrast *ta-da-ba-bu-u-ni* (pres.), ibid. r.10. For the gemination of the first radical and the anaptyctic vowel see LAS II p. 47 and cf. *aq-qa-ba-kan-ni* i 16, *šá-ad-da-lu-pu-ka* and *nag-ga-la-pa-a-a*, no. 9:16 and 18. i 15-17 → vi 7-12. i 15 See coll. i 17 *zi*!!: tablet NAM, scribal error. i 19 Cf. AfO 3 156:10 (Aššur-dan II), "I flayed (*a-ku-uṣ*) PN, king of Katmuhi, and draped his skin over the walls of Arbela." *ú-ka-a-ṣa*!, miscopied by Pinches (1891) as *ú-ka-a-a* and consequently misinterpreted in most previous editions, was correctly copied by Smith (1875).

20′ *a-da-na-ka* [[*x*]] *a-na-ku*
21′ ^{d}15 *ša* URU.*arba-ìl*
22′ *ina pa-na-tu-u-ka*
23′ *ina ku-tal-li-ka*
24′ *a-la-ka la ta-pa-làh*
25′ *at-ta ina* ŠÀ-*bi mu-gi*
26′ *a-na-ku ina* ŠÀ-*bi* u_8*-u-a*
27′ *a-ta-ab-bi ú-šab*

[20] I am Ištar of Arbela. I will go before you and behind you.

[24] Fear not! You are paralysed, but in the midst of woe I will rise and sit down (beside you).

28′ *ša pi-i* $^{m!d}$15*—la—ta-ši-ia-aṭ*
29′ DUMU URU.*arba-ìl*

[28] By the mouth of Issar-la-tašiyaṭ of Arbela.

1.2 SINQIŠA-AMUR

30′ LUGAL KUR*—aš-šur la ta-pa-làh*
31′ *na-ak-ru ša* MAN KUR*—aš-šur*
32′ ⌜*a*⌝!-*na ṭa-ba-ah-hi a-da-na*
33′ [*ina*] ⌜É⌝*—re-du-te-ka*
34′ [*ú-ta-q*]*a-an-ka*
35′ [*ú-ra-ba*]*-ak-ka*
36′ [*x x x* GA]L-*tu a-na-ku*
37′ [*a-na-ku* ^{d}15 *š*]*a* URU.*arba-ìl*
38′ [*x x x x x* T]A! ⌜ŠÀ-*bi*⌝-*šú*
39′ [*x x x x x x x*]*x-šú*
II beginning (about 6 lines) destroyed
1′ [*x x*] *x*[*x x x x x x x*]
2′ *a*[*i*]!-ʾ*u*! *x*[*x x x x x x*]
3′ *la áš-me-k*[*a na-ka-ru-te*]
4′ *ina si-ga-r*[*a-te sa-al-mu-ti*]
5′ *ina ma-da-*[*na-ti x x*]
6′ *na-kar*^{ar}*-ka ina*! Š[À? *qa-ra-bi*]
7′ *e-da-ni-*ʾ*e ak-t*[*a-šá-ad*]
8′ *ú-ta-ki-il-ka la uš-ba-*[*ku*]

[30] King of Assyria, have no fear! I will deliver up the enemy of the king of Assyria for slaughter. [I will] keep you safe and [*make*] you [*great* in] your Palace of Succession.

[36] I am the Gr[eat *Lady*. I am Ištar o]f Arbela

[38] [......] from *his* midst

(Break)

[ii 2] What [......] I would not have heard you? [The enemies ...] in neckst[ocks, [the vassals] under tribu[te]; I defea[ted] your enemy in a single [*encounter*].

[8] I have given you faith, I do not sit (idle)!

9′ *ša pi-i* MÍ.*si-in-qi-šá—a-mur*
10′ DUMU.MÍ URU.*arba-ìl*

[9] By the mouth of the woman Sinqiša-amur of Arbela.

---

i 20 Traces of erased ŠI before *a-na-ku* (see coll.). i 22ff Cf. Streck Asb p. 48:100f, "I (Ištar of Arbela) will go before Assurbanipal, the king whom my hands created"; Isa. 45:2, "I (Yahweh) will go before you (Cyrus) and level the swelling hills." i 25ff The king is here pictured as a baby crying violently (to the point of paralysis) in its distress, the god as mother rushing to help it. Cf. nos. 2 iii 32f, 3 ii 12ff, and 9:26, and see Introduction, p. XXXVIff. i 27 The parallel passage no. 9:26 indicates that *a-tab-bi* refers to the god's attack on the king's enemy. Cf. Isa. 14:22 and Jer. 46:8. i 28 The scribe started writing the name of the prophet with the feminine determinative MÍ, but then changed his mind and wrote the masculine and divine determinatives ^{md} over the MÍ sign; see coll. The prophet was accordingly not a woman (thus most previous editions and translations) but a man. Cf. note on ii 40. i 31f Cf. i 19 and no. 9:26. i 32 See coll. i 33f Cf. no. 7:6. i 35 Or: "[I will rear] you" (cf. nos. 2 iii 27, 7 r.11, and ABL 1249:4). i 36 Cf. lines 11f. Restoring ^{d}GAŠAN is not possible, however, since *three* not two signs are missing before GA]L-*tú* (the missing signs take the space of *na-ak-ru* in line 31). *rabītu* "great" is otherwise attested in the corpus only in no. 1 iii 16, where it refers to Ištar as the king's "midwife." i 38 The referent of the suffix *-šu* remains unclear; the parallel in col. vi 19ff is not pertinent, since "palace" was feminine in NA (cf., e.g., É.GAL SUMUN-*ti*, GPA 68 r.9). ii 1f See coll. Smith's copy is here superior to Pinches'. ii 3f For the restorations and the passage in general cf. no. 2 iii 23f. There is room for [*-ka*] "your" at the end of line 3 (cf. ii 6). ii 5 Cf. SAA 3 8:19, "Tribute from [all la]nds enters there" (i.e., Arbela). The line is spaced out, and there is no room for [*ub-ba-la-ka*] ending the parallel passage in no. 2 iii 24. ii 6 See coll.; *na-kar*^{ar}*-ka* is clear on the tablet, though it is probably a scribal error for *na-kar-u-ti-ka* (see Introduction, p. LVI and cf. i 19 etc.). The restoration is conjectural but agrees with the traces and the available space; see also Introduction, p. LXXIII. ii 7 For restoration see nos. 2 i 23 and 3 iv 17; space considerations require restoring two signs (*šá-ad*) rather than one (*šad*). ii 8 Cf. iv 1f, *ú-ta-ki-i*[*l-ka*] *la ú-ba-áš-*[*ka*]. Despite this parallel, the tablet clearly reads *la uš-ba-*[*ku*] "[I] do not sit," possibly an allusion to the statue of Ištar "seated" (*uš-bat*) on her lion in Arbela (SAA 3 8 r.5). Despite Hecker, TUAT II/1 p. 51, there is no trace of, and also no room for, either *-ka* or *-ak* at the end of the line.

11′ *ri-i-šá-ak* TA* ^{m}*aš-šur*—PAB—AŠ
12′ LUGAL-*ia ri-i-ši* URU.*arba-ìl*

13′ *ša pi-i* MÍ.*re-mu-te—al-la-te*
14′ *ša* URU.*da-ra—a-hu-u-ia*
15′ *ša bir-ti* KUR.MEŠ-*ni*

16′ *la ta-pa-làh* ^{m}*aš-šur*—PAB—AŠ :$^{!}$
17′ *a-na-ku* ^{d}EN *is-si-ka*
18′ *a-da-bu-bu*
19′ GIŠ.ÙR.MEŠ *ša* ŠÀ-*bi-ka*
20′ *a-ha-ri-di ki-i* MÍ.AMA-*ka*
21′ *tu-šab-šu-ka-ni*
22′ 60 DINGIR.MEŠ GAL.MEŠ *is-si-ia*
23′ *it-ti-ti-su it-ta-ṣar-u-ka*
24′ ^{d}30 *ina* ZAG-*ka* ^{d}UTU *ina* 150-*ka*
25′ 60 DINGIR.MEŠ GAL.MEŠ *ina bat-ti—bat-ti-ka*
26′ *i-za-zu* MURUB$_4$-*ka*$^{!}$ *ir-tak-su*
27′ *ina* UGU *a-me-lu-ti la ta-tak-kil*
28′ *mu-tu-uh* IGI.2.MEŠ-*ka*
29′ *a-na a-a-ši du-gul-an-ni*
30′ *a-na-ku* ^{d}15 *ša* URU.*arba-ìl*
31′ *aš-šur is-si-ka ú-sa-lim*
32′ *ṣe-he-ra-ka a-ta-ṣa-ak-ka*
33′ *la ta-pa-làh na-i-da-a-ni*
34′ *ai-ʾu*$^{!!}$ *šu-ú na-ak-ru*
35′ *ša i-di-ba*$^{!}$*-kan-ni*
36′ *a-na-ku qa-la-ku-u-ni*
37′ *ur-ki-ú-te lu-u ki-i pa-ni-u-te*
38′ *a-na-ku* ^{d}PA EN *qar—ṭup-pi*
39′ *na-i-da-a-ni*

40′ *ša pi-i* MÍ.*ba-ia-a* DUMU URU.*arba-ìl*

1.3 REMUTTI-ALLATI

11 I rejoice with Esarhaddon, my king! Arbela rejoices!

---

13 By the mouth of the woman Remutti-Allati of Dara-ahuya, a town in the mountains.

1.4 BAYÂ

16 Fear not, Esarhaddon!

17 I am Bel. (Even as) I speak to you, I watch over the beams of your heart.

20 When your mother gave birth to you, sixty great gods stood with me and protected you. Sin was at your right side, Šamaš at your left; sixty great gods were standing around you and girded your loins.

27 Do not trust in man. Lift up your eyes, look to me! I am Ištar of Arbela; I reconciled Aššur with you. When you were small, I took you to me. Do not fear; praise me!

34 What enemy has attacked you while I remained silent? The future shall be like the past. I am Nabû, lord of the stylus. Praise me!

---

40 By the mouth of the woman Bayâ, 'son'(!) of Arbela.

---

ii 11f Or: Rejoice, Arbela! Cf. SAA 3 8 r.18ff, "Arbela rejoices (*ri-ša*)! The people are rejoicing (*i-ri-*[*šá*]) [...]! The Lady rejoices (*ri-šat*) ... The Lady of the House of Arbela rejoices (*i-ri-šá*)"; Zech. 9:9, "Rejoice, rejoice, daughter of Zion, for see, your king is coming to you, his cause won, his victory gained." ii 14 This town is not otherwise known, but may be compared with Dara-abuya (written URU.*da-ra-bu-u-a*), a town in the vicinity of Dur-Šarruken (DŠ 32-17a+ i 6 and ii 4). ii 17 → col. iii 24, and see Introduction, p. XVIII. ii 20f Cf. Ezek. 16:4ff, "When you (Jerusalem) were born, (...) I (Yahweh) spoke to you, there in your blood, and bade you live. I tended you like an evergreen plant ..."; also cf. S. of S. 3:7, "Sixty warriors round it, all of them trained ... swords ready at their loins" [Weinfeld]. ii 22f Cf. SAA 3 3:14f, "As a child the great gods guided me (Assurbanipal), going with me on the right and the left." ii 24f Cf. Jer. 8:2, "They shall expose them to the sun, the moon, all the host of heaven, whom they loved and served and adored, to whom they resorted and bowed in worship, " and see Weinfeld *Deuteronomy*, p. 140. ii 27 Cf. Ps. 146:3, "Put not your faith in rulers, or in the son of man, in whom there is no salvation," and Jer. 17:5ff, "A curse on the man who trusts in man .... Blessed is the man who trusts in YHWH, and rests his confidence upon him." → no. 2 ii 17. ii 31 Cf. no. 2 ii 3 and iii 20, and see Introduction, p. XLIII and n. 153. ii 32 Cf. Hos. 11:1ff, "When Israel was a boy, I (Yahweh) loved him... It was I who taught Ephraim to walk, I who had taken them in my arms; but they did not know that (...) I had lifted them like a little child to my cheek, that I had bent down to feed them." See also Introduction, p. XL. ii 34 Cf. col. i 6. The second sign is not KÁM (thus both copies and earlier editions) but rather an aleph written over an (unerased) *i*, see coll. ii 36 For other NA examples of *qâlu* "to remain silent" with the implication of doing nothing, see, e.g., SAA 1 98 r.4, 220 r.1, and SAA 5 149 r.5. ii 38 The epithet "lord of the stylus" (also in BBR 45 vi 3, ABL 716:4 and 717:3) refers to Nabû as the recorder of sins and determiner of fates on the day of judgment, see Pomponio, *Nabû*, p. 182 and Parpola, JNES 52 (1993) 204f. Cf. Streck Asb p. 364 o 2, where Nabû is called "keeper of the writing-board, holder of the stylus (GI—*ṭup-pi*) of fates"; AnSt 33 78:10, where he presents a "tablet of sins" to Bel; and ABL 545:8ff, referring to the "life-giving writing-board" of Nabû consulted on the day of "the settling of accounts." On the "book of life" opened before God on the New Year's day see also TB *'Arakhim* 10b [Weinfeld]. ii 39 Right after *-da-*, there are shallow traces of an erased *a*, written before the scribe decided to space out the line (see coll.). ii 40 On the question of the sex of this prophet (both the female determinative and the sign DUMU "son" are clear on the tablet) see Introduction, pp. XXXIV and IL.

III beginning (about 14 lines) destroyed

1′ *ku*-[*x x x x x x x x x*]
2′ *a-na-*⌜*ku a*$^{?!}$⌝-[*x x x x*]
3′ *at-ta tal*-[*x x x* (*x*)]
4′ *a-na-ku* ^{d}N[IN$^{!}$.LÍL (*x*)]

5′ *ša pi-i* MÍ.DINGIR-*sa—a-m*[*ur*]
6′ URU.ŠÀ—URU-*a*$^{!}$-[*a*]

7′ *a-na-ku* ^{d}15 *ša* UR[U.*arba-ìl*]
8′ ^{m}*aš-šur*—PAB—AŠ MAN KUR—*a*[*š-šur*]
9′ *ina* URU.ŠÀ—URU URU.NIN[A]
10′ URU.*kal-ha* URU.*arba-ì*[*l*]
11′ UD.MEŠ *ar-ku-u-t*[*e*]
12′ MU.AN.NA.MEŠ *da-ra-t*[*e*]
13′ *a-na* ^{m}*aš-šur*—PAB—AŠ LUGAL-*i*⌜*a*⌝
14′ *a-da-an-na* [0]
15′ *sa-ab-su-ub-ta-k*[*a*]
16′ *ra-bi-tu a-na-ku*
17′ *mu-še-ni*[*q*$^{!}$]-*ta-ka*
18′ *de-iq-tú a-na-ku*
19′ *ša* UD-*me ar-ku-te*
20′ MU.AN.NA.MEŠ *da-ra-te*
21′ GIŠ.GU.ZA-*ka ina* KI.TA AN-*e*
22′ *ra-bu-te uk-ti-in*
23′ *ina ma-si-ki ša* KUG.GI
24′ *ina* MURUB$_4$ AN-*e a-ha-ri-di*
25′ *nu-ur ša il-me-ši*
26′ *ina* IGI ^{m}*aš-šur*—PAB—AŠ MAN KUR—*aš-šur*
27′ *ú-šá-na-ma-ra*
28′ *ki-i a-ge-e ša* SAG.DU-*ia*
29′ *a-ha-ri-su*
30′ *la ta-pa-làh* LUGAL
31′ *aq-ṭi-ba-ak*
32′ *la as-li-k*[*a*]
IV 1 *ú-ta-ki-i*[*l-ka*]
2 *la ú-ba-áš-*[*ka*]

1.5 ILUSSA-AMUR

(Break)

iii 2 I will [......]
3 you shall [.....].
4 I am Mu[llissu (...)].

---

5 By the mouth of the woman Ilussa-am[ur] of the Inner City.

1.6 UNKNOWN PROPHET

7 I am Ištar of [Arbela].

8 Esarhaddon, king of A[ssyria]! In the Inner City, Nineveh, Calah and Arbela I will give long days and everlasting years to Esarhaddon, my king.

15 I am your great midwife; I am your excellent wet nurse. For long days and everlasting years I have established your throne under the great heavens.

23 I watch in a golden chamber in the midst of the heavens; I let the lamp of amber shine before Esarhaddon, king of Assyria, and I watch him like the crown of my head.

30 Have no fear, my king! I have *spoken to* you, I have not lied to you; I have given you faith, I will not let you come to shame. I will

iii 4 The traces after ^{d} agree with the beginning of NIN in col. iv 6; 15, EN, PA and *aš* are excluded (see coll.). There is no room for [*na-i-da-ni*] at the end of the line, despite the parallel passages nos. 1 ii 39 and 2 iv 8. iii 5 See Introduction, p. L. iii 6 See coll. iii 7ff Cf. 2 Sam. 7:8ff and Ps. 89:3f and 19ff. iii 9-12 Cf. iv 15-17 and see relevant note. The four cities mentioned here are the "four doorjambs of Assyria" of no. 3 iii 20 and iv 15. iii 13 See coll. iii 15 Since *šabsūtu* "midwife" is a loan from Sum. šà-zu, the present (otherwise unattested) form with an extra *b* is generally considered a scribal error. The signs are clear, however, and the possibility of a true NA linguistic variant cannot be excluded. iii 17 Cf. SAA 3 39:19, "Ištar of Durna (= Nineveh) is ... the wet nurse of Bel." The third sign is not *ṣu*, as copied by Pinches, or NIN (Weippert, ARINH [1981] p. 22 n. 22), but simply a damaged *niq* (see coll.). The right half of the sign is almost totally eroded, but the traces agree with UR in col. iii 25. iii 19-22 Cf. Ps. 89:4, "I will establish your posterity for ever, I will make your throne endure for all generations," and ibid. 29, "I will establish his posterity for ever, and his throne as long as the heavens endure"; cf. also Isa. 9:6. iii 23-27 This passage refers to the abode of Bel in the middle heaven, see Introduction, n. 248. iii 24 On God as "the Watcher" of the king see Introduction, n. 249. Cf. col. ii 17, and note that the "Watcher" there identifies himself as Bel. iii 25 *nūru* can also mean "light," but the parallel passage in SAA 3 39:32, where the word is replaced by *buṣinnu*, indicates that "lamp" is the intended meaning here. Cf. Ps. 18:28, 132:17, and Job 29:2, "when God was watching me, when his lamp shone above my head, and by its light I walked through the darkness." On the connection between "the lamp of *elmešu* (amber)" and "the likeness of *hašmal* (Septuagint: *elektron*) glowing in the midst of fire" of Ezek. 1:4 and 27, see Introduction, n. 249. iii 31-iv 2 Cf. Ps. 89:33-36; 2 Sam. 7:15. iii 31 Or: "I have trusted you," taking *aq-ṭi-ba-ak* as a form of *qiāpu* with syllable metathesis (*aqṭīpka* → *aqṭīpak*, cf. *ušēṣa* → *ú-še-aṣ*, ADD 1194 r.4) and voicing of the last radical (cf. LÚ.*qe-e-bi*, SAA 2 5 iii 13, LÚ.*qe-ba-a-ni*, ABL 442:14). The rendering "I have spoken to you" (cf. col. i 16, vi 8, and no. 7:14) presupposes apocopation of the final vowel of *aqṭibakka*, which is otherwise not attested (note, however, *issūku* → *i-su-uk*, GPA 180 r.8). Despite Weippert, ARINH (1981) p. 85 n.27, *aqṭibakka* is a normal NA suffixed pf. form of *qabû*, cf. e.g. *aq-ṭi-ba-áš-šu*, ABL 471:20. iv 1f → col. ii 8. Cf. Zeph. 3:11; Ps.

ÍD *ina tu-qu-un-ni*
ú-še-ba-ar-ka
^{m}*aš-šur*—PAB—AŠ *ap-lu*
ke-e-nu DUMU ^{d}NIN.LÍL
ha-an-ga-ru ak-ku
ina ŠU.2-*ia*
LÚ.KÚR.MEŠ-*ka*
ú-qa-at-ta
^{m}*aš-šur*—PAB—AŠ MAN KUR—*aš-šur*
ka-a-su šá ma-lu-u qi-il-te
ka-la-pu ša 2 GÍN
^{m}*aš-šur*—PAB—AŠ *ina* URU.ŠÀ—URU
UD.MEŠ *ar-ku-u-ti*
MU.MEŠ *da-ra-a-ti*
a-da-nak-k[*a*]
^{m}*aš-šur*—PAB—AŠ *ina* ŠÀ-*bi* URU.*arba-ì*[*l*]
a-ri-it-ka de-iq-tú a-[*na-ku*]
^{m}*aš-šur*—PAB—AŠ DUMU.UŠ *k*[*e-e-nu*]
DUMU ^{d}NIN.[LÍL]
hi-is-sa-at-[*ka*]
ha-sa-[*ku*]
ar-ta-am-k[*a*$^{!}$]
a—*dan-*[*niš*]
ina ki-zir-ti-k[*a*]
ina AN-*e* GAL.⸢MEŠ⸣
ú-kal-ka
ina ZAG-*ka*
qut-ru ú-qa-at-t[*ar*]
ina KAB-*k*[*a*]
IZI *ú-*⸢*šá*⸣*-*[*haz*]

take you safely across the River.

iv 5 Esarhaddon, rightful heir, son of Mullissu! With an angry dagger in my hand I will finish off your enemies.

11 O Esarhaddon, king of Assyria, cup filled with lye, axe of two shekels!

14 Esarhaddon! I will give you long days and everlasting years in the Inner City. O Esarhaddon, I will be your good shield in Arbela.

20 Esarhaddon, ri[ghtful] heir, son of Mul[lissu]! I am mindful of you, I have loved you greatly.

26 I keep you in the great heavens by your *curl*. I make smoke rise up on your right side, I kindle fire on your left.

71:1; SAA 3 12 r.13, "(O Nabû), do not let me come to shame (*la t*[*u-b*]*a-šá-a-ni*) in the assembly." iv 3 As already pointed out by R.F. Harper *apud* Banks, AJSL 14 (1898) 273, n.2, this probably refers to the crossing of the river Tigris, the last obstacle in Esarhaddon's thrust to power in late 681 (see Introduction, p. LXXIII). iv 5f Cf. Ps. 89:27; 2 Sam. 7:14; ABL 442 r.1ff, "you (Esarhaddon) are the legitimate seed of Sennacherib"; → col. vi 27ff, no. 2 ii 13f. iv 7 For *ha-an-ga-ru* "dagger" (von Soden, Or. 46 [1977] 187 no. 188) cf. Syr. *ḥangrā* "pugio" (Brockelmann, Lex. Syr. p. 244) and Arab. *ḫanǧar* "dagger"; note also Ištar's "pointed sword" (*namṣaru zaqtu*) in Streck Asb p. 116:55. *ak-ku* is taken as an unvoiced variant of *aggu* "angry," cf. *a-kap-pi* for *agappi* in no. 2 ii 6, and Ištar's anger (*uggugat*) in Streck Asb p. 118:76; von Soden, loc. cit. 184 no. 174 compares Syr. *ʾakketā* "Zorn." iv 12 Cf. Mal. 3:2, "He [God] is like the refiner's fire, or like the fuller's lye"; Jer. 23:15, "I will give them ... a bitter poison to drink"; Jer. 51:7, "Babylon has been a gold cup in YHWH's hand to make all the earth drunk"; Ezek. 23:32, "You (Jerusalem) shall drink from your sister's (Samaria's) cup"; and see Weinfeld *Deuteronomy*, p. 143. The idea is that Esarhaddon is the "cup of poison" called to avenge the criminals who assassinated Sennacherib and "spread a godless spirit over all the land" (see Introduction, p. LXXII). For the rendering of *ma-lu-u qi-il-te* see LAS II p. 313. iv 13 Cf. Isa. 7:20 and 10:15, where the king of Assyria functions as the "razor" and "axe" of God. A deified axe (^{d}*ka-la-pu*) of Aššur was kept in the god's temple at Assur (see CAD s.v. *kalappu* and ABL 896:11); in the present passage, Esarhaddon is the personification of this divine weapon, called to annihilate the god's enemies. The qualification "of two shekels" can in principle be taken either as a weight (thus Weippert, ARINH [1981] p. 87, followed by Hecker, TUAT II/1 [1986] p. 59) or a price indication; since a miniature axe of 32 grams (1 oz.) hardly makes a formidable weapon, the latter alternative, with the connotation "expensive (quality) axe," seems more likely. Reading GÍN as *pāšu* and rendering the passage as "two-edged axe" (Deller *apud* Weippert, OBO 64 [1985] 59 n.10, an idea originating with me) is unlikely, since the equation GÍN = *pāšu* was not current in NA outside lexical texts and there is no evidence that *pāšu* "axe" could actually mean "blade." iv 14-17 This passage recalls the blessings invoked upon the king at coronation ceremonies in Assur (the "Inner City") and the concomitant divine meal (*tākultu*), cf. SAA 3 11 r.1f, "Give (pl.) our lord Assurbanipal long [days], copious years ...," and Frankena Takultu p. 9 x 9f, "Open the gate(!) of wisdom to the city of Assur, give (pl.) long days and everlasting years ... to the king, our lord." → col. iii 9-14 and no. 3 i 6. Note that while the above prayers are addressed to a *plurality* of gods, the blessings are here in fact granted by a single god, and see Introduction, p. XXI. iv 19 Cf. Gen. 15:1, "Fear not, Abram, I am your shield"; Zech. 9:15, "YHWH of Hosts will be their shield"; Isa. 31:5, "YHWH of Hosts (...) will be a shield over Jerusalem." iv 22-25 Cf. Ps. 89:24. iv 26 Reading *-i*[*a*] at the end of the line is excluded (see coll.). iv 29-32 This passage refers to the victorious progress of Esarhaddon's campaign, cf. TCL 3 261 (Sar.), "I set fire to their elaborate houses and caused smoke from them (*quturšunu*) to rise and cover the heavens like mist"; Streck Asb 132 viii 4, "they set fire (IZI *ušāhizū*) to the tents, their dwellings, and burnt them down." Note also Isa. 9:18, "Wicked men have been set ablaze like a fire,... they are wrapped in a murky pall of smoke." iv 34 Probably to be restored *da-aʾ-*[*na-at*] "is strong" (or *da-ʾu-*[*na-at*], "strengthened"), but the meaning of the passage remains obscure. The "partially preserved" *ur*

33 LUGAL-*tú ina* UGU [*x x* (*x*)]
34 *da-a*ʾ-[*x x*]
35 *ina* ⌜UGU *da*⌝-[*x x x*]
rest (about 14 lines) destroyed

[33] The kingship [*is*] *stro*[*ng*] on [......]
(Break)

1.7 ISSAR-BELI-DA''INI

V 1 TA* *pa-ni-šú*
2 *la i-ma-har*
3 *ka-kiš-a-ti*
4 *pu-uš-ha-a-ti*
5 *šá i-da-ba-bu-u-ni*
6 *ina* IGI GÌR.2-*šú*
7 *ú-bat-taq-šú-nu*
8 *at-ti at-ti-ma*
9 LUGAL *šar-ri-ma*

---

10 *ša pi-i* MÍ.15—EN—*da-i-ni*
11 *še-lu-tu ša* LUGAL

[v 1] [......] shall not receive [...] from him. I will cut the conspiring weasels and shrews to pieces before his feet.

[8] You (f.) are you. The king is my king!

---

[10] By the mouth of the woman Issar-beli-da''ini, a votaress of the king.

1.8 AHAT-ABIŠA

12 *a-na-ku* ᵈ*be-let—arba-ìl*
13 *a-na* AMA—LUGAL
14 *ki-i ta-hu-ri-ni-ni*
15 *ma-a ša* ZAG
16 *ša šu-me-li*
17 *ina su-ni-ki ta-sak-ni*
18 *ma-a ia-ú*
19 *ṣi-it*—ŠÀ-*bi-ia*
20 EDIN *tu-sar-pi-di*
21 *ú-ma-a* LUGAL *la ta-pa-làh*
22 LUGAL-*tú ik-ku-u*
23 *da-na-nu ik-ku-u-ma*

---

24 *ša pi-i* MÍ.NIN—AD-*šá*
25 DUMU.MÍ URU.*arba-ìl*

---

[12] I am the Lady of Arbela.

[13] To the king's mother:

[14] Because you implored me, saying: "You have placed the ones at the (king's) right and left side in your lap, but made my own offspring roam the steppe" —

[21] Now fear not, *my* king! The kingdom is yours, yours is the power!

---

[24] By the mouth of the woman Ahat-abiša of Arbela.

1.9 UNKNOWN PROPHET

26 DI-*mu a-na* ᵐ*aš-šur*—PAB—AŠ MAN KUR—*aš-šur*
27 ᵈ15 *šá* URU.*arba-ìl*
28 *a-na* EDIN *ta-at-tu-ṣi*

[26] All is well with Esarhaddon, king of Assyria.

[27] Ištar of Arbela has gone out to the

following *a*ʾ in 4 R^2 41 is in fact the tail of *a*ʾ. v 3ff The rendering of *kakkišu* is based on Syr. *kākuštā* "weasel, polecat" (Payne Smith, p. 214), that of *pušhu* on the equation *hu-li-i* = *pu-uš-hu* in STT 402 r.20, cf. CAD s.vv. *hulû* and *kakkišu*. The "conspiring weasels and shrews" were Esarhaddon's domestic adversaries, cf. ABL 965:8-10, "The governorship of Uruk is yours, I will not give it to anybody else; and I will put into your hands all those who conspired against you." → SAA 10 352 = LAS 280 r.2ff. v 8 The woman addressed in the 2nd person is certainly Esarhaddon's mother, Naqia, cf. line 13, no. 2 i 13 and iv 28, no. 5:4, and see Introduction, p. XLIII. Though Naqia in these other oracles (excepting no. 5) appears as a secondary addressee after her son, the grouping of the present oracle with 1.8 suggests that it also began with an address to her, and thus has to be separated from 1.6. v 10 See Introduction, p. L. v 15f I.e., Esarhaddon's rebel brothers, the eldest and second-eldest sons of Sennacherib. Cf. SAA 10 185 = LAS 129:7ff, "You (Esarhaddon) have girded a son of yours with a diadem and entrusted to him the kingship of Assyria; your eldest son you have set to the kingship in Babylon. You have placed the first on your right, the second on your left side!" → no. 3 iv 23f and Gen. 48:13ff. v 18 *ia-ú* does not mean "where" (thus all previous editions) but is the NA 1st person sg. possessive pronoun serving to emphasize the hereditary contrast between Esarhaddon and his half-brothers. v 20 "Roaming the plain" is a metaphor for Esarhaddon's flight from Nineveh before the murder of Sennacherib, see Borger Esarh. p. 40 and Parpola, CRRAI 26 (1980) p. 175, with n.39 on p. 178. → no. 9:8 and 25. v 22f Cf. Mt. 6:13, "Yours is the kingdom and the power and the glory," and Isa. 9:6f, "A boy has been born for us... Great shall the dominion be, and boundless the peace bestowed on David's throne and on his kingdom." See also Introduction, p. LXVIII. v 26, 29 → no. 3 i 9ff, ii 8 and 26, and see Introduction, p. LXIV on *šulmu* "(oracle of) well-being, salvation." The different spellings of the word (DI-*mu* and *šul-mu*) do not imply a difference in meaning (such as "greeting" vs. "well-being"), cf. SAA 10 194:2ff (*lu* DI-*mu* vs. *šul-mu a-na*), 223:3ff (*lu-u šul-mu* vs. DI-*mu a-na*), and 217:2ff (*lu* DI-*mu* vs. DI-*mu a-na*). v 27f This is a reference to the procession of Ištar to a chapel called "Palace of the Steppe" outside Arbela (see Streck Asb p. 248:6; → no. 5:8) in anticipation of a subsequent triumphal return to the city together with the king, waiting for the goddess in the city; see LAS II pp. 158f and 192f. Such

29 *šul-mu a-na mu-ri-šá*
30 *a-na bi-rit* URU *ta-sap-ra*
31 *a-na ú-ṣe-*⸢*e*⸣*-*[*šá*?]
32 *šá ú-*[*x x x x*]
33 LÚ.[*x x x x* (*x*)]
34 *mu-x*[*x x x x x*]
35 *ki-*⸢*i*?⸣ [*x x x x x x*]
36 *x*[*x x x x x x*]
rest (about 8 lines) destroyed
VI 1

steppe and sent (an oracle of) well-being to her calf in the city.

31 *At* [*her*] coming out [......]

(Break)

1.10 LA-DAGIL-ILI

2 [*a-na-ku* ^{d}*be-let*—URU.*arb*]*a-ìl*
3 [^{m}*aš-šur*—PAB—AŠ *šá*] *ina* DÙG.GA
4 [^{d}15] *šá* URU.*arba-ìl*
5 *ha-bu-un-šú*
6 *tu-mal-lu-u-ni*
7 *da-ba-bu pa-ni-u*
8 *šá a-qa-ba-kan-ni*
9 *ina* UGU*-hi la ta-zi-zi*
10 *ú-ma-a*
11 *ina* UGU *ur-ki-i*
12 *ta-za-az-ma*
13 *na-ʾi-da-an-ni*
14 *ki-i* UD*-mu*
15 *i-ši-ṣu-u-ni*
16 *zi-qa-a-ti*
17 *lu-ki-il-lu*
18 *ina pa-ni na-ʾi-da-an-ni*
19 [*n*]*i*!*-ir-ri-ṭu*
20 [T]A ŠÀ É.GAL*-ia*
21 ⸢*ú*⸣*-še-ṣa*
22 *ak-lu taq-nu ta-kal*
23 A.MEŠ *taq-nu-ti*
24 *ta-šá-at-ti*
25 *ina* ŠÀ*-bi* É.GAL*-ka*
26 *ta-taq-qu-un*
27 DUMU*-ka* DUMU—DUMU*-ka*
28 LUGAL*-u-tú*
29 *ina bur-ki šá* ^{d}MAŠ
30 *ú-pa-áš*

vi 1 [I am the Lady of Arb]ela.

3 [O Esarhaddon, whos]e bosom [Ištar] of Arbela has filled with favour! Could you not rely on the previous utterance which I spoke to you? Now you can rely on this later one too.

13 Praise me! When daylight declines, let them hold torches! Praise me before them!

19 I will banish trembling from my palace. You shall eat safe food and drink safe water, and you shall be safe in your palace. Your son and grandson shall rule as kings on the lap of Ninurta.

triumphal celebrations were arranged only after major military victories, so the present passage almost certainly relates to Esarhaddon's victory over his rebel brothers (→ no. 3 iv 23 and Introduction, n. 197). v 29 On the king as the "calf" of Ištar see Introduction, p. XXXVIf; → nos. 2 iv 20 and 7 r.11. v 31 Cf. SAA 3 7:12, "at the coming out (*a-na* È*-šá*) of the Lady of Nineveh (all the gods rejoice)." The spacing of the line requires restoring one sign only in the break. v 34f See coll. vi 2 Restored from no. 2 i 36. vi 3 The interpretation of DÙG.GA as *ṭābtu* "(divine) favour" (referring to the victory over the brothers, cf. no. 3 iii 18ff) can be supported by the spelling EN—DÙG.GA of *bēl ṭābti* in SAA 10 198 r.9 and 227:27; note also *pi-i-ka am-mì-u ša* DÙG.GA, SAA 3 13:13 and 26. The restoration of *šá* at the end of the break imposes itself, there being no room for *šá* (required by the subjunctive predicate) in the following line. vi 5 The rare literary word *habūnu* occurs in a similar context in Tammuz-Ištar love lyrics, where the goddess refers to the bosom of her lover ("your [i.e., Tammuz's] bosom is full of ..." Pallis Akitu p. 8:18), and is therefore likely to carry the same connotation here too. See Introduction, p. XXXIII. vi 7-12 Cf. col. i 15ff. and Isa. 48:3-6, "Long ago I announced what would first happen, I revealed it with my own mouth; suddenly I acted and it came about ... I told you of these things long ago, and declared them before they came about, so that you could not say, 'This was my idol's doing ... he ordained them.' You have heard what I said; consider it well, and you must admit the truth of it. Now I show you new things, hidden things which you did not know before." See also note on no. 3 ii 17. vi 13ff → nos. 2 ii 21ff and 3 iii 25ff, by the same prophet, also containing cultic demands. vi 19-30 → no. 2 ii 11-14 (by the same prophet). On Assyrian crown princes as incarnations of Ninurta, see Introduction, p. XXXIXff. Cf. Isa. 9:6, "A boy has been born for us, a son given to us to bear the symbol of dominion on his shoulder; and he shall be called in purpose wonderful, in battle God-like, Father for all time, Prince of Peace," and see M. Weinfeld, *Social Justice in Ancient Israel and in the Ancient Near East* (Jerusalem 1955), p. 71. vi 27ff Cf. Ps. 2:7, rendering with Tur-Sinai, "I will put you in my lap" // Ruth 4:16, see Weinfeld, *The Promise of the Land* (1993), p.

31 *ša pi-i* ᵐ*la—da-gíl*—DINGIR
32 DUMU URU.*arba-ìl*

---

blank space of 5 lines
rest (about 8 lines) broken away

[31] By the mouth of La-dagil-ili of Arbela.

---

243 n. 87.

Collection Two

FIG. 24. *Birds circling around a tree (reign of Sargon II, cf. oracle 2.3).*
BM 118829.

2. Oracles Concerning Babylon and the Stabilization of the King's Rule

K 12033 (unpub.) + 82-5-22,527 TI pl.2f+

2.1 [NABÛ]-HUSSANNI

I beginning (about 5 lines) destroyed
1′ [*x x x x x x-b*]*u*$^{!}$*-bu-ni*
2′ [*x x x x x ú-da-ʾ*]*i*$^{!}$*-i-nu*$^{!}$
3′ [*x x x x x x x x*]*-ši-na*
4′ [*x x x x x*] *a-da-an*
5′ [*x x a-na-ku*$^{?}$] ⌜^{d}⌝*ba-ni-tu*
6′ [*x x x x x*] *ú-ta-qa-an*
7′ [GIŠ.GU.ZA$^{?}$ *ša* ^{m}*aš-šur*—PAB]—AŠ$^{!}$ *ú-ka-na*
8′ [*x x x x x x*] *a-ni-nu* ^{d}IŠ.TAR.MEŠ
9′ [*x x x x i*]*na* É.SAG.ÍL
10′ [*x x x x* ^{m}]*aš-šur*—PAB—AŠ MAN KUR—*aš-šur*
11′ [LÚ.KÚR.MEŠ-*ka*] ⌜*ú*⌝*-sa-pa-ak*
12′ [*ina* GÌR.2-*ia*] *ú-kab-ba-as*
13′ [*la ta-pa-a*]*l*$^{!}$*-li-hi* AMA—MAN
blank space (slightly less than a line)
14′ [TA* *pi-i* ^{md}PA]—*hu-sa-an-ni* URU.ŠÀ—URU-*a-a*

(Beginning broken away)

i 1 [...... *sp*]*oke*
2 [... have *stre*]*ngthened*
3 [......] their
4 [......] I will give
5 [... *I am*] the Creatress.
6 I will put [...] in order and consolidate [the *throne* of Esarha]ddon.
8 [......]. We are the goddesses
9 [...... i]n Esaggil.
10 Esarhaddon, king of Assyria! I will seize [your enemies] and trample [them under my foot].
13 [Be not a]fraid, mother of the king.
14 [From the mouth of *Nabû*]-hussanni of the Inner City.

2.2 [BAYÂ]

15′ [*la ta-pa*]*-làh* ^{m}*aš-šur*—PAB—AŠ
16′ [*a-ki* LÚ.M]Á$^{!}$.LAH$_4$ *dam*$^{!}$*-qí ina ka-a-ri* DÙG.GA
17′ [GIŠ.MÁ *ú-k*]*al-la a-ki šá pa-ni-ti*
18′ [*lu ina u*]*r*$^{!}$*-ki-ti ina bat-bat-ti-ka*
19′ [*a-sa-hu*]*r*$^{!}$ *ma-ṣar-ta-ka a*$^{!}$*-na-ṣar*

15 [Have no fe]ar, Esarhaddon!
16 [Like a] skilled pilot [I will st]eer [the ship] into a good port. [The fu]ture [shall] be like the past; [I will go] around you and protect you.

---

2 Photo pls. IV-V. Copy Langdon, TI (1914), pls. 2-3. The fragment K 12033 was identified and joined to 82-5-22,527 by the editor in June, 1969, and March, 1971. Collated by the editor in July, 1992 (82-5-22,527 also in November, 1966). i 2 Or, less likely, *ú-za-ʾ*]*i-i-nu* "have ado]rned." i 5 Despite the reference to Esaggil in line 9, the broken first sign is not *za*]*r* but DI]NGIR (coll.); cf. the corresponding sign forms in col. ii 6 and 14. Banitu ("Creatrix," actually an appellative of Belet-ili, see CAD B 95 s.v. *bānû* A; Tallqvist Götterepitheta, pp. 70f and 275; Deller, Assur 3 [1983] 142) was worshiped as an independent deity in the Aššur temple of Nineveh (see STT 88 ii 6). i 7 Restoration based on no. 1 iii 21′; cf. col. ii 5′. i 8 See Introduction, p. XVIII. i 9 → col. ii 24 and iv 4′, and see Introduction, pp. XLIV and LXIX. i 11 The rendering of ⌜*ú*⌝*-sa-pa-ak* is based on Syr. *sbk* "to fasten upon, assail, attack; (Pa.) to cling, seize, lay hold, catch" (Payne Smith, p. 357f); cf. SAA 2 6:589 (referring to the catching of beasts). For the devoicing of the middle radical cf., e.g., *abiktu* → *a-pi-ik-te*, ABL 158:22, and see LAS II p. 257. Taking ⌜*ú*⌝*-sa-pa-ak* as a form of *šapāku* "to pour" (thus Nougayrol, Syria 33 [1956] 159 n. 6) is of course impossible. i 13 Cf. col. iv 28 and see note on no. 1 v 8. i 14 For the restoration of the prophet's name see Introduction, p. LI. i 16f Cf. JNES 33 (1974) 284:5, "I am a ship, [I do not know] at which quay I put in" (royal *dingiršadibba* psalm), and Cicero's famous metaphor of "the ship of state rocked in the open sea by the storms of seditions and discords" (*pro Sestio* 20:46); see also Introduction, n. 296, for other occurrences of this metaphor in Mesopotamian and Classical literature.
i 17 The verb *kullu* normally means "to keep, hold," but this meaning would make no sense in an oracle promising *relief* from a stormy political situation (cf. col. iii 9′ and 33′, and see Introduction, p. LXIX). The required meaning "to drive, steer" is rare but attested in BBSt. no. 6:27 and 37 (referring to a chariot), see CAD *kullu* 1b. i 17f → no. 1 ii 37. i 18 Cf. col. ii 7′f; the traces before *ma-* preclude restoring [*a-la-ab-b*]*i*.

20′ [*ma-ṣar-tú šá*] KUR.KUR *da*!*-an-na-at a—dan-niš*
21′ [60 DINGIR.MEŠ *ina* ZAG]-*ia* 60 DINGIR.MEŠ *ina* KAB-*ia*
22′ [*i-za-zu* ^{m}]*aš-šur*—PAB—AŠ MAN KUR—*aš-šur*
23′ [LÚ.KÚR.MEŠ-*k*]*a*! *a-ka-šá-ad*
24′ [*x x x x x x*]*x* EN-*šú-nu a-na-ku*
25′ [*x x x x x* TA Š]U.2-*ia mah-ru*
26′ [*x x x x x x x*] ⌜*ú*⌝-*da-in-an-ni-ni*
27′ [*x x x x x x x x* ^{m}]*aš-šur*—PAB—AŠ
28′ [*x x x x x x x x*].MEŠ *šá* AN-*e*
29′ [*x x x x x x x x x*]*x par-šá-mu-tú*
30′ [*x x x x x x x x*]*x ú-šal-lak-šú*
31′ [*x x x x x x x x*]*x ú-ka-na*
32′ [*x x x x x x x ú-šá-a*]*n*!*-mar*
33′ [*x x x x x x š*]*ul-me* ⌜*šá*⌝ [^{m}*aš-šur*—PAB]—AŠ!
34′ [*x x x x x x*] *ú-x*[*x x*]*x*
35′ [TA* *pi-i* MÍ.*ba-ia*]-⌜*a*⌝ URU.*arba-ìl*-⌜*a-a*⌝

[20] [The watch over] the lands is very strong. [Sixty gods are standing at] my [right side], sixty gods at my left.

[22] Esarhaddon, king of Assyria! I will vanquish yo[ur enemies].

[24] [......] I am their lord

[25] [... from] my hand they have received

[26] [......] strengthened me

[27] [......] Esarhaddon

[28] [......]s of the heavens

[29] [......] old age

[30] [......] I will make him go

[31] [......] I will consolidate

[32] [...... I will l]ight

[33] [...... the w]ell-being of [Esarhadd]on

[34] [......] I will [...].

[35] [From the mouth of Bay]â of Arbela.

2.3 LA-DAGIL-ILI

36′ [*a-na-ku* ^{d}*b*]*e-let—arba-ìl*
37′ [^{m}*aš-šur*—PAB—AŠ MAN] ⌜KUR⌝—*aš-šur*
38′ [*la ta-pa-làh x x x x x*]-⌜*ti*⌝
rest (about two lines) destroyed
II beginning (3-4 lines) destroyed
1′ ⌜LÚ⌝.KÚR.MEŠ-*ka mar*! [*šu-nu-ni x x* (*x*)]
2′ *ina* ŠÀ-*bi* É.GAL-*ka lu* [*kam-mu-sa-ka*?]
3′ KUR—*aš-šur*.KI *is-si-ka* ⌜*ú*⌝-[*sal-lam*]
4′ *ša kal*—UD-*me kal-la-ma-r*[*i ma-ṣar-ta-ka*]
5′ *a-na-ṣar a-gu-ka* ⌜*ú*!⌝-[*ka-na*]
6′ *a-ki iṣ-ṣur a-kap-pi ina* U[GU! AMAR-*šú*]
7′ *ina* UGU-*hi-ka a-ṣab-bur ina bat-*⌜*bat*⌝-[*ti-k*]*a*
8′ *a-la-ab-bi a-sa-hu-ur*
9′ *a-ki mu-ra*!!*-ni dam*!!*-qí ina* É.GAL-*ka*
10′ *a-du-al* LÚ.KÚR.MEŠ-*ka ú-ṣa-a-na*
11′ *ina* É.GAL-*ka ú-ta-qa-an-ka*
12′ *ni-kit-tu ni-ir-ri-ṭu ú-šá-an-ṣa-ka*

[36] [I am the La]dy of Arbela. [Esarhaddon, king of] Assyria, [fear not!]

(Break)

[ii 1] [*I will annihilate*] whatever enemies you [have]. *As for* [*you, stay*] in your palace; I will [reconcile] Assyria with you. I will protect [you] by day and by dawn and [consolidate] your crown.

[6] Like a winged bird ov[er its *young*] I will twitter over you and go in circles around you. Like a beautiful (*lion*) cub I will run about in your palace and sniff out your enemies.

[11] I will keep you safe in your palace; I will make you overcome anxiety and trem-

i 21f → no. 1 ii 24′ff. i 23 Cf. col. iii 32′. i 24 See coll. The topmost horizontal of the sign before EN is too long for -*k*]*u* or -*k*]*i*, implying -*m*]*a*, -*a*]*t*, -*š*]*u*, or the like. i 25 Cf. Introduction, p. XXIVf. i 28 Possible restorations include MUL].MEŠ "stars," MUŠEN].MEŠ "birds," DINGIR].MEŠ "gods." i 29-34 See coll. Lines 34′f are written in smaller script than the rest of the column, and the two lines appear to be compressed into the space of one normal line. i 32 → no. 1 iii 27. i 35 For the restoration see Introduction, p. IL. ii 1 See coll. ii 2 For the restoration cf. ABL 1217 r.22, Streck Asb p. 116 v 64 (Introduction, p. XLVII), and SAA 10 89 r.7. Restoring *lu-*[*taq-qi-in-ka*] on the basis of col. ii 10f is unlikely since all other 1st person forms in this prophecy are in the indicative present; cf. no. 11 r.4f. ii 3 Cf. iii 20 (angry gods reconciled with Assyria) and no. 1 ii 31 (Aššur reconciled with the king). ii 5 Cf. YOS 1 72:40, "May he (Sin) establish (*lu-ki-in*) my royal crown (*a-ge-e šar-ru-ti-ia*) forever on my (Nabunaid's) head." ii 6f Cf. Deut. 32:10f, "He guarded him as the apple of his eye, as an eagle watches over its nest, hovers over its young" [Weinfeld]; Isa. 31:5, "Thus YHWH Zebaoth, like a bird hovering over its young, will be a shield over Jerusalem"; the idiom "winged bird" has an equivalent in biblical *ṣpwr knp* (Ps. 148:10). Besides AMAR, "young," one could, of course, also restore *qin-ni-šú* "its nest," cf. the examples cited CAD s.v. *qinnu*. ii 9 Tablet: *mu-*ṢI*-ni* NIN-*qí*; scribal error (see coll.). Cf. Isa. 31:4, "As a lion or a young lion growls over its prey..., so shall YHWH of Hosts come down to do battle for Mount Zion." The word *mūrānu* can also mean "young dog, puppy" (see CAD s.v. *mirānu*), but this would make less sense in the present context where the "cub" clearly represents a mortal danger to the king's enemies (cf. line 20). Note also the adjective *damqu* "beautiful" attached to the word, and see Introduction, fig. 10, for the lion as the emblematic animal of Ištar (goddess of beauty). ii 10 *ú-ṣa-a-na* is D pres. of *eṣānu* "to smell, to scent" (CAD E 344f) with coordinative pitch on the final syllable (see LAS II p. 26, note on no. 18 r.8); the D stem is required by the plurality of the object (see ibid. p. 129, note on r.8). ii 11-14 Cf. no. 1 vi 19-30 (same prophet). ii 12 *maṣû* is usually intransitive in NA, but the present transitive usage has a parallel in Syriac, where *mṣ*ʾ ethpe. means both "to

13′ DUMU.UŠ-*ka* DUMU.UŠ—DUMU.UŠ-*ka*
14′ LUGAL!-*u-tu ina* IGI ^{d}MAŠ *up-pa-áš*
15′ *ta-hu-ma-a-ni ša* KUR.KUR
16′ *ú-ga-am-mar a-da-nak-ka*
17′ *a-me-lu-tu ṭùl-lu-ma-a*
18′ *a-na-ku ši-i qa-bi-tu e-pi-is-su*
19′ DUMU.MÍ *hu-bur-tu a-na-ku*
20′ *ú-ṣa-a-na ú-*⌜*ba*!*-ra ad-da*⌝-[*nak*]-*ka*!
21′ *at-ta a-na a-a-ši na-i-da-an-ni*
22′ *di-ib-bi-*⌜*ia*!⌝ *an-nu-ti* TA* ŠÀ URU.*arba-ìl*
23′ *ina* É-*a-nu-uk-ka e-si-ip*
24′ DINGIR.MEŠ *ša* É.SAG.ÍL *ina* EDIN HUL! *bal-li*!
25 *šar-bu-bu ar-hi-iš* 2 GIBÍL.MEŠ
26′ *ina pa-ni-šú-nu lu-še-ṣi-ú lil-li-ku*
27′ *šu-lam-ka li-iq-bi-u*
28′ TA* *pi-i šá* ^{m}*la—da-gíl*—DINGIR URU.*arba-ìl-a-a*

bling. Your son and grandson shall rule as kings before Ninurta.

15 I will abolish the frontiers of all the lands and give them to you.

17 Mankind is deceitful; I am one who says and does. I will sniff out, catch and give you the 'noisy daughter.'

21 As for you, praise me! Gather into your innards these words of mine from Arbela:

24 The gods of Esaggil languish in the 'steppe' of mixed evil. Quickly let two burnt offerings be sent out to their presence, and let them go and announce your well-being!

28 From the mouth of La-dagil-ili of Arbela.

2.4 URKITTU-ŠARRAT

29′ *a-ki ta-ap-pa-la la ke-nu-ti*
30′ *a-bat* ^{d}15! *šá* URU.*arba-ìl a-bat šar-ra-ti* ^{d}NIN!.LÍL
31′ *a-da*!*-gal as-sa-nam-me*
32′ *ú-ha-a-a-a-ṭa*! *la ke-nu-ti*
33′ *ina* ŠU.2 LUGAL-*ia a-šá-kan*

29 *Thus shall you* answer the disloyal ones!

30 The word of Ištar of Arbela, the word of Queen Mullissu:

31 I will look, I will listen, I will search out the disloyal ones, and I will put them into the

be able" and "to prevail over, overcome" (see Payne Smith, p. 293). ii 15 Cf. Isa. 10:13, "I (the king of Assyria) have removed the frontiers of nations and plundered their treasures." → no. 7:13. ii 17f Cf. Jer. 10:14-16, "All men are brutish and ignorant... God, Jacob's creator, is not like these," and, for Mesopotamia, the *dingiršadibba* passage JNES 33 (1974) 284:6, "the iniquities, [sins, and transgressions] of mankind are more numerous than the hairs of his head" (// Ps. 40:12, "my iniquities ... are more than the hairs of my head" [Weinfeld]). *ṭùl-lu-ma-a* is an Aram. loanword, see von Soden, Or. 37 (1968) 261, and cf. Syr. *ṭolûm*, *ṭolûmô* "unjust, faithless, ungrateful," and *ṭlm* "to oppress, wrong, cheat, defraud, deceive, deal falsely, treat wrongly, unjustly" (Payne Smith p. 174f). The meaning "treacherous, deceitful" implied by the context also fits ABL 281 r.4 *šú-nu ṭùl-lu-um-ma-a*ʾ (referring to the Elamites). → no. 1 ii 27ff. ii 19 → ii 31f. 'Noisy daughter' is certainly a metaphor for "corrupt men" (with 'daughter' referring to mankind as God's creation), cf. Isa. 5:14, "Therefore Sheol gapes with straining throat, down go nobility and common people, their noisy bustling mob." The same idea occurs in the Babylonian Flood story (see Lambert-Millard, *Atra-hasis*, pp. 72 and 106-121), where the "noise" (*hubūru*) of mankind corresponds to the "corruption of the world" of Gen. 6:11-13 (cf. my remarks in JNES 52 [1993] 199 n. 147). See also Introduction, n. 14. The insertion of *anāku* after the object is unusual and probably served for emphasis; the word order is paralleled by SAA 5 56 r.4ff, LÚ.TIN.[MEŠ ... *a*]*-na-ku a-ti-din*, and NL 31:8ff, *ma-qar-ra-a-ti ša ku-pe-e a-na-ku ... ú-se-bi-la*. ii 22ff → nos. 1 vi 13ff and 3 iii 25ff, by the same prophet, also containing cultic demands. ii 24 A reference to the damaged images of gods deported to Assyria after the destruction of Babylon, see Introduction, p. LXXIV. The 'steppe of evil' is likely to be a metaphor for the "exile" of the gods; cf. no. 1 v 20, where "steppe" refers to Esarhaddon's own exile, and Borger Esarh. p. 23 Ep. 32, where the images are said to have suffered "evil desecration" (*šalputtu lummuntu*). At the end of the line, *-li* is absolutely clear (see coll.) and reading *bal-ti* "thistle" (Nougayrol, Syria 33 [1956] p. 59 n. 6) is excluded. It is unlikely that *bal-li* is a mistake for *balliṭ* "revive!", since the standard NA spelling of the latter was *bal-liṭ* (81 examples), not *bal-li-iṭ* (1 example, SAA 10 185 r.25). ii 25 For *maqlūtu* "burnt offering, sacrifice of atonement" see LAS II p. 157, note on 167 r.7. While these offerings evidently were to be performed before the images in the 'steppe,' their real destination, of course, was heaven. Cf. Borger Esarh., p. 14, Ep. 8: "(At the destruction of Babylon), the gods and goddesses who dwelt within it abandoned their shrines (var. flew off like birds) and ascended to heaven." The reading of GIBÍL as *maqlūtu* (not *qilūtu*, *kiskibirru*, or the like) is confirmed by the Asn. passages cited CAD M/1 252a, where GIBÍL.MEŠ alternates with *ma-aq-lu-te* and GIBÍL-*te* in the phrase *ana maqlūte ašrup*. ii 27 The idiom *šulmu qabû*, lit. "to announce the well-being," is otherwise attested twice in NA, in contexts showing that it could mean both "to greet" (see SAA 5 108:4) and "to report on somebody's health" (see SAA 10 304:9). In the present case, the king's well-being implied the well-being of the entire cosmos (cf. no. 3 i 9ff and Introduction, p. LXIV), so announcing it to the gods of Babylon effectively meant putting an end to their exile, i.e. the period of disrupted cosmic harmony initiated by the destruction of Babylon. ii 29 Or: "How do you/does she answer ...," taking *a-ki* as a scribal error for *a-ke-e* "how" and *tappala* as a 3rd sg. f. form referring to Ištar. For *akī* "thus" cf. SAA 10 277 r.8 (written *a-ki-i*), and see also LAS II p. 249:13 for two instances of *a-ke-e* meaning "thus." ii 30 Cf. SAA 3 7:11, "Out comes the Lady of the Land, queen Mullissu" (^{d}NIN.LÍL *ša*[*r-r*]*a-tú*), there referring to Ištar of Nineveh, and see Introduction, p. XVIII; → no. 7:2. ii 31 For the rendering of *as-sa-nam-me*, cf. line 35 showing that the Gtn stem of *šm*ʾ in NA could simply mean "to listen," without any iterative or frequentative connotation. Cf. also SAA 3 14 r.31f. ii 32 *ú-ha-a-a-a-ṭa* (sic): see coll. Despite coll. Wiseman *apud* Deller, Or. 27

34′ *a-da*!*-ab-ub*!! *a-na ma-a*ʾ*-[du-ti]*
35′ *si-ta-am-me-a na-pa-ah*! [^{d}UTU-*ši*]
36′ *ra*!*-ba*! ^{d}UTU!*-ši a*!*-x[x x x x]*
37′ *a-*⸢*ba*⸣!*-an-ni [x x x x x]*
38′ *a-bat* ⸢^{d}15⸣ [*šá* URU.*arba-ìl*]
39′ *a-*⸢*na x*⸣ *[x x x x x x]*
about two lines broken away
III beginning (about two lines) destroyed
1′ *lu-u et-k[a-ka x x x x x x]*
2′ LÚ.*da-gíl*—⸢MUŠEN⸣.[MEŠ *x x x x*]
3′ *a-na-*⸢*ku*⸣*-ma bi-[x x x x x]*
4′ *a-g*⸢*a-lal*⸣ *ma-a*ʾ*-d[u-ti x x x x]*
5′ *a-bi-ar* ⸢*ú*⸣*-b[a]-r[a x x x x x]*
6′ *a-*⸢*na-ku*⸣ *x[x x x]x* ⸢*a*⸣*-x[x x x x]*

7′ ⸢*a*!*-ke*⸣!*-e*! *a*!*-ke-e ša a-na*! LÚ!.[ERIM?.MEŠ]
8′ *ma-a*ʾ*-du-ti ú*!*-[[sa?]]-na-*ʾ*u-[x-ni]*
9′ *ma-a im—ma-ti* KUR *na-ku-ru ib-ba-áš-ši*
10′ *ma-a ina* URU.*kal-hi* NINA.KI *lu la nu-šab*
11′ *at-ta lu qa-la-ka* ^{m}*aš-šur*—PAB—AŠ

12′ LÚ.*ṣi-ra-ni* NIM.MA.KI*-a-a*
13′ KUR.*man-na-a-a a-bi-ar* KUR.URI*-a-a*
14′ *ši-iṭ-ri-šú a-bar-ri-im*
15′ *i-gi-ib ša* ^{m}*mu-gal-li*! *ú-bat-taq*

16′ *man-nu* LÚ.*e-du man-nu* LÚ.*ha-ab-lu*
17′ *la ta-pa-làh ina* GIŠ.MI ^{m}*aš-šur*—PAB—AŠ MAN KUR—*aš-šur*

18′ TA* *pi-i* MÍ.*ur-kit-tu—šar-rat* URU.*kal-hi-tú*

hands of my king.

34 I will speak to the multi[tudes]:

35 Listen, sunr[ise] and sunset! I will create [......].

38 The word of Ištar [of Arbela] to [......]
(Break)

iii 1 Be on [your] guard [......]
2 the augur[s ......]
3 I myself [......]
4 I will roll many [......]
5 I will choose and *catc[h* ......]
6 I [......].

7 How, how (to answer) those who ... many [*men*], saying, "When will the change in the land come about? Let us not stay in Calah and Nineveh!" As for you, keep silent, Esarhaddon!

12 I will choose the emissaries of the Elamite and the Mannean. I will seal the writings of the Urarṭian. I will cut off the ... of Mugallu.

16 Who (then) is the lone man? Who is the wronged man? Have no fear! Well sheltered is Esarhaddon, king of Assyria.

18 From the mouth of the woman Urkittu-šarrat of Calah.

2.5 [SINQIŠA-AMUR]

19′ ^{m}⸢*aš-šur*—PAB—AŠ⸣ *la ta-pa-làh* KUR—*aš-šur ú-ta-qa-an*
20′ DINGIR.MEŠ ⸢*ze*!*-nu*!*-ti*⸣! [T]A! ⸢KUR!—*aš-šur*!⸣ *ú*!*-sal*⸣!*-[l]am*!
21′ *ṣi-ip-pu-tu ša* LÚ.⸢KÚR.MEŠ⸣*-ka a*!*-na*!*-sa-ah*

19 Esarhaddon, have no fear! I will put Assyria in order and reconcile the angry gods with Assyria.

21 I will pull away the *cover* of your

(1958) 121, the last sign certainly is DA not *ša*, which in this tablet is consistently written with four horizontals. Cf. the form of DA in lines 31 and 34. ii 34 *a-da-ab-ub*!!: tablet *a-da-ab-*BI, scribal error. For the spelling cf. *ak-tar-ar*, no. 3 iii 30. ii 35 Cf., e.g., Isa. 1:2, "Hark you heavens, and earth give ear, for YHWH has spoken"; 8:9 "Listen, all you distant parts of the earth"; Mic. 1:2, "Listen, you peoples, all together; attend, O earth and all who are in it." → no. 3 i 27. ii 36 See coll. ii 37 Reading *a-*⸢*ka*⸣*-an-ni* excluded. ii 39 See coll. The broken sign after *a-na* is either MAN "king" or KUR "land." iii 2ff See coll. iii 4 Cf. Bibl. *gll*, mostly referring to a stone rolled unto or away, but also metaphorically to grief etc., e.g. Josh. 5:9, "Today I (Yahweh) have rolled away from you the reproaches of the Egyptians." iii 6 See coll.; the last sign of *a-*⸢*na-ku*⸣ cannot be read ⸢*ṣar*⸣, as the traces are incompatible with those of *ṣar* in line 23. iii 8 See coll.; the sign after the erased sign cannot be read *ba*. iii 8-10 Similar echoes of the voices of domestic critics and opponents are also found in biblical prophecy, e.g. Jer. 18:12 and 18. iii 9 Lit., "When will changing the land take place?"; for a similarly structured phrase see, e.g., PKTA pl. 36 ii 8-13, GIŠ.IG.MEŠ *pa-tu-ú* ... LÚ.*láh-hi-nu pu-tu-hu na-ši* "opening the doors ... is the responsibility of the temple steward." The present passage implies a prolonged period of disorder in Assyria after Esarhaddon's accession. Cf. Gilg. X 316, "Does hostility exist forever in the country?", and 2 Sam. 2:26, "Will the sword devour forever?" [Weinfeld]. iii 15 *i-gi-ib*: possibly, though unlikely, to be connected with *ikkibu* "sacred thing (or place)," or with SB *eqbu*, Syr. *eqb* "heel, hoof" (cf. Isa. 9:13, "Therefore YHWH cut off from Israel head and tail"). On Mugallu, king of Melid (Melitene), see SAA 4 p. LVIIf and cf. no. 3 i 35. iii 16 Cf. SAA 3 12 r.15, "May the lone one (*e-du*) who has called to you, Lord, not die!" Note that the god appealed to in this royal prayer is not Ištar but Nabû, and see Introduction, p. XVIII. iii 19f → line 33f. iii 20 See coll. iii 21f Cf. Ezek. 32:6, "I will drench the land even to the mountains with your flowing(?) blood (*ṣptk mdmk*), and the watercourses shall be full of you." The rendering of *ṣipputu* is based on Syr. *ṣipptô* "a mat, matting" (Payne Smith p. 483), rabb. *ṣippetā* "Decke, Matte" (Dalman Aram. Wb. p. 367); none of the different meanings assigned to Akkadian *ṣippatu* in CAD ("orchard," a vegetable, a metal or alloy, a reed) fit the present

22′ *da-me ša* LÚ.KÚR.MEŠ *ša* LUGAL-*ia a-tab-ba-ak*
23′ *šar-ri a-na-ṣar* LÚ.KÚR.MEŠ *ina* GIŠ$^{!}$.*si-ga*$^{!}$-*ra-te*
24′ LÚ.*sa-al-mu-ti ina ma-da*$^{!}$-*na-ti*
25′ *ina* IGI GÌR.2-*šú ub-ba-la*
26′ *a-na-ku* AD-*ka* AMA-*ka*
27′ *bir-ti a-gap-pi-ia ur-ta-bi-ka*
28′ *né-ma-al-ka am-mar*
29′ *la ta-pal-làh* ^{m}*aš-šur*—PAB—AŠ
30′ *bir-ti i-zi-ri-ia am-ma-te-ia*
31′ *a-šá-kan-ka ina* ŠÀ-*bi u*$_{8}$-*a*
32′ LÚ.KÚR.MEŠ *ša* LUGAL-*ia a*-⸢*ka*⸣-[*šá-a*]*d*$^{!}$
33′ KUR—*aš-šur ú-ta-qa-an* ⸢LUGAL⸣-[*u-tu ša*]
34′ AN$^{!}$-*e ú-ta-qa-a*[*n x x x x*]
35′ [*na*]-⸢*pa*$^{!}$⸣-*ah* ^{d}UTU-*š*[*i x x x x*]
36′ [*ra-ba* ^{d}UTU-*š*]*i*$^{!}$ ⸢*x*⸣ [*x x x x*]
rest (about 5 lines) destroyed

IV beginning (2-3 lines) destroyed
1′ [*x x x x x x še*]-⸢*tu*$^{?}$⸣-*qi*
2′ [*x x x x x-a*]*l* ^{d}*aš-šur*
3′ [*x x x x x x x a*]*t-ta*
4′ [*x x x* É.SAG.Í]L KÁ.DINGIR.KI
5′ [*x x x x x x e*]*t-ka-ku*
6′ [*x x x x x x x*] ⸢*x x x*⸣ LU[GAL$^{?}$]

7′ [*x x x x*] *a-ti-din*
8′ [*a-na-ku* ^{d}*ur-k*]*i*$^{!}$-*tú na-id-a-ni*

9′ [*bé-et tal-la-k*]*u*$^{!}$-*u-ni a-na-ṣar*$^{!}$-*ka*
10′ [*x x x*]-*ra-ka*
11′ [*x x x x x*] *na-i-da-an-ni*
12′ [(*x*) *x x x*] ⸢*a*$^{!}$⸣—*dan-niš*
13′ [*x x x x d*]*a-ʾa-at-tú at-ta*
14′ [*x x x x l*]*a ta-pa-làh*
15′ [*x x x x x x* I]GI$^{!}$.2-*ka*
16′ [*x x x x š*]*ak*$^{!}$-⸢*na*⸣
17′ [*x x x x x x*]-⸢*du*$^{!}$⸣
18′ [*x x x x x x*]-⸢*ši*$^{!}$⸣
19′ [*x x x ú-sa-a*]*l*$^{!}$-*lam*
20′ [*la ta-pa-làh*] *mu-u-ri*
21′ [(*x*) *x x x x*] *gat*$^{!}$-*ta-ka a-ši*$^{!}$-*al*

enemies and shed the blood of my king's enemies. I will protect my king; I will bring enemies in neckstocks and vassals with tribute before his feet.

26 I am your father and mother. I raised you between my wings; I will see your success.

29 Have no fear, Esarhaddon! I will place you between my arm and my forearm. In woe I will vanquish the enemies of my king. I will put Assyria in order, I will put the kin[gdom of] heaven in order. [...]

35 [t]he sunri[se ......]

36 [the sunse]t [......]

(Break)

2.6 UNKNOWN PROPHET

iv 1 [...... *to a*]*vert*
2 [......] Aššur
3 [...... y]ou
4 [... Esaggi]l, Babylon
5 [......] I am on my guard
6 [...... to *my*] king
7 I gave [......].
8 [I am Urk]ittu. Praise me!
9 [Wherever you g]o, I will guard you.
10 [......] you
11 [......]. Praise me!
12 [......] very
13 [...... s]trong, you
14 [......] Have no fear!
15 [......] your eyes
(Break)
19 [I will re]concile [......]
20 [Have no fear], my calf!
21 I will cover your figure [......].

context, so an Aramaic loanword is very likely to be in question. → no. 3 ii 22f. iii 23ff → no. 1 ii 3ff. Cf. Ezek. 19:9, "They brought him in neckstocks (*bswgr*) ... to the king of Babylon" [Weinfeld], and Borger Esarh. p. 54:30, "My troops threw RN with his men into irons and brought them to me. I put them in neckstocks (GIŠ.*ši-ga-ru*) and fettered them beside my city gate." This practice had a long history in Mesopotamia reaching back to the mid-third millennium BC, see I.J. Gelb, "Prisoners of War in Early Mesopotamia," JNES 32 (1972) 70ff, esp. p. 73: "Captives were put in *neckstocks* (Sumerian GIŠ.*si-gar*, Akkadian *šigarum*), as expressed by the sentence 'Sargon took captive Lugalzagesi, king of Uruk, and brought him in a neckstock (Sumerian GIŠ.*si-gar-ta e-túm*, Akkadian *in si-gar-rìm u-ru-uš*) to the gate of Enlil.' iii 24 *sa-al-mu-ti*, lit. "peaceful ones" (i.e. those who have chosen peace, submitted to Assyrian rule, Aššur); cf. Arab. *aslama* "submit to God's will." iii 26f Cf. Isa. 66:13, "As a mother comforts her son, so will I myself (Yahweh) comfort you," and SAA 3 3:13ff, "I (Assurbanipal) knew no father or mother, I grew up in the lap of my goddesses." → nos. 1 ii 32′ and 7 r.6ff, and see Introduction, p. XL. iii 30 → col. iv 20′-23′. For *izirû* (certainly a WSem. loanword in NA, see CAD s.v.) cf. Hebr. *ʾezrōᶜ/zᵉrōᶜ* and Aram. *drāᶜā* (Syr. *drōᶜô*), both "arm, shoulder (portion)." iii 31 → nos. 1 i 26f and 9:2" iii 32 → no. 3 i 28. iii 33f Cf. line 19f. On the "kingdom of heaven" see Introduction, p. XLIII and n. 25; the reading ⸢LUGAL⸣ is certain, and the restoration agrees perfectly with the available space (coll.). iii 35f → col. ii 35f. iii 36 The partially preserved sign after -*ši* is either MAN or KUR. iv 2 See coll.; the traces of -*al* agree with those in line iv 21. iv 4 See coll. → col. i 9, ii 24. iv 6 Small script; the break goes through the line. iv 8 See Introduction, p. XVIII. iv 9 Cf. 2 Sam. 7:9, "I have been with you wherever you have gone." iv 10 Line spaced out. iv 13 See LAS II p. 202, note on 206:8. iv 15ff See coll. iv 20 For restoration see no. 7 r.11. iv 21 The reading *a-ši-al* is certain, and the coll. *a-pi*$^{!}$-*al* cited in CAD Š/1 p. 283 (under *šâlu* B "to coat,

22′ [*bir-ti i-z*]*i*$^{!}$*-ri-ia*
23′ [*am-ma-te-ia a-n*]*a-ṣar-ka*

24′ [*x x x x x*] *ke-e-ni*
25′ [*x x x tu-b*]*a*$^{?}$*-ʾa-a-ni*
26′ [*x x x-b*]*i*$^{?}$ *ina pa-ni-ia*

27′ [*x x x x* L]UGAL*-ta-ka ú-ta-qa-an*
28′ [*x x x x l*]*a*$^{!}$ *ta-pal-li-hi*

29′ [*x x x x t*]*u-kul-ti* ^{d}*aš-šur*
30′ [*x x x x l*]*a ta-pa-làh*
31′ [*x x x x x x x*]⌜*x*⌝[*x*]*x*
rest (about six lines) destroyed

22 [I will sh]elter you [between my uppe]r arm
23 [and my forearm].
24 [......] righteous
25 [...... *you s*]*eek me*
26 [......] in my presence
27 [......] I will put your kingdom in order.
28 [*As for you, mother of the king*], have no fear!
29 [......] the support of Aššur.
30 [*Esarhaddon*], have no fear!
(Rest destroyed)

smear") should be disregarded. iv 22f → col. iii 30f. iv 24 Possibly "rightful [heir]," cf. no. 1 iv 5. iv 25f See coll. iv 30 The name of Esarhaddon is to be restored either in this or the following line.

FIG. 25. *Tame lion roaming in a park (reign of Assurbanipal, see oracle 2.3).*
BM 118916.

Collection Three

FIG. 26. *Sennacherib facing Aššur/Enlil and Ištar/Mullissu in the Maltai rock relief.*
ORIGINAL DRAWING II, 28.

3. The Covenant of Aššur

K 2401

I 1 [*x x x x x x x x x x*]
2 [*x x x x x x x x x x*]
3 [*x x x x x x x x*]-⌈*an*!?⌉
4 [*x x x x x x x x*]-*nu*!-*ni*
5 [*x x x x x x x*] *ṭa*!-*ab-tú*
6 [*x x x x x x x*]*x di-na*!
7 [*x x x x i*]*h-ti-ṣi-in*!
8 [*x x x-šú-n*]*u*! *us-se-li-a*
9 [DI-*mu a*]-*na* AN-*e u* KI.TIM
10 [DI-*m*]*u*! *a-na* É.ŠÁR.RA
11 [DI-*mu*] ⌈*a*!?⌉-*na* {m}*aš-šur*—PAB—AŠ MAN KUR—*aš-šur*
12 [*šul-m*]*u šá* {m}*aš-šur*—PAB—AŠ
13 [*iš-kun*]-*u*!-*ni*! *ina* UGU GÌR.2 *lil-lik*
14 [*i-sin-nu ina*] ⌈É⌉.ŠÁR.RA {d}*aš-šur is-sa-kan*
15 [(*x*) *x x*] *ša* URU!.ŠÀ—URU

16 [*x x x* {m}*aš*]-⌈*šur*!—PAB!?⌉—AŠ
17 [(*x*) *x x x x x x x x-n*]*i*
18 [*x x x x i-n*]*a*!-*áš-ši*
19 [*x x x x x x x*] KUR.KUR

20 [*x x x x*]-⌈*ti*⌉ *ina* IGI {d}*aš-šur*
21 [*x x x*]-⌈*a*?⌉-*ni* TA* {m}*aš-šur*—PAB—AŠ
22 [*x x x*] *il-lak-u-ni*
23 [*x x x x*]-*šú i-šar-ru-pu*

ABRT 1 22f

3.1 INTRODUCTION

(Beginning destroyed)

i 5 favour [......]
6 *give* [......]!
7 He has taken care of [...],
8 he has promoted th[eir ...].
9 Heaven and earth are [well]; Ešarra is [wel]l; Esarhaddon, king of Assyria, is [well].
12 [May the well-b]eing which Esarhaddon [has established] *gain footing*!
14 Aššur has arranged [*a feast* in] Ešarra.
15 [......] of the Inner City
16 [...... Es]arhaddon
17 [......]
18 [...... *l*]*ifts up*
19 [......] the lands
20 [......] before Aššur
21 [......] with Esarhaddon
22 [......] they come
23 [......] they burn

3 Photo pls. VI-VII. Copy Strong, BA 2 (1893), 637-643 (cols. ii and iii only) and Craig, ABRT I (1895), pls. 22-25, with corrections in Vol. II, pp. ix-x. Collated by the editor in November, 1966, and July, 1992. i 4ff If *di-na* in line 6 is the imperative of *tadānu* "to give," the text probably began with a blessing resembling those invoked at the Assyrian coronation ritual and *tākultu* ceremony, see note on no. 1 iv 14ff and Introduction, p. LXIV. The fragmentary verbal form at the end of line 4 is then possibly to be restored *id-di*]-*nu-ni* "[who has gi]ven," cf. Frankena Takultu p. 26 iv 9 // p. 8 x 19. i 6 See coll. Excepting the imp. *di-na* "give!", the only words in the SAA database ending in *di-na* are *i-di-na, id-di-na, li-di-na, lid-di-na, ta-di-na, ú-di-na, ud-di-na*, as well as the toponyms URU.*a-ra-di-na* and URU.*ṣa-i-di-na*. None of these words can be reconciled with the horizontal wedge preceding *di-na*. i 7 Objects of *haṣānu* "to take care of" attested in contemporary texts include various types of destitute people (deserters, refugees, slave-girls) and pack-animals, see ABL 210:13-16, SAA 2 2 iii 13f, Iraq 16 pl.6 ND 2307:45f, and NL 71:7. i 8 See coll. Note the ventive suffix in *us-se-li-a* "promoted" and see LAS II p. 106:14f. i 9-12 See note on no. 2 ii 27 and Introduction, p. LXIV. i 10 See coll. i 12 For the restoration see coll. and note on no. 1 v 26; the break at the beginning of the line is too wide for restoring DI-*mu*, as in lines 9-11. Restoring [*ṭè-m*]*u* "order" would be epigraphically possible but would make less sense. i 13 "Gain footing": lit., "go/become footed." This idiom is also attested (in fragmentary context) in CT 53 226:9′, and must not be confused with *ina šēpi alāku* "to go on foot," see SAA 10 294 r.14 and 18. Cf. *ana pāni alāku* "to improve" (SAA 10 329 r.3) and *ina muhhi issēt šēpi uzuzzu*, "to stand upon one foot, be infirm" (SAA 1 244 r.12). i 14 For the restoration cf. col. iv 6 and *šá-ki-in i-sin-nu* Gilg. I 211; *isinna ... kî taškunu*, EA 3:18. Note, however, PKTA pl.27:14f, referring to the *akītu* chapel of Assur (not Ešarra) as the place of "Aššur's festival" (*i-sin-ni* AN.ŠÁR). i 18 Traces of *n*]*a* as elsewhere in this column; see coll. The restoration *i-n*]*a-áš-ši* is based on the fact that only forms of *našû* end in *-na-áš-ši* in the SAA database. In Assyrian royal rituals, the verb mostly refers to the king lifting up the crown (*agû*) of Aššur and the weapons of Mullissu, see KAR 216+ ii 15 (coronation ritual), Or. 21 135:35 and r.5, CA pl.3 ii 22′f and r. iii 3, KAR 215 i 6′, or his jewelry (*dumāqī*), see Menzel Tempel T88:18 and T94:8. i 21 See coll. i 23 This line certainly referred to the burning of aromatics (ŠEM.MEŠ) during the ritual acts described (cf., e.g., the royal *naptunu* ritual MVAG 41 6 r. i 44f, ŠEM.MEŠ ... *i-šar-ru-pu*, and below, col. ii 31). The latter seem to have involved [sacrifices?] before the image of Aššur (line 20), followed by a procession lead by the king (lines 21f).

24 [*x x a-n*]*a*! *ga-ri-ni-šú*
25 [*x x x l*]*u*? MUN! 3! *tim-me*
26 [*x x x* IG]I.2?-*šú ú-še-taq*

24 [... t]o his mother
25 [...] ... three pillars
26 [...] he runs his [*ey*]*e* over [...].

---

27 [*si-ta-am*]-*me-a* DUMU.MEŠ KUR—*aš-šur*
28 [LUGAL LÚ.K]ÚR-*šú ik-ta-šad*
29 [LUGAL-*ku-n*]*u* LÚ.KÚR-*šú*
30 [*ina* KI.TA G]ÌR.2-*šú is-sa-kan*
31 [TA* *ra-b*]*a*! ^{d}UTU-*ši*
32 [*a-di na-pa-a*]*h* ^{d}UTU-*ši*
33 [TA* *na-pa-a*]*h* ^{d}UTU-*ši*
34 [*a-di ra*]-*ba* ^{d}UTU-*ši*
35 [URU.*me-li-d*]*i a-hap-pi*
36 [*x x x a-ha*]*p*!-⌜*pi*!⌝
37 [*x x x x x x x*]
II 1 [KUR].*gi-mir-a-a ina* ŠU!-*šú a*-⌜*šá*!-*kan*!⌝
2 ⌜*i*⌝-*šá-tu ina* KUR.*el-li-pi um-ma-ad*
3 *kip-pat erbe-tim* ^{d}*aš-šur it-ta-na-šú*
4 TA* É *i-nap-pa-ha-an-ni*
5 É *i-rab-bu-u-ni*
6 LUGAL *mi-hir-šú la-áš-šú*
7 *a-ki ṣi-it*—^{d}*šá-maš na-mir*
8 *an-ni-u* (sup. ras.) *šul-mu ša ina* IGI ^{d}EN—TÙR
9 *ina* IGI DINGIR.MEŠ-*ni šá-ki-nu-u-ni*

3.2 FIRST ORACLE OF SALVATION

27 [List]en, O Assyrians!

28 [The king] has vanquished his enemy. [You]r [king] has put his enemy [under] his foot, [from] sun[se]t [to] sun[ris]e, [from] sun[ris]e [to] sun[se]t!

35 I will destroy [*Meli*]*d*,

36 [I will de]stroy [...],

37 [*I will* ......],

ii 1 I will deliver the Cimmerians into his hands and set the land of Ellipi on fire.

3 Aššur has given the totality of the four regions to him. From sunrise to sunset there is no king equal to him; he shines as brilliantly as the sun.

8 This is the (oracle of) well-being placed before Bel-Tarbaṣi and the gods.

---

10 *an-nu-rig* LÚ.*sar-sar-a-ni*! *an*!-*nu*-⌜*ti*!⌝
11 *us-sa-ad-bi-bu-ka us-se-ṣu-nik*!-*ka*
12 *il-ti-bu-ka at-ta pi-i-ka*

3.3 SECOND ORACLE OF SALVATION

10 Now then, these traitors provoked you, had you banished, and surrounded you; but

i 24 See coll.; *garinnu* is taken as a variant of *agarinnu* "mother" (referring to Naqia), with apheresis of the initial vowel as in *alahhinu* → *lahhinu*, *alappānu* → *lappānu*, *ašarittu* → *šarissu*, etc. Cf. Borger Esarh. p. 115 § 82:8, "[Belet-ili created me while I was] in the womb of the mother (*a-ga-ri-in-ni*) who bore me," a topos already found in MA royal inscriptions (see Weidner Tn. no. 60:2). i 25 The broken sign before MUN is like *lu* in col. ii 17 and 24; the sign before *tim* is certainly 3 and cannot be read *ku* (see coll.) i 26 See coll. and cf. SAA 10 72 r.4. i 27 → no. 2 ii 35. Cf. Am. 3:1, "Listen, Israelites, to these words that YHWH addresses to you"; Joel 1:2, "Listen, you elders; hear me, all you who live in the land"; Mic. 3:1, "Listen, you leaders of Jacob, rulers of Israel"; Jer. 2:4, "Listen to the word of the LORD, people of Jacob, families of Israel, one and all"; also Jer. 10:1, Isa. 1:10, Hos. 4:1 and 5:1. i 25 A verbatim allusion to the royal victory ritual Menzel Tempel T88 r.16f. → no. 2 iii 32ff. The "enemy" here refers to Esarhaddon's rebel brothers, see col. iv 23f. i 29f Cf. Josh. 10:24; Ps. 110:1 [Weinfeld]. i 35 The restoration is based on no. 2 iii 15 and agrees with the traces and the available space. → no. 8:9. i 36 See coll.; the traces of *a-hap-pi* exactly match those in the preceding line. ii 1 *a*-⌜*šá*!-*kan*!⌝ "I will place" at the end of line is certain; delete the reading *a*-⌜*di*!⌝ and the interpretation *addi* "I have put" in Weippert, ZAW 84 (1971) 474 n.61, and Hecker, TUAT II/1 (1986) 60. (Apart from the fact that the verb *nadû* was obsolete in NA, note also that preterit forms could not function as predicates of positive statements in NA). Thus the reference to the Cimmerians does not point to year 679 (the year of Esarhaddon's victory over the Cimmerians) as a terminus post quem (thus Weippert, ARINH [1981] p. 96) but as a terminus *ante* quem. ii 3 Cf. Ps. 89:25, "I will extend his rule over the Sea and his dominion as far as the River." ii 4 See coll. ii 7 Cf. Mt. 17:2, "In their presence he (Jesus) was transfigured; his face shone like the sun," and Rev. 1:16, "his face shone like the sun in full strength," and see Introduction, n. 209. For *ṣi-it* ^{d}*šá-maš* "sunshine" (as opposed to *ṣīt šamši* "sunrise," wr. ^{d}UTU.È.A) see CAD s.v. *ṣētu*. ii 8f See coll. On *šulmu* "(oracle of) well-being, salvation" see Introduction, p. LXIV. Bel-Tarbaṣi ("Lord of the Pen") was a statue in the Aššur temple, see Menzel Tempel T149:45. The text does not say that the oracle quoted originated with this "Gatekeeper of Ešarra" (thus Weippert, ARINH [1981] p. 75) but that (a copy of) it was placed before the statue. Note that according to SAA 1 76 r.6, the ratification of vassal treaties apparently also took place in the "Pen" (courtyard) of Ešarra. → line 26. ii 10ff On the historical background of this oracle see Introduction, pp. XLIII and LXXIIf. ii 10 *sarsarru* is most likely a *paspass* formation (GAG § 57b) from *sarru* "criminal," comparable to *dandannu* "overpowering" and *kaškaššu* "almighty," derived from *dannu* "strong" and *kaššu* "mighty." As noted by Weippert, ZAW 84 (1972) 481 n. 102, this interpretation is supported by the NB letter ABL 1341:6ff, where the word (spelled *šá-ar-šá-ra-nu*) is preceded by *mušamhiṣu* "instigator of armed rebellion"; for NB *š* = NA *s* see Parpola, *Assur* 1 (1974) 4 n.13. Reading the word LÚ.*šar-šar-a-ni* and interpreting it as "would-be-kings" (Weippert, ARINH [1981] p. 94) or "kings-of-kings" (Hecker, TUAT II/1 [1986] p. 60) seems less likely in view of the spelling (note the determinative LÚ and the predominantly logographic spellings of *šarru* "king" as opposed to the predominantly syllabic spellings of *sarru*). Note also that the

13 *tap-ti-ti-a ma-a a-ni-na* ^{d}*aš-šur*!
14 *a-na-ku kil-la-ka as-se-me*
15 TA* ŠÀ-*bi* KÁ.GAL AN-*e*
16 *at-ta-qa-al-la-al-la*
17 *la*!-*ak-ru-ur i-šá-tu lu-šá-kil-šú-nu*
18 *at-ta ina bir-tu-šú-nu ta-za-az*
19 TA* *pa*!-*ni-ka at-ti-ši*
20 *a-na* KUR-*e us-se-li-šú-nu*
21 NA$_{4}$.MEŠ *aq-qul-lu ina* UGU-*hi-šú-nu a-zu-nu-un*
22 LÚ.KÚR.MEŠ-*ka uh-ta-ti-ip*
23 *da-me-šú-nu* ÍD *um-tal-li*
24 *le-mu-ru lu-na-i*!-⸢*du*⸣-*ni*
25 *a-ki* ^{d}*aš-šur* EN DINGIR.MEŠ *a-na-ku-ni*
26 *an-nu-u šul-mu šá ina* IGI *ṣa-al-me*

you opened your mouth (and cried): "Hear me, O Aššur!"

14 I heard your cry. I issued forth as a fiery glow from the gate of heaven, to hurl down fire and have it devour them.

18 You were standing in their midst, so I removed them from your presence. I drove them up the mountain and rained (hail)stones and fire of heaven upon then.

22 I slaughtered your enemies and filled the river with their blood. Let them see (it) and praise me, (knowing) that I am Aššur, lord of the gods.

26 This is the well-being (placed) before the Image.

rebel brothers are referred to as "rebels/usurpers (*hammā'u*), instigators of revolt and rebellion" in Borger Esarh. p. 44:82. ii 12 *il-ti-bu-ka* is a regular NA pf. form of *labû* "to surround" (cf. simply SAA 5 93:3ff, "his magnates surrounded him ([*i*]*l-ti-bi-ú-šu*) and killed him"), and there is absolutely no reason to connect it with either *le'ābu* or *liāpu* (thus Weippert and Hecker, loc. cit.), neither of which is attested in NA. ii 13-23 Cf. Ps. 18:6-13. ii 13 *a-ni-na* is taken here as a loan from Aram. *ᶜanīnī*, cf. Syr. *ᶜanīnī mor'ō* "hear me, O Lord!", from *ᶜn'/y* "to answer, respond; hearken, hear" (Payne Smith p. 419; Jastrow Dict. p. 1093); this meaning fits all attestations of the word in NA. The replacement of the final *-i* with *-a* is paralleled by NA *udini* → *udīna* "yet" and probably due to the need to avoid confusion with *anīni* "we." Connecting the word with Aram. *ḥanīnā* "pity, mercy, compassion" (Dalman Aram. Wb. p. 153b, Payne Smith p. 149b) is not possible, since the latter is regularly spelled with an initial *ha* in NA names (see Zadok West Semites p. 88, and cf. ibid. p. 244). ii 14 Cf. no. 5:3, and note that in this text it is Mullissu, not Aššur, who hears the king's cry. Cf. note on line 21 and see Introduction, p. XIX. ii 15f In Mesopotamian cosmic geography, "gate (KÁ.GAL) of heaven" denoted the two points at which the path of the sun cuts through the horizon; cf. En. el. V 9 with the passages cited CAD s.v. *ṣēlu* 2a, and see F. Rochberg-Halton, JNES 42 (1983) 214 for passages associating the heavenly gates with Šamaš and showing "the opening of the locked doors of heaven to be a poetic metaphor for the breaking of the day" (ibid.). On the other hand, the word *anqullu* (line 21) referred in contemporary texts to an ominous fiery glow of the sky at sunrise or sunset (thus, at "the gate of heaven"), taken to portend massacres and the defeat of an army; see SAA 10 79 = LAS 64 and the commentary in LAS II p. 68. This is what actually happened in the present case (lines 21ff); accordingly, the enigmatic *at-ta-qa-al-la-al-la* (cf. AHw. s.v. *qalālu* II) can be explained as a denominative from *anqullu* indicating the *appearance* of the said portent, while line 17 (corresponding to an omen apodosis) explains its significance. The difficulties with connecting the verb with *šuqallulu* "to hover" were already pointed out by von Soden, Or. 20 (1951) 262. ii 17 Lit., "let me hurl down ..." The precative indicates the divine will manifested by the omen, to emphasize that the latter was sent as a premonition of the coming events (lines 21ff) so that these could unequivocally be recognized as God's work (cf. lines 24f and note on no. 1 vi 7ff). The idiom *išātu karāru* "to set fire" combined with *akālu* "to consume" is also attested in GPA 188:4ff, "your servants set fire (IZI ... *ik-tar-ru*) to the steppe, and it consumed (*ta-ta-kal*) the whole steppe up to GNN." Cf. Am. 1:10, 12, etc., "I (YHWH) will send/set fire upon/to GNN, fire that shall consume (*'kl*) ...," and the occurrences of the corresponding SB idiom *išāta nadû* in NA royal inscriptions (CAD s.v. *išātu*, p. 230). In the present passage, *išātu* is the object of both *karāru* and *šākulu* and therefore placed between the two verbs (cf. nos. 2 ii 32f and 3 iii 36). ii 18ff Cf. Gen. 19:21f, "I (YHWH) grant your (Lot's) request; I will not overthrow this town you speak of. But flee there quickly, because I can do nothing until you are there." The verb *ta-za-az* does not refer to the future (thus Weippert, ARINH [1981] 94, and Hecker, TUAT II/1 [1986] 61) but to the situation at the appearance of the omen, cf. no. 1 ii 26 (*i-za-zu* ... *ir-tak-su*) and SAA 10 363 = LAS 290:7ff. ii 19 See coll. ii 21 Cf. Streck Asb p. 78:79ff, "Ištar, who dwells in Arbela, clothed in fire, bearing sheen, rained flames (*nablu*) upon the Arab land." Note that Ištar here takes the place of Aššur of the text, and see Introduction, p. XIX. Cf. also Gen. 19:23f, "The sun had risen over the land as Lot entered Zoar; and then YHWH rained down fire and brimstone from the skies on Sodom and Gomorrah"; Ezek. 38:22, "I will pour down teeming rain, hailstones hard as rock, and fire and brimstone, upon him and his squadrons." The soteriological significance of the present passage was based on the fact that it referred to events that actually took place. Thus it implies that the defeat of the numerically superior rebel forces was accomplished in the midst of and perhaps thanks to a violent thunderstorm and a torrent of hail (see CAD *abnu* mng. 6) following the ominous sunrise alluded to in lines 15f. Note that *anqullu* is explained as *išāt šamê* "fire of heaven" in LTBA 2 1 iv 28ff and alternates with *nablu* "flame" in the phrase *išāt anqulli/nabli*, Hruška Anzu 170:10f. ii 22f → no. 2 iii 21f. ii 24 Cf. Ezek. 38:23 (continuing the passage quoted above), "Thus will I prove myself great and holy and make myself known to many nations; they shall know that I am YHWH (*ydᶜw ky 'ny yhwh*)"; ibid. 13:13f, "In my rage I will unleash a stormy wind; rain will come in torrents in my anger, hailstones hard as rock in my fury, until all is destroyed ... thus you shall know that I am YHWH"; Jer. 16:21 "Once and for all will I teach them my power and my might, and they shall learn that my name is YHWH"; Isa. 12:1 "You shall say on that day: I will praise thee, O YHWH"; ibid. 4, "You shall all say on that day: Give thanks to YHWH ... declare that his name is supreme." Note especially Isa. 45:5ff, "I will strengthen you (Cyrus) though you have not known me, so that men from the rising and the setting sun may know that there is none but I: I am YHWH, there is no other. I make the light, I create darkness... I, YHWH, do all these things." → col. iv 7-9 and 20. ii 26 The contents of the preceding oracle imply that the Image meant here was that of Aššur

27 *ṭup-pi a-de-e an-ni*!*-u šá* ^{d}*aš-šur*
28 *ina* UGU *ha-ʾu-u-ti ina* IGI LUGAL *e-rab*
29 Ì—DÙG.GA *i-za-ar-ri-qu*
30 UDU.SISKUR.MEŠ *ep-pu-šú*
31 ŠEM.HI.A *il-lu-ku*
32 *ina* IGI LUGAL *i-sa-as-si-u*

[27] This covenant tablet of Aššur enters the king's presence on a *cushion*. Fragrant oil is sprinkled, sacrifices are made, incense is burnt, and they read it out in the king's presence.

3.4 THE MEAL OF COVENANT

33 *a-bat* ^{d}15 *šá* URU.*arba-ìl*
34 *a-na* ^{m}*aš-šur*—PAB—AŠ MAN KUR—*aš-šur*
35 DINGIR.MEŠ AD.MEŠ-*ia* ⌈ŠEŠ.MEŠ!-*ia*!⌉ *al*!-*k*⌉*a*!-*ni*
36 *ina* ŠÀ *a-d*[*e-e x x x x*]
possibly one line missing
III 1 [*x x x x x x x x x x x*]
2 *ina* UGU [*tam-l*]*e-e hi-*⌈*ir*⌉*-ṣ*[*u*! *x x x*]
3 A.MEŠ *ṣar-ṣa-ri ta-si-qi-šú-*⌈*nu*!⌉
4 DUG.*ma-si-tú ša* 1BÁN
5 A.MEŠ *ṣar-ṣa-ri tu-um-ta-al-li*
6 *ta-at-ta-an-na-šú-nu*
7 *ma-a ta-qab-bi-a ina* ŠÀ*-ku-nu*
8 *ma-a* ^{d}15! *pa*!*-aq-tú ši-i*
9 *ma-a tal-la-ka ina* URU.MEŠ*-ku*!*-nu*
10 *na-gi-a-ni-ku-nu* NINDA.MEŠ *ta-ka-la*
11 *ta-maš-ši-a a-de-e an-nu-ti*
12 *ma-a* TA ŠÀ A.MEŠ *an-nu-ti*
13 *ta-šat-ti-a ta-ha-sa-sa-ni*
14 *ta-na-ṣa-ra a-de-e an-nu-ti*
15 *ša ina* UGU ^{m}*aš-šur*—PAB—AŠ *áš-kun-u-ni*

[33] The word of Ištar of Arbela to Esarhaddon, king of Assyria:

[35] Come, gods, my fathers and brothers, [enter] the cove[nant ......]

(Break)

[iii 2] [She *placed*] a slice ... on the [ter]race and gave them water from a cooler to drink. She filled a flagon of one seah with water from the cooler and gave it to them with the words:

[7] "In your hearts you say, 'Ištar is slight,' and you will go to your cities and districts, eat (your) bread and forget this covenant.

[12] "(But when) you drink from this water, you will remember me and keep this covenant which I have made on behalf of Esarhaddon."

3.5 WORD OF IŠTAR OF ARBELA

16 *a-bat* ^{d}15! *šá* URU.*arba-ìl*
17 *a-na* ^{m}*aš-šur*—PAB—AŠ MAN KUR—*aš-šur*

[16] The word of Ištar of Arbela to Esarhaddon, king of Assyria:

in the holy of holies of Ešarra. ii 28 See Weippert, ARINH (1981) 95 n. 54, and the discussion in CAD Ḫ 163a s.v. *hawû* ("seat cover for thrones"). ii 32 Cf. Ex. 24:7, "Then he (Moses) took the book of the covenant and read it aloud for all the people to hear"; 2 Kgs. 22:10, "He read it (the book of the law) out in the king's presence." ii 35 See coll. and Introduction, pp. XIXf and XXIIIf. ii 36 This line, missing in Craig's copy, appears correctly in Strong's copy. iii 2 See coll. A "terrace" (*tamliu*) located immediately outside the Royal Gate of Ešarra (leading to the cella of Aššur) is mentioned in the coronation ritual KAR 216+ ii 42ff and occurs as a scene of cultic activities in the royal rituals PKTA pl.12f and van Driel, CA p. 194. The word *hirṣu* is otherwise attested three times in Neo-Assyrian, once in the meaning "cut, incision, track (of a wheel)," see SAA 10 68 = LAS 59 r.10 (*hi-ir-ṣi mugirri*), and twice in the meaning "cut, slice (of meat or bread)," see PKTA pl.32:33 (UZU.*hir-ṣu* of a sacrificed bull) and CT 53 46 r.3f ("we ate the *hi-ir-ṣu* of our sons and daughters"). iii 3-6 Line iii 15 implies that the ambiguous predicates in these lines refer to Ištar and cannot be taken as 2nd m. forms (referring to Esarhaddon); for other 3rd f. pf. forms in narrative sections of the present corpus similarly referring to Ištar see nos. 1 v 28, 30, and 7:12. While the passage can be understood as recounting a vision or dream seen by the prophet (cf. no. 11), the possibility that it represented a mythical *topos* well-known to the audience and recited on similar occasions seems more likely, see Introduction, p. . iii 3 Cf. Šurpu III 62, *ma-mit ina ṣar-ṣa-ri* A.MEŠ *šá-tu-u* "(Asalluhi will undo) the oath (taken by) drinking water from a *ṣarṣāru*." This parallel shows that *ṣarṣāru* cannot here mean "cricket" (CAD *ṣarṣaru* A = rabb. *ṣarṣūr* "chirper, cricket," Jastrow Dict. p. 1305) but a container for water storage (CAD *ṣarṣaru* B), to be compared with rabb. *ṣarṣūr/ṣirṣūr* "Krug, Flasche; a stone vessel containing a strainer and having an inverted (comb-like) rim; a sort of cooler" (Dalman Aram. Wb. p. 368; Jastrow Dict. p. 1305 with refs., e.g., Ab. Zar. 73a, "If one pours forbidden wine from a small cooler into the wine pit"). The semantics of the rabbinical word provides a key to the interpretation of the passage. As shown by lines 12f, the drinking ceremony described in it was intended to have a mnemonic function, which fits the fact that *cooled water* played a prominent part in *libations* to gods and divine statues (see simply CAD K 268 s.v. *kaṣû* "cool, cold"). Note the affinity of *ṣarṣāru* to NA *ṣarruru* "to libate" and *ṣurāru* "libation" (CAD Ṣ 106a and 256a), and the incipit of the *tākultu* ritual, "[Aššur], drink! Enlil (and other gods), drink!" (KAR 214:1ff, see Frankena Takultu p. 25, and cf. above, notes on col. i 4ff and no. 1 iv 14-17). iii 4 → line 33. iii 5ff Cf. Mt. 26:26ff, Mk. 14:22ff, Lk. 22:17ff, and see Introduction, p. LXIV. iii 8 See coll.; *pa* is written over an erasure, as indicated in Craig's copy, but the reading is certain and Strong's copy gives a realistic idea of what is on the tablet. For the rendering of *pāqtu* cf. [tu-ur-tu-ur] TUR.TUR = *pa-a-qu* "narrow" Diri I 266, grouped with *rabbu* "soft" and *dallu* "small"; it is assumed that the passage refers to the stature of Ištar (as a feminine apparition) rather than her powers or sphere of influence (which of course were not "slight, narrow"). iii 12 See coll. iii 12ff Cf. Lk. 22:17-20. iii 15 ^{d}15 is correctly copied by Strong.

18 *a-ki šá me-me-ni la e-pa-šú-u-ni*
19 *la a-di-nak-kan-ni*
20 *ma-a* 4 *si-ip-pi šá* KUR—*aš-šur*
21 *la ak-pu-pa-a la a-di-nak-ka-a*
22 LÚ.KÚR-*ka la ak-šu-du*
23 LÚ.*gi-ṣi-ṣi-ka a-a-bi-ka*
24 [*a-ki gu*]*r!-ṣip-ti la al-qu-tú*
25 [*at-t*]*a! a-na a-a-ši mi-nu ta-di-na*
26 [*a-k*]*a!-li ša qa-ri-te*
27 *l*[*a!-áš-šú*] *ša ak la!* É—DINGIR
28 *a*[*k-ka-l*]*i a-ka-li*
29 *ak-k*[*a*]-⌜*li*!⌝ *ka-a-si*
30 *ma-a ina! pa!-ni a-da-gal*
31 IGI.2 *ina* UGU-*hi ak-tar-ar*
32 *ma-a ket-tu-ma* 1BÁN *a-kal a-ṣu!-di*
33 1BÁN DUG.*ma-si-tú ša* KAŠ DÙG.GA
34 *ke-in* Ú.*ur-qí a-ku-su*
35 *la-áš-ši-a ina pi-ia la-áš-kun*
36 *lu-mal-li ka-a-su ina* UGU-*hi la-as-si*
37 *la-la-a-a lu-tir-ra*
IV 1 [*x x x x x x x x x x*]
2 [*x x x x x x x x x*]-*ni*
3 [*x x x x x x x*] *la-áš-ši*
4 [*x x x x x x la-a*]*l-lik*
5 [*x x x x x*] *e-ta-li-a*

[18] As if I did not do or give you anything!

[20] Did I not bend the four doorjambs of Assyria, and did I not give them to you? Did I not vanquish your enemy? Did I not collect your haters and foes [like but]terflies?

[25] [As for yo]u, what have you given to me?

[26] [There is no fo]od for my banquet, *as if there were* no temple; I [am depri]ved of my food, I am d[ep]rived of my cup! I am waiting for them, I have cast my eye upon them.

[32] Verily, establish a one-seah bowl of food and a one-seah flagon of sweet beer! Let me take and put in my mouth vegetables and soup, let me fill the cup and drink from it, let me restore my charms!

(Break)

iv 3 let me lift [......]

[4] [let m]e go [......]

[5] I went up [......]

iii 18f Weippert, ARINH (1981) p. 88, takes this passage as a rhetorical question similar to lines 20-24, but this is rendered impossible by the subjunctive suffix and the lack of interrogative marking in *a-di-nak-kan-ni*. iii 20 "The four doorjambs" probably refers to the four urban centers of Assyria, Assur (the "Inner City"), Nineveh, Calah and Arbela, see no. 1 iii 9-10; the present passage suggests that the activity of the prophets of Ištar of Arbela had been instrumental in winning these pivotal cities, each of which was an important centre of Ištar's cult, over to Esarhaddon's side (cf. also col. iv 13-15). For *sippu* "doorjamb" as a metonym for "entrance" see CAD s.v. iii 21 The present nuance of *kapāpu* "to bend" is paralleled by Syr. *kpp* "to bend, curve, bow (knee, head, or oneself)," (ethpe.) "to be bent or bowed down" (Payne Smith p. 221) and Bibl. *kpp* "to bend (back), bow (head), subdue, depress" (cf. Isa. 58:5 and Ps. 145:14). iii 24 The reading *gu*]*r-ṣip-ti* suggested in AHw. 512a s.v. *kurṣiptu* is confirmed by collation; despite Weippert, ARINH (1981) p. 87 n.32, the traces do not fit *ku-u*]*r-ṣip-ti*, and this reading would not leave enough room for *a-ki* in the break. iii 25ff → nos. 1 vi 13ff and 2 ii 21ff, by the same prophet, also containing cultic demands. Cf. Hag. 1:4-8, "Is it a time for you [Zerubbabel and Joshua] to live in your own well-roofed houses, while this house lies in ruins? ... Consider your way of life. Go up into the hills, fetch timber, and build a house acceptable to me, where I can be honoured." iii 26 On *qarētu* "(divine) banquet" see LAS II p. 81f. For two catering contracts pertaining to the banquet of Ištar of Arbela, both from the reign of Sennacherib, see BT 116 and 117 (Iraq 25, 94f), and cf. Deller, Or. 34 [1965] 169 and Postgate, TCAE (1974) pp. 71ff and 358f; the texts are dated Ab 1, 686, and Kislev 20, 682. A letter probably addressed to Esarhaddon (ABL 876) also relates to the matter; the author expresses the fear that Ištar of Arbela, characterized as "powerful" in the text, may kill him unless he provides for the festival.

iii 27 For the first sign see coll. and cf. *la* at the beginning of lines 19 and 21. *ak* as a proclitic variant of *akī* is attested in *la ak an-ni-e* ABL 390 r.15, and *ak* (*an*)-*ni-im-ma* ABL 84 r.15; the apocopation of *i* may be due to an intentional play with words, note the assonance of *ak la* to *a-ka-li* and see notes on lines 28 and 32f. The expression *ša ak la* "as if not(?)" is not otherwise attested; cf. *kī lā libbi ilāni* "against the will of gods," and *ša lā ilāni* "godlessly," Borger Esarh. p. 41:26 and 29. Note *ak la* as a NA variant to SB *balu* "without" in Gilg. X 85. iii 28 Note the rhyme and assonance of *akkalli akāli* and its structural parallelism and assonance to the following line. For the final *-i* in *ak-ka-li* (pres. of *kl*ʾ N) cf. MÚD.MEŠ *ik-ka-li-u* SAA 10 322 = ABL 108 r.16f, and see GAG § 105q. iii 30 *ina pa-* written over an erasure. iii 31f M.-C. Perroudon, SAAB 6 (1993) 41ff, draws attention to the sequence *ma sūtu – aṣūdi – massītu* in these lines and argues that this peculiar sequence of sounds (combining sibilants and dentals with "dark" vowels) served to underline the angry tone of the passage. iii 32 The suffix *-ma* serves to differentiate *kettumma* "verily" (also in SAA 10 284 = LAS 213 r.8) from *kettu* "really," which often has the connotation "nevertheless" (see the examples listed in SAA 10 p. 341 s.v.). iii 32ff The dishes enumerated in these lines resemble those listed in contemporary documents as (offerings for) "the wedding night of Mullissu," see SAA 7 207-210 and 215-218. "Bowl of food" corresponds in these texts to "a bowl (DUG.*a-ṣu-du*) of *haršu* and fruit," "a flagon of sweet beer" to "flagons (DUG.*ma-si-tú*) of bittersweet (*lappānu*) and bruised beer," and "vegetables and soup" to bags of chick-peas, sesame, and mixed kernels, cups of small onions, quinces and olives, and various confections and yoghurts(?). iii 34 See coll. The determinative Ú is normally omitted in syllabic spellings of *urqu* "vegetable" (e.g., GIŠ.SAR *ur-qí*, "vegetable garden," ADD 906 r. ii 1.5) but is quite common in logographic spellings of the word, e.g., Ú.SAR = *ur-qí*, AfO 18 p. 328:56, GIŠ.SAR Ú.SAR, ADD 471:8. The meaning "soup" of *akussu* is established by its juxtaposition with *mê šīri* "bouillon" in contemporary lists of offerings, e.g. SAA 7 209:8f. iii 36 The rendering of this line follows Ylvisaker, LSS 5/2 (1912) 62 n.3. iv 1-4 The precative predicates suggest that this passage continues the discourse of the previous column. iv 5 The irregular pf. form *e-ta-li-a* (with *-ta-* replacing normal *-te-*) is rare in NA and for some reason almost exclusively limited to contexts involving a festival of Ištar; see ABL 876:12, ABL

6 [*x x x i-sin*]*-nu a-sa-kan*
7 [*a-ki ina* ŠÀ*-bi*$^{?}$] *a-na-ku-ni*
8 [*ma-a nu-da*$^{?}$] *a-ki* ^{d}15
9 [*šá* URU].⸢*arba-ìl*⸣ *at-ti-ni*
10 [*a-na* KUR—*aš*]*-šur ut-ta-am-me-šá*
11 [*né-mal*$^{?}$*-k*]*a la-mu-ur* KUR.MEŠ*-ni*
12 [*ina* GÌR.2*-ia*$^{?}$] *la-ak-bu-us*
13 [*la-ad-bu*$^{?}$]*-ub ina* UGU ^{m}*aš-šur*—PAB—AŠ
14 [*ú-ma*]*-*⸢*a*⸣ *ri-iš* ^{m}*aš-šur*—PAB—A
15 [4 *si-ip-p*]*i ša* KUR—*aš-šur*
16 [*ak-tap-p*]*a at-ta-nak-ka*
17 [LÚ.KÚR*-k*]*a ak-ta-šá-ad*
18 [UN$^{?}$.MEŠ *š*]*a is-si-ka i-za-zu-ni*
19 [*ṭè-en*$^{?}$*-šú-n*]*u na-bal-ku-ut*
20 [*ina* ŠÀ *an-ni-t*]*i ta-am-mar*
21 [*a-ki* ^{d}15 *šá* URU].*arba-ìl a-na-ku-ni*
22 [*ki-ma* LÚ.LUL$^{?}$.MEŠ$^{?}$ *u*]*s-sa-di-du-ni*
23 [*ša i-mit-ti*] *ša šu-me-li*
24 [*ši-ip-ṭu*$^{?}$] *na-ṣu i-za-z*[*u*]
25 [LÚ.*man-za-az*]—É.GA[L]
26 [LÚ.ARAD]—⸢É⸣.GAL *šu-*⸢*nu*⸣
27 [*ša ina* UGU]*-ka i-si-hu-ni*
28 [*al-ti*]*-bi-a ina* UGU *šin-ni-šú-nu*
29 [*a-na* GIŠ].*za-qi-ba-a-ni*
30 [*as*]*-sa-kan-šú-nu*
blank space of about 2 lines
31 [^{m}*la—da-gíl—*DI]NGIR$^{!}$ ⸢LÚ.*ra*⸣*-gi-mu*
32 [URU.*arba-ìl*]*-*⸢*a-a*⸣
33 [*x x x x x x*] ^{d}15
34 [*x x x x x x*]*-lu-ni*
35 [*ir-tu-gu-um*] (blank)
(end of column)

[6] and arranged [*a fea*]*st* [...].

[7] [*When*] I was [*there, they said: "We know*] that you are Ištar [of A]rbela."

[10] I set out [for As]syria to see yo[ur *success*], to tread the mountains [*with my feet*], [and to *spea*]*k* about Esarhaddon.

[14] [No]w rejoice, Esarhaddon! [I have be]nt [the four doorjamb]s of Assyria and given them to you; I have vanquished yo[ur enemy. The *mood* of the *people*] who stand with you has been turned upside down.

[20] [From thi]s you shall see [that] I am [Ištar of] Arbela.

[22] [*As soon as the traitors*] have been dragged forth, [the 'ones at the right and] left side' shall be there to bear [the *punishment*].

[25] (As for) those cou]rtiers and palace [personnel who] rebelled [against] you, [I have sur]rounded them and impaled them *by* their *teeth*.

[31] [La-dagil-i]li, a prophet of [Arbela, *prophesied* (*this*) *when* ......] Ištar [......].

1103:4, SAA 3 14 r.11 and SAA 10 273 r.10. iv 6 Cf. col. i 14. iv 8ff, 20 See note on col. ii 24. iv 9ff See coll. iv 11 For restoration see no. 2 iii 28. iv 12 Restoration conjectural; cf. Hab. 3:6. iv 13 For restoration see note on col. iii 20. iv 14 See coll. The sign *iš* has an extra horizontal wedge at the bottom, but is clearly different from *ša* in the next line and *da* in line iii 30. iv 15ff Restored from col. iii 20ff. iv 19 Restoration conjectural; for the rendering see CAD *nabalkutu* mng. 2d. iv 20f For the restorations see ABL 896:24 and col. ii 24f. iv 22 *u*]*s-sa-di-du-ni* is pf. 3m pl. vent. of *šadādu* D; cf. the corresponding G-stem form in SAA 5 91 = ABL 144:10, "they have dragged forth (*i-sa-du-ú-ni*) the rest of the people involved in the plot." In the present context, the D-stem form implies a plural object, see the note on no. 2 ii 10. Since the rebel brothers of Esarhaddon evidently managed to escape punishment, at least for some time, it is necessary to restore *ki-ma* at the beginning of the line and take the passage iv 22-24 as a prophecy. iv 23 For the restoration see no. 1 v 15f; the width of the break calls for a syllabic spelling of *imittu*. As a matter of fact, with the exception of SAA 10 185 = LAS 129:12, NA syllabic spellings of *šumēlu* are otherwise regularly paired with syllabic spellings of *imittu*, cf. SAA 8 489 = RMA 145 r.4, SAA 10 358 = LAS 286 r. 6, and SAA 3 3:15, 4 i 4 and 18:4. iv 24 Restoration conjectural, cf. CAD N/2 pp. 104 and 108 s.v. *hīṭu* and *šērtu našû*; the usual NA word for "punishment" was *šipṭu*, which alternates with *hiṭṭu* in the idiom *hiṭṭu/šipṭu emādu/šakānu* "to punish." The pl. stative *na-ṣu* (lacking the ventive suffix) is otherwise attested in NA only in the idiom *pūtuhu našû* "to bear responsibility," see TH 15:10 and PKTA pl.38 i 7 and 22. iv 28 The meaning of the reference to the "teeth" escapes me and the suggested translation is conjectural. iv 29f For the restorations see ABL 967:9f, SAA 1 22:11f and SAA 10 350 r.11. iv 31 The reading of the last element of the prophet's name is certain; the restoration of the other elements is justified by the width of the break, by the fact that no other prophet name in the present corpus ends in the element DINGIR, by the prominent stature of La-dagil-ili, which is compatible with the importance of the text, and by the affinities of the text with the other oracles by La-dagil-ili (see Introduction, p. LI). iv 32 For restoration see no. 2 ii 28 and cf. above. iv 35 For restoration see no. 6 r.12.

Collection Four

FIG. 27. *Rebels cast down for flaying (reign of Sennacherib, cf. oracle 1.1).*
BM 124908-9.

4. Fragment of a Collection of Encoragement Oracles

83-1-18,839

beginning (possibly one line only) destroyed

1′ [*x x x x x*] ⸢*x x*⸣ [*x x x x*]

2′ [^{m}*aš-šur*—PAB—A]Š MAN KUR—*aš-šur* [*x x x x*]

3′ [*ka-ki*]*š-a-ti* ⸢*ú*⸣-[*ba*$^{?}$-*ra*$^{?}$]

4′ [*ina* IGI] GÌR.2-*ka* ⸢*a*⸣-[*kar-ra-ar*]

5′ [*at-t*]*a*$^{?}$ *la ta-p*[*al-làh x x*]

6′ [*x x*]*x ur-ki-u-te a-k*[*aš*$^{?}$-*šad*$^{?}$ *x x x*]

7′ [*x x-k*]*a tap-ta-an-*[*x x x*]

8′ [*x x-t*]*i a-šá-*[*kan x x*]

9′ [*x x x*]*x-*⸢*ka-bar*⸣ *ina x*[*x x x*]

rest destroyed

83-1-18,839

(Beginning destroyed)

2 [Esarhaddo]n, king of Assyria! [......]

3 I will [*catch* ... and wease]ls, (and)

4 I will [cast them before] your feet.

5 [As for yo]u, fe[ar] not! [......]

6 I will *v*[*anquish*] the later [......]

7 You shall ... yo[ur ......]

8 [...] I will p[ut ......]

10 [...] *massive* in [...]

(Rest destroyed)

4 Photo pl. VIII. Previously unpublished; identified and transliterated by the editor in June, 1969. Collated in July, 1992. Not part of no. 2 or no. 3. Cf. no. 1 v 3-7 and no. 2 ii 19f and 32f. 4 Cf. no. 1 i 14. 6 Or: "I will ch[oose] (*a-b*[*i-ar*]) the future [...]"; cf. no. 2 iii 5 and 15. 7 Obscure; hardly [*pi-i*]-*ka tap-ta-an-*[*at-ti* "you shall keep opening your mouth." 8 → no. 2 ii 33 and 3 ii 1. 9 See coll. The traces after *bar* cannot be read *ti* (cf. the form of *ti* in line 3).

Oracle Reports

Reports to Esarhaddon

FIG. 28. *Cow suckling and licking her calf (ivory panel from Calah/Nimrud, see p. XXXVI).*
ND 6310(B).

5. An Oracle to the Queen Mother

K 6259

1 *a-bat* ^{d}15 *ša* URU.*arba-ìl* [*x x x x x x*]

2 *kin-ṣa-a-a kan-ṣa a-n*[*a*$^{!}$ *x x x x x x x*]
3 ^{d}NIN.LÍL *a-na kil-li* [*ša mu-ri-šá ta-se-me*]
4 *qab-le-ki ru-uk-si x*[*x x x x x x*]
5 *ša* ^{m}*aš-šur*—PAB—AŠ MAN KUR—*aš-šur* [*x x x x x x*]
6 [[1]] ^{d}NIN.URTA 15 *u* 150 *š*[*a*$^{?}$ *x x x x x*]
7 *a-a-bi-šú ina* KI.TA$^{!}$ GÌR$^{!}$.2$^{!}$-[*šú x x x x x x*]

8 *ina* É.GAL EDIN *ú-*[*ṣa x x x x x x*]
e.9 *tu*$^{!}$*-qu-un a-na* ^{m}[*aš-šur*—PAB—AŠ MAN KUR—*aš-šur*]
10 [*a*]*d-dan* LÚ$^{!}$.[KÚR.MEŠ-*šú*]
r.1 *ina* ŠÀ$^{!}$ *x*[*x x x x x x x x x x*]
2 *ú-*⌈*ba*⌉-[*x x x x x x x x x x*]

3 LÚ.KÚR *š*[*a x x x x x x x x x*]
4 LÚ.KÚR ⌈*ša lum*$^{?}$ *x*⌉ [*x ina* IGI GÌR.2.MEŠ-*šú*]
5 *ni*$^{!}$*-ik*$^{!}$*-ru-ur*$^{!}$ *ni-i*[*l*$^{!}$*-x x x x x x*]
6 ^{d}NIN.LÍL ⌈*dul*$^{?}$⌉*-la* [*x x x x x x*]
7 [*š*]*a*$^{?}$ ^{d}UTU *ši-na* EN AD$^{!}$*-u-a ú-*⌈*za*$^{?}$⌉-[*x x x x x x*]

TI pl.4

1 The word of Ištar of Arbela [*to the king's mother*: ...]

2 My knees are bent fo[r ......].
3 Mullissu [has heard] the cry [of *her calf*].
4 Gird (f.) your loins! [......]
5 of Esarhaddon, king of Assyria [......]
6 Ninurta [*shall go*] at the right and left side *o*[*f* ....]
7 [*shall* put] his enemies under [his] foot [......]

8 I will g[o out] to the Palace of the Steppe [...]
9 I will give security for [Esarhaddon, king of Assyria.]
10 [His] e[nemies]
r.1 within [......]
2 I will [......]

3 The enemy *who* [......]
4 the enemy who ... [...]
5 we will cast [before his feet] and *g*[*o* ...].
6 Glorify (pl.) [...] Mullissu! [......]
7 *are those of* Šamaš, *until* my father [......].

5 Photo pl. VIII. Copy Langdon, TI (1914), pl. 4. Collated by the editor in July, 1992. 1 The feminine suffixes in line 4 and the fact that Esarhaddon is nowhere in the extant portion of the text addressed in the 2nd person suggest that this oracle was addressed to the queen mother. Accordingly, the beginning of the break could be restored *a-na* AMA—LUGAL in accordance with nos. 1 v 13, 2 ii 38f, and no. 3 ii 33f and iii 16f, where *abat Issār* is directly followed by an address formula. Note, however, that in no. 2 ii 30, *abat Issār ša Arbail* is coupled with *a-bat šar-ra-ti* ^{d}NIN.LÍL; the occurrence of ^{d}NIN.LÍL in line 3 could be taken to indicate that this formula is to be restored here too. See also the note on no. 1 v 8. At the end of the line possibly restore: [*a-na man-ni*] "for whom (are my knees bent)?"; cf. no. 2 iii 16. 2 Possibly restore: *a-n*[*a* ^{m}*aš-šur*—PAB—AŠ LUGAL-*ia*] "for [Esarhaddon, my king]"; cf. no. 1 ii 12 and iii 13. 3 For restoration cf. nos. 3 ii 14 and 7 r.11. 4 See LAS II p. 161:23. 6 There is an erased vertical wedge before ^{d}NIN.URTA; see coll. 7 → no. 3 i 30. 8 See note on no. 1 v 28. 9 Cf. *ina tu-qu-un-ni* "in safety," no. 1 iv 3, and *tuq-nu bi-la* "bring safety," SAA 3 13:17. *tu-qu-un* can be taken both as a variant of *tuqnu* (cf. *ú-zu-un* = *uznu*, CT 53 41 r.1) and *tuqunnu* (cf. *nu-ur* = *nūru*, no. 1 iii 25). 10 Line spaced out. r.4 See coll. For restoration see no. 1 i 13f. r.5 The plural "we" probably refers to Ištar of Arbela and Mullissu, cf. nos. 2 i 8 and 9:3. r.6 *dul-la* is taken as imp. pl. of *dalālu* "to glorify" (addressing Naqia and Esarhaddon), cf. ABL 514 r.12f, *a-na* ^{d}30 *du-ul-lu ... a-da-lál.* r.7 See coll. The first (badly obliterated) sign differs from *ša* in r.3f but does resemble the one in obv.5. The rendering of the line should be taken as tentative only.

6. An Oracle from Tašmetu-ereš of Arbela

Bu 91-5-9,106 + Bu 91-5-9,109 (unpub.)

1 ^{d}15 *ša* URU.*arba-*[*ìl ma-a x x x x x x x x x*]
2 *ma-a ú-ta-qa-*[*an x x x x x x x x x x x*]
3 *ú-ta-qa-an* [*x x x x x x x x x x x x*]
4 [*x*]*-ru-bi x*[*x x x x x x x x x x x x x x*]
5 *ma-a* ⸢URU⸣.[*x x x x x x x x x x x x x x*]
6 *in-ta-*[*x x x x x x x x x x x x x x*]
7 *e-tar-b*[*u x x x x x x x x x x x x x*]
8 *ša* LUGAL [*x x x x x x x x x x x x x*]
9 *i-du-k*[*u x x x x x x x x x x x x x x*]
e.10 *a-ka-*[*x x x x x x x x x x x x x*]

r.1 [*m*]*a-a la* ⸢*a*⸣*-x*[*x x x x x x x x x*]
2 ⸢*ú*⸣*-su-tú* [*x x x x x x x x x x x x x*]
3 *a-se-me a-tan-*[*x x x x x x x x x x x*]
4 LÚ*.KÚR.MEŠ-*ka* [*x x x x x x x x x x x*]
5 *an-ni-i* [*x x x x x x x x x x*]
6 ⸢*ir*⸣*-gu-mu-*[*u-ni x x x x x x x x x x*]
7 [*ina* Š]À-*bi* ⸢*ru*⸣*-x*[*x x x x x x x x x x*]
8 *ša ir-gu-m*[*u-u-ni x x x x x x x*]
9 *ina* ⸢*pa*⸣*-an ku-d*⸢*u*⸣*-*[*x x x x x x x*]
10 ⸢*a*⸣*-*[*d*]*i* LÚ*.KÚR.[MEŠ-*ka x x x x x x*]
11e [0 ^{m}]⸢^{d}⸣LÁL—KAM-*eš* ⸢LÚ⸣.[*ra-gi-mu x x x x*]
12e [*ina* Š]À URU.*arba-ìl ir-t*[*u-gu-um* 0]

Bu 91-5-9,106+

1 Ištar of Arbe[la has said: ......]
2 "I will put in order [......]
3 I will put in order [......]
4 ... [......]
5 "the city [......]
6 th[ey ...]ed [......]
7 they entered [......]
8 of the king [......]
9 they killed [......]
10 I will *c*[*ast* ......]
r.1 "I do not [......]
2 help [......]
3 I heard and [......]
4 your enemies [......]
5 this [......]
6 prophes[ied ......]
7 [wit]hin [......]
8 who prophes[ied ......]
9 before [......]
10 until [your] enemi[es ......].
11 [T]ašmetu-ereš, a [prophet *of* ......],
12 pro[phesied] (this) in the city of Arbela.

6 Photo pl. VIII. Both fragments previously unpublished. Identified and joined by the editor in March, 1968; collated in July, 1992. 1 For restoration see no. 7:1f. 2f → no. 2 iii 33f and iv 27. 4 Possible restorations include [*qar*]*-ru-bi* "to present" and [*še*]*-ru-bi* "to bring in." 7, 9 These lines have no parallels in the present corpus. r.1 *ú-su-tú* is taken as the nom. sg. of *usātu* "help" (Ass. *usatu*, see AHw. 1437b), cf. MA gen. *ú-si-ti*, KAJ 46:5. The word was hitherto attested only in names in NA. r.6-8 This passage, clearly part of the oracle, seems to refer to earlier oracles from other (rival?) prophets and as such is unique in the corpus. r.10 See coll. r.11f These lines are written in smaller script on the upper edge and clearly constitute a colophon. The name Tašmetu-ereš is otherwise unattested in NA (see APN 235), but the traces are clear and exclude the well-known Tuqunu-ereš (e.g., ^{m}LAL—KAM-*eš* ADD 50:2, ^{m}LAL-*un*—KAM-*eš* ADD 672 r.7; see coll. For the restorations see no. 3 iv 31ff.

Reports to Assurbanipal

FIG. 29. *Below: Elamite troops being defeated at Til Tuba (reign of Assurbanipal). Above: Victory procession in Arbela.*
ORIGINAL DRAWING VII, 11.

7. Prophecies for the Crown Prince Assurbanipal

K 883

1 [MÍ].^{d}NIN.LÍL—*kab-ta-at* MÍ.*ra-gi-in-tú*
2 [*ma*]-*a a-bat* LUGAL ^{d}NIN.LÍL *ši-i ma-a la ta-pal-làh* ^{m}*aš*$^{!}$-*šur*$^{!}$—DÙ—A
3 [*ma*]-*a a-di ki-i šá aq-bu-u-ni ep-pa-šu-u-ni ad-da-nak-kan-ni*
4 [*ma*]-⌜*a*⌝ *a-di ina* UGU DUMU.MEŠ *šá šá*—SU$_6$.MEŠ *ina* UGU *hal-pe-te šá* LÚ.SAG.MEŠ
5 [*at-t*]*a* LUGAL-*u-tú ina* UGU-*hi-šú-nu tu-up-pa-šú-u-ni*
6 [*a-ha-ṣ*]*i*$^{!}$-*in*$^{!}$-*ka* *ina* É—UŠ-*u-ti*
7 [*ma-a* AD-*ka x x*]*x-a-ti* TÚG.*pi-tu-tu i-rak-kas*
8 [*ma-a x x* LUGAL].MEŠ *šá* KUR.KUR *a-na a-he-iš i-qab-bu-u-ni*
9 [*ma-a al-ka-ni ni*]-*il-lik ina* UGU ^{m}*aš*$^{!}$-*šur*$^{!}$—DÙ—A LUGAL *ši-i-bi ra-ši* ⌜*x*⌝
10 [*ma-a mi-i-nu šá* DINGIR].MEŠ *a-na* AD.MEŠ-*ni* AD—AD.MEŠ-*ni i-ši-mu-u-ni*
11 [*ma-a ú-ma-a šu*]-⌜*ú*⌝ *ina bir-*⌜*tu-un*⌝-*ni lip-ru-us*
12 [*ma-a* ^{d}NIN.L]ÍL *taq-ṭi-bi ma-a* [LUGAL.ME]Š *šá* KUR.KUR
e.13 [*ta-pi-a*]*l ta*$^{!}$-*hu-ma-a-ni tu*$^{!}$-*kal-lam*$^{!}$-⌜*šú*$^{!}$-*nu*$^{!}$⌝ [KA]SKAL$^{!}$.MEŠ *ina* GÌR.2-*šú-nu*$^{!}$ GAR-*an*
14 [*ma*]-⌜*a*$^{!}$⌝ *šá-ni-tú laq-bak-ka ma-a ki-i* KUR.NIM.KI KUR.*gi-mir a-*⌜*ga*$^{!}$⌝-*mar*$^{!}$

ABRT 1 26f

1 The prophetess Mullissu-kabtat (has said):

2 "This is the word of Queen Mullissu: Fear not, Assurbanipal!

3 "Until I have done and given to you what I promised, until you rule as king over the sons of the bearded courtiers and the successors of the eunuchs, [I will look af]ter you in the Palace of Succession; [*your father*] shall gird the diadem [...].

8 "[The ... king]s of the lands shall say to one another: ['Come, let us] go to Assurbanipal! The king has witnesses! [Whatever the god]s decreed for our fathers and forefathers, [let him now] arbitrate between us.'

12 "[Mullis]su [has] said: [You shall ru]le over [the king]s of the lands; you shall show them their frontiers and set the courses they take.

14 "Secondly, let me tell you: I will finish the land of Gomer like (I finished) Elam.

7 Photo pls. IX and XIII. Copy Strong, BA 2 (1893), 645; Craig, ABRT I (1895), pls. 26-27, with corrections Vol. II, p. x. Collated by the editor in July, 1992. → SAA 10 185. 2 LUGAL here certainly stands for *šarratu*, a standing epithet of Mullissu, cf. no. 2 ii 30 and relevant note. It is unnecessary to assume a connection with *abat šarri*, "king's word," and impossible to take LUGAL as a "genetivus objectivus" rendering "a word for the king," as done by Weippert, ARINH (1981) p. 77, Hecker, TUAT II/1 (1986) p. 62, and earlier translators. 4 The reference is to the new government of the future king, the sons of the uncastrated officials taking the place of their fathers and new eunuchs replacing their predecessors, who could not have sons (see LAS II p. 20f). For *hal-pe-te* (hapax legomenon, certainly an Aram. lw.) see von Soden, Or. 46 (1977) 187 no. 43, and cf. Syr. *ḫalp*^{e}*tā* "something given in exchange, a substitute," from *ḫlp* "to exchange, substitute; (ethpa.) to be changed, succeed" (Payne Smith, p. 144f), and Arab. *ḫalīfa* "deputy; successor; caliph." 6 See coll.; for the restoration see AHw. 331b, followed by Hecker, TUAT II/1 (1986) p. 62 n.6 and Ivantchik, N.A.B.U. 1993/2, 40. Restoring [*lu-taq-q*]*i-in-ka* on the basis of no. 1 i 34, vi 26, and 2 ii 11 is epigraphically possible but is rendered unlikely by the fact that precative predicates are otherwise not found in divine promises (see Introduction, p. LXVI). 7 As shown by SAA 10 185 = LAS 129:7f, the girding of the diadem signalized the official investiture of the crown prince. For the sign at the break (hardly *š*]*á*) see coll. 8 Possibly restore DUMU.(MEŠ)—LUGAL, "sons of the kings." The rendering of the passage assumes that *i-qab-bu-u-ni* is a vent. form, as e.g. in SAA 5 40 r.1, 289:7 and 294:8. 9 For the restoration cf. NL 43 r.6ff, "I said to him, 'Come, let us go (*muk alka nillik*) ... and let me see'"; CT 53 55:9f, "he said, 'Come, let you and me go (*mā alka atta anāku nillik*) and bring them forth'"; cf. also Isa. 2:2f, "All the nations shall come streaming to it (Jerusalem), and many peoples shall come and say, 'Come, let us climb up to the mountain of YHWH'"; Jer. 18:18, "'Come, let us decide what to do with Jeremiah,' men say." For *alāku ina muhhi* "to go to" see, e.g., ABL 884:15, NL 43 r.5 (king), and ABL 1058:8 (PN); for the word order cf. ABL 471:20 (*alka issēja ina* UGU *karāri ša uššē*). The broken sign at the end of the line is most likely ⌜*ma*⌝, see coll. 11 Cf. Isa. 2:4: "He will be judge between nations, arbiter among many peoples"; SAA 1 29 12ff, "[Until the ki]ng comes, [I (Sennacherib) will ar]bitrate between you (two vassal kings)." 12 Cf. Isa. 3:7: "Once again YHWH spoke to Ahaz and said"; Jer. 3:11, "YHWH said to me ..." 13 For restoration see the passages from NA royal inscriptions cited CAD s.v. *bêlu* 1a-1′. → no. 2 ii 15f. 14 See coll.

r.1 *[ma]-a ta-al-la gi-ṣu a-šab-bir ma-a mur-din-nu a-na ni-ip-ši a-nap-pa-áš*
2 *a-dam!-mu-ma-a-te a-na sar-bi ú-ta-ra*
3 *hal-la-la-at-ti en-gur!-a-ti*
4 *at-ta ta-qab-bi ma-a mi-i-nu hal-la-la-at-ti en-gur!-a-ti*
5 *hal-la-la-at-ti ina!* KUR.*mu-ṣur e-rab en-gur!-a-te ú-ṣa-a*
6 *ma-a šá* ^{d}NIN.LÍL AMA-*šú-ni la ta-pal-làh šá* GAŠAN—*arba-ìl ta-ri-su-ni la ta-pal-làh*
7 *ma-a ki-i ta-ri-ti ina* UGU *gi-iš-ši-ia* ÍL!-*ši-ka*
8 *ma-a* GIŠ.HAŠHUR!.KUR.RA *ina bi-rit* UBUR.MEŠ-*ia a-šak-kan-ka*
9 *šá mu-ši-ia e-rak an-ṣar-ka šá kal*—UD-*me hi-il-pa-ka ad-dan*
10 *šá kal-la-ma-ri un-na-ni-ka ú-ṣur ú-ṣur up-pa-áš-ka*
11 *⸢ma-a⸣ at-ta la ta-pal-làh mu-u-ri šá ana-ku ú-rab-bu-u-ni*

r.1 "... I will break the thorn, I will pluck the bramble into a tuft of wool, I will turn the wasps into a squash.

3 "Like a centipede, like a ...! You say, 'What does it mean, like a centipede, like a ...?' Like a centipede I will enter Egypt, like a ... I will come out.

6 "You whose mother is Mullissu, have no fear! You whose nurse is the Lady of Arbela, have no fear!

7 "I will carry you on my hip like a nurse, I will put you between my breasts (like) a pomegranate. At night I will stay awake and guard you; in the daytime I will give you milk; at dawn I will play '*watch, watch your* ...' with you. As for you, have no fear, my calf, whom I (have) rear(ed)."

→ no. 8 r.1f and see the discussion in LAS II p. 192f. r.1 The first sign in this line has hitherto been read ⸢*e*⸣ and combined with the following signs into ⸢*e*⸣*-ta-al-la*, a difficult form rendered either "I will go up" (Strong [1893], Jastrow [1912], Langdon [1914], Pfeiffer [1950], Ivantchik [1993]), or "lordly" (CAD E [1958], AHw. s.v. *etellu*, Huffmon [1974], Hecker [1986]); both renderings involve grave grammatically difficulties. As a matter of fact, the break before the first sign is much too wide for an *e*, and there is no trace of the required horizontals (see coll. and photo). Thus the sign probably is not ⸢*e*⸣ but *a*. There is just enough room for [*ma*] in the break, and the restored [*ma*]*-a* is perfectly aligned with [*ma*]-⸢*a*⸣ in the preceding line. The interpretation of *ta-al-la* (signs clear) remains a crux. Cf. Isa. 10:17, "The light of Israel shall become a fire and his Holy One a flame, which in one day shall burn up and consume his thorns and his briars" (referring to the king of Assyria). r.2 For the rendering of this line see Landsberger, *Fauna* p. 132 and Parpola, OLZ 74 (1979) 29 s.v. *nipšu*. r.3ff A prophecy on the impending (671) conquest of Egypt, see Introduction, p. LXX. For *hallalatti* (an adverb derived from *hallulāja* "centipede") see von Soden, ZA 45 (1939) 63f and Farber, Festschrift Reiner (1987), p. 102ff; in discussing the role of the centipede in Lamaštu rituals, Farber notes that this poisonous tiny beast is dreaded in Iraq like the scorpion for its painful bite, ominous hissing motion, and clandestine nocturnal activity. The reading and interpretation of the other adverb, which is a hapax legomenon, remains enigmatic; cf. perhaps *engurru* "underground waters" or *imgurru* "envelope," or read EN.GUR-*a-ti* and cf. *adudillu* "a mantis grasshopper." An interesting structural parallel to the passage is provided by John 16:16ff: 'A little while, and you see me no more; again a little while, and you will see me.' Some of his disciples said to one another, 'What does he mean by this: "A little while, and you will not see me, and again a little while, and you will see me."' r.5 The sign *ina* (omitted by Craig) appears correctly in Strong's copy. r.6ff See Introduction, pp. XXXVI and XL, and cf. Isa. 66:11-13, "Then you may suck and be fed from the breasts that give comfort, delighting in her plentiful milk. For thus says YHWH: 'I will send peace flowing over her (Jerusalem) like a river, and ... it shall suckle you, and you shall be carried in their arms and dandled on their knees. As a mother comforts her son, so will I myself comfort you, and you shall find comfort in Jerusalem.'" Cf. also SAA 3 39:22, "The Lady of Liburna (= Arbela) is the dry nurse (UM.M[E.D]A!) of Bel." r.7 Cf. Num. 11:12, "Am I (Moses) their mother? Have I brought them into the world, and am I called upon to carry them in my bosom, like a nurse with her babies?" The sign ÍL at the end of the line (miscopied by Craig) appears correctly in Strong's copy. r.8 See coll. The context implies that "pomegranate" here refers to a pomegranate-shaped pendant hanging from the neck of the goddess; for specimens of such pendants see J. Börker-Klähn, "Granatapfel," RlA 3, pls. I-II on p. 628f, and pp. 618:11-18, 619:28 and 4-5, 621:22 and 625ff. The pomegranate itself is well attested as an attribute of female deities (Kubaba, Aphrodite, Artemis, Juno etc.) in the classical world, and goddesses wearing pomegranate pendants are actually depicted in Greek and Roman art (ibid. p. 625). The association of the king (here pictured as the child of the goddess) with the pomegranate has a parallel in Adonis statuettes holding pomegranates in their hands, found in Cypriote sanctuaries of Astarte-Aphrodite, see ibid. p. 626. For the symbolic meaning of the pomegranate (fertility, life, unity, regeneration) see ibid. and A. de Vries, *Dictionary of Symbols and Imagery* (1974), p. 371. See also Introduction, n. 46. r.9 → SAA 3 13 r.8; cf. Ps. 121:4f [Weinfeld]. r.10 In view of the context and the vocalization, it seems unlikely that *un-na-ni-ka* (hapax legomenon) is to be connected with the well-known poetic word *unnennu* "prayer," as assumed in previous translations; the context rather points to an otherwise unattested vocable of child language (sg. *unnu*). The phrase *un-na-ni-ka uṣur uṣur* grammatically functions as the object of *uppaška* and may with Deller (*apud* Ivantchik, N.A.B.U. 1993/2, p. 41) well have been "une interjection que les nurses utilisaient pour calmer un infant." r.11 Cf. Isa. 1:2 (referring to kings of Israel), "I (Yahweh) have sons whom I reared and brought up, but they have rebelled against me." The verbal form *ú-rab-bu-u-ni* is ambiguous and can refer to the present or future (see no. 1 i 35) as well as to the past (see no. 2 iii 27). → nos. 1 v 29, 2 iv 20, and ABL 1249:4.

8. Words Concerning the Elamites

K 1545

1 *dib-bi* [*ša* KUR.NIM.MA.K]I$^{!}$-*a-a*
2 *ki-i an-*[*ni-i* DINGIR] ⌜*i*⌝-*qab-bi*
3 *ma-a at-t*[*a*$^{!}$-*lak at*]-*tal-ka*

4 5-*šú* 6-*šú iq-*[*ṭi-b*]*i id—da-a-te*
5 *ma-a* TA* UGU GIŠ.[*nàr*]-*an-ti at-tal-ka*
6 *ma-a* MUŠ *ša ina* ŠÀ-*bi-šá as-sa-ad-da*
7 *ab-ta-taq ù ma-a* GIŠ.*nàr-an-tu*

8 *ah-te-pi ù ma-a* KUR.NIM.MA.KI
e.9 *a-hap-pi* :. 0$^{!}$ Á.2.MEŠ-*šú* TA* *kaq-qir*
r.1 *i-sap-pan ma-a ki-i an-ni-i*
2 KUR.NIM.MA.KI *a*$^{!}$-*gam-mar*

rest uninscribed

ABL 1280

1 Words [concerning the Elam]ites.
2 [*God*] says as follows:
3 "I have go[ne and I ha]ve come."
4 He s[ai]d (this) five, six times, and then:
5 "I have come from the [m]ace. I have pulled out the snake which was inside it, I have cut it in pieces, and I have broken the mace."
8 And (he said): "I will destroy Elam; its army shall be levelled to the ground. In this manner I will finish Elam."

9. Words of Encouragement to Assurbanipal

K 1292 (ZA 24 169) + DT 130 (unpub.)

1 [*ki-din*]-*nu šá* ^{d}N[I]N.LÍL
2 [(*x*) *x x*] *ša* ^{d}GAŠAN—URU.*a*[*r*]*ba-ìl*
3 [*ši-na-m*]*a ina* DINGIR.DINGIR *dan-na*
4 [*i-ra-ʾ*]*a*$^{!}$-*a-ma u* ÁG-*ši*$^{!!}$-*na*
5 [*a-na*] $^{m!}$AN.ŠÁR—*ba-an*—A DÙ-*ut* ŠU.2-*ši-na*
6 [*il-t*]*a-nap-pa-ra šá* TI.LA-*šú*
7 [*ú-šá-á*]*š-ka-na-šu* ŠÀ-*bu*

ZA 24 169+

1 [*O proté*]*gé* of Mullissu, [...] of the Lady of Arbela!
3 [They] are the strongest among the gods; they [lov]e and keep sending their love [to] Assurbanipal, the creation of their hands. [They g]ive him heart for the sake of his life.

8 Photo pls. X and XIII. Copy Waterman, AJSL 29 (1912) 16; Harper, ABL XIII (1913), no. 1280. Collated by the editor in July, 1992. → Weippert, ARINH (1981), pp. 73 and 96. As noted below, this text has several points of contact with the biblical book of Obadiah, with which it was approximately contemporary (see Introduction, p. LXX).
1 Restored from r.2; the traces of K]I (see coll.) agree with KI in r.2. 2 Comparison with r.1 indicates that there is room for only one sign in the break after *an-*[*ni-i*; the restoration DINGIR "God" accordingly imposes itself. Cf. Ob. 1:1, "The vision of Obadiah: what the Lord GOD has said concerning Edom"; Mic. 6:1, "Now hear what the LORD is saying." 3 See coll. There is room for one sign only between -*t*[*a*- and *a*[*t*-; the traces of the latter agree with the preceding *at*. 4 Only one sign is missing between *iq*- and -*b*]*i*. 6 In view of lines 8ff, the "snake" here is certainly a symbolic expression for Elam. No textual evidence for this association seems to be extant, but note the general prominence of the snake in Elamite religion and art (cf. W. Hinz, *Das Reich Elam*, Stuttgart 1964, p. 35ff) and the ophidian snake gods Nirah and Ištaran worshipped in Der (on the Elamite border), on which see McEwan, Or. 52 (1983) 221ff. 8f Cf. Jer. 49:37, "I will break Elam" [Weinfeld]; Ob. 1:3 "You (Edom) say to yourself, 'Who can bring me to the ground?'" and ibid. 8: "I will destroy all the sages of Edom." 9 See coll.; the sign *ina* preceding Á in the two published copies does not exist (and never did exist) on the tablet.
9 Photo pls. XI-XII. No previous copy; the exclamation marks pertain to Zimmern's transliteration in ZA 24 (1910) 169. The fragment DT 130 was identified and joined to K 1292 by R. Borger in March, 1973. Collated by the editor in July, 1992. 1 For restoration cf. ABL 186 r.12ff, "I have sent to the king, my lord, the protection (*ki-din-nu*) of Mullissu and the Lady of Kidimuri, the mothers who love you"; for examples of *kidinnu* in the extended meaning "man under protection, protégé," see CAD K 344a and cf. Introduction, p. LXIIf. 3 Cf. SAA 3 3:1ff, "Exalt and glorify the Lady of Nineveh, magnify and praise the Lady of Arbela, who have no equal among the great gods" (Assurbanipal's hymn to Mullissu and Ištar of Arbela). 4 Tablet ÁG-*me-na* (scribal error). 5 Cf. r.2 and Streck Asb p. 48:100f, "I (Ištar of Arbela) will go before Assurbanipal, the king whom my hands created"; ibid. p. 274:3, "(Assurbanipal) the creation of her (Mullissu's) hands." Note, on the other hand, that in SAA 3 3:23, the hymn to Mullissu and Ištar just quoted, Assurbanipal calls himself "the creation of the hands (*binūt qāti*) of the great gods," and that in the extispicy reports from Assurbanipal's time the king is called the creation (*binūt qāti*) of Šamaš (see Starr, SAA 3 Index p. 326 *binūtu*); in Streck Asb p. 20 ii 12 and Borger Esarh. p. 45 ii 16, he is presented as "the creation of Aššur" (AN.ŠÁR DINGIR DÙ-*ia*, *binūt* AN.ŠÁR). This variation reflects the Assyrian concept of God discussed in Introduction, pp. XVIII and XXIff. 7 Cf. SAA 3 12 r.2, "I give heart to myself (*libbu raminī ašakkan*), but what have I got to give?"; and see ibid. p. XXVI on the identification of the sufferer with Assurbanipal, and above, p. LXXI, on the connections between SAA 3 12-13 and the present text.

8 *[ba-la]-ṭa-ka er-šá-a-ku-ma a-rap-pu-da* EDIN
9 *[e]-⸢ta⸣-nab-bir* ÍD.MEŠ *u tam-tim*.MEŠ
10 *⸢e-ta⸣-na-at-ti-iq* KUR.MEŠ-*e hur-sa-a-ni*
11 *e-⸢ta⸣-nab-bir* ÍD.MEŠ *ka-li-ši-na*
12 *e-⸢ta⸣-nak-kal-a-ni ia-a-ši*
13 *ṣe-[t]a-a-te sa-rab-a-te*
14 *il-ta-nap-pa-ta ba-nu-ú la-a-ni*
15 *an-ha-[k]u$^{!}$-ma šá-ad-da-lu-pu-ka la-a-ni-ia*
16 *ina* UKKIN$^{!}$ DINGIR.MEŠ *ka-la-me aq-ṭi-bi ba-la-ṭa-ka*
17 *dan-na rit-ta-a-a la ú-ram-ma-ka ina* IGI DINGIR.MEŠ
18 *nag-ga-la-pa-a-a har-ru-ud-da*
19 *it-ta-na-áš-šá-a-ka a-na ka-a-šá*
20 *⸢ina⸣$^{!?}$* NU[NDU]N$^{!}$.MEŠ$^{!}$-*[t]e$^{?}$-ia$^{!}$ e-ta-nar-riš$^{!}$* TI.LA-*ka*
21 *[x x x x x]* TI.LA-*ka* TI.LA *tu-šá-tar*
22 *[x x x x x]* $^{⸢d⸣+}$AG *li-ih-da-a* NUNDUN.MEŠ-*ka*
23 *[ina* UKKIN DINGIR.MEŠ*] ka-la-a-me*
24 *[aq-ṭa-nab]-bi dam-qa-a-te-ka*
25 [TI.LA-*ka er-šá]-ku-ma a-rap-pu-da* EDI[N]

26 *[ina* ŠÀ *u$_8$-a a-t]a-bi a-a-ab-ka a-ṭa-[ba-ah]*
27 *[x x x x x x]x-ma a-na* KUR-*šú i-tu-r[a]*
28 *[x x x x x x x]-u-ni a-šá-x[x x x]*
about 4 lines broken away
Rev. about 8 lines obliterated or uninscribed
1′ *[x]* ^{d}[NIN].⸢LÍL⸣ *u* $^{⸢d⸣}$GAŠAN—*arba-ìl*.KI
2′ *[a-na]* ^{m}AN.ŠÁR—DÙ—A ⸢DÙ⸣-*ut* ŠU.2.MEŠ-⸢*ši*⸣-*na*
3′ *⸢lu⸣$^{!}$-ú-bal-liṭ-ṭa a-na [d]a-⸢a⸣-r[i]*
blank line
4′ *ša* ⸢KA⸣$^{!}$ MÍ$^{!}$.KALAG$^{!}$-*šá—a-mur*
5′ [DUMU.MÍ URU.*arba*]-⸢*ìl*⸣$^{!}$
6′ ITI.BAR⸢AG⸣$^{!}$ UD-18$^{!}$-KAM *lim-mu* ^{m}EN—KUR-*u-a*
7′ LÚ.GAR.KUR *ṣur-ri*
rest (about 8 lines) destroyed

[8] I roam the desert desiring your life. I cross over rivers and oceans, I traverse mountains and mountain chains, I cross over all rivers. Droughts and showers consume me and affect my beautiful figure. I am worn out, my body is exhausted for your sake.

[16] I have ordained life for you in the assembly of all the gods. My arms are strong, they shall not forsake you before the gods. My shoulders are alert, they will keep carrying you.

[20] I keep demanding life for you with my lips; [...] your life; you shall increase life.

[22] *[O favourite of]* Nabû, may your lips rejoice! I keep spe]aking good words about you [in the assembly of] all [the gods]; I roam the desert [desiri]ng [your life].

[26] *[In woe* I will r]ise and slau[ghter] your enemy; [your ...] will [...] and retur[n] to his country.

(Break)

[r.1] May Mullissu and the Lady of Arbela keep Assurbanipal, the creation of their hands, alive for ever!

[4] By the mouth of the woman *Dunna*ša-amur [of Arbe]la.

[6] Nis[an] 18, eponymy of Bel-šadû'a, governor of Tyre (650).

[8] A clear allusion to Gilg. IX 5, *mūta aplahma arappud ṣēra* "I feared death, roaming the steppe," a line also recurring as a refrain in the 10th tablet of the Epic. → obv.25. [9-11] Cf. Gilg. X 251ff, "I came circling through all the lands, I traversed (*ētettiqa*) difficult mountains, I crossed all the seas (*ētebbira kalīšina tâmātu*)." [12-14] Cf. Gilg. X 122ff and refrains, "How would my cheeks not be emaciated (*aklā*) ... my face not 'burnt' by showers (*sarbi*) and droughts (*ṣēti*)." On the rendering of *sarbu* and *ṣētu* see Landsberger, ZA 42 (1934) 161f and JNES 8 (1949) 252 n.30. [15] Cf. Gilg. X v 28ff, "My face did not get enough good sleep, I have worn myself out through sleeplessness (*ina dalāpi*)," and I 7, "He came a long way, was exhausted (*anih*) and found relief." *šá-ad-da-lu-pu-ka* is stat. 3 pl. of *dalāpu* Š with an anaptyptic vowel and secondary gemination, on which see note on no. 1 i 14 and cf. *nag-ga-la-pa-a* obv. 18.
[16] On the assembly of gods see Introduction, pp. XXI, XXIIIf and n. 136. [18f] → nos. 1 ii 32 and 2 iii 30. The curious gemination of the last radical in *har-ru-ud-da* has a parallel in r.3. [20] See coll. [22ff] → SAA 3 13:24-26. [26] For restoration see nos. 1 i 26 and 2 iii 31; note also no. 1 i 31f (an oracle by Sinqiša-amur, cf. note on r.4). [r.1] Cf. SAA 3 3 r.14ff, "The Lady of Nineveh, the mother who gave birth to me, endowed me with unparalleled kingship; the Lady of Arbela ordered everlasting life for me to live." [r.4] Or: Sinqiša-amur (see Introduction, p. IL). [r.5] Despite Weippert, ARINH (1982) p. 73 n.6, the month name is certainly Nisan not Kislev (coll.); note the three initial wedges of BARAG, clearly visible in the photo. The date places the text in the middle of the Šamaš-šumu-ukin rebellion, see Introduction, p. LXXI.

10. Fragment of a Prophecy

83-1-18,726

beginning broken away
1′ *s[i-x x x x x x x x x]*
2′ *is-[x x x x x x x x x]*
3′ *nu-[x x x x x x x x x]*
4′ *né-me-[el x x x x x x x x]*
5′ *ina* IGI *[x x x x x x x x]*
6′ *pa-ni [x x x x x x x x]*
7′ *gu-[x x x x x x x x]*
rest broken away
Rev. beginning broken away
1′ *[x i]b-ba-áš-[ši x x x x]*
2′ *ú-še-ṣa-an-ni [x x x x x x]*
3′ LUGAL-*u-tú id-dan-[x x x x x x]*
4′ *ša* KUR.KUR *gab-b[u x x x x x]*
5′ UD-*mu ša tap-x[x x x x x x]*
6′ *u šá ke-n[u-ni x x x x x]*
7′ *lu-ur-r[i-ik x x x x x]*
8′ *ú-[x x x x x x x x x]*
rest destroyed
s.1 *[x x x x]* MÍ.KALAG-*šá—a-mur ma-a [x x x x x x x x]*
2 *[x x x x x] ma-a* MÍ.GUB.BA *šá ra-[x x x x x x x x]*

CT 53 946

(Beginning destroyed)

3 we [......]
4 because [......]
5 before [......]
6 *face* [......]
(Break)

r.1 shall be [......]
2 *shall bring me* out [......]
3 *shall give* the kingship [......]
4 of all lands [......]
5 the day when you [......]
6 and those who are lo[yal ......]
7 I will lengt[hen ......]
(Break)
s.1 [...] the woman *Dunna*ša-amur (said): "[......]
2 [...] the prophetess who [......]

11. Report on a Vision and an Oracle to Assurbanipal

K 1974

Obv. completely destroyed
r.1 *[x x]x it-tal-[x x x x x x x x x x x]*
2 *[la-a] tal-li-ki a-n[a x x x x x x x x x]*
3 *[ma]-⸢a⸣* UD-*me i⸢n ni?⸣ ú ⸢kin⸣ [x x x x x x x]*
4 [L]Ú.KÚR *a-kaš-šad šá ^{m}aš-šur*—DÙ—A *[x x x x x x]*
5 *[ma]-⸢a⸣ ši-bi* KUR.KUR *ú-taq-qa-[an x x x x x]*
6 *[m]a-a ina di-gi-li-ia p[a-ni-i x x x x x]*
7 *[a]—dan-niš kak-kab-tú šá* KUG.GI *a⸢n?⸣-[x x x x x]*
8 [GIŠ].BANŠUR 1 *qa* NINDA *dan-ni ina* UG[U *x x x x x x*]
9 [DU]G.*síh-ha-ru sa-ʾu mat [x x x x x x]*

CT 53 219

(Beginning destroyed)

1 [...] *wen[t ......]*
2 *did you/she [not]* go t[o ......]
3 "*days* ... [......]
4 "I will vanquish the enemy of Assurbanipal [......]
5 "Sit down! I will put the lands in orde[r ......]
6 "In my pr[evious] vision [......]
7 "very [much]; a golden star ornament [......]
8 [a t]able, *one 'litre' of strong bread* upon [it ......]
9 a ... platter [......]

10 Photo pl. XIII. Copy S. Parpola, CT 53 (1979) pl.210. No previous edition or translation. Identified by the editor in June, 1969; collated in July, 1992. r.2 Or: "[who] brings in." r.3 Or: "[who] gives the kingship." r.5 See coll. s.1 Or: Sinqiša-amur.

11 Photo pl. XIII. Copy S. Parpola, CT 53 (1979) pl.66. No previous edition or translation. Collated by the editor in July, 1992. Judging from the curvature, about 1/3 of line 8 is missing; the number of missing signs in the other lines has been estimated accordingly. 4 → nos. 1 ii 6f, no. 2 i 23, iii 32, and no. 3 iii 22 and iv 17. 5 Cf. Streck Asb p. 116 v 64, "You shall stay here ... until I (Ištar) go and accomplish that task" (Introduction, p. XLVII); → no. 2 ii 2f and iii 32ff. 6 → SAA 10 363:16-r.2 and 365:5-12; CT 53 17:10ff and 938:10ff.

10 [*x x*]*x-ma-ni šá šad-du-*[*ni x x x x x x x*]
11 [*šá*]*-pal kak-kab-tú šá* [KUG.GI *x x x x x x x*]
12 [*ina*] *re-še-ia x*[*x x x x x x x x x x x*]
13 [M]UL.M[EŠ? *x x x x x x x x x x x x x x*]
rest broken away

10 [...]s *pulled taut* [......]
11 [un]der the [golden] star ornament [......]
12 [at] my head [......]
13 [s]tar[s ......]
(Rest destroyed)

12 See coll.; both *še* and KUR seem possible.

GLOSSARY AND INDICES

Logograms and Their Readings

A.MEŠ → *mê;* Á.2 → *ahu B;* AD → *abu;* AD—AD → *ab abi;* ÁG → *raʾāmu;* AMA → *ummu;* AMA—LUGAL, AMA—MAN → *ummi šarri;* AMAR → *marʾu;* AN → *šamê;* ARAD → *urdu;*

^{d}AG → *Nabû;* ^{d}EN → *Bēl;* ^{d}EN—TÙR → *Bēl tarbiṣi;* ^{d}GAŠAN → *Bēlet;* ^{d}IŠ.TAR → *ištāru;* ^{d}MAŠ → *Inurta;* ^{d}NIN.LÍL → *Mullissu;* ^{d}NIN.URTA → *Inurta;* ^{d}PA → *Nabû;* ^{d}UTU → *Šamaš, šamšu;* ^{d}15 → *Issār;* ^{d}30 → *Sīn;*

DI → *šulmu;* DINGIR, DINGIR.DINGIR → *ilu;* DÙ → *binūtu;* DÙG.GA → *ṭābtu, ṭiābu;* DUMU → *marʾu;* DUMU—DUMU → *mār marʾi;* DUMU.MÍ → *marʾutu;* DUMU.UŠ → *aplu, marʾu;* DUMU.UŠ—DUMU.UŠ → *mār marʾi;*

É → *bēt rēdūti, bētānu, bētu;* É—DINGIR → *bēt ili;* É.GAL → *ekallu;* É.SAG.ÍL → *Esaggil;* É.ŠÁR.RA → *Ešarra;* É—UŠ → *bēt rēdūti;* EDIN → *ṣēru;* EN → *adi, bēlu;*

GAL → *rabû;* GAR → *šakānu;* GAŠAN → *Bēlet Arbail;* GIBÍL → *maqlūtu;* GÍN → *šiqlu;* GÌR.2 → *šēpu;* GIŠ.BANŠUR → *paššūru;* GIŠ.GU.ZA → *kussiu;* GIŠ.HAŠHUR.KUR.RA → *armannu;* GIŠ.MÁ → *eleppu;* GIŠ.MI → *ṣillu;* GIŠ.ÙR → *gušūru;*

HUL → *lumnu;*

ÍD → *nāru;* IGI → *pānu;* IGI.2 → *ēnu;* ÍL → *našû;* ITI.BARAG → *nisannu;* ITI.SIG$_4$ → *simānu;* IZI → *išātu;* Ì—DÙG.GA → *šamnu ṭābu;*

KA → *pû;* KÁ.DINGIR.KI → *Bābili;* KÁ.GAL → *abullu;* KAB → *šumēlu;* KASKAL → *hūlu;* KAŠ → *šikāru;* KI.TA → *šapal;* KI.TIM → *kaqquru;* KUG.GI → *hurāṣu;* KUR, KUR.KUR → *mātu, šadû;* KUR.NIM.KI, KUR.NIM.MA.KI → *Elamtu;* KUR.URI → *Urarṭu;*

LÚ.ARAD—É.GAL → *urdu ekalli;* LÚ.ERIM → *ṣābu;* LÚ.GAR.KUR → *šaknu;* LÚ.KÚR → *nakru;* LÚ.LUL → *parriṣu;* LÚ.MÁ.LAH$_4$ → *mallāhu;* LÚ.SAG → *ša rēši;* LUGAL → *šarratu, šarru, šarrūtu;*

MAN → *šarru;* MÍ.AMA → *ummu;* MÍ.GUB.BA → *raggintu;* MU → *šumu;* MU.AN.NA → *šattu;* MUL → *kakkubu;* MUN → *ṭābtu;* MURUB$_4$ → *qablu;* MUŠ → *ṣerru;*

NA$_4$ → *abnu;* NIM.MA.KI → *Elamtu;* NINA.KI → *Nīnua;* NINDA → *kusāpu;* NUNDUN → *šaptu;*

SAG.DU → *kaqqudu;*

ŠÀ → *libbu;* ŠEM.HI.A → *riqiu;* ŠEŠ → *ahu A;* ŠU, ŠU.2 → *qātu;*

TA → *issi/u;* TI.LA → *balāṭu;* TÚG → *pitūtu;*

UBUR → *tulû;* UD → *ūmu;* UDU.SISKUR → *niqiu;* UGU → *muhhu;* UKKIN → *puhru;* URU → *ālu;* URU.NINA → *Nīnua;* URU.ŠÀ—URU → *Libbi āli;* Ú → *urqu;*

ZAG → *imittu;*

5 → *hanšīšu;* 6 → *šeššīšu;*

1BÁN → *sūtu;* 15 → *imittu;* 150 → *šumēlu*

Glossary

abnu "stone; hail": NA$_4$.MEŠ 3 ii 21,
abu "father": AD-*ka* 2 iii 26, 7:7, AD.MEŠ-*ia* 3 ii 35, AD.MEŠ-*ni* 7:10, AD-*u-a* 5 r. 7,
abullu "(city) gate": KÁ.GAL 3 ii 15,
abutu "word, matter": *a-bat* 2 ii 30, 38, 3 ii 33, iii 16, 5:1, 7:2,
ab abi "grandfather": AD—AD.MEŠ-*ni* 7:10,
adammumu "wasp": *a-dam-mu-ma-a-te* 7 r. 2,
adanniš "very": *a—dan-niš* 2 i 20, iv 12, *a—dan-[niš]* 1 iv 25, *[a]—dan-niš* 11 r. 7,
adê "treaty, covenant": *a-de-e* 3 ii 27, iii 11, 14, *a-d[e-e* 3 ii 36,
adi "until, plus": *a-di* 7:3, 4, *a-[d]i* 6 r. 10, *[a-di* 3 i 32, 34, EN 5 r. 7,
agappu "wing": *a-gap-pi-ia* 2 iii 27, *a-kap-pi* 2 ii 6, *a-qa-pu-šú* 1 i 7,
agarinnu "mother": *ga-ri-ni-šú* 3 i 24,
aggu "angry": *ak-ku* 1 iv 7,
agû "crown, tiara": *a-ge-e* 1 iii 28, *a-gu-ka* 2 ii 5,
ahāiš "each other": *a-he-iš* 7:8,
ahāzu "to grasp; (Š) to attach, kindle": *ú-šá-[haz]* 1 iv 32,
ahu A "brother": ŠEŠ.MEŠ-*ia* 3 ii 35,
ahu B "arm, (pl.) army": Á.2.MEŠ-*šú* 8 e. 9,
aiābu "enemy": *a-a-ab-ka* 9:26, *a-a-bi-ka* 3 iii 23, *a-a-bi-šú* 5:7,
aiāši "me": *a-a-ši* 1 ii 29, 2 ii 21, 3 iii 25, *ia-a-ši* 9:12,
aiu "what, which?": *ai-ʾu* 1 ii 34, *a[i]-ʾu* 1 ii 2, *[a]i-ʾu* 1 i 6, *ai-ú-te* 1 i 15,
akālu "to eat, consume; food": *a-kal* 3 iii 32, *a-ka-li* 3 iii 28, *[a-k]a-li* 3 iii 26, *e-ta-nak-kal-a-ni* 9:12, *lu-šá-kil-šú-nu* 3 ii 17, *ta-ka-la* 3 iii 10, *ta-kal* 1 vi 22,
akappu see *agappu,*
akê "how?": *a-ke-e* 2 iii 7,
akī "as; as if; thus": *a-ki* 2 i 17, ii 6, 9, 29, 3 ii 7, 25, iii 18, iv 8, *[a-ki* 2 i 16, 3 iii 24, iv 7, 21, see also *kî,*
akku see *aggu,*
ak lā "without(?)": *ak—la* 3 iii 27, see also *akī,*
aklu "bread, loaf": *ak-lu* 1 vi 22, see also *kusāpu,*
akussu "soup": *a-ku-su* 3 iii 34,
alāku "to go, come": *al-ka-ni* 3 ii 35, 7:9, *at-tal-ka* 8:5, *at]-tal-ka* 8:3, *at-t[a-lak* 8:3, *a-la-ka* 1 i 24, *il-lak-u-ni* 3 i 22, *il-lu-ku* 3 ii 31, *it-tal-[x* 11 r. 1, *la-a]l-lik* 3 iv 4, *lil-lik* 3 i 13, *lil-li-ku* 2 ii 26, *ni]-il-lik* 7:9, *tal-la-ka* 3 iii 9, *tal-la-k]u-u-ni* 2 iv 9, *tal-li-ki* 11 r. 2, *ú-šal-lak-šú* 2 i 30,
ālu "city, town": URU 1 v 30, URU.MEŠ-*ku-nu* 3 iii 9,
amāru "to see, behold": *am-mar* 2 iii 28, *la-mu-ur* 3 iv 11, *le-mu-ru* 3 ii 24, *ta-am-mar* 3 iv 20,
amēlūtu "mankind": *a-me-lu-ti* 1 ii 27, *a-me-lu-tu* 2 ii 17,
ammutu "forearm, cubit": *am-ma-te-ia* 2 iii 30, *[am-ma-te-ia* 2 iv 23,
amurdinnu "bramble": *mur-din-nu* 7 r. 1,
ana "to": *a-na* 1 i 32, ii 29, iii 13, v 13, 26, 28, 29, 30, 31, 2 ii 21, 34, 39, iii 7, 3 i 10, 11, ii 20, 34, iii 17, 25, 5:3, e. 9, 7:8, 10, r. 1, 2, 9:19, 27, r. 3, *a-n[a* 5:2, 11 r. 2, *a-n]a* 3 i 24, *a]-na* 3 i 9, *[a-na* 3 iv 10, 29, *[a-na]* 9:5, r. 2,
anāhu "to be exhausted": *an-ha-[k]u-ma* 9:15,
anāku "I": *ana-ku* 7 r. 11, *a-na-ku* 1 i 11, 12, 18, 20, 26, 36, ii 17, 30, 36, 38, iii 2, 4, 7, 16, 18, v 12, 2 i 24, ii 18, 19, iii 6, 26, 3 ii 14, *a-na-ku]* 2 i 5, *a-[na-ku]* 1 iv 19, *[a-na-ku* 1 i 37, vi 2, 2 i 36, iv 8, *a-na-ku-ma* 2 iii 3, *a-na-ku-ni* 3 ii 25, iv 7, 21,
anīna "hear me!": *a-ni-na* 3 ii 13,
anīnu "we": *a-ni-nu* 2 i 8,
anniu "this": *an-ni-i* 6 r. 5, 8 r. 1, *an-[ni-i* 8:2, *an-ni-t]i* 3 iv 20, *an-ni-u* 3 ii 8, 27, *an-nu-ti* 2 ii 22, 3 ii 10, iii 11, 12, 14, *an-nu-u* 3 ii 26,
annurig "now": *an-nu-rig* 3 ii 10,
anqullu "glow, fire": *aq-qul-lu* 3 ii 21, see also *naqallulu,*
apālu "to answer": *ta-ap-pa-la* 2 ii 29,
aplu "heir": *ap-lu* 1 iv 5, DUMU.UŠ 1 iv 20,
aqappu see *agappu,*
aqqullu see *anqullu,*
arāku "to be long; (D) to lengthen": *ar-ku-te* 1 iii 19, *ar-ku-u-t[e]* 1 iii 11, *ar-ku-u-ti* 1 iv 15, *lu-ur-r[i-ik* 10 r. 7,
arhiš "quickly": *ar-hi-iš* 2 ii 25,
arītu "shield": *a-ri-it-ka* 1 iv 19,
arku see *arāku,*
armannu "pomegranate": GIŠ.HAŠHUR.KUR.RA 7 r. 8,
aṣû see *uṣû,*
aṣūdu (a bowl for fruit and dough): *a-ṣu-di* 3 iii 32,
ašābu see *ušābu,*
atta "you": *at-ta* 1 i 25, iii 3, 2 ii 21, iii 11, iv 13, 3 ii 12, 18, 7 r. 4, 11, *a]t-ta* 2 iv 3, *[at-t]a* 3 iii 25, 7:5,
atti "you": *at-ti* 1 v 8, *at-ti-ma* 1 v 8, *at-ti-ni* 3 iv 9,
baʾāru "to catch": *ú-ba-ra* 2 ii 20, *ú-b[a]-r[a* 2 iii 5,
baʾāšu "to come to shame": *ú-ba-áš-[ka]* 1 iv 2,
baʾʾû "to seek": *tu-b]a-ʾa-a-ni* 2 iv 25,
balālu "to mix": *bal-li* 2 ii 24,
balāṭu "life; to live": *ba-la-ṭa-ka* 9:16, *[ba-la]-ṭa-ka* 9:8, *lu-ú-bal-liṭ-ṭa* 9 r. 3, TI.LA 9:21, TI.LA-*ka*

9:20, 21, [TI.LA-*ka* 9:25, TI.LA-*šú* 9:6,
banû A "to create": *a-ba-an-ni* 2 ii 37,
banû B "to be beautiful": *ba-nu-ú* 9:14,
barāmu "to seal": *a-bar-ri-im* 2 iii 14,
bašû "to exist, (Š) to give birth, (N) to come about": *ib-ba-áš-ši* 2 iii 9, *i]b-ba-áš-[ši* 10 r. 1, *tu-šab-šu-ka-ni* 1 ii 21,
batāqu "to cut off": *ab-ta-taq* 8:7, *ú-bat-taq* 2 iii 15, *ú-bat-taq-šú-nu* 1 v 7,
battibatti "around": *bat-bat-ti-ka* 2 i 18, *bat-bat-[ti-k]a* 2 ii 7, *bat-ti—bat-ti-ka* 1 ii 25,
beālu see *piālu,*
bēlu "lord": EN 1 ii 38, 3 ii 25, EN-*šú-nu* 2 i 24, see also *piālu, Bēl,*
bētānu "inside": É-*a-nu-uk-ka* 2 ii 23,
bētu "house; (in st. constr.) where": [*bé-et* 2 iv 9, É 3 ii 4, 5,
bēt ili "temple": É—DINGIR 3 iii 27,
bēt rēdūti "Succession Palace": É—*re-du-te-ka* 1 i 33, É—UŠ-*u-ti* 7:6,
biālu see *piālu,*
biāru "to examine, choose": *a-bi-ar* 2 iii 5, 13,
binūtu "creation": DÙ-*ut* 9:5, r. 2,
birti "between, in the midst of": *bir-ti* 1 ii 15, 2 iii 27, 30, [*bir-ti* 2 iv 22, *bir-tu-šú-nu* 3 ii 18, *bir-tu-un-ni* 7:11, *bi-rit* 1 v 30, 7 r. 8,
burku "knee, lap": *bur-ki* 1 vi 29,
da'ānu "to be strong; (D) to strengthen": *d]a-'a-at-tú* 2 iv 13, *ú-da-']i-i-nu* 2 i 2, *ú-da-in-an-ni-ni* 2 i 26, see also *danānu,*
dabābu "to talk, plot; (Š) to incite, provoke": *a-da-ab-ub* 2 ii 34, *a-da-bu-bu* 1 ii 18, *da-ba-bu* 1 vi 7, *i-da-ba-bu-u-ni* 1 v 5, [*la-ad-bu*]*-ub* 3 iv 13, *us-sa-ad-bi-bu-ka* 3 ii 11,
dagālu "to look": *a-da-gal* 2 ii 31, 3 iii 30, *du-gul-an-ni* 1 ii 29,
dāgil iṣṣūri "augur": LÚ.*da-gíl*—MUŠEN.[MEŠ 2 iii 2,
dalālu "to glorify": *dul-la* 5 r. 6,
dalāpu "to be sleepless": *šá-ad-da-lu-pu-ka* 9:15,
damāqu "to be good, beautiful, skilled": *dam-qí* 2 i 16, ii 9, *de-iq-tú* 1 iii 18, iv 19,
damiqtu "good word, recommendation": *dam-qa-a-te-ka* 9:24,
damqu see *damāqu,*
dāmu "blood": *da-me* 2 iii 22, *da-me-šú-nu* 3 ii 23,
danānu "to be strong": *dan-na* 9:3, 17, *dan-ni* 11 r. 8, *dan-ni-te* 1 i 1, *da-an-na-at* 2 i 20, *da-na-nu* 1 v 23, see also *da'ānu,*
dannu "strong" see *danānu,*
darû "everlasting": [*d*]*a-a-r*[*i*] 9 r. 3, *da-ra-a-ti* 1 iv 16, *da-ra-te* 1 iii 20, *da-ra-t*[*e*] 1 iii 12,
dātu "after": *id—da-a-te* 8:4,
dibbī "words": *dib-bi* 8:1, *di-ib-bi-ia* 1 i 15, 2 ii 22,
diglu "vision": *di-gi-li-ia* 11 r. 6,
duāku "to kill": *i-du-k*[*u* 6:9,
duālu "to run about": *a-du-al* 2 ii 10,
ebāru "to cross": *e-ta-nab-bir* 9:11, [*e*]*-ta-nab-bir* 9:9, *ú-še-ba-ar-ka* 1 iv 4,
ēdānīu "single": *e-da-ni-'e* 1 ii 7,
ēdu "single, lone": LÚ.*e-du* 2 iii 16,
ekallu "palace": É.GAL 5:8, É.GAL-*ia* 1 vi 20, É.GAL-*ka* 1 vi 25, 2 ii 2, 9, 11,
eleppu "boat, ship": [GIŠ.MÁ 2 i 17,
elmešu "amber": *il-me-ši* 1 iii 25,
elû "to go up; (Š) to remove, set aside": *e-ta-li-a* 3 iv 5, *us-se-li-a* 3 i 8, *us-se-li-šú-nu* 3 ii 20,
emādu "to impose, lean": *um-ma-ad* 3 ii 2,
enguratti: *en-gur-a-te* 7 r. 5, *en-gur-a-ti* 7 r. 3, 4,
ēnu "eye, eye-stone, spring": IGI.2 3 iii 31, I]GI.2-*ka* 2 iv 15, IGI.2.MEŠ-*ka* 1 ii 28, IG]I.2-*šú* 3 i 26,
epāšu "to do, make, perform; (D) to do, practice, exercise": *ep-pa-šu-u-ni* 7:3, *ep-pu-šú* 3 ii 30, *e-pa-šú-u-ni* 3 iii 18, *tu-up-pa-šú-u-ni* 7:5, *up-pa-áš* 2 ii 14, *up-pa-áš-ka* 7 r. 10, *ú-pa-áš* 1 vi 30,
ēpissu "doer": *e-pi-is-su* 2 ii 18,
erābu "to enter": *e-rab* 3 ii 28, 7 r. 5, *e-tar-b*[*u* 6:7,
erāšu "to request, desire": *er-šá-a-ku-ma* 9:8, *er-šá*]*-ku-ma* 9:25, *e-ta-nar-riš* 9:20,
erbettu "four": *erbe-tim* 3 ii 3,
êru "to be awake": *e-rak* 7 r. 9,
esāpu "to gather, collect": *e-si-ip* 2 ii 23,
eṣānu "to smell, scent": *ú-ṣa-a-na* 2 ii 10, 20,
etāku "to be alert": *et-k*[*a-ka* 2 iii 1, *e*]*t-ka-ku* 2 iv 5,
etāqu "to pass, move on; (Š) to transfer, avert": *e-ta-na-at-ti-iq* 9:10, *še*]*-tu-qi* 2 iv 1, *ú-še-taq* 3 i 26,
gabbu "all": *gab-b*[*u* 10 r. 4,
galālu "to roll": *a-ga-lal* 2 iii 4,
gamāru "to finish; (D) to abolish": *a-gam-mar* 8 r. 2, *a-ga-mar* 7:14, *ú-ga-am-mar* 2 ii 16,
garinnu see *agarinnu,*
gaṣṣiṣu "hater, foe": LÚ.*gi-ṣi-ṣi-ka* 3 iii 23,
gattu "form, stature": *gat-ta-ka* 2 iv 21,
giṣṣiṣu see *gaṣṣiṣu,*
giṣṣu "thorn": *gi-ṣu* 7 r. 1,
giššu "hip": *gi-iš-ši-ia* 7 r. 7,
gurṣiptu "butterfly": *gu*]*r-ṣip-ti* 3 iii 24,
gušūru "log, roof-beam": GIŠ.ÙR.MEŠ 1 ii 19,
ha'ūtu "cushion": *ha-'u-u-ti* 3 ii 28,
habālu "to wrong": LÚ.*ha-ab-lu* 2 iii 16,
habūnu "bosom": *ha-bu-un-šú* 1 vi 5,
hadû "to be glad": *li-ih-da-a* 9:22,
hallalatti "like a centipede": *hal-la-la-at-ti* 7 r. 3, 4, 5,
halputu "successor": *hal-pe-te* 7:4,
hangaru "dagger": *ha-an-ga-ru* 1 iv 7,
hanšīšu "five times": 5-*šú* 8:4,
hapû "to break, destroy": *ah-te-pi* 8:8, *a-hap-pi* 3 i 35, 8 e. 9, *a-ha*]*p-pi* 3 i 36,
harādu "to watch, attend, (D) to warn, alert": *a-ha-ri-di* 1 ii 20, iii 24, *a-ha-ri-su* 1 iii 29, *har-ru-ud-da* 9:18,
harrānu see *hūlu,*
hasāsu "to remember": *ha-sa-*[*ku*] 1 iv 23, *ta-ha-sa-sa-ni* 3 iii 13,
haṣānu "to take care": *a-ha-ṣ*]*i-in-ka* 7:6, *i*]*h-ti-ṣi-in* 3 i 7,
hatāpu "to slaughter": *uh-ta-ti-ip* 3 ii 22,
hiāṭu "to weigh; (D) to search out": *ú-ha-a-a-a-ṭa* 2 ii 32,
hilpu "milk": *hi-il-pa-ka* 7 r. 9,
hirṣu "cut, slice": *hi-ir-ṣ*[*u* 3 iii 2,
hissutu "reminder": *hi-is-sa-at-*[*ka*] 1 iv 22,
hubburu "noisy": *hu-bur-tu* 2 ii 19,
hūlu "road, way": [KA]SKAL.MEŠ 7:13,
hurāṣu "gold": KUG.GI 1 iii 23, 11 r. 7, [KUG.GI

11 r. 11,

hursānu "mountain": *hur-sa-a-ni* 9:10,

iāši see *aiāši,*

iāu see *ijû,*

iddāti see *dātu,*

igib (mng. uncert.): *i-gi-ib* 2 iii 15,

ijû "mine": *ia-ú* 1 v 18,

ikkillu "scream, cry": *kil-la-ka* 3 ii 14, *kil-li* 5:3,

ikkû "yours": *ik-ku-u* 1 v 22, *ik-ku-u-ma* 1 v 23,

ilmešu see *elmešu,*

ilu "god": DINGIR] 8:2, DINGIR.MEŠ 1 ii 22, 25, 2 i 21, ii 24, iii 20, 3 ii 25, 35, 9:16, 17, DINGIR.MEŠ] 9:23, DINGIR].MEŠ 7:10, DINGIR.MEŠ-*ni* 3 ii 9, DINGIR.DINGIR 9:3,

imittu "right side": *i-mit-ti*] 3 iv 23, ZAG 1 v 15, ZAG]-*ia* 2 i 21, ZAG-*ka* 1 ii 24, iv 29, 15 5:6,

immati "when?": *im—ma-ti* 2 iii 9,

ina "in": *ina 1 i 10, 14, 17, 22, 23, 25, 26, ii 4, 5, 6, 24, 25, 27, iii 9, 21, 23, 24, 26, iv 3, 8, 14, 18, 26, 27, 29, 31, 33, 35, v 6, 17, vi 3, 9, 11, 18, 25, 29, 2 i 16, 18, 21, ii 2, 6, 7, 9, 11, 14, 23, 24, 26, 33, iii 10, 17, 23, 24, 25, 31, iv 26, 3 i 13, 20, ii 1, 2, 8, 9, 18, 21, 26, 28, 32, 36, iii 2, 7, 9, 15, 30, 31, 35, 36, iv 7, 13, 27, 28, 4:9, 5:7, 8, r. 1, 4, 6 r. 9, 7:4, 5, 6, 9, 11, 13, r. 5, 7, 8, 8:6, 9:3, 16, 17, 20, 10:5, 11 r. 6, 8, ina*] 3 i 14, *i]na* 2 i 9, [*ina* 2 i 12, 3 i 30, iv 12, 20, 4:4, 6 r. 7, 12, 9:23, 26, [*ina*] 1 i 33, 11 r. 12,

isinnu "festival": *i-sin*]-*nu* 3 iv 6, [*i-sin-nu* 3 i 14,

issi "with": *is-si-ia* 1 ii 22, *is-si-ka* 1 ii 17, 31, 2 ii 3, 3 iv 18,

issi/u "with/from": TA 1 ii 11, v 1, 2 i 25, ii 22, 28, iii 18, 3 i 21, ii 4, 15, 19, iii 12, 8:5, e. 9, T]A 1 i 38, [TA 2 i 14, 35, 3 i 31, 33, [T]A 1 vi 20, 2 iii 20,

iṣṣūru "bird": *iṣ-ṣur* 2 ii 6,

išātu "fire": *i-šá-tu* 3 ii 2, 17, IZI 1 iv 32,

ištāru "goddess": ^{d}IŠ.TAR.MEŠ 2 i 8,

izirû "(upper) arm": *i-zi-ri-ia* 2 iii 30, *i-z*]*i-ri-ia* 2 iv 22,

kabāsu "to tread upon, trample": *la-ak-bu-us* 3 iv 12, *ú-kab-ba-as* 2 i 12,

kakkabtu "star-shaped object, rosette": *kak-kab-tú* 11 r. 7, 11,

kakkišu "weasel": *ka-kiš-a-ti* 1 v 3, *ka-ki*]*š-a-ti* 4: 3,

kakkubu "star": [M]UL.M[EŠ 11 r. 13,

kalāma "all, everything": *ka-la-a-me* 9:23, *ka-la-me* 9:16,

kalappu "axe": *ka-la-pu* 1 iv 13,

kallumu "to show": *tu-kal-lam-šú-nu* 7:13,

kalu "all": *ka-li-ši-na* 9:11,

kalû "to hold back": *ak-k*[*a*]-*li* 3 iii 29, *a*[*k-ka-l*]*i* 3 iii 28,

kal amāri "early morning": *kal-la-ma-ri* 7 r. 10, *kal-la-ma-r*[*i* 2 ii 4,

kal ūmi "daytime": *kal*—UD-*me* 2 ii 4, 7 r. 9,

kamāṣu "to kneel": *kan-ṣa* 5:2,

kammusu "to sit, live, stay": [*kam-mu-sa-ka*] 2 ii 2,

kapāpu "to bend, subdue": *ak-pu-pa-a* 3 iii 21, [*ak-tap-p*]*a* 3 iv 16,

kaqqudu "head": SAG.DU-*ia* 1 iii 28,

kaqquru "earth, ground": *kaq-qir* 8 e. 9, KI.TIM 3 i 9,

karāru "to throw, cast": *ak-kar-ru-u-ni* 1 i 14, *ak-tar-ar* 3 iii 31, *a-*[*kar-ra-ar* 4:4, *la-ak-ru-ur* 3 ii 17, *ni-ik-ru-ur* 5 r. 5,

kāru "port, harbour": *ka-a-ri* 2 i 16,

kasāpu "to break": *ak-su-pu-u-ni* 1 i 7,

kāsu "cup, chalice": *ka-a-si* 3 iii 29, *ka-a-su* 1 iv 12, 3 iii 36,

kāša "you": *ka-a-šá* 9:19,

kašādu "to conquer, vanquish": *ak-šu-du* 3 iii 22, *ak-ta-šá-ad* 3 iv 17, *ak-t*[*a-šá-ad*] 1 ii 7, *a-kaš-šad* 11 r. 4, *a-k*[*aš-šad* 4:6, *a-ka-šá-ad* 2 i 23, *a-ka-*[*šá-a*]*d* 2 iii 32, *ik-ta-šad* 3 i 28,

kēnu "true" see *kuānu,*

kettumma "verily": *ket-tu-ma* 3 iii 32,

kî "as": *ki-i* 1 i 9, ii 20, 37, iii 28, v 14, 35, vi 14, 7:3, 14, r. 7, 8:2, r. 1, see also *akī,*

kidinnu "protection; protégé": [*ki-din*]-*nu* 9:1,

killu see *ikkillu,*

kīma "when, as soon as": [*ki-ma* 3 iv 22,

kinṣu "knee": *kin-ṣa-a-a* 5:2,

kipputu "circle, circumference": *kip-pat* 3 ii 3,

kizirtu "curl(?)": *ki-zir-ti-k*[*a*] 1 iv 26,

kuānu "to be firm, loyal, true; (D) to confirm, establish": *ke-e-ni* 2 iv 24, *ke-e-nu* 1 iv 6, *k*[*e-e-nu*] 1 iv 20, *ke-in* 3 iii 34, *ke-n*[*u-ni* 10 r. 6, *ke-nu-ti* 2 ii 29, 32, *uk-ti-in* 1 iii 22, *ú-ka-na* 2 i 7, 31, *ú-*[*ka-na*] 2 ii 5,

kuāṣu "to flay": *ú-ka-a-ṣa* 1 i 19,

kullu "to hold; to steer": *lu-ki-il-lu* 1 vi 17, *ú-kal-ka* 1 iv 28, *ú-k*]*al-la* 2 i 17,

kusāpu "bread": NINDA 11 r. 8, NINDA.MEŠ 3 iii 10, see also *aklu,*

kussiu "throne, seat": [GIŠ.GU.ZA 2 i 7, GIŠ.GU.ZA-*ka* 1 iii 21,

kutallu "rear, back": *ku-tal-li-ka* 1 i 23,

lā "not": *la* 1 i 7, 17, 24, 30, ii 3, 8, 16, 27, 33, iii 30, 32, iv 2, v 2, 21, vi 9, 2 ii 29, 32, iii 10, 17, 19, 29, 3 iii 18, 19, 21, 22, 24, 27, 4:5, 6 r. 1, 7:2, r. 6, 11, 9:17, *l*]*a* 2 iv 14, 28, 30, [*la* 1 i 5, vi 1, 2 i 13, 15, 38, iv 20, [*la-a*] 11 r. 2,

labû "to go around, surround": [*al-ti*]-*bi-a* 3 iv 28, *a-la-ab-bi* 2 ii 8, *il-ti-bu-ka* 3 ii 12,

lalû "charm, pleasure": *la-la-a-a* 3 iii 37,

lānu "body, figure": *la-a-ni* 9:14, *la-a-ni-ia* 9:15,

lapātu "to touch, affect": *il-ta-nap-pa-ta* 9:14,

laqātu "to pick, pluck": *al-qu-tú* 3 iii 24,

laššu "is not": *la-áš-šú* 3 ii 6, *l*[*a-áš-šú*] 3 iii 27,

libbu "heart": ŠÀ 1 vi 20, 2 ii 22, 3 ii 36, iii 12, iv 20, 5 r. 1, 9:26, š[À 1 ii 6, Š]À 6 r. 12, ŠÀ-*bi* 1 i 25, 26, iv 18, vi 25, 2 ii 2, iii 31, 3 ii 15, ŠÀ-*bi*] 3 iv 7, Š]À-*bi* 6 r. 7, ŠÀ-*bi-ka* 1 ii 19, ŠÀ-*bi-šá* 8:6, ŠÀ-*bi-šú* 1 i 38, ŠÀ-*bu* 9:7, ŠÀ-*ku-nu* 3 iii 7,

limmu "eponym year": *lim-mu* 9 r. 6,

lū "let, may, be it": *lu* 2 ii 2, iii 10, 11, *l*]*u* 3 i 25, [*lu* 2 i 18, *lu-u* 1 ii 37, 2 iii 1,

lumnu "ill fate": HUL 2 ii 24,

mā "thus": *ma-a* 1 v 15, 18, 2 iii 9, 10, 3 ii 13, iii 7, 8, 9, 12, 20, 30, 32, 6:1, 2, 5, 7:2, 12, 14, r. 1, 4, 6, 7, 8, 11, 8:3, 5, 6, 7, 8, r. 1, 10 s. 1, 2, [*ma-a* 3 iv 8, 7:7, 8, 9, 10, 11, [*ma*]-*a* 7:2, 3, 4, 14, r. 1, 11 r. 3, 5, [*m*]*a-a* 6 r. 1, 11 r. 6,

maʾādu "to be much": *ma-aʾ-du-ti* 2 iii 8, *ma-aʾ-d*[*u-ti* 2 iii 4, *ma-aʾ-*[*du-ti*] 2 ii 34,

maddattu "tribute": *ma-da-na-ti* 2 iii 24, *ma-da-*[*na-ti* 1 ii 5,

mahāru "to accept, receive; to turn to, implore":

i-ma-har 1 v 2, *mah-ru* 2 i 25, *ta-hu-ri-ni-ni* 1 v 14,

mallāhu "boatman, pilot": LÚ.M]Á.LAH$_4$ 2 i 16,

malû "to be full; (D) to fill": *lu-mal-li* 3 iii 36, *ma-lu-u* 1 iv 12, *tu-mal-lu-u-ni* 1 vi 6, *tu-um-ta-al-li* 3 iii 5, *um-tal-li* 3 ii 23,

mannu "who?": *man-nu* 2 iii 16,

manzāz ekalli "courtier": [LÚ.*man-za-az*]—É.GA[L] 3 iv 25,

maqlūtu "burnt-offering": GIBÍL.MEŠ 2 ii 25,

mar "as much/many as": *mar* 2 ii 1,

marʾu "son; young (of a bird)": AMAR-*šú*] 2 ii 6, DUMU 1 i 29, ii 40, iv 6, 21, vi 32, DUMU-*ka* 1 vi 27, DUMU.MEŠ 3 i 27, 7:4, DUMU.UŠ-*ka* 2 ii 13, see also *aplu,*

marʾutu "daughter": DUMU.MÍ 1 ii 10, v 25, 2 ii 19, [DUMU.MÍ 9 r. 5,

mār marʾi "grandson": DUMU—DUMU-*ka* 1 vi 27, DUMU.UŠ—DUMU.UŠ-*ka* 2 ii 13,

massītu (a jar for liquids, "flagon"): DUG.*ma-si-tú* 3 iii 4, 33,

massuku "chamber": *ma-si-ki* 1 iii 23,

maṣṣartu "watch, guard": *ma-ṣar-ta-ka* 2 i 19, *ma-ṣar-ta-ka*] 2 ii 4, [*ma-ṣar-tú* 2 i 20,

maṣû "(Š) to make overcome": *ú-šá-an-ṣa-ka* 2 ii 12,

mašû "to forget": *ta-maš-ši-a* 3 iii 11,

matāhu "to lift": *mu-tu-uh* 1 ii 28,

mātu "land, country": KUR 2 iii 9, KUR-*šú* 9:27, KUR.KUR 1 i 4, 2 i 20, ii 15, 3 i 19, 7:8, 12, 10 r. 4, 11 r. 5,

mê "water": A.MEŠ 1 vi 23, 3 iii 3, 5, 12,

memmēni "anybody, anything": *me-me-ni* 3 iii 18,

mihru "equal, counterpart": *mi-hir-šú* 3 ii 6,

mīnu "what?": *mi-i-nu* 7:10, r. 4, *mi-nu* 3 iii 25,

muggu "paralysis": *mu-gi* 1 i 25,

muhhu "top, on": UGU 1 ii 27, iv 33, 35, vi 11, 3 i 13, ii 28, iii 2, 15, iv 13, 28, 7:4, 9, r. 7, 8:5, UG[U 11 r. 8, U[GU 2 ii 6, UGU-*hi* 1 i 17, vi 9, 3 iii 31, 36, UGU-*hi-ka* 2 ii 7, UGU-*hi-šú-nu* 3 ii 21, 7:5, UGU]-*ka* 3 iv 27,

mūrānu "cub": *mu-ra-ni* 2 ii 9,

murdinnu see *amurdinnu,*

mūru "calf": *mu-ri-šá* 1 v 29, 5:3, *mu-u-ri* 2 iv 20, 7 r. 11,

mušēniqtu "wet nurse": *mu-še-ni*[*q*]-*ta-ka* 1 iii 17,

mūšu "night": *mu-ši-ia* 7 r. 9,

naʾādu "(D) to praise": *lu-na-i-du-ni* 3 ii 24, *na-ʾi-da-an-ni* 1 vi 13, 18, *na-id-a-ni* 2 iv 8, *na-i-da-an-ni* 2 ii 21, iv 11, *na-i-da-a-ni* 1 ii 33, 39,

nabalkutu "to turn upside down": *na-bal-ku-ut* 3 iv 19,

nagarruru "to roll": *i-tan-ga-ra-ru* 1 i 10,

nagiu "district": *na-gi-a-ni-ku-nu* 3 iii 10,

naglubu "shoulder": *nag-ga-la-pa-a-a* 9:18,

nakāru "to be hostile; (D) to change": *na-ku-ru* 2 iii 9,

nakru "enemy": LÚ.KÚR 5 r. 3, 4, [L]Ú.KÚR 11 r. 4, LÚ.KÚR-*ka* 3 iii 22, [LÚ.KÚR-*k*]*a* 3 iv 17, LÚ.KÚR.MEŠ 2 iii 22, 23, 32, LÚ.KÚR.MEŠ-*ka* 1 iv 9, 2 ii 1, 10, iii 21, 3 ii 22, 6 r. 4, LÚ.KÚR.[MEŠ-*ka* 6 r. 10, [LÚ.KÚR.MEŠ-*ka*] 2 ii 11, [LÚ.KÚR.MEŠ-*k*]*a* 2 i 23, LÚ.[KÚR.MEŠ-*šú*] 5 e. 10, LÚ.KÚR-*šú* 3 i 29, LÚ.K]ÚR-*šú* 3 i 28, *na-ak-ru* 1 i 31, ii 34, *na-kar*^{ar}-*ka* 1 ii 6, *na-ka-ru-te-ka* 1 i 8, 13, 19, *na-ka-ru-te*] 1 ii 3,

namāru "to be bright, (Š) to let shine": *na-mir* 3 ii 7, *ú-šá-a*]*n-mar* 2 i 32, *ú-šá-na-ma-ra* 1 iii 27,

nammušu "to set out": *ut-ta-am-me-šá* 3 iv 10,

napāhu "to blow, ignite, light up; to rise": *i-nap-pa-ha-an-ni* 3 ii 4, *na-pa-ah* 2 ii 35, *na-pa-a*]*h* 3 i 32, 33, [*na*]-*pa-ah* 2 iii 35,

napāšu "to comb, pluck apart": *a-nap-pa-áš* 7 r. 1,

naqallulu "to issue as fiery glow": *at-ta-qa-al-la-al-la* 3 ii 16, see also *anqullu,*

narʾantu "mace": GIŠ.[*nàr*]-*an-ti* 8:5, GIŠ.*nàr-an-tu* 8:7,

nāru "river": ÍD 1 iv 3, 3 ii 23, ÍD.MEŠ 9:9, 11,

nasāhu "to pull out, uproot": *a-na-sa-ah* 2 iii 21,

naṣāru "to watch, guard": *an-ṣar-ka* 7 r. 9, *a-na-ṣar* 2 i 19, ii 5, iii 23, *a-na-ṣar-ka* 2 iv 9, *a-n*]*a-ṣar-ka* 2 iv 23, *it-ta-ṣar-u-ka* 1 ii 23, *ta-na-ṣa-ra* 3 iii 14, *ú-ṣur* 7 r. 10,

našû "to lift, carry, take": *at-ti-ši* 3 ii 19, *a-ta-ṣa-ak-ka* 1 ii 32, *it-ta-na-áš-šá-a-ka* 9:19, *i-n*]*a-áš-ši* 3 i 18, ÍL-*ši-ka* 7 r. 7, *la-áš-ši* 3 iv 3, *la-áš-ši-a* 3 iii 35, *na-ṣu* 3 iv 24,

nēmel "since": *né-me-*[*el* 10:4,

nēmulu "profit, gain": [*né-mal-k*]*a* 3 iv 11, *né-ma-al-ka* 2 iii 28, *né-me-*[*el* 10:4,

nikittu "fear, worry": *ni-kit-tu* 2 ii 12,

nipšu "tuft of wool": *ni-ip-ši* 7 r. 1,

niqiu "offering, sacrifice": UDU.SISKUR.MEŠ 3 ii 30,

nirriṭu "trembling": *ni-ir-ri-ṭu* 2 ii 12, [*n*]*i-ir-ri-ṭu* 1 vi 19,

nisannu (Nisan, name of the first month): ITI.BARAG 9 r. 6,

nišē "people": [UN.MEŠ 3 iv 18,

nūru "lamp": *nu-ur* 1 iii 25,

palāhu "to fear": *ta-pal-làh* 2 iii 29, 7:2, r. 6, 11, *ta-p*[*al-làh* 4:5, *ta-pal-li-hi* 2 iv 28, *ta-pa-a*]*l-li-hi* 2 i 13, *ta-pa-làh* 1 i 24, 30, ii 16, 33, iii 30, v 21, vi 1, 2 i 38, iii 17, 19, iv 14, 30, *ta-pa-làh*] 2 iv 20, *ta-pa*]-*làh* 2 i 15, *t*]*a-pa-làh* 1 i 5,

pānāt "fore": *pa-na-tu-u-ka* 1 i 22,

pānīu "previous, former": *pa-ni-ti* 2 i 17, *pa-ni-u* 1 vi 7, *pa-ni-u-te* 1 ii 37,

pānu "face, presence": IGI 1 i 10, 14, iii 26, v 6, 2 ii 14, iii 25, 3 i 20, ii 8, 9, 26, 28, 32, 5 r. 4, 9:17, 10:5, IGI] 4:4, *pa-an* 6 r. 9, *pa-ni* 1 vi 18, 3 iii 30, 10:6, *p*[*a-ni-i* 11 r. 6, *pa-ni-ia* 2 iv 26, *pa-ni-ka* 3 ii 19, *pa-ni-šú* 1 v 1, *pa-ni-šú-nu* 2 ii 26,

parāsu "to separate, decide": *lip-ru-us* 7:11,

parriṣu "traitor, criminal": LÚ.LUL.MEŠ 3 iv 22,

paršumūtu "old age": *par-šá-mu-tú* 2 i 29,

paššūru "table": [GIŠ].BANŠUR 11 r. 8,

patû "to open": *tap-ti-ti-a* 3 ii 13,

piālu "to rule, hold sway over": [*ta-pi-a*]*l* 7:13,

piāqu "to be narrow, slight": *pa-aq-tú* 3 iii 8,

pitūtu "diadem, headband": TÚG.*pi-tu-tu* 7:7,

pû "mouth, utterance": KA 9 r. 4, *pi-i* 1 i 28, ii 9, 13, 40, iii 5, v 10, 24, vi 31, 2 i 14, 35, *ii* 28, iii 18, *pi-ia* 3 iii 35, *pi-i-ka* 3 ii 12,

puhru "assembly": UKKIN 9:16, 23,

pušhu "shrew": *pu-uš-ha-a-ti* 1 v 4,

qablu "middle (parts), loins": MURUB$_4$ 1 iii 24, MURUB$_4$-*ka* 1 ii 26, *qab-le-ki* 5:4,

qabû "to say, tell": *aq-bu-u-ni* 7:3, *aq-qa-ba-kan-ni* 1 i 16, [*aq-ṭa-nab*]-*bi* 9:24, *aq-ṭi-ba-ak* 1 iii 31, *aq-ṭi-bi* 9:16, *a-qa-ba-kan-ni* 1 vi 8, *iq-*[*ṭi-b*]*i*

8:4, *i-qab-bi* 8:2, *i-qab-bu-u-ni* 7:8, *laq-bak-ka* 7:14, *li-iq-bi-u* 2 ii 27, *qa-bi-tu* 2 ii 18, *taq-ṭi-bi* 7:12, *ta-qab-bi* 7 r. 4, *ta-qab-bi-a* 3 iii 7,

qaqqadu see *kaqqudu,*

qaqqaru see *kaqquru,*

qarābu "battle, fight": *qa-ra-bi]* 1 ii 6,

qarītu "banquet": *qa-ri-ti* 3 iii 26,

qarṭuppu "stylus": *qar—ṭup-pi* 1 ii 38,

qatāru "to smoke": *ú-qa-at-t[ar]* 1 iv 30,

qatû "to end": *ú-qa-at-ta* 1 iv 10,

qātu "hand": ŠU-*šú* 3 ii 1, ŠU.2 2 ii 33, ŠU.2-*ia* 1 iv 8, Š]U.2-*ia* 2 i 25, ŠU.2.MEŠ-*ši-na* 9 r. 2, ŠU.2-*ši-na* 9:5,

qīltu "lye": *qi-il-te* 1 iv 12,

qû "litre": *qa* 11 r. 8,

quālu "to be silent": *qa-la-ka* 2 iii 11, *qa-la-ku-u-ni* 1 ii 36,

qutru "smoke": *qut-ru* 1 iv 30,

ra'āmu "love; to love": *ar-ta-am-k[a]* 1 iv 24, ÁG-*ši-na* 9:4, *[i-ra-']a-a-ma* 9:4,

rabābu "to yield; (Š) to languish": *šar-bu-bu* 2 ii 25,

rabiu see *rabû A,*

rabû A "to be great, grow; (D) to raise, bring up": GAL.MEŠ 1 ii 22, 25, iv 27, GA]L-*tu* 1 i 36, GAL-*tú* 1 i 11, *ra-bi-tu* 1 iii 16, *ra-bu-te* 1 iii 22, *ur-ta-bi-ka* 2 iii 27, *[ú-ra-ba]-ak-ka* 1 i 35,

rabû B "to set": *i-rab-bu-u-ni* 3 ii 5, *ra-ba* 2 ii 36, *ra-b]a* 3 i 31, *ra]-ba* 3 i 34, *[ra-ba* 2 iii 36,

ragāmu "to shout, prophesy": *ir-gu-mu-[u-ni* 6 r. 6, *ir-gu-m[u-u-ni* 6 r. 8, *ir-t[u-gu-um* 6 r. 12, *[ir-tu-gu-um]* 3 iv 35,

raggimu "prophet": LÚ.*ra-gi-mu* 3 iv 31, LÚ.*[ra-gi-mu* 6 r. 11,

raggintu "prophetess": MÍ.GUB.BA 10 s. 2, MÍ.*ra-gi-in-tú* 7:1,

rakāsu "to bind, attach, gird": *ir-tak-su* 1 ii 26, *i-rak-kas* 7:7, *ru-uk-si* 5:4,

rammû "to leave, release": *ú-ram-ma-ka* 9:17,

rapādu "to run, roam": *a-rap-pu-da* 9:8, 25, *tu-sar-pi-di* 1 v 20,

rapāšu "to be wide, extensive": *rap-šat* 1 i 2,

rašû "to get, obtain": *ra-ši* 7:9,

rēšu "head, top, beginning": *re-še-ia* 11 r. 12,

riāšu "to rejoice": *ri-iš* 3 iv 14, *ri-i-šá-ak* 1 ii 11, *ri-i-ši* 1 ii 12,

riqiu "aromatic": ŠEM.HI.A 3 ii 31,

rittu "hand, wrist": *rit-ta-a-a* 9:17,

sa'u (mng. uncert.): *sa-'u* 11 r. 9,

sabsūtu "midwife": *sa-ab-su-ub-ta-k[a]* 1 iii 15,

sahāru "to go, turn around": *[a-sa-hu]r* 2 i 19, *a-sa-hu-ur* 2 ii 8,

sahû "to rebel": *i-si-hu-ni* 3 iv 27,

salāmu "to make peace; (D) to reconcile": *ú-sal-[l]am* 2 iii 20, *ú-[sal-lam]* 2 ii 3, *ú-sa-a]l-lam* 2 iv 19, *ú-sa-lim* 1 ii 31,

salmu "ally": LÚ.*sa-al-mu-ti* 2 iii 24, *sa-al-mu-ti]* 1 ii 4,

salû "to lie, cheat": *as-li-k[a]* 1 iii 32,

sapāku "to assail; (D) to seize, catch in": *ú-sa-pa-ak* 2 i 11,

sapānu "to level, deface": *i-sap-pan* 8 r. 1,

sarbu "cold rain, shower; squash": *sar-bi* 7 r. 2, *sa-rab-a-te* 9:13,

sarsarru "traitor": LÚ.*sar-sar-a-ni* 3 ii 10,

sasû "to read": *i-sa-as-si-u* 3 ii 32,

sigāru "neck-stock": GIŠ.*si-ga-ra-te* 2 iii 23, *si-ga-r[a-te* 1 ii 4,

sihhāru (a shallow bowl for honey, fruits, and sauces, "platter"): [DU]G.*síh-ha-ru* 11 r. 9,

simānu (Sivan, name of the 3rd month): ITI.SIG$_4$ 1 i 9,

sippu "doorjamb; entrance": *si-ip-pi* 3 iii 20, *si-ip-p]i* 3 iv 15,

sūnu "lap": *su-ni-ki* 1 v 17,

supurgillu see *armannu,*

sūtu "seah": 1BÁN 3 iii 4, 32, 33,

ṣabāru "to twitter": *a-ṣab-bur* 2 ii 7,

ṣābu "men, troops": LÚ.[ERIM.MEŠ] 2 iii 7,

ṣalmu "statue, image": *ṣa-al-me* 3 ii 26,

ṣarṣāru (a container for water storage, "cooler"): *ṣar-ṣa-ri* 3 iii 3, 5,

ṣehru "small; child": *ṣe-he-ra-ka* 1 ii 32,

ṣerru "snake": MUŠ 8:6,

ṣēru "open country, steppe": EDIN 1 v 20, 28, 2 ii 24, 5:8, 9:8, EDI[N] 9:25,

ṣēt šamši "sunshine": *ṣi-it—*[d]*šá-maš* 3 ii 7,

ṣētu "heat, light, drought": *ṣe-[t]a-a-te* 9:13,

ṣillu "shadow": GIŠ.MI 2 iii 17,

ṣipputu "cover": *ṣi-ip-pu-tu* 2 iii 21,

ṣīru "emissary": LÚ.*ṣi-ra-ni* 2 iii 12,

ṣīt libbi "offspring": *ṣi-it—*ŠÀ-*bi-ia* 1 v 19,

ša "that; what; of": *ša* 1 i 6, 9, 12, 13, 16, 18, 21, 28, 31, ii 9, 13, 14, 15, 19, 30, 35, 40, iii 5, 7, 19, 23, 25, 28, iv 13, v 10, 11, 15, 16, 24, vi 31, 2 i 7, ii 4, 15, 24, iii 7, 15, 21, 22, 32, 3 i 15, ii 8, iii 4, 15, 26, 27, 33, iv 15, 23, 5:1, 5, r. 4, 6:1, 8, r. 8, 8:6, 9:2, r. 4, 10 r. 4, 5, *ša]* 2 iii 33, *š[a* 5 r. 3, *š]a* 1 i 37, 3 iv 18, *[ša* 3 iv 23, 27, 5:3, 8:1, *[š]a 5 r. 7, šá* 1 iv 12, v 5, 27, 32, vi 4, 8, 29, 2 i 17, 28, 33, ii 28, 30, 3 i 12, ii 26, 27, 33, iii 16, 18, 20, iv 21, 7:3, 4, 8, 10, 12, r. 6, 9, 10, 11, 9:1, 6, 10 r. 6, s. 2, 11 r. 4, 7, 10, 11, *šá]* 1 vi 3, 2 i 20, *[šá* 2 ii 38, 3 iv 9,

šabāru "to break": *a-šab-bir* 7 r. 1,

šadādu "to drag, haul": *as-sa-ad-da* 8:6, *šad-du-[ni* 11 r. 10, *u]s-sa-di-du-ni* 3 iv 22,

šaddû "mountain": KUR-*e* 3 ii 20, KUR.MEŠ-*e* 9:10, KUR.MEŠ-*ni* 1 ii 15, 3 iv 11,

šahšūru "apple": *šá-ah-šu-ri* 1 i 9,

šakānu "to place, set": *[as]-sa-kan-šú-nu* 3 iv 30, *áš-kun-u-ni* 3 iii 15, *a-sa-kan* 3 iv 6, *a-šak-kan-ka* 7 r. 8, *a-šá-kan* 2 ii 33, 3 ii 1, *a-šá-[kan* 4:8, *a-šá-kan-ka* 2 iii 31, GAR-*an* 7:13, *is-sa-kan* 3 i 14, 30, *[iš-kun]-u-ni* 3 i 13, *la-áš-kun* 3 iii 35, *š]ak-na* 2 iv 16, *šá-ki-nu-u-ni* 3 ii 9, *ta-sak-ni* 1 v 17, *[ú-šá-á]š-ka-na-šu* 9:7,

šaknu "governor; prefect": LÚ.GAR.KUR 9 r. 7,

šamê "heaven": AN-*e* 1 iii 21, 24, iv 27, 2 i 28, iii 34, 3 i 9, ii 15,

šamnu ṭābu "sweet oil": Ì—DÙG.GA 3 ii 29,

šamšu "sun": [d]UTU-*ši* 2 ii 36, 3 i 31, 32, 33, 34, [d]UTU-*š[i* 2 iii 35, [d]UTU-*š]i* 2 iii 36, [[d]UTU-*ši*] 2 ii 35, see also *ṣēt Šamši, Šamaš,*

šamû "to hear, (Gtn) to listen": *as-sa-nam-me* 2 ii 31, *as-se-me* 3 ii 14, *áš-me-k[a* 1 ii 3, *a-se-me* 6 r. 3, *si-ta-am-me-a* 2 ii 35, *[si-ta-am]-me-a* 3 i 27, *ta-se-me]* 5:3,

šaniu "second, other, different": *šá-ni-tú* 7:14,

šapal "under": KI.TA 1 iii 21, 3 i 30, 5:7, *[šá]-pal* 11 r. 11,

šapāru "to send": *[il-t]a-nap-pa-ra* 9:6, *ta-sap-ra* 1 v 30,

šaptu "lip": NUNDUN.MEŠ-*ka* 9:22, NU[NDU]N.MEŠ-[*t*]*e-ia* 9:20,
šaqû "to give to drink": *ta-si-qi-šú-nu* 3 iii 3,
šarāpu "to burn": *i-šar-ru-pu* 3 i 23,
šarratu "queen, lady": LUGAL 7:2, *šar-ra-ti* 2 ii 30,
šarru "king": LUGAL 1 i 4, 30, iii 30, v 9, 11, 21, 3 ii 6, 28, 32, 6:8, 7:9, LU[GAL] 2 iv 6, [LUGAL 3 i 28, LUGAL-*ia* 1 ii 12, iii 13, 2 ii 33, iii 22, 32, [LUGAL-*ku-n*]*u* 3 i 29, LUGAL].MEŠ 7:8, [LUGAL.ME]Š 7:12, MAN 1 i 31, iii 8, 26, iv 11, v 26, 2 i 10, 22, iii 17, 3 i 11, ii 34, iii 17, 4:2, 5:5, e. 9, MAN] 2 i 37, *šar-ri* 2 iii 23, *šar-ri-ma* 1 v 9,
šarrūtu "kingship, kingdom": L]UGAL-*ta-ka* 2 iv 27, LUGAL-*tú* 1 iv 33, v 22, LUGAL-*u-tu* 2 ii 14, LUGAL-[*u-tu* 2 iii 33, LUGAL-*u-tú* 1 vi 28, 7:5, 10 r. 3,
šāru "wind": *šá-a-ru* 1 i 6,
šattu "year": MU.AN.NA.MEŠ 1 iii 12, 20, MU.MEŠ 1 iv 16,
šatû "to drink": *la-as-si* 3 iii 36, *ta-šat-ti-a* 3 iii 13, *ta-šá-at-ti* 1 vi 24,
ša-rēši "eunuch": LÚ.SAG.MEŠ 7:4,
ša-ziqni "bearded (courtier)": *šá*—SU$_6$.MEŠ 7:4,
šēlūtu "votive gift, votary": *še-lu-tu* 1 v 11,
šēpu "foot": GÌR.2 3 i 13, GÌR.2-*ia*] 2 i 12, 3 iv 12, GÌR.2-*ka* 4:4, GÌR.2.MEŠ-*ka* 1 i 10, 14, GÌR.2.MEŠ-*šú*] 5 r. 4, GÌR.2-*šú* 1 v 6, 2 iii 25, GÌR.2-[*šú* 5:7, G]ÌR.2-*šú* 3 i 30, GÌR.2-*šú-nu* 7:13,
šeššīšu "six times": 6-*šú* 8:4,
šî "she, it": *ši-i* 2 ii 18, 3 iii 8, 7:2,
šiālu "to coat, cover": *a-ši-al* 2 iv 21,
šiāmu "to decree, destine": *i-ši-mu-u-ni* 7:10,
šiāṣu "to decline, wane": *i-ši-ṣu-u-ni* 1 vi 15,
šību "witness": *ši-i-bi* 7:9,
šikāru "beer": KAŠ 3 iii 33,
šina "they": *ši-na* 5 r. 7, [*ši-na-m*]*a* 9:3,
šinnu "tooth": *šin-ni-šú-nu* 3 iv 28,
šipṭu "punishment": [*ši-ip-ṭu*] 3 iv 24,
šiqlu "shekel": GÍN 1 iv 13,
šiṭru "writing": *ši-iṭ-ri-šú* 2 iii 14,
šû "he": *šu-ú* 1 ii 34, *šu*]-*ú* 7:11,
šulmu "health, well-being": DI-*mu* 1 v 26, [DI-*mu* 3 i 9, [DI-*mu*] 3 i 11, [DI-*m*]*u* 3 i 10, *š*]*ul-me* 2 i 33, *šul-mu* 1 v 29, 3 ii 8, 26, [*šul-m*]*u* 3 i 12, *šu-lam-ka* 2 ii 27,
šumēlu "left": KAB-*ia* 2 i 21, KAB-*k*[*a*] 1 iv 31, *šu-me-li* 1 v 16, 3 iv 23, 150 5:6, 150-*ka* 1 ii 24,
šunu "they": *šu-nu* 3 iv 26, [*šu-nu-ni* 2 ii 1,
tabāku "to pour, shed": *a-tab-ba-ak* 2 iii 22,
tabû "to rise, get up, attack": *a-ta-ab-bi* 1 i 27, *a-t*]*a-bi* 9:26, *i-di-ba-kan-ni* 1 ii 35, *i-di-ba-ka-a-ni* 1 i 6,
tadānu "to give": *ad-dan* 7 r. 9, [*a*]*d-dan* 5 e. 10, *ad-da-*[*nak*]*-ka* 2 ii 20, *ad-da-nak-kan-ni* 7:3, *at-ta-nak-ka* 3 iv 16, *a-da-an* 2 i 4, *a-da-an-na* 1 iii 14, *a-da-na* 1 i 32, *a-da-nak-ka* 2 ii 16, *a-da-nak-k*[*a*] 1 iv 17, *a-da-na-ka* 1 i 20, *a-di-nak-kan-ni* 3 iii 19, *a-di-nak-ka-a* 3 iii 21, *a-ti-din* 2 iv 7, *di-na* 3 i 6, *id-dan-*[*x* 10 r. 3, *it-ta-na-šú* 3 ii 3, *ta-at-ta-an-na-šú-nu* 3 iii 6, *ta-di-na* 3 iii 25,
tahūmu "border, territory": *ta-hu-ma-a-ni* 2 ii 15, 7:13,
takālu "to trust; (D) to give confidence, faith": *ta-tak-kil* 1 ii 27, *ú-ta-ki-il-ka* 1 ii 8, *ú-ta-ki-i*[*l-ka*] 1 iv 1,
talla (mng. obscure): *ta-al-la* 7 r. 1,
tamliu "terrace": [*tam-l*]*e-e* 3 iii 2,
tāmtu "sea": *tam-tim*.MEŠ 9:9,
taqānu "to be safe; (D) to make safe, put in order": taq-nu 1 vi 22, taq-nu-ti 1 vi 23, ta-taq-qu-un 1 vi 26, ú-taq-qa-[an 11 r. 5, ú-ta-qa-an 2 i 6, iii 19, 33, iv 27, 6:3, ú-ta-qa-a[n 2 iii 34, ú-ta-qa-[an 6:2, ú-ta-qa-an-ka 2 ii 11, [ú-ta-q]a-an-ka 1 i 34,
taqnu see *taqānu,*
tārītu "(dry) nurse": *ta-ri-su-ni* 7 r. 6, *ta-ri-ti* 7 r. 7,
timmu "column, pillar": *tim-me* 3 i 25,
tuāru "to return; (D) to turn into, restore": *i-tu-*[*ra*] 9:27, *lu-tir-ra* 3 iii 37, *ú-ta-ra* 7 r. 2,
tukultu "trust, support": *t*]*u-kul-ti* 2 iv 29,
tulû "breast": UBUR.MEŠ-*ia* 7 r. 8,
tuqūnu "safety": *tu-qu-un* 5 e. 9, *tu-qu-un-ni* 1 iv 3,
ṭabāhu "to slaughter": *a-ṭa-*[*ba-ah*] 9:26, *ṭa-ba-ah-hi* 1 i 32,
ṭābtu "goodness, favour": DÙG.GA 1 vi 3, MUN 3 i 25, *ṭa-ab-tú* 3 i 5,
ṭābu see *ṭiābu,*
ṭēmu "mind": [*ṭè-en-šú-n*]*u* 3 iv 19,
ṭiābu "to be good": DÙG.GA 2 i 16, 3 iii 33,
ṭullumâ "treacherous, deceitful": *ṭùl-lu-ma-a* 2 ii 17,
ṭuppu "tablet": *ṭup-pi* 3 ii 27,
u "and": *u* 3 i 9, 5:6, 9:4, 9, r. 1, 10 r. 6, *ú* 11 r. 3, *ù* 8:7, 8, [*ù* 7:12,
ū'a "woe": *u*$_8$-*a* 2 iii 31, 9:26, *u*$_8$-*u-a* 1 i 26,
ubālu "to bring": *ub-ba-la* 2 iii 25,
udû "to know": *nu-da*] 3 iv 8,
ūmâ "now": *ú-ma-a* 1 v 21, vi 10, 7:11, *ú-ma*]-*a* 1 v 21,
ummi šarri "queen mother": AMA—LUGAL 1 v 13, AMA—MAN 2 i 13,
ummu "mother": AMA-*ka* 2 iii 26, AMA-*šú-ni* 7 r. 6, MÍ.AMA-*ka* 1 ii 20,
ūmu "day": UD-*me* 1 iii 19, 11 r. 3, UD-*mu* 1 vi 14, 10 r. 5, UD.MEŠ 1 iii 11, iv 15, UD.18.KAM 9 r. 6,
unnu (mng. obscure): *un-na-ni-ka* 7 r. 10,
urdu ekalli "palace servant": [LÚ.ARAD]—É.GAL 3 iv 26,
urkīu "later, future": *ur-ki-i* 1 vi 11, *u*]*r-ki-ti* 2 i 18, *ur-ki-u-te* 4:6, *ur-ki-ú-te* 1 ii 37,
urqu "vegetable": Ú.*ur-qí* 3 iii 34,
usutu "help": *ú-su-tú* 6 r. 2,
uṣṣunu see *eṣānu,*
uṣû "to go out, emerge; (Š) to send out, banish": *lu-še-ṣi-ú* 2 ii 26, *ta-at-tu-ṣi* 1 v 28, *us-se-ṣu-nik-ka* 3 ii 11, *ú-*[*ṣa* 5:8, *ú-ṣa-a* 7 r. 5, *ú-ṣe-e-*[*šá*] 1 v 31, *ú-še-ṣa* 1 vi 21, *ú-še-ṣa-an-ni* 10 r. 2,
ušābu "to sit, dwell": *nu-šab* 2 iii 10, *ši-bi* 11 r. 5, *uš-ba-*[*ku*] 1 ii 8, *ú-šab* 1 i 27,
utāru "to exceed": *tu-šá-tar* 9:21,
uzuzzu "to stand, to be present": *it-ti-ti-su* 1 ii 23, *i-za-zu* 1 ii 26, *i-za-z*[*u*] 3 iv 24, [*i-za-zu* 2 i 22, *i-za-zu-ni* 3 iv 18, *ta-za-az* 3 ii 18, *ta-za-az-ma* 1 vi 12, *ta-zi-zi* 1 vi 9, *ta-zi-zu-u-ni* 1 i 17,
zanānu "to rain": *a-zu-nu-un* 3 ii 21,
zaqīpu "stake": GIŠ].*za-qi-ba-a-ni* 3 iv 29,
zarāqu "to sprinkle": *i-za-ar-ri-qu* 3 ii 29,
zenû "to be angry": *ze-nu-ti* 2 iii 20,
ziqnu see *ša-ziqni,*
zīqtu "torch": *zi-qa-a-ti* 1 vi 16

Index of Names

Personal Names

Ahāt-abīša (prophetess/Arbela): MÍ.NIN—AD-*šá* 1 v 24,

Aššūr-ahu-iddina (Esarhaddon, king of Assyria): [^{m}*aš-šur*—PAB—AŠ 1 vi 3, 2 i 37, [^{m}*aš-šur*—PAB—A]Š 4:2, [^{m}*aš-šur*—PAB]—AŠ 1 i 4, 2 i 33, ^{m}]*aš-šur*—PAB—AŠ 2 i 10, 22, 27, ^{m}*aš-šur*—PAB—AŠ 1 ii 11, 16, iii 8, 13, 26, iv 5, 11, 14, 18, 20, v 26, 2 i 15, iii 11, 17, 19, 29, 3 i 11, 12, 21, ii 34, *iii* 15, 17, iv 13, 14, 5:5, ^{m}*aš-šur*—PAB—A]Š 1 vi 1, ^{m}*aš-šur*—PAB]—AŠ 2 i 7, ^{m}*aš*]-*šur*—PAB—AŠ 3 i 16, ^{m}[*aš-šur*—PAB—AŠ 5 e. 9,

Aššūr-bāni-apli (Assurbanipal, king of Assyria): ^{m}*aš-šur*—DÙ—A 7:2, 9, 11 r. 4, ^{m}AN.ŠÁR—*ba-an*—A 9:5, ^{m}AN.ŠÁR—DÙ—A 9 r. 2,

Baiâ (prophet/Arbela): MÍ.*ba-ia-a* 1 ii 40, MÍ.*ba-ia*]-*a* 2 i 35,

Bēl-šadûʾa (eponym 650): ^{m}EN—KUR-*u-a* 9 r. 6,

Dunnaša-āmur (reading uncert., prophetess/Arbela): MÍ.KALAG-*šá—a-mur* 9 r. 4, 10 s. 1, see also *Sinqīša-āmur,*

Ilūssa-āmur (prophetess/Assur): MÍ.DINGIR-*sa—a-m*[*ur*] 1 iii 5,

Issār-bēlī-daʾʾini (royal votaress): MÍ.15—EN—*da-i-ni* 1 v 10,

Issār-lā-tašīaṭ (prophet/Arbela): ^{md}15—*la—ta-ši-ia-aṭ* 1 i 28,

Lā-dāgil-ili (prophet/Arbela): [^{m}*la—da-gíl*—DI]NGIR 3 iv 31, ^{m}*la—da-gíl*—DINGIR 1 vi 31, 2 ii 28,

Mugallu (king of Melid/Melitene): ^{m}*mu-gal-li* 2 iii 15,

Mullissu-kabtat (prophetess): [MÍ].^{d}NIN.LÍL—*kab-ta-at* 7:1,

Nabû-hussanni (prophet/Assur): ^{md}PA]—*hu-sa-an-ni* 2 i 14,

Rēmutti-Allāti (prophetess/Dara-ahuya): MÍ.*re-mu-te—al-la-te* 1 ii 13,

Sinqīša-āmur (prophetess/Arbela): MÍ.*si-in-qi-šá—a-mur* 1 ii 9,

Tašmētu-ēreš (prophet/Arbela): ^{m}]^{d}LÁL—KAM-*eš* 6 r. 11,

Urkittu-šarrat (prophetess/Calah): MÍ.*ur-kit-tu—šar-rat* 2 iii 18,

Place Names

Arbail (Arbela, mod. Erbil): URU].*arba-ìl* 3 iv 9, 21, URU.*arba-ìl* 1 i 12, 18, 21, 29, 37, ii 10, 12, 30, 40, v 25, 27, vi 4, 32, 2 ii 22, 30, 3 ii 33, iii 16, 5: 1, 6 r. 12, URU.*arba-ìl*] 2 ii 38, URU.*arba-ì*[*l*] 1 iii 10, iv 18, URU.*arba-*[*ìl* 6:1, URU.*arba*]-*ìl* 9 r. 5, UR[U.*arba-ìl*] 1 iii 7, URU.*arba-ìl-a-a* 2 i 35, ii 28, [URU.*arba-ìl*]-*a-a* 3 iv 32,

Aššūr see *Māt Aššūr,*

Bābili (Babylon): KÁ.DINGIR.KI 2 iv 4,

Dāra-ahūʾa (town in Assyria): URU.*da-ra—a-hu-u-ia* 1 ii 14,

Elamtu (Elam): KUR.NIM.MA.KI 8:8, r. 2, KUR.NIM.MA.K]I-*a-a* 8:1, KUR.NIM.KI 7:14, NIM.MA.KI-*a-a* 2 iii 12,

Ellipi (kingdom in northern Luristan): KUR.*el-li-pi* 3 ii 2,

Gimir (Bibl. Gomer, Cimmerians): KUR.*gi-mir* 7:14, [KUR].*gi-mir-a-a* 3 ii 1,

Kalhu (Calah, mod. Nimrud): URU.*kal-ha* 1 iii 10, URU.*kal-hi* 2 iii 10, URU.*kal-hi-tú* 2 iii 18,

Libbi āli ("Inner City," an appellative of Assur): URU.ŠÀ—URU 1 iii 9, iv 14, 3 i 15, URU.ŠÀ—URU-*a-a* 2 i 14, URU.ŠÀ—URU-*a-*[*a*] 1 iii 6,

Manna (Bibl. Minni, kingdom S of lake Urmia): KUR.*man-na-a-a* 2 iii 13,

Māt Aššūr (Assyria): KUR—*aš-šur* 1 i 30, 31, iii 26, iv 11, v 26, 2 i 10, 22, 37, *iii* 17, 19, 20, 33, 3 i 11, 27, ii 34, iii 17, 20, iv 15, 4:2, 5:5, KUR—*aš-šur*] 5 e. 9, KUR—*aš*]-*šur* 3 iv 10, KUR—*a*[*š-šur*] 1 iii 8, KUR—*aš-šur*.KI 2 ii 3,

Melīdi (class. Melitene, now Malatya): [URU.*me-li-d*]*i* 3 i 35,

Muṣur (Egypt): KUR.*mu-ṣur* 7 r. 5,

Nīnua (Nineveh): NINA.KI 2 iii 10, URU.NIN[A] 1 iii 9,

Ṣurru (Tyre): *ṣur-ri* 9 r. 7,

Urarṭu (Bibl. Ararat, Armenia): KUR.URI-*a-a* 2 iii 13,

broken: URU.[*x* 6:5

God and Temple Names

Aššūr (national god of Assyria): *aš-šur* 1 ii 31, ^{d}*aš-šur* 2 iv 2, 29, 3 i 14, 20, ii 3, 13, 25, 27,
Bānītu ("Creatrix," an appellative of Mullissu/Ištar): ^{d}*ba-ni-tu* 2 i 5,
Bēl ("Lord," an appellative of Marduk): ^{d}EN 1 ii 17,
Bēlet ("Lady," an appellative of Ištar): ^{d}GAŠAN 1 i 11,
Bēlet Arbail ("Lady of Arbela," Ištar of Arbela): ^{d}*be-let—arba-ìl* 1 v 12, ^{d}*b]e-let—arba-ìl* 2 i 36, ^{d}*be-let*—URU.*arb]a-ìl* 1 vi 2, ^{d}GAŠAN—*arba-ìl*.KI 9 r. 1, ^{d}GAŠAN—URU.*a[r]ba-ìl* 9:2, GAŠAN—*arba-ìl* 7 r. 6,
Bēl-tarbiṣi ("Lord of the Pen," a guardian statue in Ešarra): ^{d}EN—TÙR 3 ii 8,
Esaggil (temple of Marduk in Babylon): É.SAG.ÍL 2 i 9, ii 24, É.SAG.Í]L 2 iv 4,
Ešarra (temple of Aššur in Assur): É.ŠÁR.RA 3 i 10, 14,
Inurta (Ninurta, celestial crown prince and saviour, god of victory): ^{d}MAŠ 1 vi 29, 2 ii 14, ^{d}NIN.URTA 5:6,
Issār (Ištar, goddess of love): ^{d}15 1 i 12, 18, 21, 37, ii 30, iii 7, v 27, 2 ii 30, 38, 3 ii 33, iii 8, 16, iv 8, 21, 33, 5:1, 6:1, [^{d}15] 1 vi 4,
Ištar see *Issār,*
Mullissu (wife of Aššur, queen of heaven, holy spirit): ^{d}NIN.LÍL 1 iv 6, 2 ii 30, 5:3, r. 6, 7:2, r. 6, ^{d}NIN.L]ÍL 7:12, ^{d}NIN.[LÍL] 1 iv 21, ^{d}N[IN.LÍL 1 iii 4, ^{d}N[I]N.LÍL 9:1, ^{d}[NIN].LÍL 9 r. 1,
Nabû (Nebo, son of Marduk, keeper of celestial records): ^{d}AG 9:22, ^{d}PA 1 ii 38,
Ninurta see *Inurta,*
Sīn (moon, god of purity and prudence): ^{d}30 1 ii 24,
Šamaš (sun, god of justice): ^{d}UTU 1 ii 24, 5 r. 7, see also *ṣēt šamši, šamšu,*
Urkittu ("the Urukite," an appellaltive of Ištar): ^{d}*ur-k]i-tú* 2 iv 8

Subject Index

abolish 2.3
affect 9
afraid 2.1
age 2.2
alert 9
alive 9
angry 1.6 2.5
annihilate 2.3
announce 2.3
answer 2.4
anxiety 2.3
apples 1.1
Arbela 1.1 1.2 1.3 1.4 1.6 1.8 1.9 1.10 2.2 2.3 2.4 3.4 3.5 5 6 9
arbitrate 7
arm 2.5 2.6
arms 9
army 8
arranged 3.1 3.5
assembly 9
Assurbanipal 7 9 11
Assyria 1.2 1.6 1.9 2.1 2.2 2.3 2.4 2.5 3.1 3.4 3.5 4 5
Assyrians 3.2
attacked 1.4
augurs 2.4
avert 2.6
awake 7
axe 1.6
Babylon 2.6
banish 1.10
banished 3.3
banquet 3.5
beams 1.4
bearded 7
beautiful 2.3 9
beer 3.5
bend 3.5
bent 3.3 3.5 5
bird 2.3
birth 1.4
blood 2.5 3.3
body 9
bosom 1.10
bowl 3.5
bramble 7
bread 3.4 11
breasts 7
brilliantly 3.2
brothers 3.4
burn 3.1
burnt 2.3 3.3
butterflies 3.5
Calah 1.6 2.4
calf 1.9 2.6 5 7
cast 1.1 3.5 4 5
catch 2.3 2.4
centipede 7
chains 9
chamber 1.6
change 2.4
charms 3.5
choose 2.4
Cimmerians 3.2 7
circles 2.3
circumference 3.2
cities 3.4
city 1.9 6
collect 3.5
consolidate 2.1 2.2 2.3
conspiring 1.7
consume 9
cooler 3.4
country 9
courses 7
courtiers 3.5 7
covenant 3.3 3.4
cover 2.5 2.6
create 2.4
creation 9
cried 3.3
cross 9
crown 1.6 2.3
cry 3.3 5
cub 2.3
cup 1.6 3.5
curl 1.6
cushion 3.3
cut 1.7 2.4 8
dagger 1.6
daughter 2.3
dawn 2.3 7
daylight 1.10
daytime 7
deceitful 2.3
declines 1.10
decreed 7
defeated 1.2
deliver 3.2
demanding 9
deprived 3.5
desert 9
desiring 9
destroy 3.2 8
devour 3.3
diadem 7

disloyal 2.4
districts 3.4
doorjambs 3.5
dragged 3.5
drink 1.10 3.4 3.5
droughts 9
drove 3.3
earth 3.1
eat 1.10 3.4
Egypt 7
Elam 7 8
Elamite 2.4
Elamites 8
electrum 1.6
Ellipi 3.2
emissaries 2.4
encounter 1.2
enemies 1.1 1.2 1.6 2.1 2.2 2.3 2.5 3.3 5 6
enemy 1.2 1.4 3.2 3.5 4 5 9 11
enters 3.3
eponymy 9
equal 3.2
Esaggil 2.1 2.3 2.6
Esarhaddon 1.1 1.3 1.4 1.6 1.9 1.10 2.1 2.2 2.3 2.4 2.5 2.6 3.1 3.4 3.5 4 5
establish 3.5
eunuchs 7
everlasting 1.6
evil 2.3
excellent 1.6
exhausted 9
faith 1.2 1.6
father 2.5 5 7
fathers 3.4 7
favour 1.10 3.1
favourite 9
fear 1.1 1.2 1.4 1.6 1.8 1.10 2.2 2.3 2.4 2.5 2.6 4 7
feast 3.1 3.5
feet 1.1 1.7 2.5 3.5 4 5
fiery 3.3
figure 2.6 9
fill 3.5
fire 1.6 3.2 3.3
flagon 3.4 3.5
flay 1.1
foes 3.5
food 1.10 3.5
footing 3.1
forearm 2.5 2.6
forefathers 7
forget 3.4
forsake 9
fragrant 3.3
frontiers 2.3 7
future 1.4 2.2
gain 3.1
gate 3.3
gather 2.3
gird 5 7
girded 1.4
glorify 5
glow 3.3
God 8
goddesses 2.1
gods 1.4 2.2 2.3 2.5 3.2 3.3 3.4 7 9
golden 1.6 11
governor 9
grandson 1.10 2.3
Great Lady 1.1 1.2
ground 8
guard 2.4 2.6 7
hailstones 3.3
haters 3.5
head 1.6 11
hear 3.3
heart 1.4 9
hearts 3.4
heaven 2.5 3.1 3.3
heavens 1.6 2.2
heir 1.6
help 6
hip 7
hurl 3.3
idle 1.2
Image 3.3
impaled 3.5
implored 1.8
incense 3.3
increase 9
innards 2.3
Inner City 1.5 1.6 2.1 3.1
issued 3.3
killed 6
kindle 1.6
King 1.2
kingdom 1.8 2.5 2.6
kings 1.10 2.3 7
kingship 1.6 10
knees 5
knowing 3.3
Lady of Arbela 1.8 1.10 2.3 7 9
lamp 1.6
lands 1.1 2.2 2.3 3.1 7 10 11
languish 2.3
lap 1.8 1.10
lengthen 10
levelled 8
lied 1.6
life 9
lift 1.4 3.5
lifts 3.1
light 2.2
lion 2.3
lips 9
listen 2.4 3.2
litre 11
loins 1.4 5
lord 1.4 2.2 3.3
love 9
loved 1.6
loyal 10
lye 1.6
mace 8
mankind 2.3
Mannean 2.4
manner 8
mean 7
Melid 3.2
midwife 1.6
milk 7
mindful 1.6

mixed 2.3
mother 1.4 1.8 2.1 2.5 2.6 3.1 5 7
mountain 3.3 9
mountains 1.3 3.5 9
mouth 1.1 1.2 1.3 1.4 1.5 1.7 1.8 1.10 2.1 2.2 2.3 2.4 3.3 3.5 9
multitudes 2.4
neck 1.2 2.5
night 7
Nineveh 1.6 2.4
Nisan 9
noisy 2.3
nurse 7
oceans 9
offerings 2.3
offspring 1.8
oil 3.3
one-seah 3.5
oracle 1.9 3.2
ordained 9
order 2.1 2.5 2.6 6 11
ornament 11
overcome 2.3
palace 1.10 2.3 3.5
Palace of the Steppe 5
Palace of Succession 1.2 7
paralysis 1.1
personnel 3.5
pieces 1.7 8
pillars 3.1
pilot 2.2
platter 11
pluck 7
pomegranate 7
port 2.2
power 1.8
praise 1.4 1.10 2.3 2.6 3.3
promised 7
promoted 3.1
prophesied 3.5 6
prophet 3.5 6
prophetess 7 10
protect 2.2 2.3 2.5
protégé 9
provoked 3.3
pull 2.5
punishment 3.5
Queen 2.4 7
rained 3.3
raised 2.5
read 3.3
reared 7
rebelled 3.5
receive 1.7
received 2.2
reconcile 2.3 2.5 2.6
reconciled 1.4
regions 3.2
rejoice 1.3 3.5 9
rejoices 1.3
rely 1.1 1.10
remained 1.4
remember 3.4
removed 3.3
restore 3.5
righteous 2.6
rightful 1.6
ripe 1.1
rise 1.1 1.6 9
risen 1.1
river 1.6 3.3
rivers 9
roam 1.8 9
roll 1.1 2.4
rule 1.10 2.3 7
sacrifices 3.3
safe 1.10 1.2 2.3 7
safely 1.6
scent 2.3
seah 3.4 3.5
seal 2.4
search 2.4
security 5
seek 2.6
seize 2.1
shame 1.6
shed 2.5
shekels 1.6
shelter 2.6
sheltered 2.4
shield 1.6
shine 1.6
shines 3.2
ship 2.2
shoulders 9
showers 9
shrews 1.7
silent 1.4 2.4
single 1.2
sixty 1.4 2.2
skilled 2.2
slaughter 1.2 9
slaughtered 3.3
slice 3.4
slight 3.4
smoke 1.6
snake 8
son 1.4 1.6 1.10 2.3
sons 7
soup 3.5
sprinkled 3.3
squash 7
star 11
stars 11
steer 2.2
steppe 1.8 1.9 2.3
stocks 1.2 2.5
strengthened 2.1 2.2
stylus 1.4
success 2.5 3.5
successors 7
sun 3.2
sunrise 2.4 2.5 3.2
sunset 2.4 2.5 3.2
support 2.6
sweet 3.5
table 11
tablet 3.3
taut 11
teeth 3.5
temple 3.5
terrace 3.4

thorn 7
throne 1.6 2.1
torches 1.10
town 1.3
traitors 3.3 3.5
trample 2.1
traverse 9
tread 3.5
trembling 1.10 2.3
tribute 1.2 2.5
trust 1.4
tuft 7
twitter 2.3
Tyre 9
upside 3.5
utterance 1.10
vanquish 2.2 2.5 3.5 4 11
vanquished 3.2 3.5
vassals 1.2 2.5
vegetables 3.5
vision 11
votaress 1.7
wasps 7
watch 1.4 1.6 2.2 7
water 1.10 3.4
weasels 1.7 4
well-being 1.9 2.2 2.3 3.1 3.2 3.3
wet nurse 1.6
wind 1.1
wing 1.1
winged 2.3
wings 2.5
witnesses 7
woe 1.1 2.5 9
woman 1.2 1.3 1.4 1.5 1.7 1.8 2.4 9 10
wool 7
word 2.4 3.4 3.5 5 7
words 8
worn 9
writings 2.4
wronged 2.4
years 1.6
young 2.3

Index of Texts

By Publication Number

ABL 1280	8	CT 53 219	11	4 R^2 61	1	TI pl.4	5
ABRT 1 22f	3	CT 53 946	10	TI pl.2f+	2	ZA 24 169+	9
ABRT 1 26f	7						

By Museum Number

K 883	7	K 4310	1	83-1-18,726	10
K 1292+	9	K 6259	5	83-1-18,839	4
K 1545	8	K 12033+	2	Bu 91-5-9,106+	6
K 1974	11	(DT 130+)	9	(Bu 91-5-9,109+)	6
K 2401	3	(82-5-22,527+)	2		

List of Joins

K 1292 (ZA 24 169) + DT 130 (unpub.)	10
K 12033 (unpub.) + 82-5-22,527 (TI pl.2f)	2
Bu 91-5-9,106 + Bu 91-5-9,109 (both unpub.)	6

List of Illustrations

AO 1510	11
AO 19914	23
AO 23004	18
BaM 23 357	10
Collon, First Impressions 432	11c
Fribourg 103	9
JNES 52 183, fig. 9	14
Karvonen-Kannas, Terracotta Figurines	12
Mahazari, Iran p. 21	4
ND 6310(B)	28
OBO 33, Abb. 40	19
OBO 33, Abb. 87	17
OBO 33, Abb. 118	16
OBO 33, Abb. 120	21
OBO 53, Abb. 409	15
Or. Dr. II, 28	26
Or. Dr. VII, 11	29
Tel-Aviv 9, fig. 4	3
VA 2708	2
VA Ass 1358	5
Vorderasiatisches Museum Abb. 38	11e
VS 1 Beiheft Tf. 7	2
WA 89135	13
WA 89145	22
WA 89164	Frontispiece
WA 89502	1
WA 89632	11f
WA 89769	8
WA 89810	11b
WA 105111	7
WA 118829	24
WA 118916	25
WA 124580	6
WA 124867	11d
WA 124908-9	27

Index to the Introduction, Notes and Critical Apparatus

Aaron n.213
Abbasid n.193
Abraham XXXV n.36 44 203
absolution XXXIII
Abyss n.18
Achaemenid XVI n.30
Acts of Thomas XXVIII
Adam n.77 98 193
Adam Qadmon n.41 44 193
Adapa XLVII n.127 246 p.4
Adonay n.158
Adonis n.104 123 125 127 p.39
adoration n.65
Adversus nationes n.138
Ahab XXI n.33 243
Ahura Mazda n.30
Akitu p.10 22
Alenu le-Shabeah n.63
Alkabez XXXV
Allatu LI
allegorical XXIV XXXIf n.107 116 123
allegory XXXI XXXIII XXXIX n.99 117 124
almighty p.23
altered states XVI n.143
Amarna XLVIII
amber n.248 249 p.7
Amos XLV n.54 64 214
amour libre n.100
Anael n.41
anagoge n.135
analogy XXI XXVI n.25 28 134
Anat n.41 83 92 130 165 189 199
Anathoth n.229
androgynous XXVIIIf XXXII XXXIV n.46
androgyny n.46 97 138f
angel n.40 41 65 68 140
angelic beings n.76
angelic cult n.65
angels XXII n.8 31f 36 40f 56 58 65 149
angels/gods n.31
Angimdimma n.114
animal soul n.106 133
anointed XIX n.213
anthropomorphic XXIII XLIV n.9 44 59
anthropomorphic tree XXVI n.46 133
Antiochus n.42
Anunitum n.214 220
Anzu p.24
An-Anum n.29
Aphrodite XXVIII n.6 83 140 p.39
Apocalypse n.2 36 76 84
Apocalyptic, Jewish n.2
apocalyptic and mystical tradition n.196
apocalyptic visions n.249
apocrypha n.40 56
apocryphal XXVIII n.41 84
Apocryphon of John n.9 77
apologists n.22
apostles n.130
apostles, itinerant n.257
Apostles' Creed XXVIII
apparition XXXI XXXVf n.150 p.25
appearance XXXV XLIII XLVf LXX LXXV n.98 197 257 p.24
appellative LII n.6 73 111 121 189 211 p.14
appellatives XVIII n.6
Apsû n.111
Apuleius n.132 138 189
Aramaic LXVII n.41 58 206 p.18
Aramaization n.4
Arbela XIII XIX XXXVI XL XLIII XLVIff ILf LII LXIII LXXIII n.11 103 128 170 176 235 243 p.4ff 9 24 26 39ff
Arbiel n.41
archangel n.7 196 268
archangels n.44 116
archons n.44
archontes n.31
aretalogies n.130
Aristides n.65
Ariston n.106
armor n.105
arms n.165 p.6 39
Arnobius n.138
arrow-shooting god n.66
Artemis p.39
ascend/descend n.219
ascension n.36 211
ascent XV XXXIIf XLVII n.111 114 116f 119f 124 133 141 246
ascent of the soul XXXI XXXIII n.114 135f
ascent to heaven n.41 119
ascetic XLVf L n.126 139
asceticism XVI XLV n.141
asexual XLVIII
Asherah XVI XLII n.14 34 42 46 107 138 199ff 202
asherah tree n.107
aspect XXVIII XXXVI n.91 98
aspect, destructive n.114
aspect, feminine, God's n.85 86
aspect, material n.65
aspect, sexual n.140
aspect, supernal XL
aspects XVIII XXI XXIII n.8 189
aspects of kingship n.123

assembly XXI XLV n.48 50 p.8 41
assembly, divine XXIII XXVI n.28
assembly, higher n.205
assembly of God n.32
assembly of the gods n.88
assembly of the great gods XXI
assinnu n.119 138 14f 214 220 232 244
Assurnasirpal n.186
Astarte n.92
Astarte-Aphrodite p.39
Athanasius n.71 192
Athenagoras n.40 71 97
atonement p.16
Atrahasis XLVII n.27 48f 50 57 270 p.16
Attis n.104 126f 137 139f
attributes XXI XXV n.46 114 23 116 158f p.39
attributes, divine n.22 60
attributes of divinity n.197
attributes of God XXIII
attributes of loving-kindness n.158
attributes of power n.158
Augustine n.132 134 138ff
Axial Age XVI n.4
Azriel XXXV
Baal n.30 34 138 165 200 235
Babylon XXXIX LXIX LXXI LXXV n.88 97 225 242 246 p.4 8f 16 18
Bacchic n.132
Baga n.30
Bahir n.44 98 156
Banitu XVIII n.6 p.14
baptism XV XXXII
beard XXIX n.9 97 144 234
beauty XXIX n.55 274
Beauty n.114 116
Beauty of God XXVIII n.46
beings, angelic n.76
beings, divine n.40
beings, celestial XXII
beings, spiritual n.22
belief XXXIV n.127
beliefs n.41 46
Bethel n.214
Bethlehem n.125
Bileam n.264
Binah n.55 111 116 133f 156f 201
bisexuality n.97 140
blessed n.55 p.6
blessedness n.140
blesses n.132
blessing XXXIX n.9 55 p.8 22
bliss XXXI n.126
blood n.140 p.6 17
Boaz n.201
bodies n.98 129
bodily XV XXXIV n.124 232
body XXIIIf XXVI XXXIf XLVII L LXIV n.51 135 139f 186
bond n.134 257
bondage XXXI
Book of Life n.7 p.6
bow XLVI LXXIII n.103 114 p.26
breasts XL n.89 137 165 175 p.39
breath XXVI n.69
bridal chamber XXXI n.119 120
bride XXVIIIf XXXI XXXIII n.99 111 121 274
bridegroom XXXIIf n.119 121 140
bright LXXIVf n.132 189
brightness XXIX n.98 132 150
brilliance XXIX n.97
brilliant one n.196
brother XXXIII LXX n.123 225 242
brothers XIXf XXXIX XLIII XLV LXVIII LXXII LXXIV n.172 206 229 p.9f 23 27
bullfight n.140
Bull of Heaven n.119 140
burning bush n.42
Byzantine church n.139 193
Byzantine empire n.25 191
Byzantine emperor XV n.65 191 193
Byzantine hagiographic texts n.140
Byzantine iconoclasm n.65
Byzantine patriarchs n.97
Byzantium n.191
Bît rimki n.111
cabinet, Assyrian n.25 26 56
Calah XLVIIff LII n.238 p.26
calf XXXVI XXXVIII n.162 165 187 p.10
calf-licking cow XL
calf-suckling cow XV n.165 274
caliph n.193 p.38
Canaanite XVI XLII n.107 133
Canis Maior n.114
canon law n.139
caprids n.199
captivity XXXIII
carnal sexuality XXXI
carnal man n.140
Carthage n.139
castrated n.137 140
castrates n.97 138f
castration n.126 139f
Catullus n.138
celestial and mundane realms XL n.27
celestial beings XXII
celestial Egypt n.205
celestial home XXXI
celestial imagery XXII
celestial gods n.127
celestial king-to-be XLI
celestial origin n.123
celestial pattern XL
celestial records XVIII
celestial saviour XLI n.123
celibate life n.139
cella LXIV n.240 p.25
ceremonial n.25 197
ceremonies XLV XLVII LXIV p.008
ceremony LXX p.22 25
Chaldeans n.41 106
Chaldean Cosmic Soul n.105
Chaldean Hekate/Soul n.151
Chaldean Oracles XXXI n.9 22 105f 130 134 257
Chaldean theurgy n.132
chanters n.138
chaos XXXI XLI
charms n.41
chaste XXXII
chastity XXIX n.111
cherubs n.201
cherub-flanked n.42
child-suckling XV

choirboys n.138
chosen one of Enlil n.186
chosen one of God XXXVI n.166 173
Christ XXII XXVIII XXXIII XL n.7 43 51 65 76 121 124f 127 129 134 192f 268
Christian XIV XXII XXVI XXVIII XXXI XL n.9 22 40f 60 71 97 110 127 141
Christianity XVIII XXII XXVIIIf XXXIII n.14 58 65 73 149 165
Christianity, early XLVIII n.28 40 81 97 108 196
Christians n.40 58 140
Christ-like XV
Church n.296
church, Byzantine n.139 193
Church Fathers n.40 41 65 75 97
church poetry n.111
Cicero n.296 p.14
Cimmerians LXVIII LXX p.23
City of God n.132 138ff
classical XVIf n.30 111f 138 146 p.39
classicist n.105
Clement of Alexandria n.43
Cleanthes n.30
cleaving n.28 146 151 193
climax LXVII
clothed in light n.97 120
clothes XXXII n.144 214 257
clothing XXXII n.112 140
code XV
coeternal with n.22
cognomens n.8 28
colours n.114
commentaries n.123
commentary XXXII XLVI LXIIIf LXVI n.7 75 111 172 175 219 248 268 p.24
community XLVII LII n.41 213
complementarity XL n.9
concentration XXXVI n.200
concept of God XXI XXIV XXIII XXVf IL n.9 22 55 p.40
concept of purity n.111
concept of soul n.106
conception, immaculate XXVIII XL n.211
concepts XXII XXIV n.21 31 43
cones n.197
cone-shaped n.190
consciousness XLVI n.143
consecrated n.139
consort XXVIII XLII n.126
Constantine n.125
constellation n.44 114
consubstantial n.9 134 197
consubstantiality n.9
contemplation n.200
continuity n.138
convictions XLVII
coronation LIX LXIV LXX p.8 22 25
corporate body n.51
corporeal n.144
corrupt men p.16
corruption n.111 p.16
cosmic body XXIV
cosmic bond XXV
cosmic geography XXII n.39 248f p.24
cosmic harmony XLIII LXIX LXXIV p.16
cosmic mountain n.107 114 133
cosmic order XLI
Cosmic Soul XV XXXI n.105 107 112 134
cosmic sympathy n.105
cosmic tree XV n.193 249
cosmic witch n.246
cosmogony XV
cosmos n.7 107 p.16
council XXI XXIV n.27 28 32 35
council, divine XXI XXIV n.27 31 48 136
council, heavenly XXII
covenant XIXf XXIV LXIV LXX n.51 140
covenant, book of the p.25
covenant, divine XXIV LI
cow XV XXXVIII XL XLII n.153 165 187ff 274
cow, calf-licking XL
cow, calf-suckling XV n.165 274
cow, wild XV XL XLII n.153 187ff
cow-and-calf n.165
cowhorns n.189
created n.22 23 30 40 55 103 119 175 180 183 186 192 243 p.5 23 40
creation XXXII XXXVI XXXIXf n.40 43 60 86 97 105 140 168 183 186 p.40
creation, goddess of n.186
creation, God's p.16
creations XVI XXII XXXIV XXXIX
creator n.18 40 189 p.16
Creatress n.6 190 192
Creatrix XVIII XLII LII n.6 105 155 p.14
creature XXVIII XXXVI XL n.18 28 41 134 140 270
cross n.58 103 243
crown XXXIV n.97 112 200 p.22
crowned n.191
crown prince XXXIX XLI XLV LXVIII LXX n.9 165 175 184 197 206 216 p.10 38
crown prince, heavenly XLI
crucifixion n.125
cult XV XVII XXV XXXIV n.65
cult, angelic n.65
cult, ecstatic XV n.133
cult centres XLVII LXXV
cult objects n.42
cult of Asherah XVI
cult of Attis n.126 140
cult of Cybele n.139 140
cult of Inanna XVI
cult of Isis XVI
cult of Ištar XLVII LXVII n.107 119 140 p.26
cult of Yahweh n.43
cult of Tammuz n.125
cult of the Goddess XXXI XLVII n.141 202
cult of the Hindu mother goddess n.133
cult of the Cypriote Aphrodite n.83
cult of the mother goddess XVII n.138
cult of Venus Barbata n.83 139
cult personnel n.227
cultic XLVIIff LXVII n.6 127 138 186 197 p.10 16 25f
Cutha LXXI
Cybele XVI n.92 126 132 138ff 159
Cyprian n.6
Cypriote n.83 97 139 p.39
Cypris n.6
Cyrus XIX XLIII n.173 p.5 24
Damkina n.175

darkness XV XXXI XLI n.41 104 111 130 246 p.7 24
date palm XXXIV n.55 133
daughter XXXIII XL ILf p.6 16
daughter of Anu XXIX n.114
daughter of Ea XXIX n.111 123
daughter of Enlil XLVI
daughter of the moon XXVIIIf XXXII n.111 114
daughter of the king n.274
daughters n.140 p.25
David XIX XLIII n.53 55 173 251 p.9
Davidic XXXVIII n.166
De Trinitate n.134
dead XXXIII LI n.98 107 127 129 211
death XV XXXIIIf n.7 65 106 111 114 124ff 127 130f 135 140 158 196 211 246 268 p.41
death, redemptory XXXIII n.124
death, spiritual n.111
death, waters of n.111
death of God n.22
decad n.23
defender XLI
defending n.187
defilement XXXIf n.111 112
degradation n.112
degree XXIX n.22
deified p.8
deiktérion n.123
deities XVIII XXI XXIV n.138 176 p.39
deity XVIIIf LII LXVI n.13 30 167f 248 p.14
deity, composite n.13 23
deity, oracular XVIII XLII LXVf LXXI n.11 34
deluge XXVIII LII LXXIV n.27 49 114
demonic n.117
demons n.67 68 125
demythologized XXVIII
Deo n.140
descent XV XXXII n.111 114 117 127 133 140
Descent XXXI XXXVI n.104 107f 111f 116 119 138
desecration p.16
destinies n.61 140
destruction XIX n.130 p.16
destructive aspect n.114
determiner of fates p.6
deuteronomistic n.33 42
devotee XV XXXIV XLVIIf Lf n.119 126f 138 141 232
devotees, ecstatic XLVI
dictated n.52
dictation n.279 286
Dilibat/Venus n.41
Dionysious the Areopagite n.60
Diodorus n.88 132
disciples p.39
disclosure n.141
disk of the moon n.111
disrobe XXXII
divine approval XXXIX
divine assembly XXIII XXVI n.28
divine attributes n.22 60
divine banquet p.26
divine barmaid n.111
Divine Being XVIII n.23 60
divine beings n.40
divine "body" XXIII XXVI
divine council XXI XXIV n.27 31 48 136
divine covenant XXIV LI
divine creation XL
divine determinatives p.5
divine efflux XXXVI
divine encouragement XLIII
divine endorsement n.169
divine entities n.189
divine entity XX n.146
divine favour p.10
Divine Glory n.116 144
divine help XIX LXVI
Divine Images n.9 42 58 296
divine influence n.68
divine inspiration n.67
divine institution n.9
divine judge n.125 158
divine kingship n.124 158
Divine King XXXII
divine letters LXXVII
divine light XXIX n.116 135
divine love n.167
divine meal p.8
divine message LXXVII
divine mother XXXI XXXVI XXXIXf XLII n.9
divine name XXXV n.8 46 60 116 147
divine nurse XL
divine origin XV
divine over-soul n.133
divine powers XXIff XXVf n.22 23 30f 43f 55f 63 71 86 112f 114 133 174
divine presence n.98 146
divine promises p.38
divine queen XXXVI
divine secrets n.130
divine spirit XXXIV n.146
divine statues p.25
divine substance n.40
divine support LXIV LXVI n.141
divine unity n.97 114
divine weapon p.8
divine will LXVI n.67 p.24
divine wisdom n.108
divine world n.25
divine wrath XXIV XLIII n.51
diviner/haruspex n.27 243
divinities n.30
divinity XLVI n.67
divinity, attributes of n.197
Dlibat n.41
doctrinal XVI XVIII XXIII XXXIV XL IL LII n.124 125
doctrine XV XXI XXXII XXXIXf LII n.9 51 55 112 119 126 211
doctrines XIV XVIf XLVIIf n.43 126 211
dogma XXII XL
dominion n.56 136 p.9f 23
doorkeepers n.117
doors n.37 107 p.17 24
dove XXVIII n.83 85 88f 147
dream XXXV XLVIf LXIX LXXI LXXIV n.103 119 144 234f 240 243 p.25
dressing XXXII n.8 46 97 105 114 121 138f
drink-offerings n.53
drugs LXVII
Dumuzi n.123 127

Dumuzi's Dream n.125
dying n.120
dying/dead n.123
dynastic IL LXXII
dynasty XXXVIII
eagle LXXIII p.15
ears n.177 256
earth XXI XL LXXIIIff n.9 25 30 55 77 179 193 p.8 17
earthly XV n.97 127 140
Ecbatana n.30 114
ecclesia n.51 99
eclipse n.111
ecstacy n.71 133 246
ecstatic XVI XLVI n.67 126 145 216 222 225 228f 232 242
ecstatic cult XV n.133
ecstatic devotees XLVI
ecstatic Kabbalah XXXV n.107 200
ecstatic mystery cult XXXIII
ecstatic prophecy XXVI XLII
ecstatic prophet XLV n.222 232 243
ecstatic prophetess n.220
ecstatic prophets XLV LXVIIIf LXXIIIf n.141
ecstatic prophets/prophetesses n.222
ecstatic techniques XVI
ecstatic vein XXXVI
ecstatics XLVIII LXVII n.138
Eden n.98
Edom p.40
effeminate XXXII n.139 231
Egypt LXX n.22 30 164f 205 p.39
Egypt, celestial n.205
Egyptian XVI XLII n.22 108 123 126 165
Egyptians n.214 p.17
eight-pointed star XXIX n.48 95
Elam XXXIX XLVII LXVIII LXX n.284 p.40
Elamite LXX LXXIV p.40
Elamites XLVI LXII p.16
Elammatu n.114
Elchasai n.76
electrum n.114
elektron n.249 p.7
Eleusinian n.140
Eleusis n.132 140
Elijah XLV n.200 213
Elohim n.16 30f 36 56 158
elyon n.111
elyonah n.151
emanate XXV n.111
emanation XXI XXV n.40 60 158
emasculation n.119 138ff
emperor XV XLIII LXXI n.65 191 193
emperor cult XVI
emperor-centric XIV
empire XXXIX XLI XLIII LXXI n.22 139 159
empire, Assyrian XXI LII n.139
empire, Byzantine n.25 191
empire, Roman XVI n.159
empires XVI
emulate XV XXXIV n.141
emulator n.41 213
encoded XXII XXXIV
energies n.22 60
enigmatic n.114 249 p.24 39
Enki n.57 111 189
Enkidu n.119 140
enlighten n.111
Enlil, Assyrian n.59
Enlil, chosen one of n.186
Enoch n.36 41 98 196 248
Enoch/Metatron n.46 196
entities XX n.44
entities, divine n.189
entities, lower n.205
entities, spiritual XXII
entity XXVI XXVIII XXXI n.22 98 146 192
entity, divine XX n.146
Enuma eliš 14 18 39 175 195 229 p.24
En Sof Or n.22
Ephraim p.6
epiphanies n.130 141
epithet XXIX XL n.52 72 81 91f 111 119 124 189 p.6 38
Ereshkigal n.104
Eris n.105
erotic XXXI n.99
Erra n.138 141 193
Esaggil LI LXVII LXIX LXXIVf p.14
eschatological n.213
esoteric XV XVII XXIX XL XLVIII n.46 111f 120 130 175f 193 248
esotericism XVI XXXVI n.110 132
Etana n.107
eternal life XV XXXIII L n.127
etiology XXXIII n.124 140
Eugnostos n.78
eunuch XXXIV n.97 139f p.38
eunuchlike n.140
Eusebius n.65
everflow n.44 111 133 157f
everlasting life n.128
evil XXXI XLIII LXXIIff n.88 118 136 216 246 p.4 16
Ewat n.130
ewe and lamb n.165
exaltation n.211
exalted XXV LI n.180 183
exegesis n.31 55
Exeg. Soul XXXIff n.108f 119 123 130
exile XXXII XLIII IL LXVIIIf n.125 p.16
exorcist n.243
experience, acoustic XLVII
experience, visual XXXVIII XLVII
experience, visionary n.264 286
extispicy XIV LXXII n.1 27 p.40
Ezekiel n.236
Ezekiel the Tragedian n.36 41
faith XL p.6
fallen soul n.119 124
fallen Sophia XXVIII
Fall of Sophia XXXI XXXVI n.108
fanatic XIV
fasting n.230
fast-day n.279
fate XXVIII XXXIV LII LXX LXXII n.135 270 p.6
fates, determiner of p.6
father XXXIIf XXXVI XLf XLIII IL LI LXXIIf n.9 18 52 123 172 175 180 183 189 197 206 243 254 p.18
Father XVIII XXII XXVIII XXXII n.9 22 70 119 121 134 192 197 211 268 p.10

Father-Mother-Son n.9
Fathers n.40 41 65 75 97
feast n.121
fecundity XXVI
female XVIII XXVIIIf XXXIII XLVIIIf n.9 76 98 138 14f 190 192 222 231 242 p.6 39
feminine XXVIII XXXI XXXVI L n.74 98 150 192 202 p.5 25 34
femininity n.138
fertility XVIII XXIX XXXI p.39
festival XLVI n.100 123 126f p.22 26
figurative language n.296
figurines n.88
fire XIX XLVII n.41 229 249 p.7f 24 39
fire, intellectual n.135
firmament n.249
Firmicus Maternus n.126
first-born n.119 121
flame XXVI p.24 39
flash n.101 249
flatus n.69
flesh XVI XXXIV n.140 192
flood LXXIV n.103 243
Flood XXIV XXXIV n.50 127 270 p.16
forgiveness n.20
formulation XX XXIV XXXVI LIII LXIIff LXIX n.9
forsake LXXII n.7 268
frenzy XXXIV XLVI n.67 138 219 222 231f
Gabriel n.41
Galilee n.125 130
Galli, galloi n.137 138ff
gaonic n.116
garden n.133 p.26
gardener n.123
garments XXXII LXXIII n.8 112 114 116 121
garments of Keter n.114
gate XXXII n.7 98 112 268 p.8 18 24
gate of heaven n.140
gates XXXII n.39 112 116 118
gates, heavenly XXII p.24 37
gates, seven XXXII n.114
Gates of Light n.8 20 25 28 36 38 44 46 55f 63 111 116 118 121 133 156ff 201 205
gatekeeper XXII n.37 127 p.23
gateway to the Tree of Life n.193
Gedulah n.201
gedullah n.55
gelded n.139
gematric n.111
genitals n.140
Gen.Rabba n.31
gesture n.9
gevurah n.55
Gevurah n.201
Gilgamesh XXIV XL XLV XLVII L n.72 111f 119 140 193 213
girl IL n.92
Glory, Divine n.116 144
Gnosis n.30 81 97 108f 117 12f 126 139 192 257f
gnostic XXVIII XXXIff XXXVI n.8 31 44 109 111 117 12f 126 139 192 257
Gnosticism XVIf XXVIIIf XXXIf XLVIII n.9 81 108
Gnostics n.97 108 139
god, arrow-shooting n.66
God, assembly of n.32
God, attributes of XXIII
God, Beauty of XXVIII n.46
God, chosen one of XXXVI n.173
God, concept of XXI XXIV XXIII XXVf IL n.9 22 55 p.40
God, death of n.22
God, kingdom of n.44
god, national XIV XVIII n.23
God, powers of XXII n.41 55 189
god, throne of n.248
God, unity of n.63
God, universal XXI n.22 59
God, word of n.99 192
goddess XV XXXI XL XLII LIf n.41 99 105 130 134 137 168 177 189 199f 214 220 p.9f 39
Goddess XVf XIXf XXVI XXIX XXXI XXXIIIf XXXVI XXXIX XLIII XLVIff L LXVII LXX LXXIII n.11 73 92 103 111 114 117 124 133 140f 159 189 202 206 243 257 262 270
Goddess, cult of the XXXI XLVII n.141 202
goddess, lunar n.105
goddess, oracular n.105
goddesses XXVIIIf XXXI XXXV XL LI LXXIV n.88 91 100 103 153 174f p.16 18 39
goddesses, Syrian n.138
goddess of beauty p.15
goddess of creation n.186
goddess of fertility XXIX
goddess of l'amour libre n.100
goddess of love XIV XVIII XLII
goddess of war XXVI XXIX
godhead XXXI XLVIf L LXXV n.40 240
Godhead n.134 192
gods XIV XVIIIff XXIff XXIVff XXXV XXXIXf XLIIf XLVI ILf LII LXVII LXIXf LXXIIff LXXV n.8 9 16 18 22 27 30f 34 35f 40f 50 52f 56 58f 64f 88 91 109 119 127 153 169 183 186 205 248 254 264 p.
gods, assembly of the n.88
gods, Assyrian n.8 31 189
gods, foreign XXVI n.8 56 64
gods, sum total of XXI XXIII IL n.30 31
gods, supernal n.18
God's angels n.58
God's Chosen One n.166
God's court n.136
God's creation p.16
God's familia n.36
God's feminine aspect n.85 86
God's hands n.56
God's heirs n.129
God's immanent plurality n.14
God's infinite expansion n.43
God's love XXXVI n.70 124
God's mother n.42
God's people n.153
God's power XIX
God's representative n.9 25 193
God's rule XXI
God's son XXXVI XXXVIII
God's spirit n.71
God's throne n.249
God's unity XXI n.28 46
God's work p.24
god-born XLII
god-chosen XXXVIIIf XLII
God-like p.10

god-list n.13
god-man relationship n.3 51
God-man n.134
god-raised XXXIX
god of heaven XXIX n.114
god of Israel XVIII
god of purity XXIX
god of wisdom n.111
Gomorrah p.24
gospels n.84 211 213
Gospel of Philip n.77 120 135
grace n.20
grades n.133 134
grave of the soul n.107
great gods XXIIIf XLIII LXXIIf n.23 31 34 44 48 57 166 168 186 p.6 40
great gods, assembly of the XXI
Great Heavenly Court n.36
Great Mother n.139
Greco-Roman philosophy n.105
Greco-Roman religions XVI
Greco-Roman world XXVIII n.139 140
Greece n.30 106 243
Greek n.41 45 69 73 83 92 123 139 p.39
Greeks n.106
groaning XXVIII n.70 153
guard n.116 117 132 p.15
guardians n.140
Gudea n.165
Hadriel n.41
Hafkiel n.41
Haggai n.54
Hagigah n.23 87 249
hagiographic texts, Byzantine n.140
half-Babylonian n.125
half-brothers LXVIII p.9
harlot n.119
harmony, cosmic XLIII LXIX LXXIV p.16
harmony, universal LXIV
haruspices n.243
Hasidism XXXVI
Hathor XLII n.165 198
heathen n.173
heaven XXXIIIf LXXIIIff n.25 30f 37 39 43 55 76 114 116 119 127 134 179 197 200 249 p.6 16 24
heaven, ascent to n.41 119
heaven, gate of n.140
heaven, god of XXIX n.114
heaven, highest n.127
heaven, host of XXI XXIV n.25 34 53 55
heaven, hosts of XXIV n.41 53
heaven, kingdom of XLIII LII n.25 39 205 p.18
heaven, middle n.248 249 p.7
heavenly Aphrodite n.140
heavenly bodies XXVI n.44 64
heavenly bride n.111
heavenly brightness XV
heavenly city XXII n.37
heavenly council XXII
heavenly court n.36
heavenly crown prince XLI
heavenly gates XXII p.24 37
heavenly Jerusalem n.38
heavenly mysteries n.140
heavenly oral revelation n.130
heavenly order n.25
heavenly origin XXXI
heavenly palaces XXII
heavenly paragon XLI
heavenly perfect man XV
heavenly royal court n.29
heavenly scribe n.196
heavenly tablets n.7
heavens XXII XXV XXXVIII n.37 39f 55 116 147 205 248 p.7 8 17
heavens, planetary XXXII
heaven-sent XV
heaven and earth XV LXXII n.18 41 116 132 134 179
Hebrew XXVIII n.32 41 69 74 86 92 106 149 166 206 249
Hekate XXXI n.105 130 132 134f
Hekate/Soul n.134 151
Hekhalot n.36 41
Hekhalot Rabbati n.36
Hekhalot Zutreti n.36
hell n.140 206
Hellenistic XIV XVI XXI n.30 105 110 132
helper/saviour XXXII n.119
Heno/Cosmotheismus n.30
Hermaphroditos n.97
Hermas n.196
hero XLV n.41
Herodotus n.114 189
heroic XLVI n.114
heroism n.20
Hezekiah n.243
hidden Intellect XVIII
hidden Light XVIII
hidden mother XXVIII
hidden mysteries n.140
hidden power n.76
hidden things p.10
Hidden Wisdom XXVIII n.110 130
hierodules XXXIXf
high temple n.248
High Priest n.46
higher assembly n.205
higher justice n.111
higher powers n.158
higher worlds XXXII
highest god XLVI n.46
highest grade n.153
highest heaven n.127
highest of the gods XLVI n.91
highest of the planetary spheres n.111
highest sacrament XXXI n.120
Hilkiah n.243
Hindu mother goddess XV n.133
Hinduism XXI n.22
Hippolytus n.8 14 71 106 117 126 140
Hod n.55 201
Hokhmah n.55 201
holiest/purest n.91
holiness XXIX XL n.98 139
holy XXIX XXXIII n.91 190
holy and eternal n.9
holy angels n.41
Holy Goddess XLIII
holy images n.58
holy Inanna n.91
Holy Names n.28 46

Holy of Holies n.120 p.25
Holy One n.249 p.39
Holy One of Israel XXXI
holy soul XXXVI
holy spirit XXVIII XXXI
Holy Spirit XV XVIII XXII XXVI XXVIIIf XL n.9 70f 74 76 98 111 130 134 157 191f
Holy Trinity XVIII
Holy Virgin XXXI
holy water n.197
homoousia XV n.121 272
Horace n.296
horns XV XL n.189 229
Horus XLII n.123 165
Hosea XXXVI XLII Lf n.53 54 165
hosts n.44 54 173 p.8 15
host of heaven XXI XXIV n.25 34 53 55 p.6
hosts of heaven XXIV n.41 53
hosts of heavenly stars n.41
hymn to Aššur n.17
hymn to Inanna n.111 130 138 189
hymn to Ištar of Nineveh LXVI n.114 133
hymn to Mullissu LXXf p.40
hymn to Nanaya n.6 111 130
hymn to Zeus n.30
hymns XL XLVIII
hypostases XVIII XXII n.9
hypostatized XXI n.31 98
icon n.30 59
iconoclasm n.65
iconographic XVII n.9 59 165
iconography XIV XXV XXIX XLII n.46 133
idea XV XXI XXXII XLV n.14 30 67 124 136 p.8 16 25
ideal n.97
idealization n.139
idealized XLV
identical XX XXIV XXXVI IL LII LV LXI LXIII n.55 123 146 166 197 274
identification n.59 73 140 156 158 199 p.40
identities XIX n.123
identity XVIII XXIII n.126
ideological XXXVIIIf XLII n.166
ideology, royal XIV XVI XXXIXf n.165 166 211 296
idol p.10
idolaters n.58
idolatrous n.65
idolatry XXVI n.58 64f
Igigi XXV n.91 248
image XV XIX XXI XXIII XXXI XXXVIII XL n.9 25 42 53 58f 65f 73 98 114 121 133 144 150 158 162 192 p.22 24
image of God n.133
images XIII XXXIV XXXVI n.6 9 58 65 116 127 159 p.16
Images, Divine n.9 42 58 296
images, holy n.58
imagery XV XXIf XXIV XXXI XXXVI XXXVIIIf XLVIIf LXVII n.99 117 202 296 p.39
imagine n.58 116
imitate n.137
immaculate n.111
immaculate conception XXVIII XL n.211
immanent n.192
immortal n.40 106
immortality n.126
imperfect nature n.56
imperial art XVI n.22 159
imperishable n.140
impersonate XXXIXf
impurities n.111
Inanna XVI n.92 111 125 127 130 138 189
Inanna and Enki n.130
Inanna's Descent n.91 104 119 125
Inanna-Ishtar n.90
incarnate n.67
incarnation XV XLII p.10
incense XXXIII n.127
incontinences XXXIV
incorporeal n.68
India n.22 30
Indian n.96 106 133
indwelling XXXI n.98 129
ineffable XXVIII n.110 134
infernal XXXVI n.18
influence XVI LXVII n.126 p.25
initiands n.119
initiate XXIV n.51 114 132 140
initiated n.140 p.16
initiates XV XXXIV XL n.107
initiation XLVIII n.120
innocence n.92
innocent XLIII n.124 159 206 211
innovation n.22
inspiration XV n.67 191
inspired XIV XVI n.9 286
Intellect, hidden XXVIII
intellectual fire n.135
intellectual revolution XVI
intelligences, spiritual n.40
Intelligible World n.134
intercede n.153
intercourse n.119 140
intermediary n.134
intoxication LXVII
investiture p.38
Iran n.30
Iranians n.30
Isaiah XIX XXXVI XLV LXVI n.36 54f 75 136 229 243
Isauric emperors n.65
Ishtar n.108
Isis XVI n.117 130 137 139 189
Israel XIV XVIII XXIV XXXI XXXVI XXXVIIIf XLII LI n.27 32 42 53 98f 102 114 125 149 165f 200 202 205 211 213 236 243 279 n.290 296 p.6 10 17 23 39
Israelite XXIV n.166 229 232 251
Israelites XLV n.53 p.23
Ištar, cult of XLVII LXVII n.107 119 140 p.26
Iulia Domna n.159
ivory n.165 189 199
Jachin n.201
Jehoiakim n.279
Jeremiah n.54 55 214 229 243 279 p.38
Jeroboam n.243
Jerome n.75 125
Jerusalem n.2 32 53 125f 211 214 279 p.6 8 10 15 38f
Jesse n.55
Jesus XXVIII XLIII LI n.41 76 98 124f 129 130

134 166 211 p.23
Jews n.30 41
Job XXII n.35 37 41f 66 111 249 p.7
John XXVIII n.36 38 65 71 75 165f 192 p.39
John the Baptist XLV n.213
John of Damascus n.9 44 58 296
Joshua p.26
Joshua ben Perahia n.41
Josiah n.53 65 279
Judah XXIV XXXIX n.53 125 173 279
Judaic n.41
Judaism XXII n.41 42 56
Jude n.125
Judea n.125
judge LXVII n.7 56 166 211 p.38 42
judgment LI LXXIV n.23 27f 31 106 153 158 p.6
Juno p.39
Jupiter LXIX n.114
justice XLI LXXIV n.28 36 89 111 254 p.10
Justin n.71
Kabbalah XXIIf XXXII XXXVI n.14 43f 46 55 62f 85f 98f 114ff 121 133 135f 141 144 146 149 150 151 154 156 162 193 200 205 213 230 234 249 270
Kabbalah, ecstatic XXXV n.107 200
kabbalistic XXVf n.23 43 55 114 133 249
kabbalists XXXV n.86
Kabeiroi n.132
Karo XXXV
kavod n.98
Keruv n.98
Keter XXV n.44 114 121
King XXXVI LXV n.42 53 116 193 274
king, perfect XL n.193
king, substitute n.124
kingdom XXII XXXVI n.37 p.9
kingdom of earth n.25
kingdom of God n.44
kingdom of heaven XLIII LII n.25 39 205 p.18
kingdom of light n.117
kings XXIV XXXIX n.53 169 173 p.38f
kingship XV XXXIX LXIV LXIXf LXXIIf LXXV n.9 23 166f 169f 183 186 193 211 p.9 41f
kingship, aspects of n.123
kingship, divine n.124 158
ladder XXII n.37 39 114
Lady XLVI n.180
Lady in the Window n.274
lady of Arbela XXXVI LXIII n.128 170 p.6 41
lady of Babylon n.225 242
lady of Divine Powers n.174
lady of Kidmuri n.240 p.40
lady of ladies XLVII
lady of Liburna p.39
lady of life XLII
lady of love n.72
lady of Nineveh LXXI n.133 170 182f p.10 41
lady of the Land p.16
lady of war LXXIII n.72
lamb n.124 165
Lamb of God n.165 211
lament XXXIV n.107 141
lamentation LXXIII n.138 141 232
lamentor n.232
lamp XXII n.39 43 248f p.7
lampstand n.42
lapis lazuli XXXIII n.39 248 270
Last Supper XIX XXIV n.51
Latin n.73
latreutic n.65
law n.41 139 243 p.25
legitimacy XXXIX n.168
legitimate XXXVIII XLIII p.8
legitimation XXXIX n.169
legitimize XXXVIII n.169
Levi Isaac XXXV n.162
Libat n.41
life XXXII XXXIV XLII XLV L n.7 10 98 106f 116 123f 128f 130f 133 139f 157f 180 193 203 248 268 p.6 26 39 41
Life, Book of n.7 p.6
life, celibate n.139
life, eternal XV XXXIII L n.127
life, food of n.119
life, water of XXXII n.119
life-creating power XXVIII
life-giving bosom n.180
life-giving writing-board p.6
light XXVIIIf n.14 22 28 41 59 65 98 105 111 120 124 130 150 187 p.7 24 39
light, clothed in n.97 120
light, divine XXIX n.116 135
Light, hidden XXVIII
light, kingdom of n.117
light, perfect n.120
lightning n.41 101 249
lightning arrow n.101
lights n.43
likeness n.8 41 192 249 p.7
likeness, perfect n.192
limb XXVI n.116
lion XV LXXIII p.5 15
Livy n.132
Logos XXVIII XXXII XXXIV n.8 30 119 192
lord XIX L n.18 22 52 135 254 268 p.6 8 40
Lord IL n.34 70 73 136 141 150 200 211 234 256 p.17 23f 40
Lot p.24
love XXVI XXVIIIf XXXVI Lf LXXIII n.28 41 48 53 68 70 72 105 119 124 130f 134 140 165 167 p.6 40
love, divine n.167
love, goddess of XIV XVIII XLII
love, God's XXXVI n.70 124
love, sexual XXVI XXIX
love lyrics XLVIII p.10 99
lover n.124 274 p.10
loving n.23 165
loving-kindness n.20 158
lower entities n.205
lower Shekhinah XXXVI n.156
lower Sophia n.130
lower soul n.111 126 134
lower worlds XXXVI
lower world n.200
Lo-ammi LI
Lo-ruhamah LI
Lucian of Samosata n.138
Lugalzagesi p.18
Luke LI
luminary n.153
luminosity XXIX

lunar disc n.189
lunar goddess n.105
lunar nature n.111
lunar phases n.111
Luria n.144
Lying-in-State n.123
Maashe Bereshit n.43
Maasheh Merkavah n.36
macrocosm XXIII
macrocosm/microcosm n.133
madman n.139 229
madonna XXIX XXXI n.101
magic n.41
magical-astrological n.41
magnates p.24
magnificent deeds XXIV
magnify n.170 p.40
maiden XXXII n.88
majesty n.17
Malachi n.54 290
Malkhut XXXVI n.111 133 156ff
Malkhut/Kingship n.157 158 193
Maltai n.59
man, carnal n.140
man, perfect XV XXIII XL n.41 44 121 124 126 133 193 196f 211
man, new n.140
Mandean n.41 108 130
manger n.211
manifest XXVIIIf n.22 105 123 192 p.24
manifestation XXIV XXVI XLIII n.8 14 31 146
mankind XV LIf n.27 124 270 p.16
Mannea LXVIII
man-woman n.232
man/male n.119
Mari XIV XVII XLV XLVIII n.3 4 27 32 88 127 138 214 219 232 246 254 279
Maria XIV
Mars LXIX LXXIV n.114
martial, martiality XXIX XXXI
Mary n.75 101 111 159
Marys n.125 211
masculinization n.73
mask XVIII n.8
material aspect n.65
material thoughts n.147
material world XV XXXI XXXIV n.118 257
maternal n.98 150
meal XIX XXIV LXIV
mediator XX n.134
medieval XXIIf n.56 111
meditation XVf XXXIV n.107 116 133
Mehafkiel n.41
member XXI XLVII n.35 41 139
menorah XXII n.42 43 201
menorah-shaped n.42
merciful LXXII LXXIV n.153
Mercury n.41 114 196
mercy XXXII LXXV n.20 144 158 176 p.24
Merkavah n.36 43 63 98
Messiah XXXIX XLII n.173 193 211 213
Messiah/King n.193
messianic XV XLI XLIII
Messianism n.193
metaphor XXI XXXII XXXIX IL n.28 140 296 p.9 14 16 24
metaphors XV XXIV XXXVI LXVII n.123
metaphysic XXIII
metaphysical propositions XVI
metaphysical universe n.22
Metatron n.41 43 196
Micah n.75
Micaiah XXI n.136
Michael n.7 41 196 268
Michael/Metatron n.41
Michael/Ninurta n.211
microcosm XXIII
middle heaven n.248 249 p.7
Middle Line n.46 133
Middle Platonic n.105
Midrash n.36 56
midwife XXXVI XXXIX p.5 7
milk n.165 176 p.39
minister n.56
ministering angels n.149
ministers n.40 116
miracle n.243
miraculous XL LXIX n.211
mirror XXI XL n.25 29 159
mirroring XXXII
mission XL XLIII n.211
missionary XLVIII n.257
mistress of life n.105
Mithraic n.114
moaning XXVIII n.88 89 119
model XIVff XVII XXIII LXIII
monotheism XXI XXV n.21 22 31 41 45
monotheistic XVIII XXIf n.21 30
moon XV XXVIII XL n.34 41 53 69 111 116 114 125 189 p.6
moon, daughter of XXVIIIf XXXII n.111 114
moon, full n.111
moon, waning XV n.111
moon, waxing XV
morality XLVIII
moral dimension XLVIII
moral soul n.133
mortal n.65 98 129 p.15
mortification XVI n.270
Moses XXXVI n.41 43 114 p.25 39
Most High XLVI
Mot n.165
mother XV XXVI XXXIII XXXVI XL XLIIf XLVI L LXV LXVII n.88 125 150 164f 175 180 183 186 206 211 234 p.5 9 18 23 39 40 41
Mother XXVIII n.9 139 234
motherly XXXIX
mother and child n.165
mother aspect XXVIII
mother goddess XVII XXVIII n.88 133 138
mother of the gods n.105
mother-child XV XXXVI XXXIX
Mother-Father XXVIII
mother-son n.162
motif XXXVIII n.42 165 274
mountain LI n.42 46 114 p.38
mountain, cosmic n.107 114 133
mountains XLVIII n.18 p.17 41
mourner XXXIII n.88
mourning XXVIII XXXII n.123 126f
mouth XXI XXVI XXXIVf XLVII LXIII LXXIV n.50 57 71 132 138 166 170 216 p.10 30

mouth-pieces L
Mullitu n.190
multiple n.31 192
multiplicity XVIII XXI n.22 30f 46
multitude XXI XXIV XLV
multi-layered XXIII
multi-national XXI
mundane XLf n.9
mural crown n.159
musical instruments n.71
musician n.71
mutilated n.138 139
mystai n.126
myste n.132
mysteries XLVIII n.140 174
mysteries, heavenly n.140
mysteries, hidden n.140
Mysteries, Lesser n.140
mysteries, sacred XL
mysteries of birth n.140
mysteries of Demeter n.132
mysteries of Isis n.139
mysteries of Mithras XXXII n.117
mysteries of the Kabeiroi n.132
mystery cult XIVf XVII XXXIV n.126 132 211
mystery cult, ecstatic XXXIII
mystery religion XVI
mystic XXIX XXXI XXXVf n.141 274
mystical XXIIIf XXXV XLVI XLVIII n.85 98 111 114
mystical tradition XIV XLVIII n.43 55 196 201
mystical union XXXI XXXV n.99
mysticism XL n.22 40f 56 60 63 110 114 135f
mysticism, Assyrian n.114 197
mysticism, Jewish XVIf XXIIf XXIX XXXII XXXV n.8 22 41ff 46 55 63 86 98f 106 111 114 116 121 135f 141 149 156 193 213 230 248
mystic numbers XXXIV n.111 134
myth XV XXXI XXXIII XXXIX n.104 107f 110 112 114 117 119 124 127 130 133 140 246
myths XLVII n.108 110 p.4
mythical sages n.197
mythical topos p.25
mythological XXIX XLVII LXVII n.111 123 197
mythology XIV XLI n.125 164
Naassenes n.117 126
Nabunaid n.111 p.15
Nabû XVIII LI LXXIff LXXVII n.5 7 10 69 99 106 111 153 196 268 274 p.6 8 17
Nag Hammadi XXXI n.108 130
Nahum n.54 89
naked XXXII n.229
Name n.20 28 46 83 110 193
name, divine XXXV n.8 46 60 116 147
names XXI XXVIII XLVIIff Lff LXVI n.6 8 13 16 31 40f 46 55 69 114 130 176 189 196 p.24 38
Names, Holy n.28 46
Naqia XLIII IL n.206 p.9 23 34
Naqia/Zakutu XLIII n.159
Naram-Suen XLVIII
Nathan XIX LI n.166
national god XIV XVIII n.23
Nazareth n.41
Nebuchadnezzar n.42 166 186 243
nefesh n.106 133 151
Neoplatonic XIVf XXXI n.9 22 112 151
Neoplatonism XVII XXI n.9 30 106
neshamah n.133 153 156
netherworld XV XXXIff LI n.104 107 112 114 127 134
Netiv Mizvotekha n.162
Netzah n.55 201
new man n.140
New Year LXIV LXXI n.242 197 p.6
Nicene Creed XXVIII n.73
Nietzsche n.22
Niniel n.41
Ninmah n.88
Ninsun XL n.188
Nintu n.57 88 270
Ninurta/Nabû XV XLIf n.9 196f
Nirah p.40
Nisaba n.48
Nisibis n.41
noetic realm n.135
noise, noisy n.49 p.16
non-existence n.22
novices n.119
Nudimmud n.123
number, primordial/ideal n.44
numbers, mystic XXXIV n.111 134
numerical values LXXIV n.44
numerically p.24
Nuriel n.41
nurse XXXVI XXXIXf XLII n.165 175ff p.7 39
oath XV XXXIV XXXIX LXXIIf n.50 p.25
Obadiah p.40
ocean n.135
offering n.65 88 127 140 p.16 26
Ohrid n.139
omen XIV XLVI LXIX LXXIIIf n.211 27 231f p.24
ominous p.24 39
omnipotent XXIV
omnipresent n.22
omniscient XXIV
On the Origin of the World XXVIII
ophidian p.40
opposites XXIX n.48 90 105 130 134
oracle, prophetic XIV XVII XXXIX XLV XLVIIf LVI LXXVII
oracles, Assyrian XXVI XLVIIf
Oracles, Chaldean XXXI n.9 22 105f 130 134 257
oracular deities XVIII
oracular deity XVIII XLII LXVf LXXI n.11 34
oracular goddess n.105
oracular queries n.1
oral XIV XVII XLVI LXIII LXVII LXXVII n.235 286
orchard n.123 214 p.17
order, cosmic XLI
order, heavenly n.25
Origen n.22 65 75 97 114 134
origin, Assyrian/Chaldean n.126
origin, celestial n.123
origin, divine XV
origin, heavenly XXXI
Orphic n.30
Orphism XXI
Osiris n.104 117 123 126 137 139
oversoul n.106 133
Ozar Hayyim n.200
pagan XVIII n.30 40

Palestine n.3 53 164 211
Palestinian n.83
Palladium XXXI
palm tree n.88 133 201
palmette crown n.112 114
Pamalya n.36
panegyric hymns XLVIII
panels n.165 189 199
pantheon XXIII n.23 25 29
Papsukkal XXXII
papyri n.41
parables n.121 274
paradise n.116 86
paradox XXIX XXXIII n.90 124
parallel XIIIf XXXIf XXXVI XLVIII LXII LXVI n.11 55 130 133 138 248 p.5 7 15 25 39 41
parallelism LXVII n.106 108 p.26
parallels XIV XVI XXXI XLIII XLVIII LX LXIIf LXVf LXX n.11 22 119 125 130 138 268 p.38
paranormal XXXIV
Parthian n.88
parthenos n.92
Passion story n.125
path XXXIII
pathway n.140
patriarchs n.97 139
Paul n.7 36 65 71 126
Pauline doctrine n.51
Pausanias n.106
Pazuzu n.246 p.4
penis n.114 140
penitent n.118
penitent figure XXXII
penitent sinner n.124
penitent soul XXXI
penitential psalm XLVIII p.14
perfection XV XXIX n.97 98 111 197
perfect king XL n.193
perfect light n.120
perfect likeness n.192
perfect man XV XXIII XL n.41 44 121 124 126 133 193 196f 211
perfect one n.85
permanences n.9
permutation XXXVI
perpetuate n.193
Persephone n.140
persistence n.125 139
person XVIII XX XXXIV XLIII LI LXVI LXXVII n.11 68 116 123 140 211 220 p.9 15 34
persona n.8
personification n.41 119 193 203 p.8
personify XV XXIV XXVIII XXXI n.67
pharaoh XLII n.165
Philo n.43
philosophers n.296
philosophical XVIf XLVII n.111
philosophies XVI XXI
philosophy XVI n.22 45 105
Philostratus n.83
Phoenicia XIV
Phrygian XVI n.126
physical senses n.200
physical sexual act n.119
physical universe n.22 44
physical world n.107
Physis n.105
piety L n.137
Pilate n.125
pilgrimage XLIII
pillars n.43 201
pine n.126 127
pious n.144 186
pit n.140 p.25
planetary heavens XXXII
planetary spheres n.44 111 114 117
planets n.34 41 43 111 196
Plato n.30 106 140 296
Platonic IL n.105 107
Platonism XXI
pleasures XXXIV n.140
Pleroma n.97 120
Plotinus n.30
pluralis majestatis n.31
plurality n.14 31 p.8 15
Plutarch n.137 139
pneuma n.69
polarities XXIX
pollution n.111
polytheism XXV n.14 21 31 58
polytheistic XVIII XXIf n.21 41
pomegranate XV n.46 201 p.39
pomegranate-shaped p.39
Porphyry n.30 40 58 140
portent XLIII LXIX LXXIIIf n.179 p.24
post-exilic XXII n.42
power XXI XXVIII XXXIV XXXIX ILff LII LXVIff LXIXf LXXII n.44 48 55f 58 103 130 134 158 169 172f 205f p.8 9 24
power struggle XLIII
power, God's XIX
power, hidden n.76
powers XXI XXIVf XXXII n.23 41 44 55 58 105 112 120 140 211 p.25
Powers n.8
powers, divine XXIff XXVf n.22 23 30f 43f 55f 63 71 86 112f 114 133 174
powers, higher n.158
powers, sefirotic n.44
powers of darkness n.246
powers of God XXII n.41 55 189
praise XIX XXXIII XLVII LXIV LXVI n.97 111 170 p.24 40
pray XXXV XLVI LXXIII n.118 144 153
prayer XXVI XXXII XXXV XLVI IL LXXI LXXIII n.19 20 23 27 63 88 114 116 118 128 p.39
prayers n.116 117f 141 153 p.8
praying XLVI LXXI n.41 116 141
predict XLIII LXXIV
prediction LXVI n.2
predictive XIV
premonition p.24
pre-exilic XXII XXIV XLII n.42 251
priest n.53 97 132 139 235
priestess n.226
priesthood LXXIII n.186
priestly n.213
prince XLIII LI LXX n.53 186 196
Prince of Peace p.10
principalities n.58
procession LXIV p.9 22
proclaim XIV XVIII XLV n.63 212 257

procreation XXVIII
progenitor n.10
prognosticate n.243
prohibition n.139 140
promiscuity XXXI
promise XXXIII LII LXVI LXVIII LXXf n.119 126
propagate XLIII XLVIII
prophecies XIVff XVIII XXVf XXXVI XXXIXf XLVIIf LXVff LXVIII LXX n.3 27 130 150 168f 235 296
prophecy XIIIf XVIf XXIIIf XXXV XXXIXf XLII XLVf XLVIII LIII LXI LXVI LXXf LXXVII n.1 2ff 136 157 173 246 251 264 p.15 17 27 39
prophecy, Assyrian XIV XVIff XXII XXIV XXXI XXXIV XXXVI XXXIX XLIII XLVff LIII LXIII LXVII LXXVII n.243
prophecy, biblical XIV XVI XVIII XXI XXXII XXXVI XXXVIII LXVI n.46 236
prophecy, ecstatic XXVI XLII
prophecy, royal n.243
prophets, biblical XVIII XXII XXIV XXVI XLV n.138
prophesy XXXV XLV LXIIf LXVII n.71 200 214 220 235
prophet XIX XXI XXIV XXVI XXXIVf XLVff ILff LII LXIIff n.55 136 138 141 151 189 213 216 221f 229 232 235 238 n.243 251 256 p.5f 10 14ff 25ff
prophet, ecstatic XLV n.222 232 243
prophetess XLVf ILff LII LXII LXXI n.214 221 232 243
prophetess, ecstatic n.220
prophetesses XLV XLVIIff n.244
prophetic XLVI LXIV n.240 257
prophetic acknowledgment n.211
prophetic activity XLVIII LII
prophetic encouragement XLIII
prophetic movement XLIII
prophetic oracle XIV XVII XXXIX XLV XLVIIf LVI LXXVII
prophetic rapture n.229
prophetic spirit n.69 71
prophetic state n.114
prophetic support XXXIX
prophetic texts XIV
prophetic task XXXIX
prophets XIIIf XXI XXXV XXXIX XLIII XLVff XLVIIIf LI LV LXIV LXVIf n.71 138 169 172 213 229 231 235f 238 242ff p.38
prophets, Assyrian XVIII XXV XLVIII XLV LII
prophets, biblical XVIII XXII XXIV XXVI XLV n.138
prophets, ecstatic XLV LXVIIIf LXXIIIf n.141
prophets/prophetesses, ecstatic n.222
prophets of Aššur XIII
prophets of Baal n.200
prophets of Asherah n.200
prophet/diviner n.264
prophet/prophetess LXIII
prostitute XV XXXIff n.14f
prostitution XXXIII
protection XLVII LXIII LXVI LXXIIff n.180 p.40
protector XXXI
prototype XL
protégé p.40
Proverbs XXVIII
prudence, prudent XXIX n.111 121
prosopon/persona n.8
psalms XLVIII LXVI
Pseudo-Dionysious n.60
psychic XV n.140
psychological n.116
pun n.86 88 119 140
punishment XLIII LXXIII n.55 p.27
pure XXXII XXXIV XLIII LXVII n.147 170 190 206
pure/clean/holy XXIX
pure god n.111
pure mouths LXX n.229
pure soul n.136 200
pure thought XXVI
purification XXXIV n.147
purified n.135 197
purifier n.190 197
purify/sanctify n.190
purifying n.111 197
purity XV XXIX XL n.111 211
purple n.114
Pythagoreanism n.44
qualities XXI n.23 158 189
Qudshu n.199
queen LII n.159
queen mother LXII LXVIII LXX n.9 153 159 284 p.34
Queen Mullissu XVIII LII n.104 p.16
queen of heaven XV XXXII XLII LII n.53 98 200
queen of Nineveh n.10 97
queen of the gods n.186
queries XIV n.1
Qumran n.213
rabbinic n.41 43 146
rabbinical n.31 p.25
radiance XXIX n.19 96 98
Rahmiel n.41
rainbow XV n.114
ransom XXXIII
Raphael n.41
rapture n.143
Ras Shamra n.165 199
Rav n.23 63
rays n.9
rebirth XXXII
rebirth, spiritual XXXIII n.140
reborn soul n.119
receiver XXXVI
recipient XLVII L n.244
recitation XXV
recite LXX n.63 141 p.25
reconcile LXXV n.205 p.15
reconciliation LXXIV
records, celestial XVIII
redemption XV n.124
redemptory death XXXIII n.124
redemptory role XV
reforms n.59
regeneration p.39
religion XIIIff XVI XVIII XXIf XXIVf XXXVI n.22 197 296 p.40
religions XVI XXI n.21
repentance XV XXXII n.111 118
representative XV XXI XL n.51 180
representative, God's n.9 25 193
rescued XXXIII
resurrected n.127 139
resurrection XV XXXIII n.40 126f 135 211

revelation XXXVf LII n.130 144f 234
Revelation n.36 38 41
Rhea n.92
riddles XV n.110
righteous XXXVI LXXIV n.86 121 136 162 166 186 205 209
Righteous Sufferer LXXI
righteousness LXXIV n.23 55
rightful p.19
right arm n.41
right hand n.119 140
right path n.124
right side n.138 201 211
rites XLVIII LXXIV n.140 240
ritual XXIV LVI LIX LXIV n.27 124 140 220 227 232 242 p.22f 25 39
ritual texts n.190
robbers XXXII n.116
robe n.46 138 213
rock XXXIV p.24
Roman XVI n.125 159 173 211 p.39
Romans XXVIII n.139 153
royal babies n.206
royal ideology XIV XXXIX n.165 166 211 296
royal Messiah n.213
royal psalms XLVIII LXVI
royal prayer p.17
royal prophecy n.243
royal rituals XLVIII p.22 25
ruler n.41 46
rulers n.31 52 p.6 23
Sabaoth XXVIII n.76
Sabbath n.140 234
Sabbatian messianism n.193
sacrament n.119 120
sacred XXVIIIf n.46 65
sacred grove n.125
Sacred Marriage n.125 127 202
sacred mysteries XL
sacred pillars n.53
sacred tree XVI XXIIf XXXIV n.42 133 190 199 201 202
sacred union n.86
sacrifice XXXIII n.53 83 124 214 p.16 25
Safrin XXXV n.144 150
sages n.106 25 43 111 p.40
saints XXII
salvation XV XVII XXXIf XXXIV XLVIIf n.119 124 127 140 211 257 p.6 9 23
Samaria n.125 130 165 p.8
Samaritan n.109
Samuel XIX XXXVIII n.243
sanctuaries LXXIVf n.186 p.39
Sandalphon n.43
sapphire n.249
Sargon XIV IL n.65 206 p.18
Sargonid LII n.196
Sar ha-Gadol n.196
Sasgabiel n.41
Sassanid n.193
satellite n.111
Saturn n.114
Saul n.173 229 243
saviour XV XXIV XLI XLIII LI n.76 121 123 196 211
saviour/God n.121
saviour/Michael n.76
scapegoat n.111
sea XLI n.41 88 111 211 296 p.14 23 41
seclusion XLV
Second Treatise of the Great Seth n.81
secrecy XV XXXIV n.111 132
secret XV XXIII XXVI XLVIII LXXII n.27 32 41 108 132
sect n.126
seer XXXV XLVIf n.222 231 236 251
Sefer Hekhalot n.36
Sefer ha-Meshiv n.149
Sefer Yezirah n.44
sefirah n.44 46 55 114 116 118 156 249
sefirot XXIII XXVf XXXII n.44 63 116 157 201
sefirotic equivalent n.114
sefirotic powers n.44
sefirotic tree n.107 201
Seleucid XVI n.88
self-castration IL n.119 126 139f 232
self-confidence XIV
self-identification XIX LXV
self-induced suffering XXXV
self-inflicted pain XXXIV
self-laceration n.138 270
self-mutilation XXXIV n.138
self-originate n.121
self-presentation XIX LXVI n.130
semi-divine XXXVI XL
Sennacherib XLIII LXVIII n.59 61 65 190 207 p.8 9 26 38
Sensible World n.134
separation n.14 97
Septimius Severus n.159
Septuagint n.249 p.7
seven angels n.41
seven colours n.114
seven concentric circles n.114
seven ethereal robes n.117
seven garments n.114
seven gates XXXII n.114
seven heavenly palaces n.116
seven planetary spheres n.111 114 117
seven planets n.41 43 111
seven robes n.117
seven spheres n.111 114 117
seven-branched lampstand n.42
seven-layered scheme of heavens n.248
seven-staged ziggurat XV n.114 133
sex IL p.6
sexless n.119
sexuality XXXI
sexual act n.119
sexual aspect n.140
sexual innocence n.92
sexual license XXXI
sexual love XXVI XXIX
sexual member n.114
sexual services n.140
Shakta Tantrism XV n.107 133
Shavu'ot n.145 162
Shekhinah XXXIf XXXVf n.14 42 46 85f 98f 111 116 133 144ff 149ff 153 155ff 162 200 n.201 270
Shekhinah Aila n.111 156
Shekhinah, Lower XXXVI n.156

Shekhinah, Upper XXXVI n.111 156
Shema' Israel XXV n.114
Sheol p.16
shepherd XV n.123 124 126 166 186 193 211
Shepherd, Good XL n.166
shepherdship LXXV n.183
shield p.8 15
shine XXIX LVI LXXIVf n.55 248 p.7 23
shining XLIII n.39 111 211
ship of state IL n.296 p.14
Shiur Qomah n.36
shout XLV n.212 217
shouter XLVI n.141
shrine LXXIV n.118 p.16
shrouded n.114
Siduri n.111
sighing, sighs XXXIV XLVI n.141 234
silver-coloured n.114
similes LXVII
Simon Magus n.109
sin XV XXXIIIf n.65 111 116 124 196 205 211 270 274 p.6
sinful n.49 91 270
sinless XXXIV
Sin LXXIIff LXXV n.34 41 65 91 111 114 153 183 189 p.15
Sin/Binah n.111
Sin/Moon XXIX
Sirtur n.125
sixty great gods IL n.34 p.6
Sodom p.24
Solomon n.42 55 173 201
son XV XVIII XXXVI XLIII XLVIIIf LI LXIX n.9 106 121 123f 150 153 162 165 168 173 175 234 243 279 p.6 9f 18 39
sons XLIII n.130 131 140 p.9 25 38f
Son XVIII XXVIII n.9 73 124 134 192
Son of God XXXIII XXXVI XXXVIII XL n.165 166 196
sons of God n.129
Song of Songs XXVIII XXXI n.99 111 274
Song of Songs, Assyrian n.99
Sophia XXVIII XXXI XXXVI n.108 111 117
Sophia, fallen XXVIII
Sophia, fall of XXXI XXXVI n.108
Sophia, lower n.130
Sophia of Jesus Christ n.78
soteriological p.24
soteriology XV
soul XV XXXIff XXXIV XXXVI XLII XLVII n.10 68f 99 106f 116f 119 121 123 126 133ff 136 151 153 156 193 197 200 248 268
soul, animal n.106 133
soul, ascent of the XXXI XXXIII n.114 135f
soul, concept of n.106
Soul, Cosmic XV XXXI n.105 107 112 134
soul, fallen n.119 124
soul, holy XXXVI
soul, lower n.111 126 134
soul, moral n.133
soul, pure n.136 200
soul, reborn n.119
soul, supernal n.136 151
soul, three-fold division of n.126
soul, three-graded concept of n.106 248
soul, universal n.151
souls n.106 111
south wind LXXIII n.246
Sovereignties n.8
sphere XXXII n.46 111 116 133f p.25
spheres, planetary n.44 111 114 117
spindle XXXIV XLVI n.138 232
spirit XXI XXVI XXXI n.41 55 68f 74 111 134 140 153 268 p.8
Spirit XV XXII XXVI XXVIII n.68 69ff 73 76f 98 129 153
spirit, divine XXXIV n.146
spirit, God's n.71
spirit, holy XXVIII XXXI
Spirit, Holy XV XVIII XXII XXVI XXVIIIf XL n.9 70f 74 76 98 111 130 134 157 191f
spirit, prophetic n.69 71
Spirit of Christianity XXVIII
spirit of counsel n.55
spirit of God XXVI XXVIII n.147
spirit of knowledge n.55
spirit of Nabû 69
spirit of the LORD 71
spirit of wisdom n.55
spiritual assimilation LXVII
spiritual beings n.22
spiritual bliss n.99
spiritual death n.111
spiritual entities XXII
spiritual force XXXVI
spiritual intelligences n.40
spiritual preparation XXXIV n.119
spiritual rebirth XXXIII n.140
spiritualization n.40
Spiritus Sanctus n.73
splendour n.98 129 150
spouse of Yahweh n.130
star XXIX XLVI n.48
star, eight-pointed XXIX n.48 95
stars LXXIV n.40 41 70 97 p.15
states, altered XVI n.143
stimulated XXXV
stone LXXIV n.58 111 175 248f p.17 25
string of associations n.114
stripping XXXII
struggle against desire n.139
sublimated n.140
sublime XXVI XXIX n.14 99 111
substance n.9 44 124 192
substance, divine n.40
substitute XV XXXIII n.124 p.38
substitute king n.124
suckling XXXVI XXXVIIIff n.165 175 p.39
Suen n.111
sufferer LXXI p.40
sufferer-king n.124
suffering XXXIIff XXXV n.119 124 129 137 144 150 211 270
Sufi n.141
Sumer LXXIV
Sumerian XVI n.27 88 91 104 107 112f 114 119 127 130 138 184 193 219 232 p.18
sun XV XLIII LXXV n.9 14 34 53 114 211 p.6 23f
sunshine p.23
superimposed gates n.116
supernal aspect XL
supernal force n.205

supernal gods n.18
supernal holy soul XXXVI n.136 151
supernal luminary n.249
Supernal Mother XXXVI
supernal soul n.136 151
supernal wild cow n.187
supernatural n.68
supplication n.153
supreme deity n.30
symbol XV XXIIf XXVIII n.23 42f 46 95 114 p.10
symbolic XVI XXIX n.126 p.39f
symbolically n.23
symbolism XVI XXIII
symbolize XXIX XXXIV n.43 107 111 114 126 197
symbolizing n.48 114 249
symbols XV LXXIV
sympathy, cosmic n.105
synagogue n.63
syncretistic n.41
Syria n.3 126 138 159 164 296 p.14 16
Syriac XXIX n.74 p.15
Syrian n.141 159
Syrian goddesses n.138
Syria/Assyria n.109
Tabernacle n.42
Talmud n.36 43 56 249
talmudic XXVIII n.23 58 63
talmudic-midrashic n.98
Tammuz XV XXXIII LXXI n.123 124ff 127 227 242 p.10
Tanit n.139
Tantra n.133
Tantrism XXI n.133
Tarsus n.126
Taurobolium n.140
Ta'uz n.125
teaching n.65 140
tears XLVI n.20 118 144 234
technique XXXV XLVI n.111 114 135 141 144 213
techniques, ecstatic XVI
techniques, mystical XXXV
teletai n.137
temple XXXVI XLVII Lff LXIV LXIX LXXI n.6 39 42 88 132 159 165 174 201 214 220 227 244 248 p.8 14 17 23
temple-tower n.114
temples XXXIXf XLIII XLV n.88 139f 254
tenets XXXIII n.211
term XIV XLV LXIIIf n.1 2 8 44 67 98 120 151 173f 286
terminology XIV n.67
terms XXI XXVI XXIX XXXIIf XXXVI n.22 104 111 133 147 166 211
terrestrial n.27
Teshuvah n.111
testicles n.140
Tetragrammaton n.114
tevunah n.55
theological XX IL
theophany XLVII LXXI LXXVII
theosophy XV
Theotokos n.42
theurgist n.135
theurgy n.132
Three Steles of Seth n.117
threeness n.28
throne XXIf XXVIII XLIII LI LXVI LXIXf LXXIIIf n.37 41 46 76 166 170 214 229 234 254 p.7 9
thrones n.173 p.25
throne of god n.248
thunder n.41 130
Thunder XXXIII n.130 257
thunderstorm n.55 p.24
Tiamat XLI n.49 114 229
tiferet n.55
Tiferet n.42 46 111 114 121 133f 157 249
Tiglath-Pileser XIV n.166 186
Titus n.42
tool XLIII n.23
Torah XXXII n.99 114 147 234
tradition XVII LXIV n.43 55 201 249
tradition, mystical XIV XLVIII n.43 55 196 201
traditions XVI XXII XXIX n.31 193
trance n.138 214 219f
transcend XXIV XXIX
transcendent n.22 59 112
transcendental XVf
transfigured p.23
transvestism n.138
treaties XLV LIII n.51 p.23
treaty XLVf LXX
tree XXIII XXVI XXXIV XLII n.9 42 44 46 48 55 98 107 116 123 133 140 193 203
Tree XXII n.44 46 55 60 98 107 112 133f 157 193 201
tree, anthropomorphic XXVI n.46 133
tree, cosmic XV n.193 249
tree, felled n.123
tree, sacred XVI XXIIff n.42 133 190 199 201 202
tree, sefirotic n.107 201
tree, stylized n.201
tree, three-layered n.133 248
tree, yoga n.107 133
Tree of Balance n.193
Tree of Knowledge n.157 193
Tree of Life XXII XXV XL XXIII n.42 45 98 133 157 165 193 201 249
Tree of Light n.42
triad XXVIII n.9 59
triadic n.9
Trimorphic Protennoia n.8 9 44 77 79 192
trinitarian concept of God n.9
trinitarian doctrine n.9 14
trinitarian God n.8
trinitarian Holy Spirit n.71
trinitarian oracle n.10
trinitarian plurality n.28
trinitarian scheme n.22
Trinity n.9 14 68 134 211
trinity, Assyrian XXVIII
Trinity, Holy XVIII
trinity-in-unity n.9
triumph n.197
triumphal celebrations LXIX p.9
triumphal entry n.211
triumphal processions n.197
triumphal return n.197 p.9
triumphant XLIII n.123
true essence n.140
true God XVIII n.134

true incarnation XLIII
true trinity-in-unity n.9
trunk of the tree XXXIV n.46 112 133 193
trust ILff LXXII p.7 55 p.6
Tukulti-Ninurta I XL n.19 186
two-faced XXXI n.105
two-level n.107 133
Ugarit n.30 189 199 202
Ugaritic n.41 83 92 165
ultimate reality XLII
Umayyad n.193
Ummanaldasi n.103
unbelievers n.58
unblemished n.136
uncastrated p.38
unclean n.140
Understanding n.86 111
undressing XXXII n.114
unification XXVf n.28 63 114
unifier n.105
unify XXV n.23
uninitiated XV
unio mystica n.135 136
union XXVI XXXV n.136
union, mystical XXXI XXXV n.99
union, sacred n.86
union with God XXXIV n.121 197
unite XXVI XXXI XXXVI n.119 133f 136 151 274
unity XXV LXXI n.14 28 44 p.39
unity, divine n.97 114
unity, God's XXI n.28 46
unity in multiplicity XXI
unity of divine powers XXIf
unity of God n.63
unity with God XXXIIIf
universal God XXI n.22 59
universal goddess XVIII n.130
universal harmony LXIV
universal soul n.151
universe XXI XXIII XXVIII n.9 22 30f 40 60
universe, metaphysical n.22
universe, physical n.22 44
unmarried n.97
unoriginate n.134
unorthodox n.130
unspiritual n.140
unveiling n.110
unworthy n.240
Upanishads n.30
Uriel n.41
Uruk n.46 p.9 18
Urukite XVIII LII n.6
Utnapishtim n.127
Valentinian myth XXXI
vanquisher XV
Vedic n.30
vegetation cults XVIII
vegetation god n.127
veil XV n.85
veiled XXIX n.111 117
veiling n.110 111
veneration LXVII n.58 65
Venus XXVIIIf LXIX LXXIV n.41 114
Venus Barbata n.83 97 139
vessel XXXVI p.25
victor n.196
victorious XXXI XLIII n.123 p.8
victory XXXIX XLI XLIII LXVIIIf n.23 55 211 p.6 10 23
victory celebrations n.197
virgin XXVIIIf XXXIIf n.41 76f 92 124 140
Virgin XXVIII n.41 75 101 111 140
Virgin, Holy XXXI
virginity XXXII
virgins n.77 97 121 149
virgin of light XXXI XXXVI n.149
Virgo n.114
virility XXIX
virtue XXVIII XXXII
vision XXII XXXV XLVIf LXXI LXXVII n.76 96 98 136 141 144 150 162 234ff 243 249 254 p.25 40
visionary XLVI Lff
visionary experiences n.264 286
visions XVI XXXVf XXXIX XLVIf n.141 213 230
visual arts XXIX XL
visual experience XXXVIII XLVII
visualization n.187
visualize XV XXI n.114
voice XXVI XXVIII XXXI XXXIII XXXV XLV n.9 19 105 235 257
volute n.9
wailer XLVI n.141 232
wailing XLVI n.107 127 137 211 270
Wailing Wall n.144
war XXIX XXXI XXXIV XXXIX XLIII XLVII LXVIII LXXf LXXIII n.88 205 243
warlord XXIX XXXI n.164
Watcher n.249 p.7
watching n.249 p.7 15
Watchman n.249
water XX LXXIIIf p.25
water, holy n.197
Water, Living XXVIII
water of life XXXII n.119
waters XXVIII n.111 p.39
waters of Apsû 111
waters of death n.111
water-pure n.111
waterside n.55
weapon XLVI LXXIII n.105 114 p.8 22
wedding XXXIII n.119 p.26
wedding-feast n.121
weep XXXII n.118 141
weeping XVI XXXIVf XLVI n.88 107 111 125 141 144 150 225 234 242 270
well-being XIX LXIIIf n.11 128 180 p.9 16 23
whip XXXIV n.138
white n.83 88 114 140 234
whore XXVIIIf n.81
wings XXXVI XL LXXIII n.9 107 197 206 246 p.4
winged bird n.180 p.15
winged disk XXV n.9 23 30 59f 66 101
winged sages n.190
wisdom XXIX n.23 55 86 111 119 186 189 p.8
Wisdom XXVIII n.41 86 99 111 130
wisdom, divine n.108
wisdom, god of n.111
Wisdom, Hidden XXVIII n.110 130
woman IL n.41 88 92 98 119 138 140 144 150 162 165 189 214 220 232 234 254 p.5 9
womanish n.139 231
womanly n.92

womb XXVIII XL n.105 165 186 p.23
women XLVIII L n.53 97 138f 175
Word XXVIII n.40 119 134 192
word of God n.99 192
word of Queen Mullissu XVIII LXV
word of the king LXV
word of the LORD XXI n.251 290 p.23
word of Yahweh XVIII
word of YHWH XXVI LXV n.46
word of their mouths XVIII
world XVf XVIII XXVIII XXXIf XXXIV XLf XLV XLVIII LIf n.22 23 28 40 55 98 116 124 139f 150 157f 164 192 257 p. 16 39
world, divine n.25
World, Intelligible n.134
world, lower n.200
world, material XV XXXI XXXIV n.118 257
world, physical n.107
world, upper n.111
worlds XXXII
Worlds, Sensible n.134
worlds, higher XXXII
worlds, lower XXXVI
worship XVI XXI XXIV XXVI XLVI LXX n.6 22 53 65 88 130 174 235 p.6 14 40
worshipers n.58 65 137
writing-board, life-giving p.6
Yahweh XIX XXXI XLII n.14 30f 43 56 101 202 205 p.5f 17f 39
Yahweh, spouse of n.130
Yahwists n.109
Yesod n.133
Yezirah n.44
YHVH n.28 46 56 158
yoga tree n.107 133
Yom Kippur n.111
Zarpanitu n.9 97 132 190
Zebaoth p.15
Zecheriah n.54
Zedekiah n.229 243
Zeus n.30 140
ziggurat XV n.114 133
Zion n.144 149 165 p.6 15
zodiac n.41
Zohar n.114 133 153 155 179 203
Zoroastrian n.30

Biblical Passages Cited or Discussed

Am. 1:10 p.24
Am. 1:4-8 n.101
Am. 3:1 p.23
Am. 7:10-17 n.236
1 Chron. 29:11 n.55
2 Chron. 15:1 n.71 74
Chron. 18:18-22 n.33
2 1 Cor. 11:10 n.65
2 Cor. 12:1-4 n.136
Dan. 4 n.249
Dan. 4:13 n.249
Dan. 7:9 n.37
Dan. 9:26 n.173
Dan. 10 n.230
Deut. 32:10f p.15
Deut. 32:42 n.66
Deut. 4:15f n.42
Deut. 6:4 XXV
2 Esdras 7:26 n.37
Gospel According to the Hebrews XXVIII
Ex. 3:1f n.42
Ex. 3:2 n.31
Ex. 15:20f n.258
Ex. 24:7 p.25
Ex. 24:10 n.249
Ex. 25 n.42
Ex. 25:40 n.42
Ex. 28:33ff n.46
Ezek. 1 n.66 236
Ezek. 1:4 n.249 p.7
Ezek. 6:4-8 n.64
Ezek. 7:16 n.89
Ezek. 8:14 n.125
Ezek. 10:2 n.37
Ezek. 16:4ff p.6
Ezek. 19:9 p.18
Ezek. 23:32 p.8
Ezek. 32:6 p.17
Ezek. 38:22 p.24
Ezek. 38:23 p.24
Ezek. 40f n.42 201
Josh. 5:9 p.17
Gal. 3:26-28 n.97
Gal. 4:14 n.65
Gen. 1:2 XXVIII
Gen. 1:2 n.74
Gen. 1:26 n.31
Gen. 3:24 n.201
Gen. 6:11-13 p.16
Gen. 9:13 n.114
Gen. 14:19 n.86
Gen. 15:1 p.8
Gen. 16:7 n.31
Gen. 19:21f p.24
Gen. 19:23f p.24
Gen. 28:12 n.37
Gen. 28:17 n.37
Gen. 48:13ff p.9
Hab. 3:6 p.27
Hag. 1:4-8 p.26
Hag. 2:21 n.173
Hos. 1 50
Hos. 1:1 n.290
Hos. 4:1 p.23
Hos. 8:14 n.101
Hos. 8:5f n.64
Hos. 11:1ff p.6
Isa. 1:2 p.17 39
Isa. 2:1 n.290
Isa. 2:2f p.38
Isa. 2:4 p.38
Isa. 3:7 p.38
Isa. 5:14 p.16
Isa. 6:1 n.37
Isa. 6:6 n.37
Isa. 7:20 p.8
Isa. 8:3 n.258
Isa. 8:5ff n.256
Isa. 9:6 p.7 10
Isa. 9:6f p.9
Isa. 9:13 p.17
Isa. 9:18 p.8
Isa. 10:13 p.16
Isa. 10:17 p.39
Isa. 11:1f n.71 74
Isa. 12:1 p.24
Isa. 14:22 n.101 p.5
Isa. 30:30f n.55
Isa. 31:4 p.15
Isa. 31:5 p.8 15
Isa. 40:26 n.55
Isa. 45:1 n.173
Isa. 45:2 p.5
Isa. 45:5ff p.24
Isa. 45:12 n.56
Isa. 45:20 n.64
Isa. 48:3-6 p.10
Isa. 49:15 n.165
Isa. 56:3ff n.140
Isa. 58:5 p.26
Isa. 59:11 n.89
Isa. 59:21 n.71
Isa. 66:7-13 n.165
Isa. 66:11-13 p.39
Isa. 66:13 p.18
Jer. 1:2.4.11 n.290

Jer. 2:23 n.64
Jer. 2:28 n.53
Jer. 2:4 p.23
Jer. 3:11 p.38
Jer. 5:21 n.256
Jer. 7:17f n.53
Jer. 7:2 n.214
Jer. 8:2 n.34 p.6
Jer. 10:1 p.23
Jer. 10:3-16 n.64
Jer. 10:12f n.55
Jer. 10:14-16 p.16
Jer. 17:5ff p.6
Jer. 17:7f n.55
Jer. 18:12 p.17
Jer. 18:18 p.38
Jer. 21:1ff n.243
Jer. 23:15 p.8
Jer. 23:18-24 n.136
Jer. 25:12 n.101
Jer. 27:2 n.229
Jer. 29:26f n.229
Jer. 36:2ff n.279
Jer. 46:8 p.5
Jer. 49:37 p.40
Jer. 51:1 p.4
Jer. 52:17ff n.42 201
Joel 1:1 n.290
Joel 1:2 p.23 1 John 4:9 n.124
Jon. 1:1 n.290
Josh. 10:24 p.23
1 Kgs. 6f n.42
1 Kgs. 6:29-35 n.201
1 Kgs. 14:1ff n.243
1 Kgs. 18:19ff n.200
1 Kgs. 18:26-29 n.138
1 Kgs. 18:42 n.213
1 Kgs. 22:6 n.243
1 Kgs. 22:10f n.189 229
1 Kgs. 22:19-23 n.33
2 Kgs. 1:8 n.213
2 Kgs. 19:2 n.243
2 Kgs. 22f n.65
2 Kgs. 22:10 p.25
2 Kgs. 22:12ff n.243
2 Kgs. 22:14 n.258
2 Kgs. 23:4ff n.34 53
2 Kgs. 24:13ff n.42
Lk. 13:18 n.44
Lk. 20:41-44 n.211
Lk. 23:46 n.268
1 Macc. 1:21 n.42
Mal. 1:1 n.282 290
Mal. 3:2 p.8
Mic. 1:1 n.290
Mic. 1:2 p.17
Mic. 1:7 n.64
Mic. 3:1 p.23
Mic. 6:1 p.40
Mk. 3:17 n.130
Mk. 10:13-16 n.97
Mk. 12:35-37 n.211
Mk. 14:22ff p.25
Mk. 15:34 n.268
Mt. 5:29 n.140
Mt. 5:48 n.193
Mt. 6:13 p.9
Mt. 10:19 n.70
Mt. 13:43 n.209
Mt. 17:2 p.23
Mt. 18:1-11 n.97
Mt. 18:8 n.140
Mt. 19:12 n.140
Mt. 22:1-14 n.121
Mt. 22:41-46 n.211
Mt. 25:1-13 n.121
Mt. 26:26ff p.25
Mt. 27:46 n.268
Neh. 6:14 n.258
Num. 11:12 p.39
Num. 24:2ff n.71
Num. 24:2ff n.74
Ob. 1:1 n.282 p.40
Prov. 3:19f n.55
Prov. 4:7 n.86
Prov. 8 XXVIII n.130f
Prov. 8-9 n.99
Prov. 8:22 n.86
Prov. 16:16 n.86
Ps. 2:4 n.35
Ps. 2:7 p.10
Ps. 7:12 n.66
Ps. 18 XIX
Ps. 18:6-13 p.24
Ps. 18:28 p.7
Ps. 18:51 n.173
Ps. 40:12 p.16
Ps. 46 n.37
Ps. 48:3 n.37
Ps. 68:14f n.83
Ps. 82:1-2 n.31
Ps. 89 19 XXXVIII
Ps. 89:3f p.7
Ps. 89:4 p.7
Ps. 89:5f n.37
Ps. 89:24 p.8
Ps. 89:25 p.23
Ps. 95:3 n.31
Ps. 96:4 n.31
Ps. 110:1 n.211 p.23
Ps. 121:4f p.39
Ps. 132:17 n.42
Ps. 145:14 p.26
Ps. 148:10 p.15
Rev. 1:16 p.23
Rev. 22:8-9 n.65
Rom. 5:5 n.70
Rom. 5:12-14 n.193
Rom. 8:11 n.98
Rom. 8:11-17 n.70 129
Rom. 8:26 n.70
Rom. 8:32 n.124
Ruth 4:10 n.86
Ruth 4:16 p.10
1 Sam. 9:6 n.243
1 Sam. 12:3 n.173
1 Sam. 16:6 n.173
1 Sam. 19:20 n.71
2 Sam. 1:14 n.173
2 Sam. 2:26 p.17
2 Sam. 7:7 n.166
2 Sam. 7:8ff p.7

2 Sam. 7:9 p.18
2 Sam. 7:12-16 n.166
2 Sam. 7:15 p.7
2 Sam. 24:11ff n.251
S. of S. 3:7 p.6
S. of S. 6:10 n.111
1 Thess. 5:19-20 n.71
Zech. 1:1.7 n.290
Zech. 4:1-14 n.43
Zech. 4:6 n.290
Zech. 8:6-13 n.210
Zech. 9:9 p.6
Zech. 9:14 n.66 101
Zech. 9:15 p.8
Zech. 13:4 n.213
Zech. 13:6 n.138
Zeph. 1:1 n.290
Zeph. 1:4 n.101
Zeph. 13 n.54

COLLATIONS

Text	Line	Collation
1	i.3	(end) *dan-ni*
	i.6	*šá-a-ru*
	i.7	*-pu-šu la ak-* *-pu-ni*
	i.15	*-te*
	i.20	*a-da-na-ka* *a-na-ku*
	i.28	*ša pi-i*
	i.32	*ṭa-ba-ah-hi*
	ii.1	
	ii.2	
	ii.6	*na-kar-*
	ii.34	
	ii.39	*na-i-*
	iii.4	*a-na-ku*
	iii.6	URU.ŠÀ
	iii.13	(end)
	iii.17	
	iv.26	(end)
	v.34	
	v.35	
2	i.24	[EN-*šú-nu*
	i.29	[*par-šá-mu-tú*
	i.30	[
	i.32	[
	i.33	[
	i.34	[
	ii.1	(end)
	ii.9	*a-ki*
	ii.24	(end) *ina* EDIN
	ii.32	*ú-ha-a-a-*
	ii.36	(end)
	ii.39	
	iii.2	LÚ.*da-gíl*
	iii.3	
	iii.4	*ma-aʾ-d[u-*
	iii.5	*a-bi-ar ú-*
	iii.6	
	iii.8	*ma-aʾ-du-ti*
	iii.20	DINGIR.MEŠ
	iv.2	[^{d}*aš-šur*
	iv.4	[.DINGIR.KI
	iv.15	(end) *-ka*
	iv.16	(end)
	iv.17	(end)
	iv.25	[*-ʾa-a-ni*
	iv.26	[*ina pa-ni-ia*
3	i.6	[
	i.8	[*-se-li-a*
	i.10	[
	i.11	[
	i.12	[
	i.18	[
	i.21	[
	i.24	[*ga-ri-ni-šú*
	i.25	[
	i.26	[
	i.35	[
	i.36	[
	ii.4	É
	ii.8	*an-ni-* *šul-mu*
	ii.19	*pa-ni-ka*
	ii.35	(end)
	iii.2	*ina* UGU
	iii.8	*ma-a*
	iii.12	TA* written
	iii.27	
	iii.34	
	iv.9	[*šá* URU
	iv.10	[
	iv.14	[
	iv.15	[
4:	9	[
5:	6	^{d}NIN.URTA

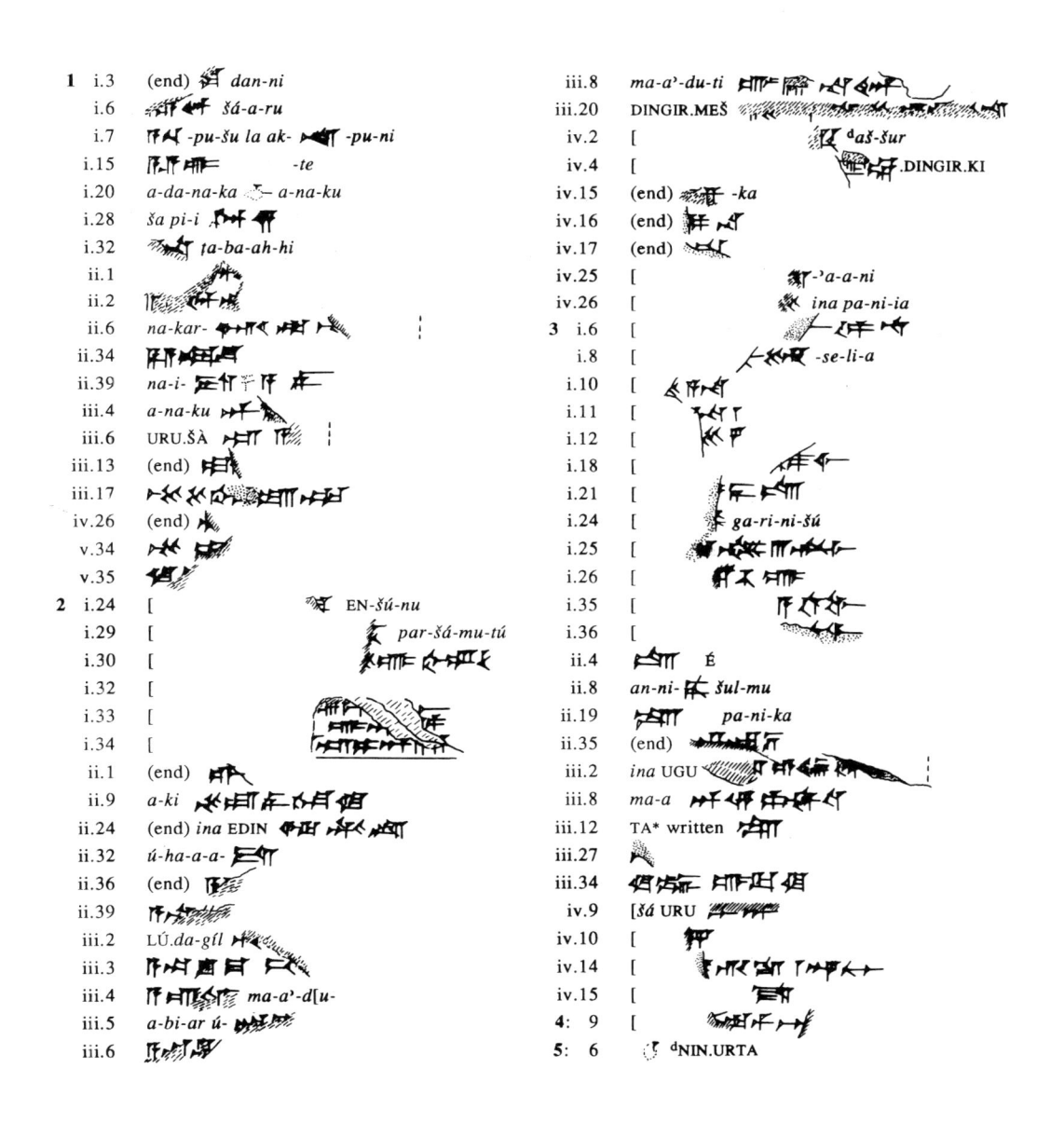

r.4 LÚ.KÚR *ša*
7
6 r.10 LÚ*.KÚR
11
12
7: 6 [
7 [*ma-a* -*a-ti*
9 (end) *ra-*
14 (end)
r.1 -*al-la*
8 *ma-a*
8: 1 *dib-bi* [*ša* KUR.NIM.MA -*a-a*
3 *ma-a at-* -*tal-ka*
9 *a-hap-*
9: 20 *e-ta-nar-riš*
10 r.5 UD-*mu šá*
11: 12 [*ina*] *re-* -*ia*

PLATES

PLATE I. K 4310 (= No. 1), Obv.

PLATE II. K 4310 (= No. 1), Rev.

Col. III Col. IV

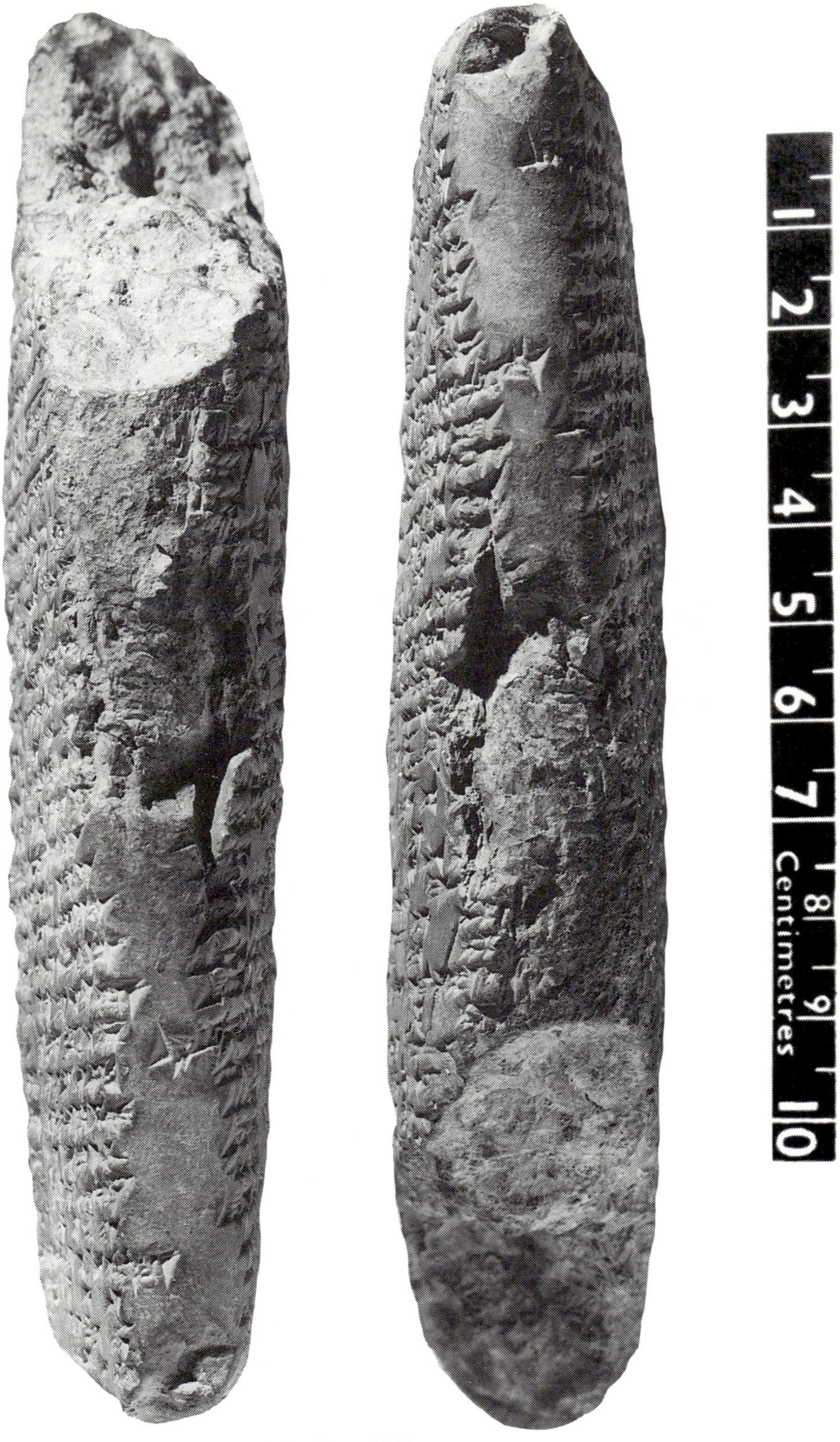

PLATE III. K 4310 (= No. 1), Right Edge (Cols. III and IV)

PLATE IV. K 12033 + 82-5-22,527 (= No. 2), Obv.

PLATE V. K 12033 + 82-5-22,527 (= No. 2), Rev.

PLATE VI. K 2401 (= No. 3), Obv. and Right Edge (Col. II)

PLATE VII. K 2401 (= No. 3), Rev. and Right Edge (Col. III)

K 6259 (= No. 5)

Bu 91-5-9,106+109 (= No. 6)

Obv.

Lower Edge

Rev.

Rev.

Upper Edge

83-1-18,839 (= No. 4)

PLATE VIII. 83-1-18,839 (= No. 4), K 6259 (= No. 5) and Bu 91-5-9,106+ (= No. 6)

Obverse

Lower Edge

Reverse

PLATE IX. K 883 (= No. 7)

Obverse

Edge

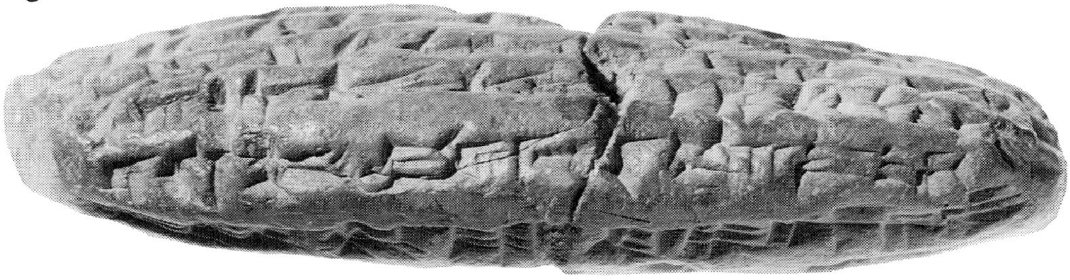

Reverse

PLATE X. K 1545 (= No. 8)

PLATE XI. K 1292 + DT 130 (= No. 9), Obv.

PLATE XII. K 1292 + DT 130 (= No. 9), Rev.

83-1-18,726 (= No. 10)

Obv.

Rev.

K 1974 (= No. 11)

83-1-18,726

Left Side

K 883 (=No.7)

K 1545 (= No. 8)

PLATE XIII. 83-1-18,726 (= No. 10) and K 1974 (= No. 11). K 883 (= No. 7) and K 1545 (= No. 8), Right Edge.

State Archives of Assyria

VOLUME I
THE CORRESPONDENCE OF SARGON II, PART I
Letters from Assyria and the West
Edited by Simo Parpola
1987

VOLUME II
NEO-ASSYRIAN TREATIES AND LOYALTY OATHS
Edited by Simo Parpola and Kazuko Watanabe
1988

VOLUME III
COURT POETRY AND LITERARY MISCELLANEA
Edited by Alasdair Livingstone
1989

VOLUME IV
QUERIES TO THE SUNGOD
Divination and Politics in Sargonid Assyria
Edited by Ivan Starr
1990

VOLUME V
THE CORRESPONDENCE OF SARGON II, PART II
Letters from the Northern and Northeastern Provinces
Edited by Giovanni B. Lanfranchi and Simo Parpola
1990

VOLUME VI
LEGAL TRANSACTIONS OF THE ROYAL COURT OF NINEVEH, PART I
Tiglath-Pileser III through Esarhaddon
Edited by Theodore Kwasman and Simo Parpola
1991

VOLUME VII
IMPERIAL ADMINISTRATIVE RECORDS, PART I
Palace and Temple Administration
Edited by F. M. Fales and J. N. Postgate
1992

VOLUME VIII
ASTROLOGICAL REPORTS TO ASSYRIAN KINGS
Edited by Hermann Hunger
1992

VOLUME IX
ASSYRIAN PROPHECIES
Edited by Simo Parpola
1997

VOLUME X
LETTERS FROM ASSYRIAN AND BABYLONIAN SCHOLARS
Edited by Simo Parpola
1993

VOLUME XI
IMPERIAL ADMINISTRATIVE RECORDS, PART II
Provincial and Military Administration
Edited by F. M. Fales and J. N. Postgate
1995

VOLUME XII
GRANTS, DECREES AND GIFTS OF THE NEO-ASSYRIAN PERIOD
Edited by L. Kataja and R. Whiting
1995

State Archives of Assyria Studies

VOLUME I

Neuassyrische Glyptik des 8.-7. Jh. v. Chr.
unter besonderer Berücksichtigung der Siegelungen
auf Tafeln und Tonverschlüsse
by Suzanne Herbordt
1992

VOLUME II

The Eponyms of the Assyrian Empire 910–612 BC
by Alan Millard
1994

VOLUME III

The Use of Numbers and Quantifications
in the Assyrian Royal Inscriptions
by Marco De Odorico
1995

VOLUME IV

Nippur in Late Assyrian Times
c. 755–612 BC
by Steven W. Cole
1996

VOLUME V

Neo-Assyrian Judicial Procedures
by Remko Jas
1996

VOLUME VI

Die neuassyrischen Privatrechtsurkunden
als Quelle für Mensch und Umwelt
by Karen Radner
1997

VOLUME VII

References to Prophecy in Neo-Assyrian Sources
by Martti Nissinen
1998